HUMAN RESOURCE MANAGEMENT

HUMAN RESOURCE MANAGEMENT

a managerial perspective

SECOND EDITION

Nelarine Cornelius

THOMSON
™
LEARNING

Australia • Canada • Mexico • Singapore • Spain • United Kingdom • United States

Human Resource Management: A Managerial Perspective

Copyright © 2001 Introduction and selection © Nelarine Cornelius; individual chapters © individual contributors

The Thomson Learning logo is a trademark used herein under licence.

For more information, contact Business Press, Berkshire House, 168–173 High Holborn, London, WC1V 7AA or visit us on the World Wide Web at: http://www.thomsonlearning. co.uk

British Library Cataloguing-in-Publication Data
A catalogue record for this book is available from the British Library.

ISBN 1–86152–610–5

First edition published 1999 by International Thomson Business Press
Reprinted 1999
Second edition published 2001 by Thomson Learning

Typeset by J&L Composition Ltd, Filey, North Yorkshire
Printed in Great Britain by TJ International, Padstow, Cornwall

Contents

Foreword to the first edition

Over the years, the profile of students studying human resource management has changed significantly. Not so long ago, the emphasis was much more on specialist professional development courses or specialist pathways on a limited number of undergraduate and postgraduate programmes in business or management.

However, there has been a significant growth in the popularity of generalist undergraduate courses and in particular post-experience management programmes at the DMS and MBA levels. There has also been a growth in the number of postgraduate degrees in general or international management. On such courses, human resource management is one of many important topics and, therefore, hard choices need to be made about what realistically the generalist student can be introduced to and, equally important, what is relevant. We have sensed a growing appreciation of human resource management as a core activity on these courses, but one for which line managers are expected to do more themselves, often with reduced support from specialist human resource management professionals: indeed, often some key specialist functions have been outsourced out of the organization altogether.

Rather than being driven by the personal preferences of the then small fledgling writing team, we did two things: reviewed the literature available and conducted a small survey amongst post-experience DMS and MBA students. What we found confirmed what we had sensed: that we needed a core of what we were already delivering on these programmes – what we can think about as a 'core curriculum'. There was also a great deal of interest in specific applications of human resource management, such as international resource management and human resource management within the context of small to medium-sized companies.

Clearly, our final decisions about what should and should not be included were always going to be a compromise. However, we did make the decision to ensure that we would write informatively beyond our core curriculum, that we would involve those who had an interest in the teaching and research of human resource management issues, and who held primary research and practitioner interests in related disciplines, such as employment law, information technology, international management policy and strategy, and the management of small to medium sized enterprises.

We have taken the 'dedicated specialist' route. All of the writers have taught and researched in the areas they have written about, many have worked in these fields prior to undertaking an academic career and continue working as consultants in these areas. All have considerable expertise in teaching post-experience students and many have written materials for and taught on distance learning programmes at certificate, diploma and masters levels of instruction. This expertise has shaped the structure and many features of the book. There are clear learning objectives and self-test questions for each chapter. A detailed glossary of key terms is also available at the end of the text. We felt that it was particularly important that the sections on employment law, which take the form of 'Legal briefings' at the end of each chapter, should have more frequent updates. The resources area of the Thomson Learning website at *www.thomsonlearning.co.uk* will include annual updates of all the legal briefings covered in the book. Sets of the key diagrams and tables included in the text are also available to download from the Internet as full-sized overhead transparencies.

Although every effort has been made to avoid burdening the reader unnecessarily, we have taken particular pains to ensure that our writing is underpinned with theories and concepts drawn not only from the mainstream human resource management literature but more broadly, including organizational behaviour, strategic and international management, information technology, small business theory and change management theory.

We would anticipate that this book would be particularly suitable for students on post-experience programmes, but would also be suitable for the student reading for a general business or management degree. Throughout, we have tried to relate theory to practice, and would anticipate that the line manager with significant responsibilities for human resourcing issues will also find much to interest them.

Acknowledgments

A number of HRM practitioners, line managers and academic staff have helped shape the content of this book through critical reading of chapters or through detailed discussions. We would like to express our thanks in particular to Dr Bert Rolf of the Hanzehogeschol, Groningen, the Netherlands; Dr Dominic Bessant of the University of Lille, France; Mr Freddy Lelie of Digital Europe, Brussels, Belgium; Dr Susan Maxwell of the Fire Service College, Moreton in Marsh, Gloucestershire, United Kingdom; Diversity and HR Solutions; Professor Adrian Furnham, University of London.

Thanks to the staff at Thomson Learning for their help throughout this project.

The editors and publishers wish to thank the following for permission to use copyright material. Professor Charles Handy for the article 'Life's a job and then you die', originally published in 'The Director' 1977. Figure 7.2 is reproduced with the permission of PWA Personnel Systems Ltd, Marlow.

Every effort has been made to trace all the copyright holders, but if any have been inadvertently overlooked the publishers will be pleased to make the necessary arrangements at the first opportunity.

Foreword to the second edition

Within this second edition, we have updated key areas of HRM theory and practice where we felt that there was a clear consolidation of certain ideas that the line manager with responsibility for delivering HRM could be usefully introduced to. The areas where we have felt the greatest pressure for such updates include the impact of information technology (particularly in the area of management systems and development and HR administration); the development of models of strategic HRM; the management of workforce diversity and inclusion. In addition, the chapter on Training and Development has been completely rewritten from a more strategic and continuous development perspective. There is also an entirely new chapter on Negotiations.

In addition, there is a range of general updates across all of the chapters and the Introduction and Conclusions. For the Introduction, we have added a section on ethics and HRM, and ethical questions posed at the end of each chapter related to some of the ethical issues and dilemmas that may arise in these fields. Over and above the content, we have also attempted to improve the layout and overall impact of the book, and Web-based information has been updated. There are now Web-based annual updates to the Legal Briefings at the end of each chapter also.

We hope that the changes leave the strengths of the first edition intact, while the updates continue to be relevant to those interested in HRM from a line manager's perspective. This group has turned out to be largely as we anticipated: students on post-experience programmes as well as those on general management and business degrees and finally, line managers with significant responsibility for HRM.

Pen portraits

Alan Blackburn

Alan Blackburn is Principal Lecturer in Human Resource Management at Oxford Brookes University School of Business. He began his career at Vickers Engineering Group, Newcastle, as a Technician Apprentice before moving into the Personnel Department at Gateshead Metropolitan Borough Council. Here he acted in a consultancy role to council departments on various organizational issues. In 1995, he moved to Cranfield Institute of Technology and worked predominantly for the Ministry of Defence. He moved to Oxford Brookes University in 1990 and has managed and played a leading role in the development of postgraduate Diploma Courses within the School of Business. Alan teaches Human Resource Management on the DMS and MBA programmes and Employee Relations and Employee Rewards on DPM. He has undertaken training and consultancy activities for a number of organizations including, Interforward Logistics, Rank Leisure, Oxford Radcliffe Hospital and Unipart. He is presently researching models of management in Hospital Trusts. Alan graduated in Business Studies from the University of Northumbria and was awarded an MA in Industrial Relations by the University of Warwick. He is also a corporate member of the Institute of Personnel and Development.

Nelarine Cornelius

Dr Nelarine Cornelius is a Lecturer in Human Resource Management and Organizational Behaviour and heads the Organizational Changes and Development Subject group in the School of Business and Management at Brunel University. She received her doctorate from the University of Manchester and subsequently an MBA from the Open University.

Prior to entering higher education, she worked as an international consultant and manager for General Motors, both in the UK and in Europe, and also in local government. She has acted, and continues to act, as an external consultant for a variety of small through to global organizations, in the private, public and voluntary sectors, as well as local and central government and the European Union. She is a chartered psychologist, whose research interests include the management of diversity; management and organizational learning; management and decision-making; and scenario planning. She has taught on a wide variety of post-experience programmes for managers, has been part of curriculum design teams for the Certificate and Diploma courses in management and was part of the design team for the new MBA programme at Brunel University. She has also written modules for these programmes. She has acted as External Examiner to the Universities of Reading, Hertfordshire and Westminster. She is a fellow of the Institute of Personnel and Development and the Royal Society of Arts, an Associate Fellow of the British Psychological Society, and a member of the Steering Comittee for the Knowledge and Learning Special Interest Group of the British Academy of Management.

Suzanne Gagnon

Suzanne Gagnon lectures in the Faculty of Management at McGill University. Formally she was Senior Lecturer in the School of Business and Management at Oxford Brookes University. She does research in the areas of ethics and HRM, diversity, and reward systems. She teaches on a variety of postgraduate courses, including Strategic HRM, Innovation and Change from an HR Perspective, and Reward Management, as well as International HRM at the undergraduate level. She is joint programme manager of the Master of Arts in HRM.

Suzanne graduated from Oxford University with a Master of Science in Management (HRM and Industrial Relations) in 1994. She worked for a major management consultancy firm, specializing in HR and organizational development, prior to entering academia on a full-time basis. Her previous experience was as a policy and communications advisor in the Canadian government in Ottawa, including two years in the Prime Minister's Office. Suzanne holds a Bachelor of Journalism degree from Carleton University and a BA in Political Science from the University of British Columbia.

Larraine Gooch

Larraine Gooch is a Principal Lecturer in Human Resource Management at Oxford Brookes University School of Business. She is the Head of the Management Development and Human Resource Management Unit. She teaches across a wide range of programmes, which involve teaching both personnel specialists and line managers; these programmes include the University Certificate in Management, the Diploma in Management Studies, the Diploma in Personnel Management, the Masters in Human Resource Management and the Masters in Business Administration.

Larraine gained her MA in Human Resource Management from Thames Valley University in 1993 and became a Fellow of the Institute of Personnel and Development in 1995. She has experience of personnel management both in the public and the private sector, having spent a number of years as a personnel manager in organizations which include J. Lyons (now Allied Lyons) and BBC Television. Larraine's research interests are in two main areas: first, issues of diversity in the workplace and second, the role of line managers in managing diverse organizations in partnership with human resource specialists. In addition, Larraine leads the 'reward' module on the University IPD Professional Qualification Scheme and has a particular interest in the relationship between performance and reward.

Beryl Grant

Beryl Grant is a law graduate of the London School of Economics and was called to the Bar by Grays Inn. Her long-term interest in labour law dates from university days and is reflected in the research thesis that gained the postgraduate Diploma in Law from Oxford University: 'The Sex Discrimination Act, 1975: the establishment of unlawful discrimination by individual complainants'. She has been a member of the Industrial Law Society since its inception in the early 1970s.

She was invited to join the steering committee that was setting up the Oxford Institute of Legal Practice and contributed the unit on 'Business Law and Practice' to the course. She sits as an Oxford Brookes University appointee on the Board of Studies.

Until her recent retirement, she held the post of Senior Lecturer in Law at the School of Social Sciences and Law, Oxford Brookes University. Her teaching commitments have included contributions to the Diploma in Personnel Management and the Human Resource Management component of the MBA. She contributed the law section to the student materials provided for the Oxford Brookes University Open Learning MBA.

Current interests include the law of companies, international trade and intellectual property.

Sheila B. Healy

Sheila Healy was a researcher at Aberdeen Business School, part of the Robert Gordon University, having obtained an MSc in Occupational Psychology from the Queen's University of Belfast. Her PhD research focuses on the measurement of small business success and failure. In addition to her research, she has been involved in teaching Organizational Behaviour and Managing Change courses at tutorial level and has also taught human resource management to Level One IPD students. She has previously worked in Human Resources and is a Graduate member of the British Psychological Society. Sheila is currently working as a trainer in Limerick, Ireland.

Matthew Lynas

Matthew Lynas has held senior positions in general and specialist management in private and quasi-government sectors and in higher education. He holds a doctorate from Brunel University. Matthew is a Fellow of the Institute of Personnel and Development and Associate Tutor on Distance Learning at Henley Management College.

His experience has covered a range of industries, including agriculture, and a wide involvement with small and medium sized businesses in consultancy and general advisory roles. Within the field of higher education, there has been extensive involvement with teaching and development of MBA programmes in Organizational Behaviour in Small Business areas, including distance learning material.

Willian Scott-Jackson

Dr William Scott-Jackson is Chief Executive of CSA Management Consultants, which specializes in the strategic application of Human Resource Management to maximize profitability and shareholder value. William's research contributions include the development of business-focused HR Strategy, methods for assessing and building individual change competence and a process for analysing opinions via open-ended questions. His PhD was gained after an extensive study into resource-based HR strategy and included the development of both a process and new capabilities for human resources. CSA Management Consultants is a highly regarded Human Resources consultancy whose Divisions provide a complete range of advanced services to international organizations. These include Strategic HR, research and selection and HR effectiveness. William's expertise, together with that of his consulting colleagues, has been applied extensively to maximize the success and benefits of many of the recent high-profile mergers and acquisitions in the finance and IT markets. With toolkits for every stage, from due diligence to evaluation, the approach allows HR to take its place in driving strategies for dealing with one of the most significant areas of business activity.

William is now also MD for a new Internet company, Pointsthree Ltd, which offers HRM provision for small businesses.

Clive Wildish

Clive Wildish is a Principal Lecturer in International Management at the Oxford Brookes University School of Business. Clive is a Course Manager for an undergraduate degree in Business and International Management and also teaches International Management and Business at postgraduate level on the MBA, International Management MSc and Human Resource Management MA programmes. Clive is a member of the Institute of Management and a Graduate Member of the Institute of Personnel Development.

Prior to joining the School of Business at Oxford Brookes in 1991, Clive worked for ten years as a Marketing Manager and Project Leader within the world of academic publishing. He has worked with a number of leading publishers in the field, specializing latterly in acquisition studies across the industry. Between 1989–90, Clive studied on a full-time MBA programme at the University of Bradford Management Centre, specializing in Human Resource Management. Clive's current research interest is in the globalization of the publishing and newspaper industries, with specific reference to the role of electronic publishing as a significant driving force for change.

David Wilson

We live in exciting times. As a freelance business author and tutor, my role is to make sense of the flood of technology-induced changes occurring in business right now. The computer-based communications technologies such as Electronic

Data Interchange and the Internet are creating a new business environment of 'co-opetition', in which commercial advantage can be gained through greater openness and more trusting relationships, both within and between organizations.

My day-job since leaving Oxford Brookes University School of Business, is lecturing for the EAP European School of Management with bases in Paris, Oxford, Berlin and Madrid. The students who are on Masters programmes in European Business and Management, are fluent in three European languages, and end up with business theory and work experience gained in those three European countries.

In between lecturing I write about information technology and its impact on business, trying to clarify principles so they can perhaps be exploited more widely. I try for a style which connects with the experience and concerns of managers, who often know more than I do about some aspects of technology, but who occasionally lack the wider perspective of developments in other organizations, and other industries.

I have two books published by Butterworth Heinemann in association with the Institute of Management. They are Managing Information (1997) 2nd Ed and Managing Knowledge (1996). My main interest is in how computers should be used to exploit the knowledge resource, by building on foundations of TQM, BPR, and above all, HRM.

Introduction and overview

Nelarine Cornelius with Suzanne Gagnon

HRM themes addressed in this book

In this textbook, rather than accepting or rejecting specific models of HRM or indeed personnel management as appropriate or not, we have identified a number of themes that we believe provide important insights into systems of employment management. These reflect changes in the theories and practice of the world of work to which the line manager or those interested in general management need to be attuned in order to understand how such changes can be tackled from a 'people management' perspective.

We do not claim that these themes are a definitive list, but have opted to select themes which appear on the surface at least to be attracting the attention of those who work or research in the area of HRM and also those who are in fields in which an appreciation of the significance of effective employment management is growing (Figure 0.1).

The first of these themes concerns the relationship between the line manager, his or her subordinates, and the HRM or personnel professional. The **line manager–HR professional relationship** can be represented on a continuum from a great degree of specialization and tight lines of demarcation of roles and responsibilities

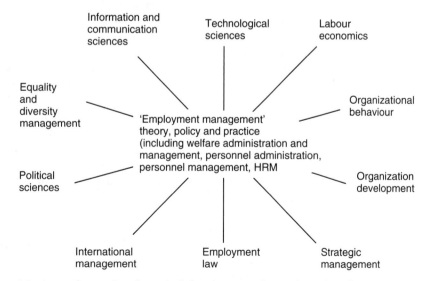

Figure 0.1 Areas of research and practice informing our understanding of employment management.

with the HR professional in 'large' departments, taking the primary lead and responsibility for HR issues, through to HR practice in which the line manager has full control of HR issues and the role of personnel is exclusively advisory, and there is essentially no HR department at all. Clearly, the greater the move towards line managers holding key roles and real responsibility for HR practice, the less acceptable is the 'gifted HRM amateur'. Specifically, there is an obvious training and development need for the line manager in order to be able to take on these tasks and execute them effectively.

Second, there is the theme of the **interrelatedness** and more **holistic approaches** in the practice of HRM. These interrelationships include:

- the links between general and HRM-specific strategic decision making and planning;
- the links between strategic HRM and more operational HRM;
- the interrelationship between parts of the HRM sub-systems, for example between the quality of the recruitment and selection process and the type of training and development plans that should be followed;
- the perception that traditional line and staff activities are now more difficult to separate and, indeed, that there is a greater degree of overlap reflected in increasing HR responsibilities for the line manager.

There are changes in work organizations that have been regarded by some as major step changes. These would include:

- The **impact of information technology**, which has been a primary driver in securing efficiency gains but, beyond this, potentially provides the basis for new ways of working and sources of sustainable competitive advantage. As with the introduction of most technologies, there is the potential to generate more rewarding working lives for knowledge workers but also to create Taylorist-like controls over employees, such as electronic surveillance and monitoring of employee performance.
- A combination of economic pressures to downsize or restructure, coupled with the enabling device of new technology, has led to a renewed interest in **different organizational forms**. Some of these, such as **the virtual organization** (in reality, more likely to be a virtualized part of a large, more conventional enterprise) and more broadly, **network structures** made up of associates, have captured the imagination. However, what is seen as a desirable organizational form should go beyond an uncritical consideration of short-term financial gains or pursuing the latest fashion. There have always been, and always will be, specific organizational structures that alone or in combination best suit the needs of a specific organization at a given moment in time.
- More firmly established is the **flexible organization** (Figure 0.2). Flexibility is sometimes considered in terms of **functional flexibility**, the range of skills and competences that employees possess that enable them to complete a wide range of jobs. However, organizational flexibility is usually considered in terms of **numerical flexibility**, with a core of permanent, often full-time employees, and other part-time or short-term contract workers used and the latter in particular shed as required.

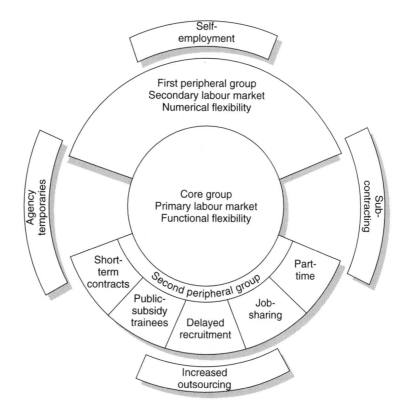

Figure 0.2   The flexible firm. *Source:* Atkinson, 1984.

Although widely used in many organizations, organizational flexibility has attracted criticism from some sources. Among scholars, the strongest criticisms have arisen from the critical HRM school, with much flexibility practice regarded as naked manipulation of the employee (e.g., Legge in Sparrow and Marchington, 1998). In addition, it could be argued that it is too often taken to the extremes in the abscence of a clear view of what is organizational core competence in terms of key knowledge, skills and experience. In other words, the costs and overheads saved in the short term through flexibility may be offset by a loss of core competence, making the maintenance of acceptable levels of service or production difficult, with the likely loss of an organization's competitive edge.

● Technological advances and a desire to exploit labour markets around the world have increasingly led to organizations undertaking **the production and delivery of goods and services from a global perspective**. This has meant that increased competence is required on the part of HRM professionals and line managers in order to cope with different approaches to people management and the difficulties that may arise when attempting to 'manage abroad' or deal with the cultural differences associated with multinational teams.

● Organizational flexibility has been accompanied by **increasing uncertainty about job security**, with a job for life becoming a thing of the past in particular industries and sectors. Against a background of heightened pressure on the welfare safety nets provided by many governments, there are also increasing anxieties about the type of support that will be secured if made unemployed, and in this climate, anxiety about the need to 'fend for oneself' is heightened. The responsibility for the management of security of employment is shifting among many from the responsibility of the employer to more proactive strategies on the part of employees to ensure that they remain employable. Therefore, the management and continual updating of **a personal portfolio of skills, knowledge and expertise** is seen as core to ensuring continuity of employment, if not continuity with a specific employer.

- Other changes in organizational structure centre around the permanent issue of deciding upon the **degree of centralization or decentralization** desirable. In recent times, many companies have moved towards decentralization, with significant reductions in headquarters and support staff. Within the context of the downsizing that often accompanies it, this means that more traditional support activities are either being contracted out and brought in when required or more support staff activities end up devolved down to the line.

- On the back of Japanese models of management there is the increasing popularity of **high commitment management and employee empowerment**. This in part reflects a shift in the industrial relations landscape of many organizations. At its most positive, commitment management may ensure more active engagement with getting the job done by heightening employee motivation. However, a more cynical view is that it represents a sophisticated form of employee manipulation with a view to securing compliance.

- Issues which have also gained importance are actual and quasi-measurement, in the form of **standard setting**, and **value for money** in management in general, and HRM is no exception to this. Added to this list is our observation that when any HR activity or intervention is introduced, set measures of success need to be established at the outset of their design, so that monitoring and evaluation can be put in train. The development of financial and non-financial measures of corporate performance at the strategic level is mirrored by a trend to monitor more closely the performance of individuals and teams. However, if well designed and managed, such systems provide important information through providing a more transparent and systematic approach to employee assessment; the setting out of expectations may also increase the expectations of employees regarding resources that the organization/manager will provide in order that these targets can be met.

- The identification of areas in which performance can be improved requires some form of assessment of the nature of the gap between desired and actual outcomes. Often, **the cost of living with below standard performance** is greater than making good the deficit, even if time and money need to be spent on improving performance. Again, the importance of **training and development** to the organization is highlighted.

The rise in **consumerism and an awareness of rights** is reflected in the workplace also. Western societies are becoming increasingly litigious, with employees often seeking **legal recourse** if they feel that they have been badly treated by their employers. For many of these employee grievances, the role of the line manager in reducing the likelihood of complaint or alternatively, being the central cause of the complaint is significant. Brewster *et al.* found in their survey that line managers were very reticent about becoming involved in legal issues (Brewster and Hegewisch, 1994). The reality is that they often have no choice. For example, many will be expected to provide key information for disciplinary action.

The themes outlined above appear throughout the chapters in the book, and are illustrated in Figure 0.3.

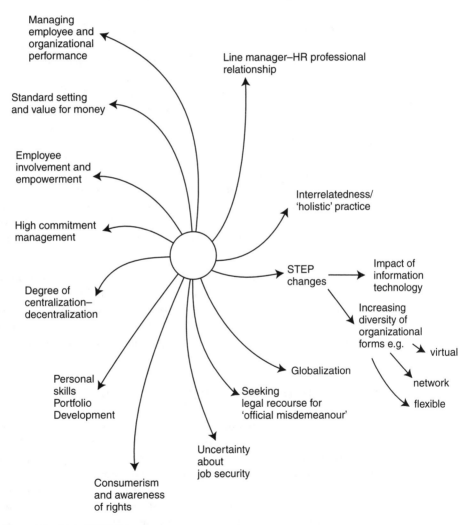

Figure 0.3 Main HRM themes.

Managing employees: 'landmark' developments

In the history of the policies and practices for managing people in organizations, there have been many significant, radical and controversial developments. Landmarks include:

- The massive increases in organizational size and complexity associated with the technological advances that occurred during the **Industrial Revolution** of the nineteenth century.
- The introduction of '**Scientific Management**' or '**Taylorism**', a system of organization of work in manufacturing industry in which workers' jobs were broken down into simple, repetitive tasks, with managers taking primary responsibilities for making decisions and controlling the flow of work, and in which it was believed that the primary motivation of workers was to earn money.
- '**Fordism**', which involved the introduction of the production line and mass production techniques into manufacturing industry, initially the production of cars. Like Taylorism, Fordism radically increased worker productivity. The volume of cars that could be produced per hour increased dramatically, and coupled with economies of scale and tight controls of the unit cost of production, there was increased availability to a wider population of what was, until this point, a luxury item.
- Criticism and reaction to 'Taylorism' and 'Fordism', which many considered de-skilled and alienated workers, was encapsulated in the **Human Relations** movement, and later developed into social science-based interventions in work organizations in order to improve **productivity and employee well-being**, in what became known as **organization development**.
- An interest in the interaction between social groupings and technical systems in the workplace in the form of **socio-technical systems** research and interventions.

These and other changes, including important social and political changes that have taken place over the past two hundred years in Western economies, are listed in Figure 0.4. However, these developments are usually viewed as more reflective of changes which inform our understanding of the development of general management theory and practice, not **employment management practice** specifically.

Employment management: definitions and debates

Human resource management theory and practice has been informed by all of these developments, but our attention will now turn to the development of **employment management** systems which are more normally thought of as mainstream **personnel or human resource management**.

There are a wide range of definitions of human resource management, reflecting its evolution and interpretation at specific moments in time. Each has its strengths and limitations, and a number of these are presented in Figure 0.5. In

There have been a number of debates and issues that have played a major role in shaping how people in organizations are managed, and some of these are outlined below.

Increase in the size of organizations during the Industrial Revolution of the nineteenth century

- Technological advances provided the opportunity for dramatic increases in productivity. The technology also required the employment of large numbers of people within a single enterprise, and with wages low there was a dramatic increase in establishment numbers and the need to coordinate their work effectively. For example, although the average size of organization in the United Kingdom grew from 137 to 191 employees between 1838 and 1897, those organizations in industries that were among the first to industrialize could be as large as 1000 as early as 1833. These larger organizations required substantial inputs in attempts to improve coordination of effort. Initially, this increase in scale was a hindrance in the growth of management until firms moved towards rationalizing their activities.
- During this period, the number of people employed in small family businesses declined, there was a move from agriculture as the primary employer to manufacturing industry, and, for many, work became separated from home for the first time.

The rise of bureaucracy

Concerns about the appropriate response to structuring large organizations was addressed by a variety of writers and researchers. One of the most noteworthy is the German sociologist, Max Weber. Weber suggested that in society, authority could be categorized into 'Traditional' (the leader has the right to rule), 'Charismatic' (the leader has a unique, special virtue) or 'Legal-rational', (based on formal written rules underpinned by law). A bureaucracy is a 'legal-rational' form of organization, which has specific characteristics, including job specialization, authority hierarchy, formal rules and regulations, impersonality (rules and regulations are applied uniformly, avoiding involvement of personality or personal preferences), formal selection of employees and career orientation for managers, who were paid professionals (rather than company owners) who pursued their careers in the organization within which they worked. Routinization of administration and decision making are key. Organizations have a 'strategic apex' and many layers of hierarchy. The strength of the bureaucracy is standardization. Although the term bureaucracy is now often used in a pejorative sense, it still remains a dominant model within many large organizations.

Worker exploitation and resultant reactions

- The consolidation of a sense of collective purpose and labour rights among workers and increasing levels of unionization, in organizations in Europe in particular, most noticeably during the latter part of the nineteenth and early part of the twentieth century.
- Models of 'benevolent capitalism' embodied in the nineteenth century by Quaker organizations such as the confectioners Cadbury's and Bournville, and the Port Sunlight enterprise, all of which exist to this day. The concern for the welfare of employees and their families at work and home is illustrated by the development of model worker villages contrasted to the slum dwellings lived in by many other factory workers. More benevolent model of managing employees.
- The importance of a welfare perspective in the workplace is embodied in the development of the embryonic Institute of Personnel and Development in the United Kingdom, which was established with the aim of addressing employee well-being (including administration of those returning from the battlefields after World War I.)

The increasing importance of the role of the manager in organizations

In the late nineteenth century, there was increasing competition between, in particular, the UK, 'Germany' and America. For all three countries, access to and the **effective management of capital** was seen as a priority, as well as **securing reliability of production** in order to ensure a steady supply of goods to increasing numbers of consumers. In the UK in particular, there was a perception that increases in organizational size was a problem, although eventually organizations did rationalize their operations.

Figure 0.4   Landmarks in the management of people in organizations.

However, concern remained about the UK's waning competitiveness against the might of the 'German' and American economies. In part, it was believed that UK companies needed to promote their goods more effectively, which fuelled a rising interest and eventually, participation and expertise in the coordination of **sales and promotional activities**. However, there remained a concern that activities in organizations were not being coordinated effectively, and interest grew in approaches that could be introduced to **improve supervisory and 'managerial' activities**.

Scientific Management

The increasing importance of the manager is embodied in models of '**Scientific Management**' developed by F.W. Taylor, in which workers' jobs were broken down into simple, repetitive tasks, which were developed by and executed under the close supervision of managers. At the heart lay a view of the worker as 'economic man', workers needing to be coerced and controlled, and their work performance optimized through the practice of careful work study at the heart of which was the simplification of complex jobs into simple repetitive tasks whose completion times were calculated and strictly enforced.

Fordism and mass production

The need to coordinate the actions of large numbers of workers as highlighted in the mass production techniques developed by Henry Ford (along with Taylor) in the 1920s. Within this system the pace of work was determined by the speed at which the assembly line flowed, not individual worker choice.

The Human Relations school

Reactions to the downside of scientific management – worker alienation and a sense that workers were merely part of the system rather than social beings in their own right – were encapsulated by the Human Relations school. Some of the earliest work was done in the 1920s, as represented by the work of Elton Mayo, and gained impetus and recognition through the work of pioneers such as Kurt Lewin at Harvard University and Eric Trist (who worked on the relationship between the impact of technology on social dynamics of groups) at the Tavistock Institute in London. These researchers created a more humane image of the worker and more humanistic models of management.

Pressure from traditionally disadvantaged groups for fairer treatment

Many groups remained on the periphery of industrial acceptance and power. Women had been in the industrial workplace since the onset of the industrial revolution but opportunities for advancement, or indeed, employment in specific industries were severely limited, and women were unlikely to receive equal pay, as their primary designated role in society was that of wife and mother. A combination of working for the war efforts of the two World Wars, universal suffrage and increasing educational opportunities sowed the seeds of discontent and created a gradual move towards greater acceptance of women in the workplace, eventually reinforced in employment law. Those from ethnic minorities have faced similar, albeit distinctive, battles for acceptance. In the United States, this pressure for fairer treatment in all walks of life, including employment, culminated in the Civil Rights movement and eventually, employment legislation. Civil unrest among immigrants to the United Kingdom in the 1950s and 1960s led to the development of Race Relations Laws which had within them implications for fair treatment in the workplace.

'Japanization' of management practice

The introduction of 'Japanese' management techniques such as Total Quality Management and continuous improvement (Kaizen) has increasingly become standard management practice and, for such practices, staff development is central.

HRM and the management of change

An argued rise in the perceived importance of systematic HRM practice, particularly in relation to the management of change which centres around such things as culture change interventions, and merger and acquisition activity.

Figure 0.4 Continued.

Below are listed definitions of HRM which reflect an 'aspirational' position (1) and (2), a more descriptive and functional view (3) and an overview of various meanings commonly in use (4).

1. **Fobrum, Tichy and Devanna, 1984**

   (HRM – the) critical management task is to align the formal structure and the HR systems (selection, appraisal, rewards and development) so that they can drive the strategic objectives of the organization.

2. **Guest, 1987**

   The main dimensions of HRM (concern) integration, employee commitment, the goal of flexibility/adaptability, and the goal of quality.

3. **Torrington and Hall, 1987**

   Human resource management is directed mainly at the management needs for human resources (not necessarily of employees) to be provided and deployed. There is a greater emphasis on planning, monitoring, and control, rather than on problem-solving and mediation. It is totally identified with management interests, being a general management activity and is relatively distant from the workforce as a whole.

4. **Storey, 1992 – a range of meanings**

   ● (HRM as) strategic interventions designed to elicit commitment and to develop resourceful humans

   ● (HRM as) strategic interventions designed to secure full utilization of labour resources

   ● (HRM as) just another term for 'personnel'

Figure 0.5 Definitions of HRM.

recent times, key debates have centred not only around developing typologies of personnel management and HRM, but also questioning the extent to which the 'new' human resource management differs from the 'old' personnel management, a debate, it could be argued, driven by a range of 'interested parties', including academics and personnel managers, with various vested interests in promoting apparently new ways of doing things (Legge, 1995).

Is HRM anything new?

Is HRM genuinely something new or merely repackaging of the old personnel way of doing things? Although we do not have time to explore this debate in any detail, many of the salient arguments have been reviewed with balanced, scholarly treatment in seminal books by Karen Legge (1995) and John Storey (1992, 1995). Some have expressed the concern that HRM is little more than a relabelling of personnel management. Others that have suggested that there are genuine demarcations between HRM and the more 'traditional' personnel management and administration include John Storey (1992) (Figure 0.6). Put simply, more 'traditional' personnel management is viewed as a support activity to line activities, closely associated with administrative tasks and coordinating and liaising between the demands of management and the concerns and needs of employees, while HRM is often regarded as a holistic, strategy-centred approach to employment management (Figure 0.7). Also, it has been suggested that, in the UK in particular, personnel management evolved against a backdrop of tough-minded, confrontational industrial relations, during which the personnel specialist often needed to adopt an implicit (if not an explicit) mediation role between management and the workforce.

However, it is argued by many that a strategy-centred, HRM approach to managing employees *should* be central to modern management practice, although there

Dimension	Personnel and IR	HRM
Beliefs and assumptions		
1 Contract	Careful delineation of written contracts	Aim to go 'beyond contract'
2 Rules	Importance of devising clear rules/ mutuality	'Can do' outlook: impatience with 'rule'
3 Guide to management action	Procedures/consistency control	'Business need'/flexibility/ commitment
4 Behaviour referent	Norms/custom and practice	Values/mission
5 Managerial task *vis-à-vis* labour	Monitoring	Nurturing
6 Nature of relations	Pluralist	Unitarist
7 Conflict	Institutionalized	De-emphasized
8 Standardization	High (e.g. 'parity' an issue)	Low (e.g. 'parity' not seen as relevant)
Strategic aspects		
9 Key relations	Labour–management	Business–customer
10 Initiatives	Piecemeal	Integrated
11 Corporate plan	Marginal to	Central to
12 Speed of decisions	Slow	Fast
Line management		
13 Management role	Transactional	Transformational leadership
14 Key managers	Personnel/IR specialists	General/business/line managers
15 Prized management skills	Negotiation	Facilitation
Key levers		
16 Foci of attention for interventions	Personnel procedures	Wide-ranging cultural, structural and personnel strategies
17 Selection	Separate, marginal task	Integrated, key task
18 Pay	Job evaluation: multiple, fixed grades	Performance-related: few if any grades
19 Conditions	Separately negotiated	Harmonization
20 Labour–management	Collective bargaining contracts	Towards individual contracts
21 Thrust of relations with stewards	Regularized through facilities and training	Marginalized (with exception of some bargaining for change models)
22 Communication	Restricted flow/indirect	Increased flow/direct
23 Job design	Division of labour	Teamwork
24 Conflict handling	Reach temporary truces	Manage climate and culture
25 Training and development	Controlled access to courses	Learning companies

Figure 0.6   Personnel management versus HRM management. *Source:* Storey, 1992.

is evidence that it may still have some way to go. A useful indicator of how seriously the activity is taken is the degree to which the function influences key decision making. Although progress seems to have been made with regards to representation at senior management level, the primary indicator of board-level representation of the HRM function has a long way to go. One survey of large companies in the UK suggests that although 30 per cent of boards in the UK now have an HRM director of some kind, a significant improvement over previous years, it is

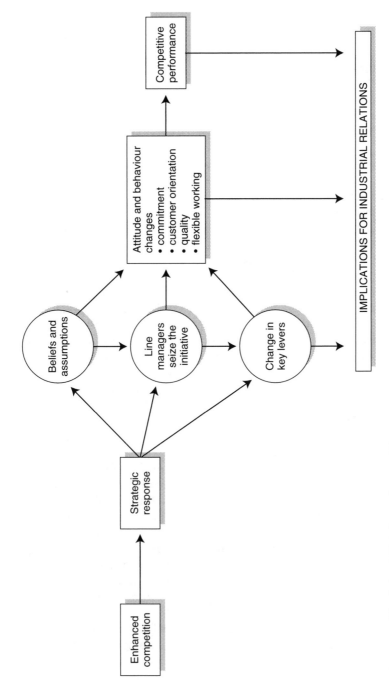

Figure 0.7 The shift to HRM. *Source:* Storey, 1992.

unlikely that any board would lack, say, a finance director, although money and people are common to all organizations (Purcell in Storey, 1995).

Fitness for purpose

What is also highlighted by a number of writers is the 'transatlantic gap' between what is considered (crudely) as 'US' theories and practice versus theory and practice in Europe. Some argue that many of the US models of HRM not only are different but that this difference is inevitable, given the different culture, ethos, industrial relations and employment law frameworks in the USA. So for example, it is argued that more 'American' models of HRM reflect a desire for a non-interventionist, unfettered free enterprise culture (see Kochan and Dyer in Storey, 1995), where managers expect that they have 'the right to manage', while in much of mainland Europe, HRM practice is more likely to be grounded in 'welfare capitalism', with a more central role for unions and their representatives, and state interventions and a more collective view of organizational life predominates (Brewster in Storey, 1995).

Furthermore, HRM can be divided into two approaches: 'hard' or 'soft' (Figure 0.8). **'Hard' HRM** is primarily financially driven, with a fairly hard-nosed view of controlling the wages bill and a directive (and sometimes manipulative) attitude towards gaining work efficiencies: it is a **utilitarian, individualistic** and **instrumental** way of managing employees in which **the company position and managerial prerogative take precedent over the collective view and the concerns and needs of employees**; it could be argued that it is the legacy of Taylorism and Fordism. In contrast, **'Soft' HRM** is centred around the development of employees and has a more humanist edge, termed **'developmental humanism'**, in which employees are viewed primarily as assets to the company, rather than as costs and liabilities, and has its foundations in the Human Relations movement (see Legge, 1995).

However, another way of considering HRM practice within organizations has less to do with the 'rhetorics and realities' of HRM or personnel management as espoused and actually practised and is more concerned with **broader interpretations of fitness for purpose**. Many writers in the field acknowledge that there is diversity of practice and that, even within 'traditional' personnel management or 'new(er)' human resource management, those with specialist responsibilities for it appear in many guises. Furthermore, although it would be foolish to ignore the difficulties that can be encountered when transplanting management practice which has developed in one culture into another culture, already the rise in the importance of global management systems and practice has put into context US–Europe differences. These differences can be regarded as one of a plethora of diversity of theory and practice that needs to be more extensively researched and understood: the gap between US and UK HRM practice is likely to be smaller than that between the USA and the rapidly developing economic power of the People's Republic of China, for example.

Ways of categorizing employment management practice and personnel practitioner style and practice are illustrated in Figures 0.9 and 0.10.

In reality, organizations do not do things by the book. It is likely that the prag-

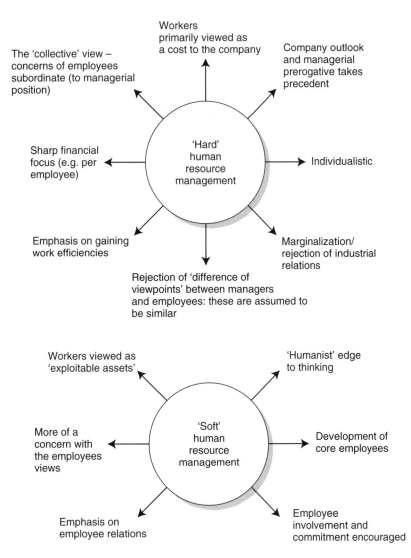

Workers
primarily viewed as
a cost to the company

The 'collective' view –
concerns of employees
subordinate (to managerial
position)

Company outlook
and managerial
prerogative takes
precedent

Sharp financial
focus (e.g. per
employee)

'Hard'
human
resource
management

Individualistic

Emphasis on gaining
work efficiencies

Marginalization/
rejection of industrial
relations

Rejection of 'difference of
viewpoints' between managers
and employees: these are assumed to
be similar

Workers viewed as
'exploitable assets'

'Humanist' edge
to thinking

More of a
concern with
the employees
views

'Soft'
human
resource
management

Development of
core employees

Emphasis on
employee relations

Employee
involvement and
commitment encouraged

Figure 0.8   'Hard' versus 'Soft' HRM: some differences.

matic response to developments in the theory and practice of employment management will be shaped by changes in corporate strategy, the economic environment, the size of the enterprise, whether there is an abundance or shortage of specific skills in the labour market, organizational ignorance, an organization's industrial context, organizational culture, and a reluctance or enthusiasm to do things differently. As with any management practice, a balanced assessment needs to be made of the reasons for apparent inconsistencies in the employment management framework of any organization. For example, organizations in transition may have both 'personnel' and HRM operating under the same roof at the same time and are no more likely to discard the 'old' system before the new one is up and running

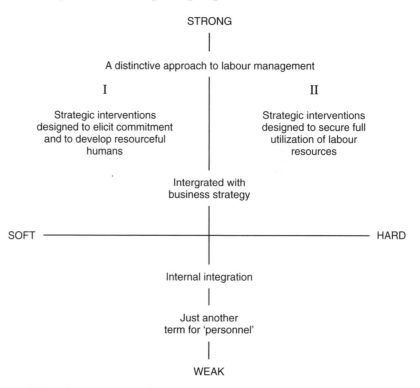

Figure 0.9 Ways of categorizing employment management practice. *Source:* Storey, 1992.

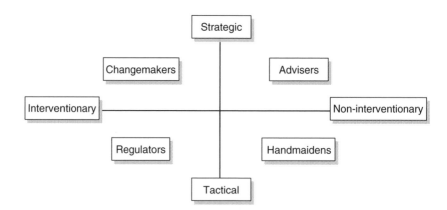

Figure 0.10 Ways of categorizing personnel practitioner style and practice. *Source:* Storey, 1992.

than they would be to throw away the old computer system before the new one is fully commissioned and teething problems sorted out. Moreover, it is likely that some organizations will 'cherry pick' their way through the best elements of personnel management and HRM, with what is emerging being new hybrid, tailored systems of employment management, developed given the external pressures on organizations, and the internal responses needed at any given time.

Line managers' involvement with 'people management'

There have been many anecdotal and researched accounts of the cynicism often held by line managers towards 'personnel' or HRM professionals, which in turn is often reflected in a cynical view of HRM. Anecdotally, it is not just a matter of personnel or HRM staff instructing line managers as to what they can and cannot do. Researchers have found that there is a perception that these professionals have been regarded as lacking in commercial awareness, or familiarity with the realities of 'life on the line', or whose views are only sought once all of the strategic and commercial decisions have been made, in order to deal with 'messy problems' like handling redundancies (e.g., Brewster and Larsen, 1992). And which of us has not come across line managers who regard employment management issues as 'nothing to do with them'?

The reality is that most line managers have always (and inevitably) had some involvement in employment management, even if formally this may have been limited to conducting annual staff appraisals and deciding who is going to get a pay rise. However, there is some evidence that line managers are *expected* to cope with these 'additional' responsibilities. In one survey, an assessment was made of the degree of 'devolvement' of what is often thought of as 'personnel work' to line managers in ten European countries (Brewster and Larsen, 1992; Brewster and Hegewisch, 1994). There was no simple correlation between the degree of devolvement to line managers and the number of personnel specialists. Although there did seem to be a relationship between an increase in line management responsibility for personnel issues and formal training, there was little evidence that organizations were providing formal training to help their line managers handle human resource issues.

Ethics and human resource management

Ethics has been defined as 'the disciplined inquiry into the morality of human conduct' (Chryssides and Kaler, 1995); 'the study of individual and collective moral awareness, judgement, character and conduct' (Petrick and Quinn, 1997); and more simply, as being about 'what is right' (Fisher and Rice, 1999). Ethical analysis may be descriptive, prescriptive or analytical, but many ethicists argue that its outcome should be fuller understanding of the conduct being examined, leading ultimately to more ethical conduct in future.

Business ethics as a subject has received increasing attention from both academic and practitioner communities in recent years. Within this, a distinctive literature of 'ethics and HRM' has begun to develop, although this has been slow compared to, say, ethical issues attached to the environment. This is in spite of the traditional view of the personnel manager or officer as the guardian of employee welfare and fair treatment. Yet persuasive arguments are now being made that 'the employment of people gives rise to unique and important ethical considerations' (Miller, 1996). In broad terms, the 'ethics and HRM' literature can be split into two streams:

● **macro-level considerations of the ethics of trends and developments in HRM and HR practice**, most often through reference to 'classical' ethical theory such as Kantian philosophy and utilitarianism, as well as discussions of the role of ethical theory in aiding our understanding of 'ethics in action' (Cornelius and Gagnon, 1999).

● **discussions of micro-level ethical dilemmas or 'moral mazes' that may confront the HR practitioner or any manager dealing with people management issues**, and development of the capacity to engage in ethical reasoning in order to better resolve these dilemmas and make ethical decisions.

The purpose of this section is to briefly review these two streams, with a view to increasing the people manager's awareness of ethics and its potential to improve practice. Then at the end of each chapter of this book, questions are raised for the reader's consideration concerning potential ethical issues surrounding the topics covered in the chapter.

Within our first 'stream' above, then, macro-level assessments have included ethical issues in human resource development, performance management, employee participation and involvement, psychometric testing, and culture change programmes (for a useful compilation of recent literature in these areas, see Winstanley and Woodall, 2000, *Ethical Issues in Contemporary Human Resource Management*, MacMillan). These studies have raised ethical questions about the fair treatment and rights of employees affected by HR practice and interventions in these areas. The ethics of human resource management itself as an approach to managing people have been analysed by Karen Legge (1998) and Paul Miller (1996). These accounts use classical ethical theory to assess the developments and trends in question. Some of the main distinctions within ethical theory are set out in Figure 0.11.

Ethical assessments of HRM and HR practice such as those of Legge and Miller have tended to have been conducted at the level of the organization as decision-maker or 'ethical actor', rather than at the level of the HR practitioner or individual line manager. Nonetheless they are of clear relevance to practitioners who, we would argue, are the decision-makers, collectively and individually, who can make ethical conduct 'happen' or not. Legge argues that only a 'soft' approach to human resource management emphasizing 'resourceful humans' can hope to approximate the most rigorous ethical standards of deontological theory, treating employees as ends in themselves. More often, she argues, HRM has been utilitarian in its ethical aims: employment practices have been designed to promote the interests of the employing organization to the exclusion of much consideration of the rights or wishes of employees. Indeed, she argues that even the softer approach in practice is based upon firms' 'enlightened self-interest' rather than higher principles. Miller takes a somewhat different view, arguing that a *strategic* approach to managing people based upon long-term planning is likely to be the most ethical one. Such an approach allows an organization the time and space to treat employees as ends in themselves. 'In the long term', he writes, 'the ethical treatment of employees has profound strategic implications; considered in the short term, employees are as expendable as the ozone layer' (1996). A 'good' or effective strategy is likely to be one

Kantian philosophy	Utilitarianism
(Immanuel Kant, Germany, 1724–1804)	*(Jeremy Bentham, Britain, 1748–1832; John Stuart Mill, Britain, 1806–1873)*
• Deontological (from Greek for duty); 'non-consequentialist' • Says: do it because it is the right thing to do, on principle • People are ends in themselves, must not be treated as means to ends, 'respect for persons' • Motives are what counts – having a 'good will', a sense of duty, makes an action right • Linked to Natural Law (Thomas Locke, Britain, 1632–1714). Precursor to 'universal human rights'	• Teleological or goal-oriented; 'consequentialist' • Actions can be judged by their consequences, 'ends justify means' • Goal is the common good, maximizing happiness • 'The greatest good for the greatest number' • Co-history with economics, cost-benefit analysis • Egoism – another consequentialist theory
Rawls' theory of justice	**'Virtue Ethics'**
(John Rawls, US, 1921–)	*(Aristotle, Greece, 5th C)*
• Distributive justice • Fair and equitable treatment of all based upon a social contract • Asks: what would you prescribe from under a 'veil of ignorance'? • Any costs or consequences are secondary to this basic focus • 'Do as you would be done by' • Link to stakeholder analysis	• We become good by practising good, not by following external rules • Human nature ethics • Aristotle's human 'potentialities' • Actions that enhance inherent human capacities are good • Can be linked to theories of moral development (e.g. Kohlberg)

Figure 0.11   Ethical Theory – a brief introduction.

that is ethical and 'delivers' to employees. This is consistent with one of the first academic models of HRM (Beer *et al.*, 1984), which said that HRM should be concerned with the well-being of society and by implication, with all of its stake-holders, as well as the business's well-being.

Within the second stream above, academic writers have begun to consider ethical issues facing individual managers responsible for HR processes and practices. Ethical analysis can assist the practitioner to deal with complicated issues ranging, for example, from alleged racist behaviour on the part of an employee, to emerging evidence that private telephone calls are not being properly claimed by a senior manager. By identifying such dilemmas as ethical in nature, managers are encouraged to resolve them using ethical reasoning. One process for ethical reasoning that might be followed has been developed by Manuel Velasquez, a renowned US business ethicist. In brief, the process follows seven steps for discussing and resolving ethical issues or dilemmas. These are:

1   Determine the facts of the matter: what is the issue, what information is relevant?
2   Identify the ethical issues: what points of debate or questions may be raised about what *ought* to be done with respect to the issue, according to your own moral standards, or those of society generally? Try to categorize the issues according to whether they concern the level of the individual, of the organization, or of society as a whole.
3   Develop alternatives for resolving the ethical issues: *how* might they be resolved?
4   Define the stakeholders for each alternative: identify any individual or group who will be affected to a significant degree by the choice of one alternative or another.
5   Evaluate the *ethics* of each alternative: using the chart in Figure 0.11 above, analyse each alternative according to the tenets of each of the major ethical theories:
    (a) the utilitarian perspective: in brief, what total benefits and costs will each alternative generate for each of the stakeholders; which alternative offers the greatest net benefits and fewest net harms?
    (b) the rights and duties perspective (Kant): what are the rights and duties of the 'moral actors' in the situation; which alternative best respects the rights of those involved?
    (c) the justice and fairness perspective (Rawls): how are the benefits and costs of each alternative *distributed* among those affected; which alternative will treat those involved in the most fair or just manner?
6   Take account of the practical constraints: are there practical factors that might prevent carrying out the preferred alternative?
7   Decide on and plan the implementation of an alternative: how will the action be carried out?
    (Source: 'Conducting an ethics case discussion', Manuel Velasquez, 1992, Business Ethics Program, Arthur Andersen and Co, SC).

This procedure may be used to help answer the ethics questions posed at the end of each chapter.

Chapter structure for Chapters 1–10

Each chapter starts with guidance on what the reader should have learned by the end of the chapter in the form of **learning objectives**. In the main body of each chapter, there are a number of illustrations and case examples included to highlight specific issues. At the end of each chapter, a **chapter summary** of the main content, along with main **conclusions**, is presented and readers have the opportunity to test their understanding of what they have learned, specifically in the form of **review questions**. A number of **library and project-based activities** are included in some of the chapters.
    At the end of the book, there is a **glossary** of the key terms used.

Chapter summaries

Chapter 1: Recruitment, selection and induction in a diverse and competitive environment

Organizations now operate in a diverse environment. That source of diversity has arisen due to increased labour market activity by those from 'traditionally disadvantaged' groups, such as women, those from ethnic minorities and those with disabilities. Increased levels of participation by these groups have been fuelled in part by legislation but this in turn reflects changes in society's attitudes. People are different from each other in many ways, and there is an increasing interest in how diversity in organizations can be viewed and marshalled in a positive way, in order to gain the most from a workforce. Not only are equal opportunities and diverse perspectives now more clearly on many organizational agendas, but the potential power of exploiting a range of differences, including cultural background, is being increasingly acknowledged within the arena of international management, particularly in the guise of the management of multinational teams, as well as improved marketing opportunities based on more specialist knowledge of the needs of, in particular, the neglected markets associated with traditionally disadvantaged groups. A number of successful organizations are exploiting the 'diversity advantage' by creating an organizational environment attractive to many beyond the 'traditional' labour pool. In part, this can be achieved through effective HRM strategies that attract, retain and develop a diversity of people and ultimately, through utilizing employees to gain competitive edge. Specifically, in this chapter, the focus is on the HRM policies, practices and strategies that can be employed to attract, recruit, retain and induct an effective workforce.

Chapter 2: Training and development

How do individuals and organizations manage employee learning and development? Over the past ten years great changes have taken place in the roles and responsibilities associated with these activities. Although in many organizations employee development is viewed primarily as the responsibility of the organization, economic recession and globalization have had a tremendous impact on shifting this responsibility much further upon the individual, with the organization playing a facilitative role in line with corporate objectives. This change in emphasis is shifting the onus for training and development through to the line manager and ultimately to the individual employee.

Within this chapter, the commercial arguments made for effective training and development strategies are presented, within the context of social and technical changes and against a background of government-led interventions attempting to improve employee competence and in turn industry effectiveness and competitiveness. The contributions that can be made in the management of training and development by various groups within organizations, including top managers, line management and employees themselves, are explored in detail.

Chapter 3: Generating commitment through involvement and participation processes

Retaining the commitment of staff is important, particularly when environmental pressures force rapid change. It has been suggested that participation and involvement processes are one of the sources of difference between traditional personnel management and human resource management approaches to managing people in organizations (Storey, 1992), and it can be argued that they play an essential part in the development of an organization's managerial climate and style. Participation and involvement processes can help managers achieve commitment, while releasing the talent of staff and creating a vehicle for a mutual exchange of obligations between managers and their work teams. In this chapter, the development of participation and involvement processes as the cornerstone of employment relations is explored.

Chapter 4: Performance management: strategy, systems and rewards

Managing employee performance is more than an annual round of staff appraisals. Evaluating performance can extend from the identification of corporate human resource performance indicators, in which the impact of the entire workforce on the bottom line is considered, through to identifying whether it is appropriate or not to link performance to pay. Moreover, pay and reward strategies need careful design, given market pressures, recruitment and retention objectives and the nature of specific jobs themselves. Furthermore, given the rise in teamwork, consideration needs to be given to developing reward systems to meet the needs of team rather than individual performance.

In this chapter, different approaches to the holistic, coherent strategies for the management of performance are outlined, and the roles and responsibilities that line managers and employees have in making company policy a reality are discussed.

Chapter 5: Managing performance and conduct

The management of employee performance needs to reflect the management of both acceptable and unacceptable performance. From time to time, employee behaviour lies on or outside the boundaries of what is required, given contracts of employment or codes of conduct. The well-briefed, well-trained manager can do much to turn a situation round informally, in the early stages of the occurrence of such incidences. Inevitably, there will be times when events may take such a turn or be of such a nature that the organization and, in turn, the manager, will have to resort to official company policy and procedures.

However, too often managers create as many problems as they seek to solve because of a lack of understanding of procedures, a failure to provide hard evidence to support their claims, ham-fisted administration and, finally, to caricature the extremes, laissez-faire or bully boy tactics.

In this chapter, the importance of managing employee conduct is highlighted and effective strategies within which practice can be executed are discussed. The focus is primarily on subordinate conduct, although as with all such procedures, line structures are such that all members of an organization may be subject to such scrutiny, and therefore the importance of being able to see things from 'both sides of the fence' really matters. The vital elements of communication, information handling and the avoidance of wrongful attribution are addressed. The management of interviewing and the manner in which specific stages of procedures should be handled are reviewed also.

Different approaches to the management of performance are outlined, and the roles and responsibilities that line managers and employees have in making company policy a reality are discussed.

Chapter 6: International human resource management within the context of the global economy

In this chapter, human resource management is considered within an international context, with particular attention paid to staffing strategies, which are reviewed within the context of location, culture, market maturity, joint ventures and new market development. Particular reference will be made to the importance of the interrelationship between corporate management, regional management and local management in international human resource management strategic decision-making processes.

Particular emphasis will be given to international management development, creating international learning organizations, the role of consultants, and cultural diversity and the management of multinational teams.

Chapter 7: Information technology – transformer of organizations and enhancer of the HRM approach

The inroads made by information technology in the world of work have been rapid. It has speeded up the liberalization and globalization of markets and intensified the competitiveness of the business environment. Information technology has also influenced the structure and size of organizations, allowing for decreases in the number of employees, often through the productivity gains achieved through the new technology, but it has also made significant impacts on the way work can be organized.

In this chapter, the way in which information technology can be used to support and enhance employment management strategies is highlighted. Particular attention will be paid to the way in which developments in computers and communications networks have irreversibly changed the global business environment, how this has resulted in new forms of organization and work allocation, and how these developments are shaping HRM policy and practice.

Chapter 8: Human resource management in the smaller business

In this chapter, the importance and uniqueness of managing human resources within the small to medium firm is highlighted. Typically, small to medium-sized firms have limited resources to support specialist approaches to people management. Further, owner-managers are often ill-equipped to decide how to deal with their specific staff development and change management problems.

There are a number of recurring concerns that are highlighted. The problems faced in finding development and training suitable for the smaller firm are considered. Also, the transition from small to medium-sized firm often creates significant corporate problems and the importance of developing coherent employment management strategies to ease such transitions is highlighted.

Chapter 9: Change and strategy in organizations

What is change and how can it be managed? In this chapter, the relationship between change and transition interventions and human resource management is considered. Some of the many HRM processes and activities that can help facilitate or generate changes are investigated and the design, development and implementation of change interventions evaluated.

Much of the literature on the management of change is focused on specialist interventionist activities. However, in this chapter, particular attention will be paid to the role of the manager in the facilitation of change in organizations and the opportunities and difficulties that he or she may face.

Chapter 10: Negotiation and HRM

This chapter is somewhat different from the others. The emphasis here is on the practice, rather than the theory, of negotiations, although the suggested practice is built on negotiation theory. Negotiations are considered along the following main lines: types of negotiation practice; outcomes of negotiations and the organization of negotiations.

It was felt that it would be useful to introduce readers to the area, as it is an integral part of the HRM practice of any line manager – this is most obvious for participation and commitment, but its potential application is much wider. Further, it is a core skill area that will better enable the line manager to get HRM 'ideas into action' in any team, department, or indeed, the entire organization.

Conclusions

We cannot know the future, but we may be able to detect trends or highlight issues that we believe merit our attention. In this final chapter, we consider a number of the choices, gaps in our understanding and possible future directions that could be taken in the management of human resources.

Each of the contributors to the book has highlighted what he or she feels are issues that merit the attention of those interested in key issues that are likely to face those with line or specialist responsibility for employment management.

References

Beer, M *et al.* (1984) *Managing Human Assets*. Free Press, New York.

Brewster, C (1995) *HRM: the European dimension*. In Storey, J (ed) (1995) *Human Resource Management: a critical text*, Routledge, London.

Brewster, C and Hegewisch, A (eds) (1994) Policy and Practice in Human Resource Management: The Price Waterhouse Cranfield Survey, Routledge, London.

Brewster C and Larsen, HH (1992) Human resource management in Europe; evidence from ten countries. *International Journal of Human Resource Management*, **3** (3), 409–434.

Chryssides, G and Kaler, J (1996) *An Introduction to Business Ethics*. International Thomson Business Press, London.

Cornelius, N and Gagnon, S (1999) From ethics by proxy to ethics in action: New approaches to understanding ethics and HRM. *Business Ethics: A European Review*, **8** (4), 225–235.

Fisher, C and Rice, C (1999) Managing messy moral matters: Ethics and HRM. In Leopold, J *et al.*, *Strategic Human Resourcing*, Pitman, London.

Fobrum, C, Tichy, NM and Devanna, MA (1984) *Strategic Human Resource Management*, John Wiley, London.

Guest, DE (1987) Human resource management and industrial relations. *Journal of Management Studies*, **24** (5), 48–51.

Kaler, J (1999) What's the good of ethical theory? *Business Ethics: A European Review*, **8** (4), 206–213.

Kochan, T and Dyer, L (1995) HRM: an American view. In Storey, J (1995) *Human Resource Management: a critical text*, Routledge, London.

Legge, K (1995) *Human Resource Management: rhetorics and realities*. Macmillan, Basingstoke.

Legge, K (1998) The morality of HRM. In Mabey, C *et al.*, *Experiencing Human Resource Management*, Sage, London.

Miller, P (1996) Strategy and the ethical management of human resources. *Human Resource Management Journal*, **6** (1), 5-18.

Petrick, J and Quinn, J (1997) *Management Ethics: Integrity at Work*. Sage, London.

Purcell, J (1995) Corporate strategy and its link with human resource management. In Storey, J (ed) (1995) *Human Resource Management: a critical text*, Routledge, London.

Sparrow, P and Marchington, M (1998) Human resource management: the new agenda, Financial Times/Pitman, St Ives.

Storey, J (1992) *Developments in the management of human resources*. Blackwell, Oxford.

Storey, J (ed) (1995) *Human Resource Management: a critical text*. Routledge, London.

Torrington, D and Hall, L (1987) *Personnel Management: a new approach*. Prentice Hall, London.

Velasquez, M (1992) Conducting an ethics case discussion. *Business Ethics Program*, Arthur Andersen and Co, SC.

Winstanley, D and Woodall, J (eds) (2000) *Ethical Issues in Contemporary Human Resource Management*. MacMillan, Basingstoke.

Legal briefing

Introduction: Line Manager's Role

It is not possible for the line manager to operate effectively these days without some knowledge of the law governing relations at work. A wrong decision, an insensitive handling of a difficult situation, a failure to act where such action is clearly required, could lead not only to expense and unwelcome publicity but also to a fracturing of industrial relations.

The law in this area has many sources: the common law, basically built up, case by case, by decisions of the judges, legislation (or Acts of Parliament) and, increasingly, the law of the European Union.

The common law

The bedrock is still the common law, which governs most aspects of the contract of employment – the basic relationship between employer and employee.

Legislation

Over the years there has been increasing intervention by Parliament, and this employment legislation can be roughly divided into three categories.

1   'Humanitarian', in which can be placed all of the health and safety legislation dating back to the early part of the nineteenth century. While this was fiercely attacked at the outset as an unwarranted interference with the freedom not only of employers but also of employees, it gradually gained acceptance as desirable for both social and economic reasons.
2   **Granting rights to employees**, typified by rights on dismissal, rights for pregnant employees, equal pay etc. It was this type of legislation that provoked the greatest opposition from employers and was seen as direct interference with management prerogative. It was also, ironically, seen in some quarters as undermining the traditional role of the trades unions and diminishing their attraction to potential members.
3   **Promoting long-term change in attitude**: the anti-discrimination statutes in particular come into this category. The best that such legislation can achieve is the outlawing of unthinking, 'institutionalized' discrimination, and the opening up of employment opportunities to all. In the last resort, an employer is free to choose whom to employ, promote, etc. The best hope is that old prejudices will be broken down as women and black employees are increasingly seen successfully tackling a variety of jobs that in former times they would not even have applied for.

Regulations

Regulations, or Statutory Instruments, are made under the direct authority of a statute, although they are not themselves debated in Parliament. They are usually drawn up in the appropriate Department or Ministry, at present, the Department for Education and Employment.

Codes of Practice

These are guidelines on good practice, and, while they are not directly enforceable, they will be consulted as a standard against which to judge the actions of an employer, employee or trade union. An example from the law of unfair dismissal would be the observance by the employer of the Code of Practice relating to warnings given of the possibilty of dismissal for bad behaviour or poor performance.

European Union law

A large number of Directives affecting employment have been issued by the Commission (after discussion in the European Parliament and agreement by the Council of Ministers), and member governments are obliged to bring their domestic law into line with them within a given time. The UK government has generally implemented these Directives in time, but has then often been challenged before the European Court of Justice for 'not getting it quite right'! Such reforms of the law will be introduced either by primary legislation (Act of Parliament) or secondary legislation (Regulation). In either event, it might not be immediately apparent, without reading any notes or preamble, that it is an enactment reflecting European law.

A significant amount of employment law already enacted in the UK has its origins in the law of the

European Union, in particular discrimination and equal pay (to be discussed in more detail in the legal briefing to Chapter 1). The stated policy of the present Labour administration is to adopt the Protocol to the Treaty of European Union relating to social policy (known colloquially as the 'Social Chapter'). The 'opt-out' for the UK was formally abolished on 1 May 2000 by the Treaty of Amsterdam. This will result over the course of time in the alteration of terms of employment to achieve goals that are deemed to be socially desirable. It will require a radical change in attitude on the part of managers. Reforms in this connection that have been introduced include the institution of a minimum wage and the right of employees to (unpaid) parental leave. The National Minimum Wage Act, 1998, was implemented on 1 April 1999, and currently sets the hourly minimum wage at £3 for workers between the ages of 18 and 21 and £3.60 for workers aged 21 and over. A minimal increase has been signalled to be paid to employees over the age of 21 from autumn 2000. The right to parental leave was included in the Employment Rights Act, 1999, and was brought into force on 15 December 1999. Please see the legal briefing for Chapter 1 for more details.

European Convention on Human Rights

Among the influences upon the development of English law must now be added the European Convention on Human Rights. As the UK government is a signatory to the Convention, it has always been possible for a citizen to take a case to the Commission and ultimately, in a very serious matter concerning the infringement of rights, to the European Court of Human Rights in Strasbourg. The UK government has usually accepted the decision of the Court (not always with enthusiasm) and has eventually amended the UK law in order to comply. Please see the case of *Lustig-Prean and others v. UK* [1999], mentioned in the legal briefing to Chapter 1. There is now on the statute book the Human Rights Act, 1998, which is due to be brought into force sometime in October 2000.

This will mark a major departure for English law. Every court and tribunal in the UK, when dealing with a right covered by the Convention, will have to take into account any judgment, decision, declaration or advi-

sory opinion of the European Court of Human Rights, or any opinion of the Commission of Human Rights. Such opinions are given in the first instance, and are of great importance if the case does not eventually go to the Court. Further, all primary and secondary legislation, that is, Acts of Parliament, ministerial Regulations etc., will have to be interpreted in a manner consistent with the Convention.

Conclusion

The law relating to employment is vast, complex and continually changing. The aim of the legal briefings accompanying every chapter is not to turn managers into self-styled lawyers; that would be both foolish and dangerous. Knowledge of law does, however, have an important purpose.

1   It will alert the manager to situations where proper legal advice should be sought.
2   It will give the manager, in the course of seeking advice, confidence to ask the right questions and argue his or her point. An intelligent client invariably gets better service from a professional, be it a medical practitioner, accountant, banker or lawyer, if the client shows some interest in and knowledge of the subject, even if only in layman's terms.

Further reading

Anderman, SD (1993) *Labour Law*, 2nd edition, Butterworths.
Deakin, S and Morris, GS (1998) *Labour Law*, Butterworths.
French, WL and Bell, CH (1999) *Organization Development: Behavioural science interventions for organization improvement*, 6th edition, Englewood Cliffs, Prentice Hall.
Lewis, D (1997) *Essentials of Employment Law*, 5th edition, IPM.
Selwyn, N (1998) *Law of Employment*, 10th edition, Butterworths.

Recommended journal for consultation:

Industrial Relations Review and Report (published twice monthly).

Recruitment, selection and induction in a diverse and competitive environment

1

Larraine Gooch and Nelarine Cornelius

Learning Objectives

After studying this chapter you should be able to:

- recognize the business advantage from recruiting, selecting and retaining a diverse workforce;
- understand the need to follow good practice in recruitment, selection and induction in a diverse and competitive environment;
- determine the impact of recruitment and selection of a diverse workforce on the culture of an organization;
- recognize the differences between diversity and equal opportunities;
- identify recruitment, selection, retention and induction processes which ensure the 'diversity advantage' is gained.

Introduction

Managers are now increasingly involved in the recruitment, selection and induction of employees for their departments and their organizations. The purpose of this chapter is to enable managers to understand key issues in recruitment, selection and induction in current organizational climates and within the legal framework that now operates in many countries around the world.

As managers take increasing responsibility for recruitment, selection and induction within their organizations, they need to recognize that the labour market from which they recruit their pool of talent is now diverse (see Box 1.1). People are different from each other in many ways – in age, gender, educational experience, values, physical ability, mental capacity, personality, experiences, culture and their attitudes and approaches towards work. We now operate in a global economy with many leading organizations operating internationally, recruiting, selecting and working with a diverse workforce not only locally but around the world to sell their services and products to diverse customers.

Box 1.1 The diverse UK labour market

Women

- Since 1975 the number of women in the labour market has increased by 34 per cent to 12.2 million in 1995, the number of men has fallen by 0.5 per cent to 15.6 million.
- Between 1994 and 2001, male employment is likely to see only a slight rise (around 3 per cent) while female employment will increase more quickly (an extra 11 per cent).

Ethnic minorities[1]

- Ethnic minority groups now make up 5.9 per cent of the population of working age (nearly 2 million people) almost half of whom were born in Great Britain.
- The greatest concentration of the ethnic working population is in the South East (61 per cent); in London almost one-fifth of the economically active population of working age is non-white and 40 per cent of these are black; the next largest concentrations are the West Midlands, the North West and the East Midlands.

Older workforce

By the year 2006 the workforce will be older, with a projected fall of 1.1 million people aged under 35 years in the labour force.

Flexible workforce

- Part-time working is increasing for both men and women: 44 per cent of all women workers are part-time but only 6 per cent of male employees work part-time. Part-time working for men is increasing at more than double the rate for women.
- An increasing number of employees work flexible hours with 10 per cent of men and 15 per cent of women working flexible hours, many of whom work to annualized working hours contracts.

- Between 1994 and 2001 part-time employment is projected to increase by 22 per cent at the same time as full-time employment decreases by 1 per cent.
- An increasing number of employees work in temporary jobs – without a permanent contract: 8 per cent of women and 6 per cent of men.
- A growing number of employees work at home (0.7 million people).

Caring responsibilities

- Two and half million men and three and half million women have caring responsibilities for elderly dependants.
- Thirty-six per cent of working-age women have dependent children under 16 years of age.

Disability[2]

Some 1.2 million disabled people are in employment; disabled people are slightly more likely than non-disabled people to work in a part-time capacity. Unemployment rates among people with disabilities is around two-and-a-half times those for non-disabled people.

Source: Labour Market Trends, February 1997.
IPD Managing Diversity Position Paper (1997a).

1 Definition of ethnic minorities used in Labour Force Survey:

   Black (Black Caribbean, Black African, Black other)
   Indian
   Pakistani/Bangladeshi
   Other (Chinese, other non-mixed, other mixed, Black mixed)

2 Definition of disability: Disability is defined in the Disability Discrimination Act (1996) as physical or mental impairment, which has a substantial and long-term effect on the ability to carry out the duties of a job.

Many successful organizations are exploiting the 'diversity advantage' by creating an organizational environment which is attractive to diverse labour markets and which is able to respond to changing social and demographic patterns. This can be achieved through effective human resource management (HRM) strategies which provide the environment and processes that attract, retain and develop a diverse workforce. Kandola and Fullerton (1994) showed that many organizations believe that diversity makes good business sense by harnessing individual differences to create a productive environment which utilizes the talents of all employees to their full potential and enables employers to gain competitive edge. Specifically, the focus of this chapter is the HRM strategies, policies and practices that managers can use to attract, recruit, retain and induct an effective and diverse workforce.

The 'diversity advantage'

Managing diversity provides competitive edge by recruiting, retaining and promoting the best people for the job regardless of their ethnicity, age, gender, or other individual characteristics. In the light of changing demographic structures and internationalization, organizations which recruit from a limited sector of the employment market will not only fail to recruit the 'best' by not choosing from a large pool of talent, but will fail to reflect their diverse customer base and will also fail to retain employees from diverse backgrounds.

As organizations often promote from within, recruiting a diverse workforce at critical entry points to the organization also ensures that the pool of talent available for promotion is the 'best'. In order to achieve this, Kandola and Fullerton (1994) show that 'organisational processes (recruitment, selection, promotion, training and career development) must be fair i.e. based on objective and job-relevant criteria and that the managers who run the processes are skilled in assessing the criteria' (p. 37). In addition, they show that in order to retain the 'best' employees, organizations need to be more flexible in their processes, systems and procedures. 'If there is not sufficient flexibility in the organization, the best will go elsewhere' (Ross and Schneider, 1992: 105).

As organizations increasingly operate in a diverse labour market, so the 'diversity advantage' comes by fully using and developing the talents of those people in that labour market. Managing diversity is about recognizing that people from different backgrounds, cultures and experiences can bring new ideas and perceptions to the workplace which can make a major contribution to the generation of new ideas, to the way work is done and to quality issues.

The 'diversity advantage' is achieved through recognition of the benefits that diversity can bring to an organization. Six major reasons why diversity matters in business have been identified by the IPD (1997a) – see Box 1.2.

If diversity is to succeed and the 'diversity advantage' to be fully utilized, it requires commitment to ownership of diversity from all the managers and employees of an organization. The manager has a key role to play in this process.

Box 1.2 Why does diversity matter in business?

- Improving customer care and increasing market share by broadening customer base both internally and externally.
- Developing organizational ethics and values which provide a guide for the organization's expectations and standards in conduct of work.
- Enhancing people management practices. Evidence shows that organizations which focus on equality and diversity are able to:

  – attract and recruit people from a wider range of talented candidates
  – retain the best talent
  – benefit from lower turnover and absenteeism
  – demonstrate greater organizational flexibility to respond to change.

- Reflecting changes in society and personal expectations of fair and equal treatment at work.
- Complying with legislation.
- Keeping up with best practice to attract and retain talent and enhance competitiveness.

Source:IPD[1] (1997a) Position Paper: *Managing Diversity*.

1 IPD: Institute of Personnel and Development

The difference between diversity and equal opportunities

Recruitment, selection and retention processess have operated for the past 20 years within a legal framework of anti-discrimination legislation.

There has been growing recognition, however, that despite 20 years of equal opportunities legislation, anti-discrimination legislation has clearly failed to deliver equality of opportunity within organizations and has led to the disillusionment of many concerned with equal opportunities in organizations (Cockburn, 1989, Ross and Schneider, 1992). For example, in the UK this disillusionment with legislation prompted attempts to change attitudes outside of legislation led by the Equal Opportunities Commission (EOC) and the Commission for Racial Equality (CRE) and joined by Opportunity 2000, the Employers' Forum on Disability, and The Employers' Forum on Age, 1996 (see Box 1.3).

How then is 'diversity' different from equal opportunities? Greenslade (1991) believes that diversity goes one fundamental step further than equal opportunities because it seeks to create a climate whereby those involved want to move beyond the achievement of mere statistical goals. There is an acceptance of the values of differences between individuals (and groups) and recognition of the benefits that multiculturalism can bring to an organization; these include innovation and change, the challenging of stereotypical opinions and of traditional assumptions.

While equal opportunities was seen to be legally driven with an emphasis on race, gender and disability, with a focus on an improvement in numbers, diversity is seen as being driven by business needs and internally initiated with an emphasis on improving the environment in which all employees work; it is proactive and embraces all differences. Its focus is on individuals rather than groups; not on equalizing the differences between groups, but on responding to individual needs and aspirations (Ross and Schneider, 1992). Further it has been suggested that perhaps the other equal opportunities or diversity management thinking need not be the only organizational option; diversity management *built* on equal opportunities

Box 1.3 Information on EOC, CRE, Opportunity 2000, Employers' Forum on Disability, Employers' Forum on Age

Equal Opportunities Commission (EOC)

A government-funded body, founded in 1976 under the Equal Opportunities Act, 1975. The EOC believes its role is to 'challenge discrimination and promote equality ... to ascertain where discrimination is taking place, and on the basis of that deciding whether to take up test cases' (Overell, 1996).

The Commission for Racial Equality (CRE)

This was set up under the Race Relations Act, 1976 with three main duties:

- To work towards eliminating racial discrimination
- To promote equality of opportunity and good race relations between people from different ethnic groups
- To keep the Race Relations Act under review

In 1984 the CRE issued a Race Relations Code of Practice in Employment which is admissable in evidence before an industrial tribunal under the Race Relations Act, 1976.

In 1995 the CRE published a new standard, 'Racial Equality Means Business'.

Opportunity 2000

Set up in 1991, Opportunity 2000 argues for equality based on the business case for equal opportunities, and on joining Opportunity 2000 an organization sets a number of objectives and measures and publishes its progress towards them. There are now 293 members, which between them employ over a quarter of the workforce (IDS, 1996).

The Employers' Forum on Disability

This makes it easier for employers to recruit, retain and develop disabled employees by:

- providing a national and international clearing house for information regarding employer best practice, specialist services and legislation;
- promoting working partnerships between employers, service providers and disabled people;
- providing help line services to member companies;
- working to improve the quality of training and work-related services available both to employers and people with disabilities.

The Employers' Forum on Age launched in April 1996

This is supported by a number of founding members including British Airways, Glaxo-Wellcome, HSBC Bank, NatWest Bank, Nationwide Building Society, WH Smith and Unigate. The forum aims to encourage employers to reconsider policies that ignore highly qualified job applicants because they are too old or target older workers first in any redundancy programmes.

can be, and is, the material reality in organizations (e,g, Cornelius, Gooch and Todd, 2000).

Diversity is the responsibility of all, not just the Equal Opportunities Officer or Personnel. Ford (1996) sees equality and diversity as interdependent, with a need to reconcile the positive image of diversity, which focuses on the individual, with equal treatment for under-represented groups. Ford's view is that diversity needs a structure of rules and to incorporate legislative requirements; however, it also needs to recognize that some specific groups have particular problems that need to be addressed.

If diversity is the responsibility of all, then the manager has a key role to play in the management of diversity within the organization. Equal opportunities is often seen as the concern of personnel and human resource practitioners. Managing diversity is seen as being the concern of all employees, especially managers within the organization. This challenge has been taken up by British Airways Management in their recruitment literature – see Box 1.4.

Creating a diverse culture

If organizations are to become truly diverse and to achieve a culture in which diversity thrives, then there needs to be a strong link between diversity objectives and the strategic plan for an organization. Organizations cannot achieve their strategic plan unless people in the organization feel valued. Part of feeling valued is that no employee receives less favourable treatment on the grounds of race, colour, nationality, ethnic or national origins, sex, marital status, sexual orientation, religious beliefs, disability, age or community background. To achieve this, executive responsibilities and commitment are essential; progress needs to be in line with organizational priorities; a coherent approach related to business needs is achieved; no one person is responsible for progress (Ross and Schneider, 1992). This commitment from the top of the organization must, however, be supported and underpinned by management.

Culture has been described as the way people think about things around here (Williams *et al.* (1993)); culture is seen as the characteristic patterns of behaviour

Box 1.4 Diversity at British Airways

- There is no such thing as a typical British Airways employee. They come from all walks of life and all types of background. Indeed our policy is one of encouraging diversity so that our teams consist of people with a wide variety of skills, experience and knowledge, learning from, and developing with, each other.
- World-wide, we employ people from almost every race and nationality, and here in the UK we are striving to ensure that the variety and diversity of our customers is reflected by our staff.
- We must reflect the demographic make-up of the UK work-force as a whole:

  - By the year 2000, we expect to have a work-force which is 50% female, with nearly 1/3 of managerial jobs held by women.
  - Having a totally diverse workforce means encouraging more people with disabilities to apply to British Airways and a subsequent commitment to disabled people in their development.

  - As lifestyles and working patterns change, we hope to strengthen our teams by recognising the additional responsibilities individuals have for family and other commitments.
  - We encourage part-time working and job-sharing responsibilities.
  - For working parents, initiatives such as our summer schools for school-age children and nursery places are designed to ease the demands of full-time work and full-time child-care.

- All these activities are aimed at one goal: that of creating a working environment that attracts, retains and develops committed people who share in the success of the company. In achieving this it will be absolutely essential for British Airways to value the differences in its employees.

Source: British Airways, 'People Powered'.

in the organization, and the rites, rituals and symbols are consequently seen as manifestations of this. In many organizations successful careers are achieved by working long and unsociable hours for organizations that expect total commitment and loyalty in return for partial job security. This type of culture discriminates against those with family or caring commitments and does not promote diversity within the workforce. Williams *et al.* (1993) identified six ways organizations can change their culture: by changing the people in the organization; by changing people's position in the organization; by changing beliefs, attitudes and values directly; by changing behaviour; by changing systems and structures; and by changing corporate image.

The strategy web developed by Kandola and Fullerton (1994) (Figure 1.1) shows that to achieve a truly diverse organization it is simply not adequate to implement policies and practices in an ad hoc way; policies and practices must be fully integrated into organizational strategy. Organizations have a range of cultures which foster diversity through attitudes, through expectations and by 'the way things are done'. Recruitment and selection play a key role in creating a diverse organization, but can only succeed in doing so if diversity is part of the business culture and 'good practice' in recruitment and selection is not 'bolted on' to organizational strategies and practices. It can only succeed if a holistic approach is taken to diversity. The reverse is also true, that an organization which sees itself as promoting diversity needs to ensure that its processes such as recruitment and selection, induction and appraisal do not deter or put barriers in the way of 'diverse' applicants. As a point of entry to organizations, all aspects of the recruitment and selection process influence company image and each can deter potential applicants (Paddison, 1990).

The management of diversity requires systematic management action and changes to working practices and organizational cultures. It is dependent on

Figure 1.1 The strategy web. *Source:* Kandola and Fullerton, 1994.

leadership and commitment from management at all levels (Bedingfield and Foreman, 1997).

To achieve a diverse culture into which a diverse group of employees are to be recruited, there must be:

Top management commitment. This is essential if the key management processes are to succeed (McEnrue, 1993 cited in Kandola and Fullerton, 1994)

Auditing and assessment of needs. This links in to an analysis of organizational 'health'. It identifies problem areas to be addressed and includes information on existing human resource systems, the attitudes and opinions of employees and data on the profile of the workforce (Cox and Blake, 1991 cited in Kandola and Fullerton, 1994). It is also essential to audit processes to ensure that one group is not being disadvantaged by the way they are being operated.

Clarity of objectives. These can include numbers or review of processes. Objectives can make it possible to show improvement and demonstrate progress (McEnrue, 1993).

Clear accountability. Every employee should be aware of their role and responsibilities for diversity; managers have a crucial role to play here. Cox and Blake, (1991) believe in the importance of accountability and claim that managing diversity should be no different from any other business activity. Rewarding managers for their achievements in achieving diversity can also be beneficial (Kandola and Fullerton, 1994).

Effective communication. It is essential to spread ownership (Ross and Schneider, 1992) and to solicit feedback on progress and processes.

Coordination of activity. A champion of diversity can be invaluable to coordinate activity (Cox and Blake, 1991) and the role of task forces across the organization.

Evaluation. Information gathered is essential to provide feedback on progress and should be shared with employees (Kandola and Fullerton, 1994).

As managers take an increasing role in the recruitment and selection process, so their involvement becomes key in creating and developing a diverse culture within the organization. Diversity cannot be achieved without management 'ownership'.

Human resource planning for diverse organizations

Human resource planning is concerned with forecasting the future needs of the organization in terms of skills, expertise and competences, of analysing the availability and supply of people, of drawing up plans to match supply to demand and of monitoring the implementation of the human resource plan (Armstrong, 1996). Human resource plans are concerned with both the external and internal supply of labour for the organization.

If we look at the external labour market, the figures given in Box 1.1 show that the external 'pool' of labour is diverse and as such has diverse demands and needs. Many people in the labour market need to be 'attracted' to work for the organization and this means recognizing and understanding that they have diverse needs. These needs might be met by flexible contracts, they might be met by 'family friendly' policies which allow a balance between home and work or they might be met by continous personal development opportunities to enable ongoing skill development to meet changing organizational needs.

Human resource planning is also concerned with the internal labour market. It is concerned with estimating the supply of human resources in the organization by analysing current skills and competencies and by analysing retirement, absence and turnover figures.

Human resource action plans arise from the gap between forecasted demand and forecasted supply of skills and competencies needed to meet corporate plans and strategies. These action plans may be concerned with the need to recruit, the need to train and develop or to retrain, with the need to improve productivity, with the need to redeploy and possibly, the need to downsize.

The recruitment plan arises out of the human resource plan and is concerned with attracting the 'right' employees to give the organization a competitive edge; it is also concerned to retain and to grow and develop those employees to enable them to make a major contribution to organizational effectiveness. If diversity is in the corporate plan, then human resource plans are concerned with diversity too. If management are involved in the recruitment, selection and retention of the 'right' people for their organizations, they need to be involved in human resource planning.

Recruitment and selection costs

The costs of recruiting and selecting the 'right' person can be high to the manager, both in financial and non-financial terms. The costs of recruitment include the obvious costs of the recruitment and selection process but also the less obvious costs of training the selected person to undertake a full and contributing role to the organization and the costs of recruiting and selecting the 'wrong' person. In their study of recruitment costs in Europe, Brewster and Hegewisch (1994, p. 69) cite Dany (1992) to show that the costs of recruitment include:

- indirect communication costs (universities, schools);
- structural cost of the personnel department (software, personnel costs, training of recruitment managers);
- variable costs related to the attraction of candidates (advertising and mailing, selection agencies);
- the examination of candidates (assessment centres, selection tests, time spent by line managers in interviewing);
- induction costs linked to the integration and training of selected candidates.

These are minimal costs as they do not reflect the less obvious costs if the 'wrong' person is selected; these include lost business, expensive mistakes, stress on the 'team' and the time and money spent in training, retraining and possibly dismissal. In the context of equal opportunities legislation, costs can also include the cost of meeting Industrial Tribunal claims if the recruitment and selection process is discriminatory. In the diversity context the costs can be loss of 'diversity advantage' by not recruiting a diverse pool of talent with the subsequent loss of innovation and potential that the talent will bring to the organization.

Recruitment and selection is clearly a costly and time-consuming exercise. It is essential, therefore, that a systematic and objective approach to recruitment and selection is applied in order to select from a diverse range of applicants and to minimize the possibility of selecting the 'wrong' person when a selection decision is reached.

Recruitment and selection processes

This section outlines eight key steps in the recruitment and selection process (see Figure 1.2). It is concerned with the way in which applicants are recruited and selected by the manager.

The recruitment process is often the first contact an individual has with an organization; bearing in mind that all applicants are already or might also become customers of the organization, it is important that the experience is a positive one.

The IPD (1997b) believes that 'Succcessful recruitment depends upon finding people both with the necessary skills, expertise and qualifications to deliver organizational objectives and with the ability to make a positive contribution to the values and aims of the organization' ... 'Selection processes should only be based on ability to do the job, ability to make a contribution to the organization's effectiveness and potential for development.'

It is important to be fully aware of equal opportunities legislation and to understand how discrimination can occur both directly and indirectly in the recruitment process (see Legal briefing). Managers need to ensure that their recruitment and selection processes are valid and non-discriminatory. At each step in the process it is important to be aware of legal requirements as well as 'good practice'. For example, the Disability Discrimination Act has a number of implications for recruitment and selection (see Box 1.5).

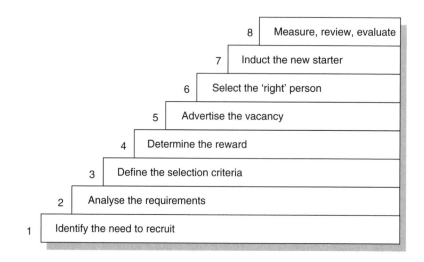

Figure 1.2   The eight steps in the recruitment and selection process.

STEP 1: Identify the need to recruit

If a proper human resource plan is drawn up then the manager will know whether there is a need to recruit. Before a decision to recruit is made, the possibility of making the requirements of the job more flexible should also be considered; this can have many advantages to an employer (see Box 1.6). Increasingly, organizations are looking at alternative ways of working and these can have an impact not only on the decision whether to recruit or not but also on the type of person who is being recruited.

The link between flexible working and diversity are clear. McEnrue (1993, cited in Kandola and Fullerton, 1994) identified that the main reason for managing diversity was to attract and retain employees in the face of labour shortages and changes in the demographic composition of the workforce. Flexible working enables organizations to attract and retain employees with diverse needs provided that those employees are treated as fairly and equitably in respect of contract terms, conditions of service and training opportunities as 'core' employees.

We have already discussed in this chapter that the pool of labour from which the manager can choose to recruit and select is increasingly diverse. The jobs for which the manager is seeking to recruit might consist of 'core' jobs, which might

---

Box 1.5 Implications of the Disability Discrimination Act 1995 for recruitment and selection

- The recruitment and selection process must begin with a thorough job analysis that focuses on the knowledge, skills and abilities required to do the job. These must be clear and accurate and any criteria that are not essential and might adversely affect disabled applicants should be avoided (e.g. good eyesight, driving licence, stamina).
- Adverts should accurately reflect the essential functions of the job and application forms should seek to gain only job-relevant information.

- The interview process should be standardized and only focus on criteria established at the outset of the recruitment campaign. Interviewers should be briefed on disability etiquette in an effort to ensure the interview runs smoothly.
- Practical arrangements should also be made with respect to the disabled person's needs, e.g. parking, access to the building.

Source: Kandola and Butterworth (1996)

Box 1.6 Flexible working practices

A survey on flexible working practices in Europe showed that the main benefits to employers of flexible working were: reduced costs, increased productivity and competitiveness, improved customer service, improved ability to recruit and retain staff, improved motivation and commitment, improved ability to manage change and improved communications (IPD, 1994).

A recent IRS survey found that employers continue to seek ways of making working time more flexible in order to increase efficiency, meet customer demands and assist employees in balancing work and personal commitments (IRS Employment Trends 603 and 608).

The Department of Employment Ten Point Plan For Employers found that 'Introducing flexible working patterns and other facilities is one of the most effective steps you can take to attract and then keep a wider range of potential employees. They will include women and men with domestic responsibilities, people with disabilities, and people with particular cultural and religious needs.'

be full-time and permanent, and 'peripheral' jobs (Atkinson, 1985) which might be temporary, part-time, job shares, contracted from outside the organization or homeworking. The jobs may require task or job content flexibility and might involve financial or remunerative flexibility. Flexible jobs should not be confined to low-skilled or poorly paid jobs but need to consider supervisory and managerial roles as well. The existence of a flexible workforce does not, in itself, create a 'diverse' organization but is an essential part of the proactive rather than reactive route to the recruitment and selection of a diverse workforce.

STEP 2: Analyse the requirements

This is the critical first stage in a recruitment and selection process. The purpose of the recruitment and selection procedure is to find the 'best' person to fill an organizational vacancy. The starting point to finding the 'best' person is to identify the criteria against which an individual is to be selected. These criteria come from an analysis of requirements.

The essence of analysis in the recruitment and selection process is to collect information systematically. Michael Armstrong (1996) identifies four main methods of collecting data:

- **Job analysis**. This is concerned with collecting data on the content of jobs in terms of the knowledge, skills and abilitites needed to achieve the job; it is also concerned with accountabilities, performance criteria, responsibilities, organizational factors, motivating factors, development factors and environmental factors.
- **Role analysis**. This is concerned with the broader aspects of behaviour linked to a role rather than a specific job; in multi-skilling, for example, a role holder may have a number of different jobs which require the same skills and attributes, e.g. working with others, working flexibly and good communication skills.
- **Attributes analysis**. This is concerned with knowledge, skill and expertise requirements.
- **Competency analysis**. This is concerned with expectations of workplace performance and the standards individuals are expected to attain; it is also concerned with behavioural competencies – the characteristics people bring to work roles.

Information can be collected using a variety of methods. The simplest methods of collecting data are:

- structured interviews with the person currently carrying out or planning the job, task or role and with their immediate supervisor and team members;
- observation (where possible);
- asking the current post holder to keep a diary or log.

It is important to analyse jobs, tasks or roles frequently in the changing environment in which organizations now find themselves as the data often becomes out of date quickly.

STEP 3: Define the selection criteria

In a fair and systematic selection process it is essential to define the criteria against which applicants are to be assessed and selected. There are a number of different ways in which the criteria for selection can be identified.

Job descriptions, role definitions and person specifications

Job and role analysis provide the information for completion of a job description or role description. The person specification is the profile of the 'ideal' person who would fill the job or role description.

Job descriptions

Job descriptions describe the tasks and responsibilities that comprise the job. They also define the place of the job in the organization and clarify the contribution the job makes to achieving organizational or departmental objectives. A valuable way of drawing up a job description is to consider outputs from the job rather than look at inputs.

Bias can easily occur in the writing of the job description; it should not overstate or understate the duties, requirements and outputs of a job, nor should it be biased towards a particular group of the working population. Tasks and responsibilities should only be included where they can be shown to be a valid and necessary function of a particular job.

Role definitions

The term job description implies a number of tasks to be completed; a role definition is concerned with what people do and how they do it rather than concentrating on narrow job content (Armstrong, 1996). Generic role definitions are becoming increasingly common as they establish criteria against which individuals can be recruited which are not specific to one job only. These role definitions allow for more organizational flexibility and multi-skilling than rather narrower job descriptions.

Person specification

The person specification is the profile of the 'ideal' person who could fill the vacant job or role; this profile needs to state the 'essential' and the 'desirable' criteria for selection and is produced from material gathered for the job description or role definition. The profile provides the criteria against which applicants can be systematically and fairly assessed.

A typical person specification would normally include the following:

● skills, aptitude, knowledge and experience;

- qualifications;
- personal qualities relevant to the job.

Unnecessarily high requirements for the person specification can lead to 'indirect discrimination' – when any requirement or condition is imposed which can be complied with by a smaller proportion of one group than another and cannot be shown to be justifiable. This includes requiring a standard of English higher than needed for safe and effective performance on the job (CRE). One of the most frequently used person specification formats is based on Rodger's Seven Point Plan (1952). This format provides a good basis for drawing up a person specification but can be discriminatory if unnecessarily high requirements are included (see Box 1.7).

Attributes

Having analysed the job or role to determine the attributes required by a successful applicant, these attributes provide the criteria against which applicants can be measured at selection. Examples of attributes which have been identified that characterize the person required for the job or role might include:

- Works well in a team
- Ability to learn from mistakes
- Good interpersonal skills
- Well organized

The selection process to match the applicants against the attribute requirements

---

Box 1.7 An example of a Person Profile – Rodger's 'Seven Point Plan'

Rodger's Seven Point Plan	Possible areas of discrimination
Physical make-up	Setting unnecessary physical standards
Attainments	Requiring standards higher than necessary, e.g. a degree when 'A' levels are adequate
General intelligence	Difficult to measure except by tests, which may, in themselves, be biased and not valid.
Special aptitudes	Education, conditions and encouragement of different activities for girls and boys tend to increase and/or create differences. It is important to identify clearly what aptitudes are required and objectively assess each applicant against them.
Interests	The person specification should record only the kind of interests which are known to further success in the job; individuals with domestic responsibilities or dependants may have no time for leisure activities.
Disposition	A diverse society can bring a range of characteristics to a job. Too narrow a definition can exclude individuals unfairly.
Circumstances	It is fair and lawful to check that all applicants are aware of the requirements of the job and can meet them. All circumstances should only include those which are essential for the job.

Sources: EOC 'Fair and Efficient Selection' Rodger (1952)

would normally include selection testing and often assessment centre techniques in the same way as competence identification.

Competence identification

Mitrani and Dalziel (1993) define a competency as 'an underlying characteristic of an individual which is causally related to effective or superior performance in a job'. They conclude that when an organization knows what aspects of performance are valued, candidates can be selected who are not only capable of filling the job but who will also be highly effective, leading to the achievement of the objectives of the organization.

By analysing the job description or role definition it is possible to elicit key behavioural characteristics which differentiate between effective and ineffective employees; those competencies which differentiate provide the criteria against which applicants can be measured at selection – often by using assessment centre selection techniques (see selection methods). Different weighting can be given to the competencies identified and this forms an important element of the assessment centre assessment decision.

Examples of valued competencies might include:

- Leadership
- Developing potential
- Customer service
- Business awareness
- Communication/presentation skills
- Workflow management
- Judgement/decision making
- Drive/motivation
- Persuasive skills
- Adaptability
- Enabling change

An additional benefit of using competence identification in recruitment and selection is that the emphasis is on assessing against competencies rather than against qualifications, education and experience; this can be less discriminating for applicants from diverse backgrounds who may not have standard career patterns. However, to be fair to applicants, attribute and competence identification should include indications of roles and responsibilities.

When establishing the criteria for selection it is important to ensure that applicants from diverse backgrounds who can bring 'different' and 'unique' approaches to the job or role should not be excluded by criteria which exclude them unnecessarily from selection. Such organizations will fail to gain competitive advantage from attracting and retaining diverse talent.

STEP 4: Determine the reward package

Having determined the criteria against which applicants are to be measured, the next step is to determine the reward package to be offered; this includes both pay and benefits.

A check on the appropriate pay rate in a local labour market can often be made simply by studying local advertisements, ringing around local recruitment agencies or consultants, contacting the Employment Agency Job Shop, forming a 'job club' in the locality of similar organizations or conducting a local market survey. However, when comparing reward packages job titles can be misleading, particularly when you are recruiting against role definitions, attributes or competencies. Comparing with a simple profile of either 2–3 lines or a capsule description of about 250 words is likely to provide more accurate comparative data. It is important to compare like with like when making a comparison – relevant factors are:

- Description of job or role or attribute or competence requirements
- Sector – whether private or public
- Location
- Size of organization (turnover, budget, number of employees)
- Range and level of responsibilities
- Impact on outputs, resources controlled, impact of error

When collecting data for comparative purposes it is important to consider all the elements of the 'reward package' (see Box 1.8).

Details of the appropriate rate for a national labour market can be obtained by checking on national and regional published surveys, from management consultants' databases and from published data in journals such as *Incomes Data Services* and *IRS Employment Review*; the *Department of Employment Gazette* is also a useful source of data, as is the *Financial Times* and other quality newspapers.

When analysing market rate data a number of simple comparisons can be made (see Box 1.9).

Box 1.8 Information to use to compare market rates for jobs

- Basic pay: gross pay before deduction of national insurance, tax and pension. It is important to check the hours worked per week or year to ensure that the comparison is equitable and to ask for information on pay review dates and likely pay increases.
- Cash bonus: received on a regular basis but not integrated into basic pay.
- Total earnings: pay plus other payments over the previous 12 months but excluding employee benefits.
- Employee benefits: these include holidays, health insurance, company cars, loans and sickness ben-

efits above the statutory minimum.
- Allowances: these include additional payments not part of basic pay for call-outs, shift work, night work, weekend work and unsocial hours.
- Total remuneration: includes the value of employee benefits and additional payments.
- Salary structure information: the salary scale or range in the structure for particular jobs.
- Date of review: is the data current or is a review due soon?

Source: Armstrong and Murlis (1995)

The level of reward package to recruit at depends not only on ability to pay but also on internal relativities and established reward policy and structure as well as perceptions of equity and fairness. The use of market surveys in isolation may be detrimental to morale and longer-term working relationships; it may also lead to the importing of discriminatory reward practices, particularly for those jobs or roles which have traditionally been held largely by women and attract a generally low market rate and benefits.

'Fair' pay means giving consideration to the market rate and also to the relationship between reward packages within the organization; it is also important to work within the legal requirements of the equal pay legislation and to judge the 'fairness' of the reward being paid. If flexibility is a key link to diversity and more and more employees are to work on non-standard contracts then it is essential that they are treated on the same basis in respect of reward as employees on full-time contracts and paid fairly for their contribution to the organization. A recruitment and selection policy which promotes and develops all members of the workforce equally, plays a major part in preventing the 'ghettoing' of women and minority groups: see Box 1.10.

STEP 5: Advertise the vacancy

The person specification or attribute or competence definition provides the information on which the recruitment advert wording is based. The image portrayed by the organization's recruitment advertising can determine the image held by customers and those applying to the organization.

Box 1.9 Methods of comparing pay data

In order to compare market rate data the following calculations provide useful data on which to base decisions:

- **Mean:** the average paid
- **Median:** the middle ranking pay
- **Range:** the range from highest to lowest
- **Quartiles:** upper 25 per cent and lower 25 per cent
- **Deciles:** upper 10 per cent and lower 10 per cent

Box 1.10 The need for reward policies that support diversity

Among both manual and non-manual workers, women are concentrated in lower-paid occupations which reduces their pay relative to men. The lowest-paid jobs where large numbers of women are employed include: hairdressing, catering, retail, care assistants and manufacturing. Despite the legislation, there is still a gap between the earnings of men and women and between full-time and part-time employees:

- **Full-time employees:** Average hourly earnings for women are around 80 per cent of those of men.
- **Part-time employees:** Women earn 64 per cent of the hourly earnings of full-time employees and men earn 70 per cent.

Source: New Earnings Survey 1996 as reported in *Labour Market Trends* (1996).

Recruiters who wish to appeal to a diverse labour market need to be aware of their organization's image. Lorraine Paddison (1990) identified particular areas for attention – advertising media which are associated with a particular section of the population can exlude others. Young white male images in adverts and brochures can exclude women, ethnic minorities, disabled and older people from applying to an organization. Confining advertisements to areas or publications which would exclude or disproportionately reduce the number of applicants from a particular group can restrict the pool of talent that can apply for a particular job; this also applies to advertising by 'word of mouth' or by 'cards in the window'. Restricting advertisements to internal applicants can also exclude diverse groups from the organization unless the 'pool of talent' from which the applicant is to be selected internally is diverse. It is important to avoid prescribing requirements which are not relevant, such as length of residence or experience in the UK, and to make it clear that comparable qualifications obtained overseas are as acceptable as UK qualifications (CRE, 1984).

Effective adverts incorporate a bold headline and reference to salary, location, job title, job functions, sector of industry and job entry requirements such as age, experience and qualifications (Duncan, 1985). Importantly, de Witte (1989) found that candidates take special notice of job entry requirements before they read further. If those are unnecessarily overstated or not valid predictors of job success, then a pool of potentially successful appointees is lost (Hill, 1994). Good practice in respect of advert content has been identified by the IPD (1997b) and is shown in Box 1.11.

Managers who complain that a diverse group of talent does not apply for their vacancies need to look at their human resource processes and practices. It can be important to develop links that encourage diverse applicants. These include working with local community groups, organizations and schools, being involved in Training Credits[1] and Modern Apprenticeship Schemes[2] through the local Training and Enterprise Council (TEC) and offering job placement and work experience opportunities. The CRE (1993) has shown that work placements and training on assessment procedures can improve selection possibilities for ethnic minorities. 'Open Days' can give potential applicants the opportunity to familiarize themselves with the organization and encourage applications.

Advertisements should appeal to all sections of the community and use positive visual images; however, it is important to recognize that images and advertisements on their own are not enough to create a diverse organization. It

Box 1.11 Good practice in the content of recruitment advertisments

Advertisements should be clear and state briefly:

- The requirements of the job or role
- The essential and desirable criteria for applicants
- The activities and working practices of the organization

- The working location
- The reward package
- Tenure (contract length)
- The application procedure

is the culture of the organization, the attitude of managers and employees, the human resource strategies, processes and procedures which support and reinforce a diverse organization.

Monitoring the response from advertisements is particularly important. Monitoring provides important information on responses, diversity of applicants and costs. These figures provide essential data for evaluating the effectiveness of the way in which advertisements are placed.

Employment agencies

It is important to apply the same principles which are applied in your own recruitment and selection procedure when using employment agencies. In order not to discriminate indirectly it is important to make it clear to 'head hunters', employment agencies, job shops, career offices and schools that they should not discriminate in their recruitment and selection procedures and should select their 'short lists' from a diverse pool of people. It is the responsibility of the line manager to establish this before finalizing the placement of a vacancy with an agency.

STEP 6: Select the 'right' person

If recruitment and selection processes are carried out systematically then there is a greater likelihood of a fair and effective selection process. A systematic process of selection collects evidence which enables the manager to measure applicants against the criteria which have been established for selection (see Figure 1.3).

Validity

All methods of selection should be validated against results and constantly reviewed to ensure they are measuring what they should measure (validity) and to ensure they are fair and reliable. Any selection test should be tested on a group of existing job holders, both good and bad performers, to see what traits it identifies in them; new appointees who initially sit the tests should be revisited at least once in their new job or role to measure their performance to test whether accurate prediction was made by the test. Selection decisions should be based on a range of selection methods and specialist training and help may be needed in some of the methods. Particular care needs to be taken with selection methods to ensure that they are 'fair' and non-discriminatory; organizations can be found guilty of discrimination if it is established that methods used had an adverse impact on particular groups.

The majority of organizations in the UK and Europe use interviews, application forms and references in the selection procedure (Smith and Abrahamson, 1994). Other methods of selection are used less frequently. The scientific validity of many methods of selection is questionable as a French study showed (Levy-Leboyer,

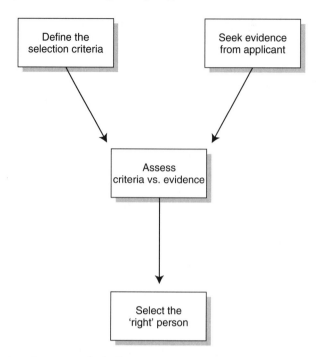

Figure 1.3   A systematic process of selection.

1990 cited in Brewster and Hegewisch, 1994) and they must, therefore, be used with care:

High validity: Work sample
                            Aptitude test
                            Assessment centre
                            Cognitive test

Medium validity: Biodata

Low validity: References
                            Interviews
                            Personality test
                            Self-evaluation

No validity: Graphology
                            Astrology

In order to increase the certainty of selecting the 'right' applicant in a 'fair' way, it is good practice to use a number of different methods of selection. The key is to match the applicant against the criteria which have been identified for selection purposes and not against each other.

The information from which to match the applicant against the criteria can be found from a number of sources; many organizations use some of these sources and others use all of them:

● Scrutinizing the application form

- Selection tests
- Assessment centres
- References
- Selection interview

These methods are each discussed in turn.

Scrutinize application forms

A number of organizations ask applicants to send in CVs; however, the application form has the advantage of asking the questions the organization wants to be answered. The application form is also an important part of the 'image' an applicant has of the organization and questions that would or might discriminate should not be asked on application forms. For example, questions that deal with age, marital status, families, ages of children, or intimate personal details can discriminate. Employers should not disqualify applicants because they are unable to complete an application form unassisted unless that is a valid test of the standard of English required for safe and effective performance on the job (CRE).

Carefully designed application forms provide a great deal of information about the applicant.

A typical application form might ask for the following basic information:

- Personal details
- Work/hours required
- Education
- Employment history
- Voluntary/charity work undertaken
- Linguistic ability
- Other skills and qualifications
- Hobbies/leisure activities
- Evidence of a work permit for non-EU residents
- Evidence of criminal offences not yet 'spent'
- Days absent from work during the last year or major illnesses
- References

When scrutinizing application forms, particularly of women, it is important to recognize that many women have breaks in their formal careers while they look after children or other dependants. In order to ensure that applicants have the opportunity to provide all relevant information, a section on the application form which enables individuals to detail voluntary or unpaid work can provide valuable information which might not otherwise have been provided.

It is important that the application form asks questions that enable the applicant to be matched against the selection criteria. Applicants who do not meet the 'essential' requirements should not be short-listed. For this reason it is essential that the selection criteria are valid for the particularly vacancy.

Biodata

In order to take the uncertainty and subjectivity out of decisions which rely on the application form, a number of organizations compare the responses to questions on their application forms with those which have been identified from other bio-graphical-type data from good performers in similar jobs or roles in their organi-zation (IRS, 1990). Biodata relates to the demands of a job or role, the most common potential predictive power being areas of education, qualifications, spare-time interests, positions of responsibility and motivation. Using this method needs great care in respect of ensuring that the organization does not simply recruit 'clones'; the problem for individuals from diverse backgrounds is that bio-data may be gathered from a largely white-dominated grouping. Particular care needs to be taken to ensure data is collected from a diverse group of employees. In non-diverse organizations this is often not possible.

Application forms can also be designed to ask questions that measure the abil-ity of the applicant against the essential attributes and competencies which have been identified in the analysis process. Examples of questions which might be asked that are not dependent on work experience include:

- Describe a time when you were faced with problems or pressures which tested your ability to cope. What did you do?
- Give an example of a time when you had to reach a decision quickly.
- Tell me about a time when you had to use fact-finding skills to gain informa-tion in order to solve a problem and explain how you analysed the infomation to come to a decision.
- Explain the ways in which you can contribute to the organization.

Administer selection tests

Research shows that the traditional method of interviewing is not necessarily very reliable and that selection testing can improve the reliability of the recruitment and selection process. A decision does have to be made, however, whether to have test results available before or after an interview. Selection test results which are avail-able after the interview can provide useful additional information for the inter-viewer on his or her assessment of the applicant. If results are available before an interview they can have the bad effect of prejudicing the interview or they can have the good effect of providing information which can be 'tested' during the interview.

However selection test results are used in the selection process, it is important that they should only be administered by trained testers and are valid predictors of performance. Saville and Holdsworth stress that if tests are being used they should be psychometrically sound; it is also important that they do not discrimi-nate. Guidelines for best practice in selection testing are given in Box 1.12. Tests can take a number of different forms:

- **Work sampling**. Work sampling has high validity (Levy-Leboyer, 1990; Wood, 1994) and can provide immediate evidence to match against criteria. Exam-ples of work sampling might include:

Word processing a report
Giving a presentation
Negotiating a sale
Watching a video and answering questions on it
Making a simple object
Taking a telephone call
Dealing with a difficult customer

Care should be taken to ensure that there is a direct link between the work sample and the selection criteria to ensure that the test is valid.

● **Psychological testing**. Psychological tests form a major component of selection testing, either alone or as part of an assessment centre. Psychological tests come in various forms but three main forms can be identified: cognitive/ability tests, personality tests and interest tests (Newell and Shackleton 1994).

Conduct assessment centres

Many organizations believe that interviews are poor predictors of performance as they tend to focus on current or previous job performance, and for this reason they use assessment centres to select the right person. The skills needed in a new job or role may be completely different and by simulating those skills assessment centres give an insight into likely future performance (IDS, 1995).

Assessment centres combine interviews with other exercises to provide a more 'complete' picture of the candidates. Usually, before an assessment centre is designed, the job or role to be filled is broken down into competencies. A typical

---

Box 1.12 Guidelines for best selection testing

● The skills or attributes the test measures should be specified and should only be those necessary to do the job; the content of the test should be similar to that found on the job.

● The level of difficulty at which the skill is measured should be appropriate to the job. Care should be taken where there is a tendency for one particular group to reach the required standard.

● Test performance must be related to job performance and a validation study must be carried out to establish that the tests correlate with job performance or other relevant criteria. Test results should be monitored for any differences in scores by different groups of applicants (sex, ethnic group, age, disabled).

● Practice items at the beginning of tests enable those less familiar with them to cope better with

the main test and allow time for questions.

● Only qualified people should administer the tests; results should be fed back to the applicant.

● Results should be evaluated in relation to the performance of a comparison 'norm' group. It is important that the 'norm' group is a diverse group.

Testing people with disabilities

The above apply but in addition special arrangements need to be made in respect of allowing practice tests; access to rooms; use of equipment; and ensuring that instructions are understood clearly. Comparing results to 'normal', non-disabled groups may not be valid.

Source: Saville & Holdsworth Ltd.

assessment centre and key competencies against which trainee managers at Pizza Hut are assessed are shown in Box 1.13.

Assesssment centres are considered by Pearn *et al.* (1987) and Schmitt (1989) to optimize efficiency and fairness – along with work samples. Wood (1994) shows that work samples are also valid and fair methods of assessment.

Assessment centres allow the assessors to judge applicants against the competencies required to fill the job successfully. Kandola and Fullerton (1994) are concerned that to ensure fairness:

- a thorough job analysis should be conducted to establish selection criteria and where possible the sample should have included a diverse group of people;
- the tasks to be carried out in the assessment centre correspond to tasks required in the job;
- the process is piloted using diverse samples;
- monitoring of processes takes place.

In addition the IDS (1995) showed that it is important to have trained assessors and to give detailed feedback to participants on their performance.

Assessment centres can be very costly in terms of time and for this reason are usually restricted to senior staff or graduate trainees. However, Haagen-Dazs uses an assessment centre to recruit crew members for its main restaurants and Pizza Hut uses them to recruit trainee managers.

Box 1.13 A typical assessment centre

- **Interviews:** Allowing areas to be probed in depth using structured interview techniques.
- **Presentations:** To enable the candidates' persuasiveness and other communication skills to be assessed.
- **Group exercises:** Assessment of problem-solving skills – the group must work together to reach consensus on the best way to tackle a problem. There is no leader and no assigned roles. Assessment of the ability to motivate and persuade through negotiation – one candidate is assigned the role of chairing and others given particular roles to pursue.
- **In-tray exercises:** These exercises simulate the problems that might face the candidates and test their ability to rank problems in order of priority and deal with them effectively.
- **Written exercises:** These exercises are to test the quality of analysis and a persuasiveness and

thoroughness of argument and might include report writing, summaries and letters.

- **Psychometric tests:** These might be objective – testing numerical, verbal and abstract reasoning. They might be personality tests – used to provide evidence of motivation and personality.

Key competencies for trainee managers at Pizza Hut

Adaptability
Quality customer service
Interpersonal communication
Team leadership
Business administration
Tenacity/commitment
Planning and organizing

Source: IDS Study 569/January 1995.

References

A number of organizations, particularly those in the public sector, take up references before short-listing applicants; however, the validity of references has been found to be low (Levy-Leboyer, 1990). This can prove particularly difficult for applicants who do not wish their current employer to know they are 'job hunting'. The demand for work references can also prove a problem for groups who have not recently been in the job market and it should be recognized that applicants may have evidence of their character and abilities from sources other than a previous employer. Employers have no obligation to give references but if they do so, they must ensure that any reference given to prospective future employers is accurate and truthful. Many managers find that the quickest way to take up a reference is by telephone but the reliability of such references is questionable. It can also be difficult to check the identity of the person giving the reference.

Selection interviews

The purpose of the selection interview is 'To obtain and assess information about a candidate which will enable a valid prediction to be made of his or her future performance ... in comparison with the predictions made for any other candidates' (Armstrong, 1996). Interviews have been shown to be unreliable predictors of future performance but when conducted by a trained interviewer in a systematic and fair way, their reliability improves. Panel interviews are often preferred to individual interviews in that the judgement of candidates can be shared, but they can be intimidating, particularly for applicants less familiar with the selection process. Sequential interviews after each other can be another way of sharing judgement but in a less threatening way.

In order to improve the reliability of the interview it is essential for the manager who is carrying out selection interviewing as part of his or her role to undertake training in selection interviewing. The learning outcomes of any training programme should enable the manager to understand the key issues of diversity, to conduct a systematic and fair recruitment and selection interview and to recognize the induction needs of the new recruit.

The purpose of the interview is to seek evidence which enables the applicant to be measured against the previously determined selection criteria. In addition, the interview provides an opportunity to clarify queries relating to information provided on the application form (e.g. gaps in career history) and to give information about the organization.

Selection interview structure

There are six key stages in a systematic interview structure (see Figure 1.4); these are:

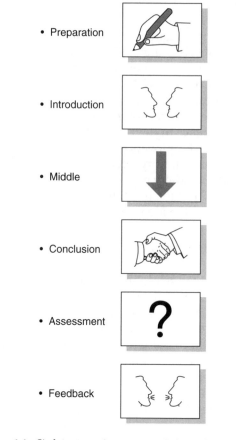

- Preparation

- Introduction

- Middle

- Conclusion

- Assessment

- Feedback

Figure 1.4   Six key stages in a systematic interview structure.

Stage 1: Preparation.

Attend recruitment and selection training.
Send out criteria against which applicant will be assessed – person specification, competency or attribute framework.
Invite applicant to visit organization prior to selection process.
Book a quiet room with no interruptions.
Arrange seating to provide a relaxing atmosphere for the applicant.
Prepare key questions which:

- clarify information provided by the application form;
- enable the applicant to be measured against the selection criteria.

Prepare an assessment sheet which clearly shows the criteria against which the applicant is being assessed and how the applicant is to be measured, e.g. scale/comments.

Stage 2: Introduction

Introduction to interviewers.
Icebreaker to settle nerves and establish dialogue.
Explanation of the interview process.

Background information concerning the organization.

Setting the applicant at ease.

Stage 3: Middle

Open and probing behavioural questions which seek to clarify information on the application form and look for evidence to enable the applicant to be matched against the previously identified selection criteria.

Active listening to what the applicant is saying; checking for understanding, not just hearing the words; being aware of non-verbal behaviour/body language which can give clues that alter the meaning of words.

Stage 4: Conclusion

A summary of the interview process; asking the applicant if they have any questions; informing the applicant of the next stage in the selection process.

Stage 5: Assessment

Measure the applicant against the predetermined selection criteria using the evidence gathered from the interview and other sources. Applicants should not be matched against each other.

Stage 6: Feedback

Information should be given to rejected applicants on their performance to help their personal action planning and development.

Questioning

Open questions enable the applicant to tell the interviewer about themselves and they begin with words like 'describe', 'tell me', 'how'. The answers to open questions need to be listened to actively and to be followed up with probing questions which follow up the answer given by the applicant. The questioning process is best thought of as a funnel (see Figure 1.5) with open questions, opening the applicant up to talk, attentive listening to responses, probing questions to find out more information and continuing the questioning process while narrowing down to specific answers. Each area of questioning is summed up by the interviewer to ensure that the answers given have been fully understood by the interviewer.

Questions which are less useful in the interview situation include 'closed' questions beginning with words like, 'do you', 'have you', 'did you'; leading questions beginning with words like 'I suppose', ' I expect', 'I should think' ; forced choice questions which force answers from fixed choices and multiple choice questions can confuse and muddle applicants. Hypothetical questions provide answers based on what a person thinks he or she would do, and need, therefore, to be used with care. Discriminatory questions which discriminate against the individual on the grounds of sex, marriage, ethnic origin, disability or age are illegal (Anderson and Shackleton, 1993). Examples of discriminatory questions which should not be asked at interview are given in Box 1.14.

Behavioural questions which seek evidence to match the applicant against the selection criteria are particularly valuable in selection interviews as they are founded on the assumption that evidence of behaviour in past performance is the best predictor of future performance (See Box 1.15). Evidence need not apply only

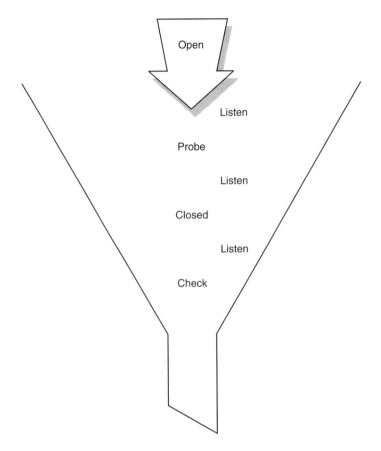

Figure 1.5 The funnel questioning process.

to the workplace and applicants without a great deal of work experience should be encouraged to think of examples outside the work environment.

Active listening is a particular skill and worrying about which question to ask next at interview can detract from actually listening. Developing the art of helicoptering can help – keeping an overview on the interview but zooming in to ask specific questions and to probe the answers given.

Box 1.14 Questions which should not be asked at interview

- Questions based upon assumptions regarding women's roles in the home and family
- Questions regarding intentions about marriage and having children
- Different questions to married and single applicants

- Questions which pry into private affairs which cannot affect the job
- Questions which are not asked of all applicants regardless of race, gender, age or disability

---

Box 1.15 Examples of behavioural questions

Selection criteria	Question
Good leadership skills	Give an example of a situation in which you were responsible for helping others to complete a task or project ... how did you obtain feedback from them on your effectiveness?
Ability to handle conflict	Describe a situation in which you were faced with conflicting views to your own ... how did you deal with it?
Problem-solving ability	Give an example of a problem you have had to solve recently ... what steps did you take in the problem-solving process?
Good customer/quality awareness	Tell me about any initiatives you have been involved in to improve quality awareness ... How did you know if they were effective?
Effective project management	Describe a project you have managed. Give details of how you managed it.

Interviewing applicants from another culture

Interviewing applicants from another culture can present the manager with particular difficulties and can be potentially unfair by disadvantaging an applicant who is unfamiliar with recruitment and selection processes. To ensure fairness in the selection process, the manager needs to have an understanding of cultural differences between the manager's own culture and the applicant's culture. It is essential, therefore, for the manager to have cultural awareness training as part of the training and development programme for recruiting and selecting.

Exploring of cultural differences openly with applicants can broaden understanding of their responses during the selection interview. Such applicants will normally benefit from visiting the organization for a familiarization visit prior to the interview and should have time spent with them prior to the interview clearly explaining the selection process and procedure.

It is also important to check assumptions and expectations clearly at the introduction stage of the interview and to check for understanding throughout the interview. Jargon and technical language should only be used if it relates to the selection criteria.

Body language can also often be misunderstood across cultures. In some cultures, to express one's opinion firmly in a team meeting is regarded as disrespectful; in others it is taken as a sign of individual initiative and is rewarded. Assumptions about understanding should be checked during the interview as the implicit message is often misunderstood across cultures (see Box 1.16).

Monitoring the recruitment and selection process

Carrying out a monitoring procedure as part of the recruitment and selection process is a valuable tool in evaluating recruitment processes. Monitoring

Box 1.16 Assessment and selection in a cross-cultural context

In addition to equal opportunities, issues relating to cross-cultural differences need careful attention and management during the assessment and selection of applicants.

Key points for consideration are:

- **Communication and misunderstandings.** National, cultural and religious differences inevitably influence use of language, argument patterns and non-verbal behaviour, possibly leading to misunderstandings from applicants from visible minorities and assessors. Some of the possible sources of misunderstanding that assessors need to appreciate include the following:
  - Degree of reticence or openness of an applicant speaking about a colleague or superior
  - Willingness or reticence to speak openly about personal or organizational strengths or weaknesses

- Degree to which body language is used when communicating and differences in the types of body language used
- Willingness to make public personal aspirations
- Willingness to disagree or say 'no' to potential superiors

- **The interview and sources of bias.** There have been few studies of the impact of race on the interpersonal dynamics of the interview process. It has been suggested that black and Asian candidates may be wrongly rated lower than white candidates on a variety of non-verbal dimensions. The reasons behind this are unclear but may relate to the different cultural and social experiences of candidates and assessors.

Sources: Echiejile (1992) and Macdonald and Hakel (1985).

---

involves collecting and analysing statistical data on existing employees, on applicants and on recruitment and selection processes. Kandola and Fullerton (1994) found that 76 per cent of the organizations they surveyed had equal opportunities monitoring in place. Where this is used the reason for requesting it should be fully explained to the applicant with a brief explanation of the organization's equal opportunities or diversity policy. Many organizations have a separate tear-off sheet attached to the application form which is removed before the application is read. These monitoring sheets are only valuable if the statistics are collected, circulated and the results used to formulate policy and practice about future recruitment and selection. An example of an ethnic monitoring form is given in Box 1.17.

All methods of selection should be validated against results and constantly reviewed to ensure fairness and reliability. Selection decisions should be based on a range of selection methods and specialist training and help may be needed in some of the methods. Particular care needs to be taken with selection methods to ensure that they are 'fair' and non-discriminatory; in the USA under the Civil Rights Acts of 1964 and 1991 organizations can be found guilty of discrimination if it is established that methods used had an adverse impact on particular groups.

STEP 7: Induct the new starter

Having selected the right person for the job from a diverse pool of talent, it is important that he or she is welcomed into a diverse organization, which has

Box 1.17 Oxfam's ethnic monitoring form

Equal Opportunities Monitoring Form

Oxfam's Equal Opportunities Policy

Our Equal Opportunities Policy is stated overleaf and in order that it is effective we need to obtain certain information. Your co-operation is sought in providing this. The information will be used only by the Human Resources Departments for the purposes of ensuring the effectiveness of our Equal Opportunities Policy. This form will be treated in the strictest confidence and will be detached before shortlisting. If you are not offered employment with Oxfam your application will be kept for up to twelve months and then destroyed. The information supplied on this form is used for statistical purposes only.

Application for:

Reference No: Date of Application:

Full Name:

Date of Birth: Age:

Where did you see this post advertised?

Are you an Oxfam volunteer?   Yes ☐   No ☐

How would you describe yourself?

These categories of ethnic origin are recommended by the UK Equal Opportunities Commission as the most appropriate for the UK. We recognise however that the specified categories may not be appropriate for everyone. If this is the case please use the last box.

Bangladeshi	☐	Irish	☐
Black African	☐	Pakistani	☐
Black Caribbean	☐	Black other	☐
		(Please specify)	
Chinese	☐	White	☐
Indian	☐	Other	☐
		(Please Specify)	

Do you consider yourself to have a disability?

Yes ☐   If yes, what is the nature of your disability?
....

No ☐   ....

Gender: Female ☐   Male ☐

Thank you for your co-operation

diverse policies and practices. The new starter's first encounter with the organization is the recruitment and selection process and the second is the induction process. Managers have a key role to play in both processes. Induction in particular is a key responsibility of managers as it is a member of their team whom they are introducing to their department and the organization. As we have already shown, recruitment and selection is an expensive process, not only in terms of placing advertisements or using selection agencies, but in terms of time and effort spent by the manager and his or her team. To spend that time and effort and then find that people leave is a very expensive process indeed.

It can be particularly difficult for people from minorities joining an organization; they often take longer to be inducted and socialized into organizations (Gordon *et al.*, 1991 and Cox and Blake, 1991 cited in Kandola and Fullerton, 1994). Gordon showed that women and ethnic minorities in particular were unaware of expectations of new employees and what was needed in order to progress within the organization.

The purpose of induction is to help new employees to adjust to their new jobs and organizational environment and to help them become fully integrated into their work teams or groups and to prevent a high incidence of early leavers (Fowler, 1990). An example of an induction process which helps new recruits adjust to their new working environment is at Daewoo Cars. New recruits are sent a video and a set of workbooks with exercises to complete before they join the organization; these deal with company philosophy, product knowledge and the no-haggle retail process. More information is then provided in the first two days of starting in the organization.

Research shows that many new employees face an 'induction crisis' in their first six weeks of joining a new organization and that turnover rates of new starters are very high during these weeks. Causes of early leaving can arise from the gap between the 'official' and 'unofficial' expectations of the employer and the expectations of the employee (see Figure 1.6). Other reasons given for leaving include false expectations during recruitment, not fitting into the organization, poor relations with managers and lack of fitting into the work group (Fowler, 1994).

In order to ensure that the new employee feels comfortable in the organization Kandola and Fullerton (1994) recommend:

● a mentoring process whereby a more experienced person can help and guide the new starter – this might be supplemented by networks which the individual can join;
● that managers are properly trained in induction techniques and recognize problems of settling into organizations, particularly for individuals from minority backgrounds.

It is also important for the manager to take responsibility for ensuring that the new starter is seen on a regular basis, that departmental and organizational expectations are clear and that opportunities exist for feedback and discussion.

It is important for the manager to take full responsibility for new starters; provide a properly planned programme for them and find them a 'buddy' or 'starter's friend' to help them find their way around during the first week. A proper induction programme should be drawn up after discussion with personnel and

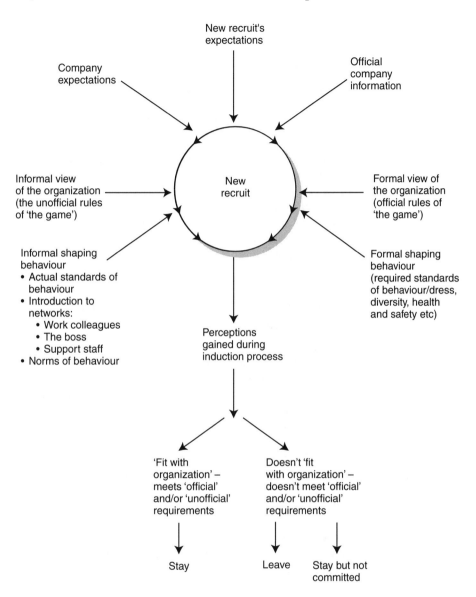

Figure 1.6   The induction dilemma.

other team members. A typical 'checklist' of issues to be covered (Fowler, 1994; Kandola and Fullerton, 1994) in the induction process might include:

● Identification of objectives
● Clarification of expectations
● Explanation of diversity practices
● Discussion of development opportunities
● Domestic information
● Health and safety
● Wages/salary information

- Conditions of service
- Working procedures
- Employee benefits
- Trade unions and employee involvement
- Employee development
- Equal opportunities
- The organization's culture/mission/core values/structure
- The industry or sector

New starters should be seen by the manager at the end of their first week and regularly during their first few weeks, to check their progress and understanding. New starters need to understand their objectives clearly and to know the standards that are expected of them. In this way, the induction process is a key part of the recruitment and selection process in that there is no point spending a lot of time and money in recruiting and selecting only to find that the individual concerned has left the organization within a few weeks.

STEP 8: Measure, review and evaluate the recruitment and selection process

The IPD (1997b) recognizes that it is simply not enough to carry out the induction process and then consider that the recruitment and selection procedure is completed. It is essential to audit, review and evaluate the recruitment and selection procedure regularly. It is important to validate the process – to track applicants – to determine their success rate. It is essential to encourage employee consultation, involvement and good communication and feedback to make sure that the organization has commitment to diversity management.

It is also important to analyse data and statistics provided from monitoring forms and from application data. A computerized personnel information system can provide invaluable statistics to help with monitoring and these can often be provided by the personnel department for each department. Exit interviews can also provide valuable sources of evidence and should always be conducted by the manager when someone plans to leave. Keeping a record of exit interviews provides valuable data for future action plans for recruitment, selection, development and induction.

Conclusion

This chapter has shown that managers are recruiting and selecting for their organizations from a diverse labour market and this provides them with opportunities to exploit the 'diversity advantage' by providing a diverse pool of talent for the organization to enable the organization to meet its existing and future objectives.

The focus for this chapter is eight key steps to recruitment, selection and induction, which provide the manager with a guide to 'best practice' to ensure that recruitment, selection and induction processes attract and retain a diverse group of applicants. Research outlined in the chapter shows that many organizations believe that diversity makes good business sense. In this respect, it underpins the role of line managers in the organization for whom 'good business' is the fundamental outcome of their organizational role. Good managers cannot operate in isolation; they must manage people within the organization; they must recruit, select and develop the right people. The basis of good management is the belief that the management of diversity develops and complements established approaches to equal opportunities. Managing diversity ensures achievement of maximum individual and organizational potential by building on the understanding and need for equality of opportunity within the organization. Within this approach, where diversity seeks to maximize the development of individuals it fits well with other initiatives which managers are concerned and involved in such as Investors in People and Total Quality Management.

The strategy web shows clearly that managing diversity is a holistic undertaking which helps to effect cultural change. Managers have a crucial role to play as front line implementers in this cultural change and their role in the key processes of recruitment, selection and induction is critical. The manager's role is to 'own' and to manage diversity and in doing this the manager helps to combat prejudice, stereotyping and other unacceptable behaviour while at the same time gaining business advantages from valuing diversity.

Managing diversity is, however, a continuous process and needs constant audit and review. The manager has a key role to play in this and no more critically than in the conduct and review of recruitment and selection processes.

Key HRM issues currently or likely to be faced

Managers are now taking increasing responsibility for recruitment, selection and induction within their organizations. We now operate in a global environment, with many leading organizations operating internationally and recruiting, selecting and working with diverse workforces around the world. In addition, the local workforce is now diverse and labour markets are reflecting changing social and demographic patterns. Organizations which harness the 'diversity advantage' will be those that benefit from harvesting the diversity of talent in the labour market and utilizing it to its full potential. This will enable those organizations to gain competitive edge.

If organizations are to become truly diverse and to achieve a culture in which diversity thrives, then there needs to be a strong link between diversity objectives and the strategic plan. This requires not only commitment from the top of the organization, but the support and 'ownership' of diversity by the line manager. Traditionally, managers have neither understood the meaning of diversity nor seen it as their responsibility. Diversity is the responsibility of all, but in particular it is managers, who are at the 'sharp' end, who can make diversity work for them and their departments.

Recruitment and selection processes play a key role in creating a diverse organization but can only succeed if diversity is part of the business culture. An applicant from a diverse background will not stay long in an environment which is clearly hostile to diversity. The manager has a clear role here to be committed to the achievement of diversity, to audit and assess needs, to have clear objectives, to be clearly accountable, to communicate policies and practices effectively, to champion diversity and coordinate activity and to evaluate and monitor progress towards diversity.

Further research

Further research is needed to look at the expectations of individuals from diverse backgrounds and the reality of organizational life. The induction crisis detailed in the chapter has shown the impact of 'formal' and 'informal' practices in organizations. Information about why people from diverse backgrounds do not apply to organizations and about their experience within them is limited by the lack of available research data. In addition, managers are often reluctant to 'own' issues of diversity and fail to recognize the value of diversity to the organization and to the achievement of organizational objectives. Further research is needed to look at the reasons for this management 'reluctance'; with increasing devolution of human resource management to line management, the effectiveness of many human resource policies and practices will be dependent on the willingness of managers to take on those responsibilities and to understand key issues such as diversity.

Implications for HRM and line managers

With the increasing devolvement of human resource management policies and practices to line managers, the human resource management of the organization is going to be very dependent on the willingness of line managers to 'manage' and to 'own' those policies and practices. The current drive of many line managers is the 'bottom line' and this is often seen as short-term cuts to achieve budget. Longer-term or broader issues, of which diversity is a key one, are frequently sidelined or seen as part of Personnel or Equal Opportunities. Managers are often unable to take the longer-term view and they are often unable to recognize the 'bigger picture'. This is not always their fault; they are pressurized from above. However, what is becoming increasingly clear is that organizations which value their people, motivate them and attract their commitment achieve competitive edge. This cannot be achieved without line management involvement in longer-term human resource policies and practices.

This involvement comes from taking the 'broader' view, from reading about current issues, from recognizing changes in demographic structure, from being willing to reflect and learn. Diversity comes within this remit; it requires that 'broader' view. There is no doubt, however, that those managers who acquire that broader view will be the managers who are able to achieve more, who will be more innovative, who will retain committed staff; these will be the managers who will achieve organizational success because the 'bottom line' will benefit from this approach as well as the members of the team.

In conclusion, good managers recognize that good people management and the 'bottom line' are compatible and take every opportunity to ensure they have the 'right' people in their team to achieve that success.

Summary

It has been argued in this chapter that as managers take increasing responsibility for recruitment, selection, retention and induction within their organizations, they need to recognize that the labour market from which they recruit their pool of talent is increasingly diverse. It has also been shown that recruiting a diverse labour force can bring significant benefits to their organization. In order to recruit a diverse labour force, managers need to have systematic and 'fair' recruitment and selection policies and practices. Eight steps in the recruitment and selection process are given in this chapter for managers to follow. Specifically we have:

- examined the diversity of the UK workforce;
- discussed the 'diversity advantage' to organizations;
- examined the differences between diversity and equal opportunities;
- considered the importance of creating a diverse culture within the organization;
- examined the link between human resource planning and recruiting and selecting a diverse workforce;
- considered the costs of recruitment and selection;
- discussed the eight steps in a 'fair' and systematic recruitment process. These steps were:

  Identify the need to recruit
  Analyse the requirements
  Define the selection criteria
  Determine the reward
  Advertise the vacancy
  Select the 'right' person
  Induct the new starter
  Measure, review and evaluate the recruitment and selection process

Checklist of key terms and concepts

You should feel confident that you understand the following terms and ideas:

- Diversity – how it differs from equal opportunities; the business case for diversity
- Diverse culture – the need for organizational culture to support diversity
- Fair and systematic recruitment and selection processes – the eight steps in the process and their relationship to diversity

- Induction and reward – their role in supporting the recruitment and selection process

Notes

1   **Training Credits** fund training for young people at work and lead to a National Vocational Qualification (NVQ), a nationally recognized qualification which assesses skill, knowledge and understanding in the workplace.
2   **Modern Apprenticeships** are available for employees who would like to develop into technicians, engineers or managers in a wide range of occupational areas. Modern Apprenticeships consist of training to NVQ level 3 or above plus the development of key working skills such as communication, information technology and working as a team.

Questions

Text related

1   Study an organization with which you are familiar and evaluate the extent to which its employment practices have created a diverse workforce which reflects the diversity of its customer base.
2   Evaluate the recruitment and selection practices of the organization you have chosen and consider whether these practices are sufficient to ensure diversity within the organization.
3   Draw up an action plan for the organization you have chosen based on the results of your conclusions from your evaluations in Questions 1 and 2.

Library and assignment based

1   Visit a number of local stores and restaurants and observe the extent to which their employees reflect the diversity of their customer base.
2   Research the Annual Reports of the organizations you visited and find out if they make any statements about diversity and equal opportunities; reflect on these statements compared with your observations.
3   Read the following:

A report on flexibility at work in Europe (IPD, 1994) showed that employers in most European countries are now employing a significant proportion of their workforce in flexible forms of work. Four main reasons were given in the report:

- Economic pressures: a positive response to increased competitiveness or to reduce costs.

- Labour market: the opportunity to draw on sections of labour markets that would not otherwise be available for work or to retain staff.
- Forced flexibility: as a result of employee pressure or union agreements; line managers' increasing responsibility for local bargaining had led to their seeking work patterns which were appropriate to the needs of their departments.
- To create change: to bring about changes in the way people thought about their work.

Now answer the following questions:

(a) Research the extent to which the reasons given in the report for the increase in flexible forms of work relate to organizations with which you are familiar.
(b) Analyse the extent to which recruitment and selection policies and practices in the organizations you have researched encourage flexible forms of work.
(c) Research the extent to which flexible patterns of work encourage diversity in the organizations you investigate. What other factors might be relevant to the achievement of a diverse organization?
(d) What ethical issues may be important in setting selection criteria? How might a manager ensure that selection criteria are ethical?

References

ACAS (1984) Advisory Booklet Number 6 *Recruitment and Selection*, Ikon Ltd.

Anderson, N and Shackleton, V (1993) *Successful Selection Interviewing*, Blackwell.

Armstrong, MJ (1996) *A Handbook of Personnel Management Practice*, Kogan Page.

Armstrong, MJ and Murlis, H (1995) *Reward Management*, Kogan Page.

Atkinson, J (1985) *Flexibility, Uncertainty and Manpower Management*, IMS Report 89.

Bedingfield, R and Foreman, J (1997) *Decentralisation and Devolution – The Impact on Equal Opportunities at Work*, The Wainwright Trust.

Brewster, C and Hegewisch, A (1994) *Policy and Practice in European Human Resource Management*, Routledge.

Cockburn, C (1989) Equal opportunities: the long and short agenda, *IRL Journal*.

Cornelius, N, Gooch, L and Todd, S (2000) Managers Leading Diversity for Business Excellence, *Journal of General Management* (**25**)3, 67–79.

Cox, TH and Blake, S (1991) Managing Cultural Diversity: Implications for Organisational Competitiveness, *Academy of Management Executive*, **5**, 45–56.

CRE (1993) *Towards Fair Selection*, CRE.

CRE (1984) *Race Relations Code of Practice For the Elimination of Discrimination and the Promotion of Equality of Opportunity in Employment*, London HMSO.

Dany, F (1992) Le cout du recruitment, *Document IRE*, October.

de Witte, K (1989) Recruiting & Advertising. In *Assessment & Selection in Organisations* (ed. P. Herriot). Wiley, Chichester.

Department of Employment (1995), *10 Point Plan for Employers*, HMSO.

Duncan, DC (1985) *The Economics of Selection: Costing for Manpower Decisions*, NFER-Nelson, Windsor, Berks.

Echiejile, IA (1992) *Equal Opportunities: Recruitment and Selection*, Book Guild.

Employment Gazette (1995) *Labour Force Survey*, February, HMSO.

EOC (undated) *Fair and Efficient Selection*, EOC.

Ford, V (1996) *People Management*, November, IPD.

Fowler, A (1990) How to plan an induction programme, September, *Personnel Plus*, IPD.

Fowler, A (1994) *A Good Start*, IPD.

Gordon, G *et al.* (1991) Managing diversity in R & D groups. *Research Technology Management*, January–February, (**34**) 1, 18–23.

Greenslade, M (1991) Managing diversity: lessons from the United States, *People Management*, December, IPD.

Hill, J (1994) Psychological dimensions in recruitment and advertising design. *British Psychological Society*, (**10**) 5, October.

Hofstede, G (1980) *Culture's Consequences*, Sage.

Incomes Data Services (IDS) Study (1995) *Assessment Centres*, January: Study 569.

Incomes Data Services (IDS) Study (1996): *Opportunity 2000*, March: Study 597.

(IPD) (1994) *Flexibility at Work in Europe*, IPD.

(IPD) (1997a) *Managing Diversity: an IPD Position Paper*, IPD.

(IPD) (1997b) *Recruitment: Key Facts*; IPD.

Industrial Relations Services (IRS) (1990) *Biodata – Past Tense, Future Perfect?* Recruitment and Development Report 1, 23 January 1990.

Kandola, R and Fullerton, J (1994) *Managing the Mosaic*, IPD.

Kandola, R and Butterworth, A (1996) The Disability Discrimination Act (1995) implications for recruiters. *British Psychological Society*, (**12**) 3, June.

Labour Market Trends, February 1996, Office for National Statistics.

Levy-Leboyer, M (1990) *Evaluation du Personnel, quelles méthodes choisir?*, Paris: Editions d'Organisation cited in Brewster and Hegewisch (1994), *Policy and Practice in European Human Resource Management*, Routledge.

Macdonald, T and Hakel, M (1985) Effects of applicants' race, sex, suitability and answers on interviewers' questioning strategy and ratings. *Personnel Psychology*, (**38**), 321–334.

Martin, J, Meltzer, H and Elliot, D (1988) *The Prevalence of Disability Among Adults*, London, HMSO.

McEnrue, MP (1993) Managing diversity: Los Angeles before & After the Riots. *Organisational Dynamics*, (**21**) 3, 18–29, Winter.

Mitrani, A, Dalziel, M and Fitt, D (1993) *Competency Based Human Resource Management*, Kogan Page.

Neathey, F and Hurstfield, J (1996) *Flexibility in Practice: Women's Employment and Pay in Retail and Finance*, IRS.

Newell, S and Shackleton, V (1994) The use (and abuse) of psychometric tests in British industry and commerce, *HRM Journal*, **1**.

Osborne, K and Nichol, C (1996) *Patterns of Pay: Results of 1996 New Earnings Survey*, Labour Market Trends, November.

Overell, S (1996) *People Management*, February, IPD.

Paddison, L (1990) The targetted approach to recruitment. *Personnel Management*, November, IPD.

Pearn, MA, Kandola, RS and Mottram, RD (1987) *Selection Tests and Sex Bias: The Impact of Selection Testing on the Employment Opportunities of Women and Men*, London, HMSO.

Rodger, A (1952) *The Seven Point Plan*, National Institute of Industrial Psychology.

Ross, R and Schneider, R (1992) *From Equality to Diversity, A Business Case for Equal Opportunities*, Pitman.

Saville & Holdsworth Ltd (Undated) *Best Test Practice in the Use of Personnel Selection Tests*, Saville & Holdsworth Ltd.

Schmitt, N (1989) Fairness in employment selection. In *Advances in Selection and Assessment* (eds M. Smith and V. Robertson), John Wiley & Sons.

Sly, F (1995a) *Ethnic Groups and Labour Market Analysis*, Spring 1994, Labour Force Survey, *Employment Gazette*.

Sly, F (1995b) *Women in the Labour Market: Results from the Spring 1995 Labour Force Survey*, Employment Gazette.

Sly, F (1996) *Disability and the Labour Market*, Labour Market Trends, September 1996.

Sly, F, Price, A and Risdon, A (1996) *Women in the Labour Market: Results from the Spring 1996 Labour Force Survey*, Labour Market Trends, March 1997.

Smith, M and Abrahamson M (1994) More data on the use of selection methods in the UK. *British Psychological Society*, (**10**) 5, October.

Williams, A, Dobson, P and Walters, M (1993) *Changing Culture – New Organisational Approaches*, IPM.

Wood, R (1994) Work sample should be used more (and will be). *International Journal of Selection and Assessment*, (**2**) 3, 166–71.

Worsley, R (1996) Only prejudices are old and tired. *People Management*, January, IPD.

Recommended further reading

Kandola and Fullerton (1994) provide an ideal introduction to the subject of diversity while Ross and Schneider (1992) provide a valuable exploration of the business case for diversity. Hofstede (1980) is widely recognized as the authority on culture. The ACAS, CRE, EOC, Department of Employment and IPD Codes of Practice also provide valuable practical guidance on key issues of good practice in recruitment and selection. Valuable reading on induction is provided by Fowler (1990, 1994).

Legal briefing

A. The contract

At the heart of the employment relationship is an individual contract between the employer and the employee. In accordance with the norm in English contract law, this agreement is not required to be recorded in a formal, signed, written document. A modicum of formality is in fact required (now contained in section 1, Employment Rights Act, 1996 – the ERA) where an employee is entitled to be given information in writing concerning vital aspects of the employment contract. This information must be furnished to each employee within two months of the commencement of the employment, and any change must be notified within one month. This obligation is owed to both full-time and part-time employees. There follows a resume of the main provisions: more details can be obtained from any of the publications listed at the end of the legal briefing to the Introduction and overview.

The statement must contain the names of the parties to the contract; the date the employment began; the rate of pay and intervals between payments; hours of work; any provisions relating to holiday pay, sick pay or pension (including any lack of provision of all or any of these payments); notice of termination of employment to be given by either side; duration of contract, if it is for a fixed term; the employee's place of work or, if there is no fixed place of work, the address of the employer; any collective agreement that affects the terms and conditions of the contract.

Other provisions will be referred to at appropriate places in this text: employees required to work outside the UK (see legal briefing to chapter 6), and matters relating to disciplinary and grievance procedures (see legal briefing to chapter 5).

Many terms of the employment contract will be

Continued on page 68

implied as a matter of law. The employee is required to render personal service and to act with honesty and in good faith and without negligence in his or her conduct of the employer's affairs. The employer is required to pay in accordance with the contract, to provide a safe system of work and to treat the employee with respect.

Some of these items require further expansion. Perhaps the most important recent development relates to the employee's obligation of confidentiality, part of the implied term of 'good faith'. The Public Interest Disclosure Act, 1998, came into force on 2 July 1999. This statute protects an employee against dismissal or any other form of discrimination in the circumstances covered by the Act. Employees who disclose information (which would otherwise be confidential) relating to specific matters laid down by the Act now have statutory protection. Examples include criminal behaviour and breaches of the health and safety laws. The disclosure must be one that is in the public interest to make, and the disclosure must be to a suitable outside body. This may, on occasion, be the press, but more often it will be an enforcement or regulatory body. The information will mainly concern breaches of the health and safety laws. This activity is strikingly, if inelegantly, known as 'whistleblowing'. Disasters such as the Piper Alpha oil platform or the Zeebrugge ferry are frequently quoted as examples of where the expressed concerns of the employees were consistently ignored by management and where the employees feared for their jobs if they took the complaints outside the company. If a 'whistleblowing' employee is dismissed for that reason after the commencement date of the Act, it will be treated as automatically unfair dismissal, no qualifying period will apply and there is no upper limit imposed on the amount of compensation awarded. 'Dismissal' is treated at greater length later on in this briefing.

The employment contract still rests on the supposition (some would say 'fiction') that it is a relationship freely entered into by the parties, and is therefore binding on them at law. While it is true that the terms offered to the employee have been devised by the employer and reflect his or her requirements for the job, those terms have been modified in accordance with powerful influences operating outside of the contract. Where there are recognized trades unions (a factor increasingly rare outside the public sector), the important terms of the employment contract will have been set by collective bargaining, and the employer will be legally bound to implement those terms as far as relevant employees

are concerned. Another factor is the large and ever-increasing amount of employment legislation. These Acts of Parliament almost always operate in favour of the employee, and are increasingly influenced by the law of the EU.

The employer's objective is often to achieve the greatest flexibility in terms of both the work to be undertaken by each employee and the variety of work contracts to be offered.

If flexibility in working practice is required, then this should be spelled out as clearly as possible in the contract. Vague terms, such as ' ... or any other tasks that the Company may require' should be avoided. If the employee may be required to change the location of his or her employment, then the contract should provide for reasonable notice of the change and for reasonable relocation expenses. Unreasonable behaviour on the part of the employer could entitle the employee to claim that he or she has been constructively dismissed for breach of the implied obligation of 'respect'. Further comments on dismissal will appear later on in this 'briefing'.

'Flexibility' in connection with a diversity in the type of contracts being offered gives rise to its own set of problems.

Not everyone who works for another for reward is, in law, an employee. It is important to grasp this fact, especially in view of the present state of the labour market, where 'peripheral' workers are increasing in number as distinct from the traditional employee employed full-time with one employer. Agency workers, self-employed, casual, temporary, part-time – these are commonly lumped together under the adjective 'peripheral'. This is an over-simplification, and can lead to dangerous assumptions with unfortunate legal consequences. The law differentiates between 'employees' and others, who, for the sake of simplicity, can be referred to as 'contractors'. The subject is sometimes referred to as the difference between a 'contract of service' and a 'contract for services'. Some peripheral workers could fall into the category of 'employees'. It depends entirely on the circumstances of each particular case, and in the event of a dispute, it is for the court to decide the status of the worker; it cannot normally be done by agreement between the parties. A clear example of the problem is furnished by the case of *O'Kelly* v. *Trust House Forte plc* [1984], where the employment status of certain individuals, designated 'regular casuals', had to be determined. They had been dismissed from Grosvenor House Hotel, almost certainly for trade union activities, and their right to compensation for unfair dismissal depended upon their being found to be 'employees' rather than 'contractors'. The decision, based on the terms of their contracts, was a very finely balanced one. The Industrial Tribunal held that they were 'contractors'; the Employment Appeal Tribunal disagreed, and held that they were 'employees'. The Court of Appeal, the final arbiter in this particular case, ruled that the original Tribunal finding had to stand as it was in accordance with the law (now contained in the Employment Rights Act, 1996) and was a decision that a reasonable Tribunal could have come to. These criteria are applied to all employment appeals, and have the general effect of making most decisions in 'run of the mill' cases difficult to overturn.

The *O'Kelly* decision can be contrasted with that in the recent case of *Carmichael v. National Power* [1998] which concerned power station guides employed on a 'casual as required' basis. These were held to be 'employees' as the court was of the opinion that there was an implied term in their contracts that the employer would provide them with a reasonable share of any work that was available, and the guides would perform a reasonable amount of any work offered. There was therefore a sufficient 'mutuality of obligation' present to create a contract of employment between the parties.

A number of guidelines on differentiating 'employees' from 'contractors' have emerged from the cases.

- What is the level of control exercised by the employer over the employee? The greater the control, the more likely it is that the worker is an employee.
- To what extent is the worker integrated into the business of the employer? The more integration, the greater the likelihood that the worker will be regarded as an employee.
- What is the 'economic reality' of the situation? This is also referred to as the 'multi-factor' test. Various matters are taken into consideration, including the extent of any personal investment by the worker in the job, and the true nature of the obligations that the worker and the employer have undertaken towards one another. This was the test used in *O'Kelly* referred to above.

The legal consequences are significant. Where the worker is, legally, an employee:

- the bulk of the employment protection legislation applies exclusively to employees;

- National Insurance contributions and benefits are affected;
- the assessment and collection of income tax is affected;
- the employer is responsible for Statutory Sick Pay and Statutory Maternity Pay;
- the employer is responsible in the civil law for damage or injury caused to third parties by his or her employees in the course of their employment;
- the employer has an implied contractual duty to provide a 'safe system of work'.

The rights of part-time employees have changed significantly in accordance with EU law, and these will be dealt with later in this briefing in the section relating to discrimination. A more wide-ranging 'framework agreement' on part-time workers has been agreed, but not yet translated in Community law. It is EU policy, in general, to equalize the rights of full-time and atypical workers and this is a trend that should be watched.

Much new UK legislation already applies to 'workers'. This term covers a wider range of personnel than 'employees'. Included are the various discrimination statutes, the protection of 'whistleblowers', the minimum wage law (recently held to apply to pupil barristers) and the Working Time Regulations. In addition, the Employment Relations Act, 1999, empowers the Secretary of State to extend, by Regulation, the ambit of all employment protected rights to those who are not, by strict definition, employees. There is also increasing evidence that UK courts are vigilant to prevent the use of atypical working patterns to deprive workers of their rights. This is illustrated by an important Court of Appeal decision in *Brown* v. *Chief Adjudication Officer* [1997]. The case concerned the status, for the purposes of Statutory Sick Pay (SSP), of an employee who was put on a series of one-day contracts which, when added together, amounted to three months continuous work. The court held that he would be deemed to be employed on an indefinite contract, terminable by notice, and therefore eligible for SSP.

B. The law relating to discrimination

Unlike the bulk of employment protection law, 'contractors' are covered equally with employees properly so called. For example, the law applies to partners in a commercial or professional partnership.

Continued on page 70

Discrimination on the grounds of sex or marriage
These grounds of discrimination at work are outlawed. Discrimination can take two forms: 'direct', which is overt, less favourable treatment, and 'indirect', which appears to apply equal treatment, but which has a discriminatory bias because members of the protected class find it difficult or impossible to comply with the requirements of the job. Direct discrimination on the grounds of sex or marriage is outlawed, except for the cases of 'genuine occupational qualification' alluded to in the legal briefing to Chapter 6. Direct discrimination can occur in the wording of job advertisements. It has even been suggested that failure to advertise but to rely on 'word-of-mouth' recommendations, 'old-boy' networks etc. could be regarded as direct discrimination. It can occur in the treatment of job applications, shortlisting and the conduct of interviews. The anti-discrimination law affects not only initial recruitment, but also promotion and dismissal.

To be realistic, it must be pointed out that in alleging discrimination as the cause of failure to obtain employment or promotion, the complainant has an uphill task. There is no generally recognized rule that an employer is obliged to appoint or promote the most qualified candidate. Appointments are still part of the prerogative of management, and are difficult to challenge except in the most blatant cases of discriminatory behaviour.

Indirect discrimination is more frequent and more difficult to deal with. The complainant will be required to demonstrate that a seemingly even-handed approach by the employer, for example setting age limits or requirements of height or job experience, or a requirement for frequent relocation for managers, is more difficult for applicants of one gender to comply with than the other. Indirect discrimination of this kind is not totally outlawed, but is subject to *justification* by the employer. What amounts to justification in the law of the UK is less clear than one would wish. Mere convenience to the employer is certainly not sufficient, but the standard falls short of the requirement of 'absolute necessity for the performance of the job'.

Employers must seriously consider their policy on suitable age for applicants because, even though there is at present no law relating to age discrimination, an age requirement that is too young may indirectly discriminate against women who are entering the labour market after a career break to raise a family. Requiring academic qualifications that are not justified by the job on offer may also discriminate against women, but that

is becoming less of a problem. It may still be regarded as an unnecessary stumbling-block in the path of some ethnic minority groups. The law relating to racial discrimination will be dealt with shortly.

'Affirmative action' – that is, giving preferential treatment to the protected class to compensate for past discrimination – is unlawful and could give rise to claims by those who have been denied employment, promotion, etc. The exception relating to training will be dealt with in the legal briefing to Chapter 3.

The UK law relating to discrimination on the grounds of sex has been greatly influenced by EU law. The impact on pay will be dealt with later on in this briefing. It is in fact the Equal Treatment Directive, in force since 1976, that has had the most profound effect. The 'equal treatment' referred to is that between men and women at work, and as this is EU law the final arbiter on its interpretation is the European Court of Justice. In two very high-profile cases brought by a health service worker, Mrs Marshall, against her employer, the Southampton and South-West Hampshire Area Health Authority, it was established that it was unlawful for an employer to impose different retirement ages on male and female employees, and that the UK statute relating to unfair dismissal (which covered enforced retirement at a 'discriminatory' age) contravened the Directive by placing a financial limit on the amount of compensation payable. As a result, employers have been required to equalize retirement ages for men and women. This left employers with contract problems with their employees already in place. They could either permit the men to retire at the (lower) female age of retirement, with consequent pressure on the pension funds, or raise the female retirement age to that of the men. The latter solution would involve 'buying' the women out of their old contracts and replacing them with new ones. This change has, coincidentally, influenced the proposal by government to equalize, sometime in the next two or three decades, the State pensionable ages for men and women.

A further result of the 'Marshall' case has been the lifting of the financial limit for compensation in dismissal cases concerning sex discrimination.

There has been a development in the law relating to the employment rights of homosexuals. The European Court of Justice had ruled, in the case of *R. v. Secretary of State for Defence ex parte Perkins,* that the Equal Treatment Directive did not affect discrimination on the ground of sexual orientation (as distinct from sex). However, a group of former military personnel challenged the policy of the Defence Department on this subject before the European Court of Human Rights, claiming that the method of interrogating them about their lifestyle, and their subsequent discharge from the Armed Services, breached their right to respect for private life under the Convention. The Court found in favour of the applicants and against the government of the UK. *Lustig-Prean and others v. UK* [1999]. A report in *The Times* for 13 December 1999 indicated that the Defence Secretary proposed lifting the ban early in the new year. Please refer to the legal briefing to the Introduction and Overview.

On a related topic, the European Court of Justice has recently held that the Equal Treatment Directive does apply to 'gender re-assignment', that is, to trans-sexuals.

Complainants are at a disadvantage, certainly in the UK and possibly in other member states, in that they have the 'burden of proof' – that is they have to establish, on a balance of probabilities, that the employer has discriminated against them unlawfully. In a draft Directive issued in 1996 (but not due to be implemented until 2001!) the burden of proof in discrimination cases will be reversed, and it will be for the employer to establish that the facts of the case do not support the allegations made by the complainant.

A combination of the 1976 Directive and the law on indirect discrimination has greatly altered the law relating to part-time employees. As most part-time employees are female, unfavourable conditions (pay, sick pay, holidays, pensions, etc.) could be seen as indirect discrimination against women and is therefore unlawful unless justified on objective grounds. These grounds must amount to something considerably more substantial than mere convenience to the employer. The former UK law, which required workers working between eight and 16 hours per week to wait five years before qualifying for redundancy pay or compensation for unfair dismissal (instead of the standard two years), with no compensation at all for those on a normal working week of less than eight hours, was declared by the highest UK court, the House of Lords, to contravene EU law, and the matter was put right by The Employment Protection (Part-Time Employees) Regulations, 1995. The statutory two–year qualifying period for unfair dismissal, now standard for all employees, both full- and part-time, has been challenged before the European Court of Justice in *R. v. Secretary of State for Employment ex parte Seymour-Smith* on the grounds that it indirectly

discriminates against women, and has not produced the desired effect of creating more jobs.

The qualifying period of employment required before an employee can make a claim for unfair dismissal has been reduced to ONE year, but this will only apply to dismissals taking effect on or after 1 June 1999. The two-year period will still apply to dismissals taking effect before that date, and a final decision has gone against the complaints in the case of *Seymour-Smith*.

When the ECJ ruled that compensation for unfair dismissal ranked as 'pay' and was therefore subject to the equal pay laws, qualification for payment fell to be decided by the national courts. It is unlikely that the two-year limit will be revised at least not on the grounds of indirect discrimination. There has also been a concession involving access by part-timers to rights in occupational pension schemes, contained in the Occupational Pensions Schemes (Equal Access to Membership) Regulations, 1995. A short period was allowed for part-timers, denied access in the past, to apply for an opportunity to 'buy' into the scheme.

The European Court of Justice has recently held that part-time workers who were deprived of access to company pension schemes may now make retrospective claims back to 1976, when the Equal Treatment Directive was implemented. This may not, in the event, turn out to be as expensive as employers fear, since the workers affected will presumably have to 'buy back' years by making suitable contributions, and some may not be willing to do this.

Hitherto, the rights of part-timers have been based on the notion of indirect discrimination on the ground of sex. It has therefore been possible for employers to justify their policies on some rational ground other than unlawful discrimination. In line with EU policy on the rights of part-timers, the Employment Relations Act, 1999, requires the Secretary of State to make Regulations to outlaw discrimination against part-time workers as regards matters to be set out in those Regulations. No details are yet known, but it might be that, in future, part-timers will have an unconditional right to equal treatment with full-timers without the need to prove unlawful discrimination on the ground of sex. Regulations are due to be implemented on 1 July 2000.

Harassment
The EU Code of Practice defines sexual harassment as 'unwanted conduct of a sexual nature, or other conduct based on sex, affecting the dignity of men and women

Continued on page 72

at work'. An employer will find himself liable to compensate a victim of harassment both in respect of his own behaviour, and that of his employees. See later in this briefing a reference to a case, in the racial context, where an employer was found liable for the unacceptable behaviour of a third party on his premises. An 'in-house code of practice' relating to discrimination in general and harassment in particular, emphasizing the serious view taken by management of such practices, will not only accord with good commercial practice but may also avoid embarrassing claims by alleged victims.

Victimization
The anti-discrimination statutes also outlaw the victimization of a person who has sought redress under the law.

Discrimination on the grounds of race, etc.
To date, the EU legislators have not concerned themselves with discrimination on racial grounds. The UK law is contained in the Race Relations Acts 1976 and 1994, and in general it closely follows the sex discrimination law, including the amendments made as a result of EU law. The Act of 1976 strikes down discrimination, both direct and indirect, on the grounds of race, colour, ethnic or national origin. Note that there is no reference to religion, but where a race or ethnic group is closely associated with a particular religion, then discrimination on religious grounds will be indistiguishable from racial discrimination. For example, employers should beware of imposing dress codes on employees that may indirectly discriminate against, for example, Muslims or Sikhs.

The one part of the United Kingdom where religious discrimination has been specifically outlawed is Northern Ireland, where the Fair Employment (Northern Ireland) Acts 1976 and 1989 prohibit discrimination in employment on religious grounds. However, there is a provision that the Secretary of State can issue a certificate to 'disapply' the Act (in effect, where Catholic employees and firms can lawfully be refused contracts) on grounds of national security. The Fair Employment and Treatment (Northern Ireland) Order, 1998, which re-enacts the Act of 1989 with amendments, has now granted a right of appeal against a 'national security' certificate.

The 'genuine occupational qualifications' relating to racial discrimination differ slightly from those applicable to sex discrimination.

Prohibitions against harassment and victimization are the same as for sex discrimination.

The case relating to employer's liability for the conduct of a third party concerns the now notorious incident where, at a private club dinner held at an hotel, the entertainer, Bernard Manning, made some racially abusive 'jokes' in the presence of black employees of the hotel. The main criterion to be applied in cases such as this where the employer was not actually 'standing by' when the incident occurred, was: 'did the employer have sufficient control over the situation to have prevented the abuse by applying good employment practice?' This gives rise, of course, to the usual legal problem of every case turning on its own facts. In the particular case under discussion, the Appeal Tribunal was of the opinion that the hotel manager could have anticipated trouble with this particular guest, and could have warned the under-manager on duty that evening to withdraw the young black waitresses if the language became abusive. In the circumstances, the failure by the manager to give any thought to the matter threw responsibility for the harassment on to the employers. *Burton v. de Vere Hotels* (1996).

Disability Discrimination Act, 1995
From 2 December 1996, it became unlawful for employers to discriminate directly against a disabled person in connection with employment. Employers of fewer than 20 employees are exempt. There is no provision for 'indirect' discrimination, and even direct discrimination can be justified in circumstances to be laid down by Regulations. Employers are required to make adjustments to the workplace to accommodate disabled workers, which include contractors. The Long Title of the Act explains its purpose:

> An Act to make it unlawful to discriminate against disabled persons in connection with employment (etc.); to make provisions about the employment of disabled persons; and to establish a National Disability Council.

This council does not have the powers of the Equal Opportunities Commission or the Commission for Racial Equality, and so enforcement of the Act may be somewhat weak.

The Act repeals the Disabled Persons (Employment) Act, 1944, so that there is no longer a statutory requirement for 3 per cent of the workforce in larger companies to be recruited from among the disabled. In any case, this Act was largely ineffective through the number of exemptions that could be applied for, and generally, through lack of effective monitoring.

An employer is under a duty to take such steps as are **reasonable in all the circumstances of the case** to ensure that disabled workers are not put at a **substantial disadvantage** in comparison with the able-bodied. The duty will include physical adjustments to the workplace and reorganization of duties, and will affect recruitment, contractual terms, promotion, transfer, training and dismissal.

The interpretation of the key provisions of the Act will be developed by the tribunals and courts deciding cases that come before them. The practicality of making adjustments to buildings and the financial burden it would impose will be among the factors to be taken into account. For example, it might be argued in a suitable case that providing wheelchair access to the ground floor and to toilet facilities might be reasonable, but installing a lift in an old building might not.

Some significant cases have already been reported in 1999. As the protection provided is to the **disabled**, the meaning of the word 'disability' in this context is of some significance. The Act itself provides as follows:

'A person has a disability if he or she has a physical or mental impairment which has a substantial or long-term adverse effect on his or her ability to carry out normal day-to-day activities'. In *Vicary v. British Telecommunications plc.* [1999], the employee's Regional Health Officer decided that the employee, a clerical officer, who suffered from an upper-arm condition that prevented her from lifting heavy weights and cutting up roast food etc., did not have a substantial impairment, and was therefore not 'disabled' within the meaning of the Act. The court held that 'substantial' in this context meant 'more than "minor or trivial", and in any event, it was ultimately for a court or tribunal to judge whether the employee was disabled within the context of the Act, and in this instance, contrary to the opinion of the company's Health Officer, Mrs Vicary was disabled and entitled to statutory protection.

MHC Counselling Services Ltd. v. Tansell [1999] deals with the important subject of agency-supplied workers where there is no direct contract between the worker and the recipient of his services: that is to say, the worker is employed by the agency which pays him, and the 'employer' to whom he is sent pays the agency for the services supplied. It was held that a disabled worker could make a claim under the Disability Discrimination Act against the 'end-user', even though there was no contract between them. This is an important decision which may well affect all aspects of the discrimination

law, and indeed, all areas where 'workers' as distinct from 'employees' are afforded protection.

Before leaving the topic of discrimination law in general, it may be pertinent to point out that according to the latest EU treaty, the Treaty of Amsterdam (in force on 1 May 1999), the Council of the EU has been granted power to combat discrimination on a number of new grounds, namely sex, race, ethnic origin, religion or belief, disability, age and sexual orientation. It will be noted that the UK has some laws to this effect in place already.

C. Pay

What constitutes 'pay' is an important topic, as it is affected by the equal pay law, and while there is a UK statute on the subject, the law ultimately derives from the European Union. It has been established long ago that individuals can make equal pay claims against their employers based directly on the relevant article of the Treaty of Rome, now Article 141, renumbered from the original 119. Decisions in such cases have established that 'pay' in this context includes redundancy pay and pensions.

Trades unions have been accorded enhanced rights to recognition under the Employment Relations Act, 1999, and it is likely that in future the pay (and other terms and conditions of employment) of a greater number of employees will be settled by the process of collective bargaining. (Please see the legal briefings to Chapters 2 and 3.)

There are comparatively few problems concerning pay where the employee is actually at work. More problematical is the situation where the employee is not attending work, but the contract of employment is still subsisting. In what circumstances must the employer continue to pay wages or salary?

Sick pay

The entitlement, or otherwise, of an employee to be paid his wages or salary, or a proportion of the same, while absent through sickness, depends entirely upon the terms of his contract. Larger employers are likely to have a sick pay scheme in place, typically starting with full pay, then after a stated interval reducing to half-pay, then no pay at all. There is no statutory obligation placed upon employers to pay contractual wages at all during sickness, and the employer's intentions in this regard are to be gleaned from the terms of the contract

Continued on page 74

itself. One of the requirements of the 'section 1' statement (see page 67 of this briefing) is an indication by the employer of whether sick pay, in this sense, is payable. Where an employer does so pay, an employee is not entitled to 'benefit unreasonably' from his or her situation, so the employer is entitled to deduct any amount that an employee receives by statutory entitlement. This is dealt with in the next section.

Statutory Sick Pay

This arises out of the Social Security (Contributions and Benefits) Act, 1992, and replaces the former 'sickness benefit' claimable from the DSS. Now, the employer is bound to pay the benefit, which is calculated according to a formula of mind-blowing complexity, which does not amount to the full contractual wage and which, since 1994, has to be paid by the employer out of his or her own resources. There is an exception for small employers, who can claim a rebate out of the employers' National Insurance contributions. SSP has been brought in as a harmonizing measure throughout the EU, and has the effect of requiring employers to pay some minimum sum by way of wages during sickness.

Statutory Maternity Pay

Maternity **leave** is now governed by EU law, but not maternity **pay**. That is governed by national law. In the UK, any employee on maternity leave who is not entitled under the terms of her contract to full pay is entitled to Statutory Maternity Pay under the same statute as SSP. Again, payment is in accordance with a formula laid down by the Act, but, at least at present, employers are able to claim a rebate out of their National Insurance contributions. This may not be the case for much longer.

Minimum wages

The National Minimum Wage Act, 1998, came into force on 1 April 1999. For details, please see the legal briefing to the Introduction and Overview.

Equal Pay Act, 1970

This Act, despite its name, applies to equal pay and conditions between men and women in the same employment. An 'equality clause' is automatically incorporated into every contract where the work is 'like, or broadly similar'; 'the work has been rated as equivalent in a job evaluation exercise'; and 'where the work is of equal value to the employer in terms of

effort, responsibility etc.' It is this last category that has caused the most problems. Here, an employee (usually female) claims that her job is the same in terms of value to the employer as a different job being performed by a man at a better rate of pay and/or conditions of service, where there has been no official job evaluation exercise.

The first successful case on this point was *Hayward* v. *Cammell Laird Shipbuilders* [1987], where a female cook successfully claimed equality in pay with male carpenters and joiners at the same shipyard. The outcome was even more alarming for the employers who, when it was pronounced that the jobs were equal in value, faced the possibility of having to put the carpenters' and joiners' sick pay and holiday schemes on a par with the cook's better provision in that area.

It is possible for an employer to justify unequal pay and conditions on objective grounds not related to the sex of the employee. An example would be the grading of jobs by way of seniority, as long as the system did not have an underlying 'sex bias' relating back to a time when women would not have been considered for the most highly paid jobs. The leading case to date is the 1999 ECJ decision in *Enderby* v. *Frenchay Health Authority*, where speech therapists claimed equality with pharmacists employed by the same Authority. It was conceded that the jobs were of equal value. The speech therapists were predominantly female and the pharmacists were predominantly male. The considerably lower pay of the speech therapists raised the presumption of unlawful discrimination in pay. The defence of the Authority was the difficulty of recruiting pharmacists to the hospital service, and the consequent need to offer higher pay. The ECJ ruled that such a claim could amount to objective justification to differences in pay scales, but the employer must give convincing evidence of it; merely to assert that he or she was responding to 'supply and demand' is not sufficient. A defence that each group of workers involved is covered by a different collective bargaining process is not acceptable.

An equivalent problem arises where there is a reorganization of the grading structure and one 'tier' is removed. Employees in this now defunct grade often have their pay and conditions preserved under a system known as 'red-circling'. Again, this will not give rise to equal pay claims unless the grading system still contains vestiges of a former regime that discriminated against women.

Article 119, Treaty of Rome [Now article 141]
The principle of equal pay for equal work is enshrined in this Article of the Treaty, which is directly enforceable in all member states by an employee against his or her employer. Over the years, the meaning of the word 'pay' has been extended. It now covers redundancy pay, thus forcing the government of the UK to equalize the age factors between men and women in redundancy payments, and occupational pensions. The landmark case of *Barber* v. *Guardian Royal Exchange* [1990] underlined the principle of equality in the ages at which men and women employees might be entitled to a pension. That case decided, to the consternation of a number of pension fund managers, that if women were permitted to take retirement with a full pension at, for example, age 60, men must be allowed the same privilege and not be required to wait until age 65, as was often the case. The ECJ ruled, however, that this provision would only take effect from the date of the case – 17 May 1990.

A more recent Dutch case before the ECJ (*Ten Oever*, 1993) has established further that survivors' pensions are also 'pay' relating to the deceased's employment, and so pension schemes may not discriminate between widows and widowers. This decision was also held to be non-retrospective.

D. Dismissal

An employee had, at common law, very few rights on dismissal. 'Wrongful dismissal', which was the only right of substance, merely provided that an employee was entitled to proper notice of dismissal or wages in lieu. Since there was no common law standard of notice, (the building trade, for instance, was notorious for putting employees on one hour's notice) the right not to be dismissed wrongfully was fairly inconsequential to a large number of employees. Only where an employee had committed a really serious breach of the employment contract was the employer entitled to dismiss without notice or payment in lieu. Due to the number of controversial cases relating to the seriousness of the employee's conduct, disentitling him to notice, employers are well advised not to exercise the power of 'summary dismissal' unless the conduct of the employee would be regarded by any reasonable employer as terminating the contract.

The recent case of *Cerberus Software Ltd.* v. *Rowley* [1999] deals with 'payment in lieu of notice' clauses in contracts (PILON). Rowley was wrongfully dismissed without notice. The employer argued that the 'payment in lieu' should be reduced by the sum that Rowley had earned during the six-month notice period to which he was entitled, but did not get. The Employment Appeal Tribunal held that an employee dismissed without cause was entitled to claim all wages or salary owed to him under the contract **in full**, without the need to mitigate his loss.

Since the mid-1960s, there has been a great deal of statutory intervention in connection with employee rights. (See the 'legal briefing' to the Introduction and Overview) Not only have minimum periods of notice been prescribed, but statutory rights on dismissal have been introduced. The employee's common law right not to be dismissed wrongfully without notice or payment in lieu has been preserved, and such payment is in addition to any statutory right to compensation.

The statutory rights on dismissal are now contained in the Employment Rights Act, 1996, which consolidates the previous law. The two aspects of termination, redundancy and unfair dismissal, are quite different concepts, but they share some common features, and impinge upon one another to a certain extent. The claiming of either right requires the claimant to prove that he or she has the requisite period of continuous service with the same, or an associated, employer, and that he or she has been dismissed according to the Act. These rights are, in essence, 'seniority rights', and depend upon qualifying periods of service. Two years' service is the standard qualification for both redundancy and unfair dismissal, but the service qualification in unfair dismissal is dispensed with in circumstances where the reason for the dismissal is deemed, by statute, to be automatically unfair. This includes dismissal for being a member or non-member of a trade union and, in the case of female employees, for reasons connected with pregnancy or childbirth.

The claimant must also demonstrate that he or she has been dismissed according to the Act. A resignation that is purely voluntary on the part of the employee is not 'dismissal', even where the employee has found alternative employment in response to a general statement by the employer that cuts will have to be made.

The statute sets out three definitions of 'dismissal':

1   the employer terminates the contract with or without notice;
2   a fixed-term contract is not renewed under the same terms (except where the contract is for one year or longer and states in writing that compensation is not payable for redundancy or unfair dismissal by reason only that the contract is not renewed);

Continued on page 76

3   the employee terminates the contract in response to the employer's conduct, amounting to a serious breach of contract.

This latter is termed 'constructive dismissal', and an implied duty placed on the employer to treat his or her employees reasonably and with respect has potentially widened the scope of this type of dismissal.

Redundancy
Rights to compensation on redundancy were first introduced in 1965, and are now contained in the Employment Rights Act, 1996. The primary purpose of redundancy pay is to compensate the employee for the loss of a valuable property in his or her job. The additional purposes of aiding job mobility and alleviating hardship are secondary. There is also the further perceived benefit of 'buying-off' conflict with the unions in the event of job cuts. Redundancy pay is calculated according to a statutory formula, and is a combination of number of years worked, age at dismissal and basic weekly pay. This is subject to a cut-off point, currently £220, revised from time to time. The maximum payable under the statutory scheme in circumstances most favourable to the employee is between £5000 and £6000 pounds. Employees, both men and women, who are dismissed after the age of 65 (or less if the normal retiring age for the employment is earlier) do not qualify for statutory redundancy pay. The sum is progressively reduced in the last year of employment before normal retirement. It is not unusual for employers who wish to reorganize and 'shake out' employees to offer compensation well in excess of the statutory minimum. Additional payments are also very often negotiated by trades unions. Employers are no longer eligible for a refund from the Redundancy Payments Fund. The Fund is still maintained and every employer contributes to it through the National Insurance Scheme, but it is now used to compensate employees who are owed wages by insolvent employers. Member states are under an EU obligation, arising out of the Insolvency Directive, to put in place such a scheme.

In order to qualify for payment, the employee must have been dismissed for reasons of redundancy. In essence, this means that the employee's job has ceased to exist, either through closure, cutting back, reorganization or by replacing employees by contractors. Where it is reasonable for employees to familiarize themselves with new technology because the method of doing the job has changed, failure to adapt may entitle the employer to dismiss fairly for lack of competence. Such employees are not redundant. The Civil Service Clerical Association tried to renegotiate the contracts of their Inland Revenue members who had to adapt to operating the new computerized system. The attempt failed. The old jobs had not disappeared to be replaced by new ones; they were the same jobs to be performed by a different method, and it was perfectly reasonable to expect the employees to adapt. *Cresswell* v. *Board of Inland Revenue [1984]*.

Where an employer makes an offer of suitable alternative employment, an employee who unreasonably refuses such an offer is no longer eligible for redundancy pay. There is a wide interpretation of what might amount to 'reasonable refusal', and includes loss of pay and status. Employees have a four-week 'trial period' in the new employment before committing themselves.

Notification of impending redundancies
This area of the law has been amended to comply with the EU Directive on Mass Redundancies. One complication is that, for this purpose, the definition of 'redundancy' has been expanded to comply with the Directive, and includes any dismissal not directly connected with the worker as an individual – that is, not connected with the conduct or capacity of the individual.

Creation of redundancies involving 20 or more employees must be notified to the Department for Education and Employment, with periods of advanced warning increasing according to the numbers involved. Failure to comply will result in a fine.

There is a duty on the part of the employer to consult representatives of affected employees involving the same numbers of redundancies to be created and the same periods of notice. In line with current EC policy on employee representation, these representatives may be official representatives of recognized trades unions or representatives elected by the workforce. Failure to comply may result in additional sums being paid to the redundant employees – the 'protective award'.

Employers will sometimes find themselves in the uncomfortable position of having to notify the Department for Education and Employment and consult with the unions before there has been any direct communication with the workforce.

Unfair dismissal
The right not to be dismissed for an unfair reason was first introduced in 1972, and is now contained in the Employment Rights Act, 1996.

The burden is on the employer to prove that he or she has a fair reason for dismissal, and after that hurdle has been overcome, the behaviour of the employer will be scrutinized to determine whether he or she has acted reasonably in all the circumstances of the case. It is possible for an employer to demonstrate that he or she had a fair reason, but to be found liable for unfair dismissal on procedural grounds. It is in this connection that regard will be had to the scrupulous use of disciplinary procedures, ACAS Codes of Practice and the like. The ACAS Code provides a 'benchmark', and will be discussed in more detail in the legal briefing to chapter 5. While it is possible in extreme cases for summary dismissal without notice or disciplinary procedures to be upheld, such a practice should normally be avoided. The case would have to be such that no reasonable employer could be expected to retain such an employee, and procedural formalities would serve no useful purpose whatever. Examples would include obtaining the employment in the first instance by fraud, false references, forged qualifications etc., conviction and imprisonment for a serious crime, or wilfully causing damage to the employer's property. (Please see legal briefing to chapter 5.)

'Fair reasons' laid down by the Act are:

- lack of capability or qualification;
- misconduct;
- redundancy;
- continued employment would breach a statutory duty – for example, it is illegal for pregnant women to be employed on certain processes;
- continued employment might breach national security;
- any other substantial reason.

After considering the fairness of the reason or reasons adduced by the employer and the fairness of the circumstances surrounding the dismissal, the Tribunal hearing the case will finally consider whether a hypothetical, reasonable employer might have dismissed in the circumstances. This has given rise to the problem of the 'range of reasonable responses'. On learning, for example, that an employee has been apprehended for shop-lifting during her lunch hour by a store detective at another establishment, one reasonable employer might regard this as a cause for dismissal, while another, equally reasonably, might give her another chance. A dismissal in these circumstances would be regarded as fair – *Moore* v. *C & A Modes* [1981].

However, in the case of *Haddon v. Van Den Bergh Foods Ltd.* [1999], the Employment Appeal Tribunal indicated that each case would be treated on its own facts, and there would be a much tighter approach adopted. This may well mean that employers in the future are more likely to be held to have acted unreasonably, and consequently unlawfully, in dismissing employees.

The usual remedy is an award of monetary compensation, which can be reduced in line with the employee's behaviour contributing to the dismissal. Thus it is that where the dismissal is found to be unfair on procedural grounds only, and the employer has a fair reason, the compensation can be considerably reduced.

There are also the possibilities of reinstatement or re-engagement which are very rarely ordered by the Tribunal. Refusal to comply will involve the employer in additional compensation.

Compensation consists of:

- a basic award consisting of the accumulated redundancy pay;
- the compensatory award, limited to £50,000;
- an additional award where the employer has refused to comply with a reinstatement or re-engagement order;
- a special award if the dismissal was connected with TU membership or non-membership or TU activities.

The £50,000 limit is in force for dismissals taking effect on or after 25 October 1999. For dismissals before that date, the limit is £12,000. The higher rate may make claimants liable to pay tax on sums in excess of £30,000. In cases involving discrimination on the grounds of sex or race, or 'whistleblowing', there is no upper limit on the amount of compensation.

There are a number of instances where dismissal is treated as automatically unfair, and no qualifying period is required. These include reasons of membership (or non-membership) of a trade union; pregnancy; refusal to work in unsafe conditions; asserting rights under the minimum pay law and working time law, 'whistleblowing' and also, since 1 September 1999, workers exercising their right to time off for study and training under the Teaching and Higher Education Act, 1998.

The employer's former power to exclude liability for unfair dismissal in written contracts for a fixed term of one year or more has been abolished with effect from 30 September 1999. The term will, however, continue to apply in all such contracts validly entered into prior to 25 September 1999. Note that the change relates only to unfair dismissal; it remains lawful for an employer to exclude liability for redundancy payments in such fixed-term contracts where they terminate without being

Continued on page 78

renewed. This enables employers to offer training contracts, for example, without having to make arrangements for 'severance pay' if the contact is not renewed.

A significant change has been in the law relating to employees who come out on strike, or who involve themselves in any other form of industrial action. The law has hitherto been quite clear on this subject: the strikers are in fundamental breach of contract and are liable to be fairly dismissed. The only protection allowed was to prevent employers from **selectively dismissing strikers**, and then only if the strike was official and the correct procedures had been followed. The Employment Rights Act, 1999, now provides that an employee who participates in a strike that has been properly called (that is, after a properly conducted ballot) and which otherwise complies with all the other criteria laid down by statute, is protected against dismissal within 8 weeks of taking industrial action. There are one or two exceptional cases covering dismissal after the end of the 8 weeks. Such dismissal will be regarded as automatically unfair, and with the recent raising of the compensatory award to a maximum of £50,000 employers may well be advised to consider very carefully the financial consequences of such a move. Of course, legal protection will only be afforded to striking employees whose actions are peaceful. Any violence or criminal damage on the part of the striker will immediately take him out of the ambit of the new protection.

Protection against unfair dismissal has been extended to employees who normally work overseas. This applies to dismissals that take effect on or after 25 October 1999.

The connection between redundancy and unfair dismissal

A redundancy that has been handled unfairly will be treated as unfair dismissal with the consequent increase in compensation payable.

- Unfair selection for redundancy consisting of selection on the grounds of TU membership or non-membership or TU activities.
- Departure from an agreed redundancy procedure, such as 'last in, first out', without a special reason to justify this.
- Selections for redundancy were made without relying on objective criteria, such as performance records, experience, conduct, etc.
- Failure to consult with or give reasonable warning to the employees.
- Failure reasonably to investigate the possibility of alternative employment.

A new voluntary arbitration scheme to settle unfair dismissal claims will be in place by the Spring of 1999 as outlined in the Employment Rights (Disputes Resolution) Act, 1998.

New rights introduced by the 1999 Act, and in force on 15 December 1999

- There are enhanced conditions for maternity leave. Ordinary leave will be extended to 18 weeks. There will, in addition, be compulsory leave of two weeks (that is, no woman may return to work within two weeks of giving birth), and additional leave in certain circumstances. The new rules apply where the expected week of childbirth begins on or after 30 April 2000.
- There is a right for an employee who is a parent of any child born, or adopted, after 15 December 1999 to take **unpaid** leave for a maximum period of 13 weeks during the first five years of the child's life, or five years after the adoption. This applies to both male and female employees who have responsibility for any such child, provided that such parent has served a minimum of one year's continuous employment with that employer. 'Procedural rules' for the taking of such leave will have to be adopted either by collective bargaining or by a 'workforce agreement'. This is presumably to ensure that employees are treated fairly. In the event of a failure to negotiate such rules, a 'default programme' has been included in the Regulations. In small establishments of 20 or fewer employees, the employer can negotiate directly with the employees. The legality of this 'cut-off' date is currently awaiting a decision by the ECJ.
- There is, further, a right for an employee to take reasonable time off, **unpaid**, to provide assistance to a dependant who is ill, or to make arrangements in respect of such a dependant who may, for example, have been involved in an accident or who may have died. This right also takes effect from 15 December 1999.
- Abuse of the above two 'family-friendly' rights is unlikely as the leave is unpaid, but many trades unions have criticized this aspect, particularly as it affects parental leave, and may mount a challenge to this in the future, possibly on the ground that it does not fully accord with the EU Parental Leave Directive.

Training and development 2

Matthew Lynas

Learning objectives

After studying this chapter you should be able to:

- understand the forces and political interest in promoting training and development;
- distinguish between training and development dimensions;
- understand the need to challenge training and development contributions within a strategic context;
- understand the importance of applying basic analytical process to identifying, designing, implementing and evaluating training and development initiatives;
- assess the roles of all levels of employee in creating effective approaches to training and understand the need for a holistic approach which integrates with business and wider HRM systems.

Introduction

The appetite for vocational training and educational opportunities, by both organizations and individuals, is pervasive. This is intensified by the increasing emphasis on individuals taking responsibility for their own career development. From an organizational perspective, investment is widely motivated by faith in the belief that maintaining strategic position is a function, in part at least, of developing employees.

The extent to which such assumptions withstand rigorous scrutiny is the purpose of this chapter. Issues of process related to identification of needs and integration of initiatives are clearly important aspects which key stakeholders need to be aware of in any planned approach to training and development. Meaning is very important too, and nowhere more so than in questioning broad statements of mission and assertions of management commitment.

Background and justification

The perspective is managerial in the sense that its intention is to generate understanding of Training and Development contributions and to raise management capabilities in challenging initiatives, within strategic and operational contexts.

The justification for such an approach can be readily understood if one considers the plethora of training and development techniques, systems and packages which the non-specialist has to attempt to make sense of, in expectation of giving commitment and support. In this sense it is not the intention to try to cover the detail of the range of concepts on offer in the training and development field, but instead provide a context for understanding the salient aspects of evolution at national level. The chapter provides a discussion of fundamental principles which affect choice of appropriate methods and an evaluation of a selected number of concepts, which dominate the current debate on training and development in the UK primarily, but increasingly being adopted internationally.

Salient issues in the history of training and development since 1964

To provide further justification of the orientation of this chapter, in relation to enhancing management understanding of training and development and its perceived contribution to strategy, some salient points, in the historical evolution since 1964, are presented. The value of being aware of such a context will enable non-training specialists to see that much of what is being offered today is not new. Historical background can be helpful in assessing whether the myriad of training and development initiatives on offer constitute a systematic and integrated approach to perceived problems and whether in fact the organizational problems being addressed are in themselves amenable to training solutions.

The Industrial Training Act of 1964 marked a major change in relation to governmental intervention within the United Kingdom. The establishment of boards covering specific sectors of industry, with powers to raise levies and award grants to encourage systematic training, was motivated by the belief that there was a dire neglect in skills development within the United Kingdom, as opposed to our continental neighbours, in particular France and Germany. France already had a levy system. The differential levies which eventually became operative in the UK seldom came anywhere near the levels statutorily applied in France, with the possible exception of engineering. In fact there was continuous opposition in many industry sectors and much compromise to keep businesses engaged.

The levy system was very widely opposed throughout United Kingdom industry. Training boards became associated with paper-laden bureaucracy. In spite of this, the aims of improving quantity and quality and spreading the cost of training did progress. The cost was in terms of deep-rooted aversion of a wide range of industrial managers, and failure to consider seriously the contribution of systematic training.

The boards shifted their emphasis from grant-linked approaches to systems-related philosophies aimed at encouraging a total process of linking initiatives into strategic thinking. Testing management commitment through a system of exemption for attaining laid-down standards of training and development across all occupational categories represented a positive attempt to reward for evidence of well-integrated T&D. In spite of these positive moves to remove the burden on business and the accompanying decision to lift the threshold for small firms obliged to pay any levy, the aversion to the perceived unwarranted intervention persisted. This led to the abolition of 28 boards at one stroke by the newly elected Thatcher government of 1979–1983. Ironically this was a government of the same political colour as the one that created the training board system, but with entirely different views on the need for intervention to encourage interest in training by statutory means.

What legacy has this historic experiment left? With the demise of the industrial training boards, with the exception of engineering and civil engineering, responsibility for encouragement of people development has gone through a multitude of forms. In the post-abolition period, voluntary associations emerged with links to the Manpower Services Commission and subsequently the Training Agency. Whether this was a manifestation of reduced bureaucracy is very much a question of debate. For industry and commerce statutory intervention had been removed and voluntary engagement substituted. The Training Agency has essentially worked through a network of third parties to further the belief in training, as a main plank in an integrated national policy. This has to a very significant degree shifted responsibility for delivery towards accredited qualifications embodied in National Vocational Qualifications. The impression is that of an umbrella belief that the most menial tasks can be covered by such recognition. With the creation of TECs (Training and Enterprise Councils in England and Wales) and LECs (Local Enterprise Councils in Scotland), the links with educational institutions, as sources for delivery of such qualifications, together with other accredited agents, have proliferated. There is no doubt that much technical education was stimulated during the training board era. Certainly significant improvements were achieved in craft and technical occupations. The question of educational involvement was carefully monitored in relation to specific industry needs and through working groups, with direct industry involvement. The current attempt to produce 'national' qualifications may arguably lack this close identification with specific sector needs.

Significant current emphasis is being placed on the Investor in People initiative to the extent of the creation of a dedicated agency for its promotion. The systems-related schemes introduced at the latter part of the training board period, combined with the exemption processes, aimed at testing the integration of training and development into strategic processes, is a clear antecedent of the 'investors' philosophy.

The burgeoning interest in MBA qualifications since the 1980s is very much a phenomenon which the educational sector has championed. It is a manifestation of the growing tendency for organizations to depend on external sources to design and deliver development opportunities. Although the contribution can be acknowledged, in some cases it remains controversial how effectively such costly development is integrated and evaluated as an investment. This point emphasizes the assertion of the need for senior managers to raise their understanding of what they should expect from training and development investment. This raising of awareness should be the starting point in moving from training and development as an 'act of faith' to that of a fully analysed contribution. In developing this perspective the following sections set out to break down the term 'Training and

Development' and present basic principles which may be regarded as fundamental in the context of planned training and development.

At the beginning of the 1990s the commentaries on inadequacy of training provision at the national level still persisted. Porter (1990) saw such inadequacies as an important factor in explaining the international disadvantage of UK firms. The Coopers and Lybrand Report of 1986, 'A Challenge to Complacency', reinforces the perception of complacency on the part of managers. Summarized, they conceded that training needed to be improved, but expressed reluctance in accepting that their organization's attitude or approach could be a contributing factor. It could be argued that the dearly held belief in volunteerism and non-government intervention contributes to training often being relegated to a subsidiary ranking, when it comes to high-level strategic decision making. This is regardless of the much-extolled mission statement that 'people development is the most important consideration for our organization'. However, a more fundamental reason may well be the need for managers to have a better understanding of the processes and basic concepts of training, and this view provides ample justification for the sections that follow.

Distinguishing between training and development

One of the most authoritative definitions of the processes of training and development and associated education comes from the *Dictionary of Management* and states:

> planning and experience and further training of members of management to develop their potential and equip them for jobs further up the (career ladder).
>
> French and Saward (1975)

However, the definition is unhelpful in that it assumes that management development is concerned only with promotion and does not tell us what the words 'management' and 'development' mean. The word development often raises difficulty for management understanding, as opposed to training or education. Development as a concept is therefore worth some considerable thought, if managers are to fully appreciate what precisely they are being asked to give their commitment to and if they are to be in a position to constructively challenge aims and purposes.

Development

The word suggests 'growth' and raises the central problem of how to define it in such a way that the concepts that lie behind it can be shared with organizations that wish to improve their management competences. Development must therefore be aimed towards an organization's purpose and obviously take place within some context. The idea of context is essential when planning, designing or facilitating management. It follows from this that context will vary from situation to situation. These variations can be characterized by elements or factors such as:

- **Society**: individual ambitions, goals, values and norms.
- **Market and economic environment**
- **Participants**
- **Systems**
- **Purpose and objectives**
- **Dominating ideas**

From this the scope of development can be regarded as:

> activities undertaken by the enterprise to release the potential of individuals in order to further the ends of the enterprise and to match the capabilities, inclinations and goals of the individuals to those ends

This definition has two paradoxes – firstly, the underlying assumption that the needs of the organization can be matched to the individual. This paradox arises because quite often individuals may not wish to accept the additional responsibilities which the investment in development often implies, or the moves and other changes which organizational philosophies project in a changing environment, for instance the compulsion towards continuous or self-development which is the current emphasis in much of the advice on career development. The evidence of resistance can be found across all types of organizations, private and public, and in the not-for-profit sector. A survey of top managers carried out by the Opinion Research Centre in the late 1970s is evidence of this reluctance and illustrates the point (Opinion Research Centre, 1978).

The second paradox can be illustrated in the suggestion that if one develops individuals according to their needs, one misses the essential synergy of organizations. Many of the approaches used in management development, such as appraisal, deal with individuals one by one and assume that by adding the individual needs together, organizational needs will be met. This is unlikely to be so!

Development therefore is a process that embraces not only specific structured inputs of skills and knowledge but activities with a longer horizon which are aimed at broadening individual capability in line with the aims of the organization, such as succession, or in relation to projected needs of the organization. This can thus involve planned job experience, shadowing, secondments and so on. It can be based as much on discovery learning as on formally based programmes and may involve various combinations, from executive development to self-development commitments.

Training, on the other hand, will normally be job specific and have shorter job horizons. The methods of delivery can, however, be equally varied as can be seen from the section on implementation.

Prerequisites of systematic training and development

Systematic T&D is distinguished by its dependence on analysis. The key aspects of this can be expressed as a training cycle, the components of which are as follows.

Identification of needs

This process involves diagnosis of problems at strategic and operational levels which are amenable to training and development solutions. By implication there is always likely to be an interaction with broader organizational issues which may have a bearing on the effectiveness of T&D processes. Such problems may almost certainly have to be resolved either before or in parallel with T&D initiatives to enable benefits to be realized.

Assessing training needs – philosophy and practice

To meet the objectives of this chapter, assessing training needs can be divided into two levels – strategic and operational. At the strategic level, the decisions should broadly relate to actions that are needed to support the core competencies, which are designed to give competitive advantage, thus providing the linkage between the strategic needs of the business and training and development actions. At the operational level, training and development needs may manifest themselves across the value and or profit–service chains. Thus needs may emerge in any or all functional activities of the business, with the main objective of enhancing the response capabilities of the organization.

Three key questions emerge at the preliminary stage of assessing training and development needs:

- What organization is required to meet existing company policy?
- What should the organization be like in future?
- How do present personnel rate against these requirements in ability and potential?

The underlying principles of any kind of needs analysis are to provide data which will allow priorities to be identified. This implies that resources are always likely to be limited and thus the focus needs to be on the possible. There are many variations to assessing needs but the key lies in the careful formulation of questions. The following are practical questions which fall into distinctive categories:

General questions on the organization of the firm

1   What are the firm's overall aims and objectives? Are changes anticipated?
2   What are the firm's resources and market potential?
3   Is the organization good enough to achieve its objectives?
4   Is the business profitable?
5   How can profitability be improved?
6   What key changes are likely to occur in the rationalization of services or markets?
7   Can the business be better managed?

General questions about manpower

Answers to this part of the assessment must obviously relate to the preceding analysis of aims and the ability to meet such aims. It may involve all aspects of the value chain or specific parts of it. The following are examples of the sort of questions which can provide specific data for feeding into more detailed programme decisions:

Operational Personnel

1   How effectively do people work as teams and individually? The responses may be influenced by the nature of the work. In some areas of commerce the emphasis is on the individual but in a wide range of organizational work, including even very small businesses, the need for project-related activities dominates. The problem-solving skills and interpersonal competencies often need to be enhanced through appropriate development processes. At a time when a great deal of project work takes place across boundaries, in various forms of partnership and collaborations, such analysis is important for effectiveness. Such emphasis is intensified in the diverse cultural context which characterizes such inter-organizational enterprises.

2   How have employees been trained and developed to date? Essentially the question raises issues of dependency on buying-in as opposed to meeting own needs. The balance between planned approaches, with the resource commitment this suggests, and ad hoc approaches are at the centre of such analysis. Management may not be convinced of the argument for investing in training and development on any significant scale.

3   Can the efficiency/effectiveness balance be improved? The implied process here is analysis of the value and/or service–profit chains of the business. Do the functional activities involved embody the competencies needed to position the organization competitively? In this period when many organizations work on an internal market principle the need will often be for non-core functions to justify their continuation as the 'preferred' resource against the possibility of being outsourced. This not only relates to secondary value-chain activities but in public service and not-for-profit organizations may mean the need to demonstrate the capability to acquire entirely different competences at relatively short notice.

4   Are employees versatile and able to tackle more than one job? Flexibility, regardless of the size of the organization, is likely to be valued as critical in responsiveness to the competitive environment. This needs to come not only from systematically identifying and meeting needs in a formal context, but, in vocational occupations, through self- and continuous development. Such considerations need to be given account by organizations in the development of human resources policies.

5   Are more people needed in any particular activity area? This question highlights the need to keep the interaction with other aspects of the human resource contribution firmly in mind. For example, recruitment and selection should provide the right level of recruits, tying in with the same analysis of

skills, knowledge and behaviours which provides the focus for training and development strategy.

The annexe to the chapter provides a checklist of areas which can be asked in relation to any process of identifying training needs. It must always be remembered that most organizations operate in intensely dynamic environments where a whole range of variables is continuously changing. The implication is obviously that such a list can be added to, in relation to such circumstances, but overall the list will be seen to have value as a diagnostic tool.

The importance of standards in defining performance standards

No advice on assessing needs would be complete without bringing to the reader's attention the importance of performance standards. This is particularly apposite at a time when performance management is becoming a central part of human resources policies in all sectors of working life.

The key idea is that if criteria can be established, preferably quantifiable, measurable objectives can be set. In practice this often proves to be difficult, but the principle is a sound one. However, in key areas such as customer service, aspects such as speed of response and ways of dealing with complaints can be measured. It is therefore important that such standards are built into training and development processes and where necessary identified deficiencies dealt with as part of such processes and wider HRM policies. This example gives an indication where proactive T&D contributions get to the heart of supporting core competencies and, by implication, competitive advantage.

Job analysis

The skills, knowledge and behaviours necessary to discharge a specific job or task need to be identified if T&D is to be correctly targeted. Many techniques have emerged over the past half-century which aim to provide analysis of skills, knowledge and, in some cases, attitudes needed to perform specific tasks. The very extensive work of Douglas Seymour in the 1960s was influential in some areas of manufacturing industry (Seymour, 1966). However, many areas such as managerial work and indeed supervisory jobs have traditionally proved very much less amenable to analysis. This does not exclude attempts to describe managerial work by theorists such as Brech and Urwick and much more pragmatically by Rosemary Stewart in the 1970s (Stewart, 1976). Techniques such as critical incident identification have also been used to try to identify the problems that supervisors have to contend with in their daily work. Much of this very detailed analysis has receded in the face of competency thinking embodied in nationally recognized qualifications, from shop floor through supervisory to management. These qualifications purport to identify a broad range of elements and their associated outputs and provide accreditation for the T&D associated with the components covered by individual trainees. Regardless of the criticisms which can be levelled at such national qualifications, from the administrative burden to the significance of content claims, this is an approach in which much is invested by key stake-holders; it is spreading on a global scale, and is likely to be a key feature of people development in the future.

For those who are still not convinced about what such frameworks offer, there are a number of guidance points which cut through to the basics of job analysis for training purposes:

- **Enlist support**: It is vital to enlist support of the key players involved in the job and/or processes. This may, depending on complexity, engage a range of interacting personnel, including management and supervision. It is a quite involved psychological process where it is vital to dispel anxieties and to develop rapport with the job incumbent.
- **Examine the job**: This means finding out in broad outline what is involved in successful job performance – the key processes being observation and questioning.
- **Analyse training requirements**: Essentially this consists of two parts – the identification of skills and knowledge required to do the job and a detailed breakdown of those skills. The elements should cover all the statements of duties in a related job description.

The depth of the analysis depends on the number of people to be trained and the inherent complexities of the job as a whole or of specific tasks within the job. Analysis may be presented in a number of ways:

- in the form of plans and sketches;
- in short descriptions;
- in multi-column breakdowns;
- as a 'faults analysis'.

Job analysis is therefore within the capabilities of even the smallest business and can be usefully self-administered, with value even to the one-person business.

Some principles of training programme design

Preparation of some kind of programme should emanate from such an analytical process. Programme design should be based on a clear statement of objective(s) of what the trainee should be able to do at the completion of training. In this way programmes can be devised which can systematically impart key skills and knowledge and the relevant behaviours related to doing a particular job. The critical inclusions in any training programme, however simple or complex, are:

- Summary of job training requirements. This typically would include basic knowledge and skills, and specific job knowledge and skills, which would include elements of tasks to be performed.
- Order of how the elements will be taught.
- Where they will be taught: internally or externally, on or off the job.

- The relevant methods to be employed.
- Other resources appropriate to delivery.
- Timing of discrete programme elements.
- Targets to be achieved at significant stages of the programme.

The basic principles provide a basis for imparting knowledge and skills in a systematic way. It provides a focus for arguably the most important and the most neglected aspect of the T&D investment – evaluation.

Evaluation of training and development

Remarkably, a very limited amount has been written on the evaluation process which is not, by and large, repetitive. For the purposes of illustration, therefore, reference to the levels of the process proposed by Kirkpatrick (1994) provide a readily applicable starting point which can provide, at the least, a qualitative perspective. Targeting and specific projects aimed at reinforcing acquired skills and knowledge are possible pointers to what has been gained by formal inputs. However, it has to be kept in mind that there may always be organizational factors that may account for performance improvements, not simply training.

The approaches to training and development are varied, some seeking objectivity through elaborate frameworks and processes. The truth is that however elaborate, evaluation as a concept seldom provides comprehensive or wholly satisfactory answers capable of isolating training from non-training contributions. However, there can be general agreement that evaluation has to be attempted. The pointers to any design components would seem to affirm the following considerations as critical success factors:

- Adopt a multi-source perspective to assessment.
- Think carefully about the importance of timing in the process (e.g. avoiding the post-course-euphoria syndrome).
- Plan integrative projects for participants before commencing the course and also the necessary integration support on return to the workplace.
- Use the evaluation process as a catalyst for ongoing learning.

The additional wisdom would see the need for evaluation design to be integrated with the wider human resource systems in terms of competences, reward and recognition arrangements and career and retention policies. The overriding need is for strategic-level reflection and debate on the perceived contribution of training and development which should ensure the necessary support decisions in relation to structures and culture. Finally, you are recommended to refer to Plath (1999), who reinforces the views presented here by warning about the dangers of over-elaboration. Systems such as the Higson and Wilson (1995) PDP model can be a great deal more bureaucratic than academic authors imagine, thus turning, as Plath rightly states, 'sound organisational innovations into just another fad'.

The competence framework

A number of lead bodies have provided competencies for a wide range of occupational categories and levels. These emphasize trainee capability to do the job. Robertson's (1995) definition clarifies this emphasis in: 'being able to perform 'whole' work roles (perform, not just know about or understand) to the standards expected in employment (not standards divorced from work expectations) in real working environments (including all the related pressures and variances of work)'. Plath in the first edition of this text gives a very good analysis of the perceived benefits of the competence movement. Equally important, he sets out very potent criticisms by writers such as Cornford and Athansou (1995). They assert that the competence framework presents a framework for under-achievement by saying that 'there are probably few involved in serious industrial training who have insights into the abilities characteristic of those at different stages of skill acquisition who would not agree that the objective for training should be aimed, at the least, at proficiency and preferably expert levels'. Plath (1999) evokes a counter-view that these authors may misunderstand the central notion that competence is 'level neutral', all that is required being to set the level high enough to achieve excellence. This in turn needs to be considered in relation to the features that Robertson (1995) projects as underpinning the development of competence. These are presented in full by Plath in the first edition of this text (page 81).

It would also be beneficial for those readers particularly interested in the underlying philosophies of the competence concept and how this is reflected in occupational standards such as NVQs (National Vocational Qualifications) again to refer to Plath's more intensive treatment of this subject (Plath, 1999). Clearly it has relevance to managers, as becoming involved does require significant resource commitment and thus key questions need to be asked on what might be expected in return. Again Plath provides very helpful insights in the form of a critical assessment of NVQs. Such reference should assist managers to develop understanding of what is often over-simplified in terms of the management commitment needed to support such initiatives. It should also help to provide insight into what has become, in a sense, an 'industry' in itself!

The changing nature of organizational work

Many of the approaches to training and development are still based on, or are derived from, the sort of analytical methods outlined in the preceding sections. However, the dynamics of organizational change, in whatever form, demand appropriate ways of disseminating and assimilating knowledge. This not only suggests more flexible technologies such as multimedia, but the transformation of organizations into what Senge (1990) and others refer to as 'the learning organization'; such a tranformation provides a synthesis of formal and informal processes of acquiring knowledge; it involves discovery by individuals of different levels of learning, self-development on a continuous basis and elevation of the concept of reflection to its rightful place in organizational learning.

The creation of a genuine learning organization needs to be predicated on the existence of a conducive culture, open to ideas and innovative approaches to acquiring knowledge, essential to maintain competitive advantage. Nor should it be concluded that such a sophisticated concept as the learning organization is the domain of highly resourced organizations! With the right style of management, small businesses can create the conditions for sharing knowledge, for reflecting on problem issues and for deriving lessons from such processes.

What are the essentials of the learning organization?

The essence of the 'learning organization' is that its culture makes it sensitive to the rapidly changing environment, and creates the capabilities to adapt to the changing demands needed to sustain competitive advantage.

Drivers for creating the learning organization are:

- Market and competitive forces create rapidly changing pressures on organizations to adapt in order to maintain competitive advantage.
- Distrust of traditional or current methods of development to deliver the kind of competencies needed to maintain competitive advantage.
- Prescriptive solutions which may reduce rather than enhance flexibility. This is important where processes such as globalization demand cross-border competencies.

Inhibitors are:

- The holistic view that organizational learning implies and the rationale underpinning its application may not be readily understood by those used to a conventional approach to T&D; this might very possibly include professional trainers.
- There may be a limited awareness at corporate level of the importance of having an integrated, strategic approach to training and development for the organization. This includes a level of commitment by top management based on a demonstration of their understanding.
- Employees may also be likely to have a limited perception of learning as opposed to conventional approaches to T&D.
- Cultural and mental models referred to by Senge (1990) tend to reinforce the conventional view of T&D as receiving inputs in a formal or semi-formal setting.
- Confusing or vague visions for learning are common, with regard to the organization of shared learning experiences. Creation of organizational learning must be seen as a process which is continuously evolving. The most powerful learning is often derived from this evolutionary and sometimes revolutionary process.
- Senge reminds us that the emphasis on team learning is widely inadequate and that the potential for optimizing available technology in learning is under-exploited.

Too often the emphasis remains with individually focused initiatives. It should be remembered that with increasing collaborative partnerships and customer orientation, the emphasis on the team concept is not confined to the internal interactions of organizations but needs to be seen as crossing boundaries, in support of strategic advantage. It is here that the power of multimedia is of future potential for organizational learning, for example in developing awareness of cultural diversity and preparing personnel in more effective ways for dealing with situations they might encounter, in the course of career moves or in responding to significant organizational change. The thinking of Senge and others reminds us of the points made earlier in this chapter on a systems approach to training and development. It provides a basis for integrating the various approaches to training and development into the strategic needs of the business.

There are obviously many streams that contribute to the creation of a learning organization, not all of them based on learning methodologies. For instance, the wider HRM and HRD activities of the organization have to be transparently reinforcing. The emergence of performance contracts in organizations such as Mobil have backing from the most senior levels of management downwards. The development and extension of this type of thinking is encapsulated in 'learning and behaviour development contracts' applied to all employees and agreed annually between an individual and his or her immediate supervisor. Clearly these processes are not unique, being found in various forms. What is possible is the application of this process to organizations, regardless of size – in fact even a mini business can apply the principles, ensuring that development opportunities are actively sought, in the ongoing process of conducting their business.

Resourcing training and development

Clearly the resourcing of training and development is a significant consideration for any management. Not only do all the processes described in this chapter take up considerable resources in terms of human resources but the implementation is likely to be constrained by approved budgets. For example, even in companies with an international profile and in areas as important as keeping up to date with IT innovation, some parts may and do fare less well than other parts, which are more accessible to customized courses and mentoring.

The scope of resources can be broadly divided into on-the-job, off-the-job, internal and external training and development.

On-the-job training

In many cases this may be the only sensible approach, either as a first resort or as a supplement to other forms of training. If it is to be effective it still requires application of the basic analytical principles set out in previous sections of this chapter. Not only can these contribute to better use of resources in a training and development context, but, certainly in smaller organizations, the process of analysis, however simple, can assist managers to clarify their thoughts about the way of doing tasks, generally.

The second principle which must be observed is how knowledge and skills are imparted on the job. The effects of picking up basic skills in a haphazard fashion from fellow workers or through the occasional attention of supervisory staff have been demonstrated as inadequate, and in many cases positively dangerous. The need for adequate coverage by a member of staff trained in the fundamentals of instruction is an essential part of the resourcing process.

Off-the-job training

The scope of off-the-job training arrangements is vast and beyond the intention of this chapter. It can obviously range from very basic in-house instruction to vastly costly external courses for all categories of staff in technical and managerial subjects. There are two principles to keep in mind when considering investment in off-the-job training and development:

- The appropriateness of the proposed training to both individual and organization. The well-worn view of courses as 'a holiday' for participants is not without foundation and has been instrumental in causing a loss of credibility in relation to such resources. Quite often courses have been used to reward and this is not only clearly wasteful but can cause long-term damage in relation to establishing credibility. Not only should those authorizing course attendance check the relevance of content to the individual and to the organization, but the credentials of the providers and their track record need to be scrutinized in relation to resource application.
- The second principle which needs to be given much more attention is how acquired knowledge, skills and behaviours are transferred and integrated into the organization. This has two dimensions – first the mechanisms, such as relevant projects, which will utilize the knowledge, skills and behaviours and secondly, very much in line with the 'learning organization' concept, provision for dissemination of such knowledge. Too often the acquired competencies remain locked up in the individual without any apparent pay-off to the sponsor.

Other approaches to meeting training and development needs

Off-the shelf courses cannot be expected to match the needs of every participant. Indeed, regardless of the post-course enthusiasm which course attendance often engenders, there will be often an admission that some parts were more relevant than others, in a particular event. It is not surprising therefore that the use of consultants in course design and follow-up is a very significant part of the training scene. It is therefore worthwhile examining the decision to employ consultants in delivering training and development initiatives.

Training consultants come in a wide variety of forms, from the one-person independent through to the services of the large international management and specialist organizations. Obviously, the ability to employ what are generally costly services is a screening mechanism and may well place their employability outside the reach of the smaller business. However, in some areas such as training associated with the introduction of IT, employing consultants may be unavoidable. Therefore some basic guidelines should be applied:

● Preliminary meetings, involving the most senior decision makers and other managers tasked with seeing projects through, should engage in evaluating any consultancy 'pitch'. Such a 'pitch' should be within broad guidelines provided by management, linked to some concept of the core competencies of the business. Where appropriate, the package may involve all the steps in the training cycle, from assessing training and development needs through to evaluation and follow-up. Whatever decision is made on specific components of consultant responsibility, the consultants need to:

1 be able to demonstrate their ability to grasp the essentials of the industry and the people involved;
2 be able to present a credible track record, including the variations in expertise which different aspects of the contract may dictate;
3 be able to assess the processes presented which will operationalize the skills, knowledge and behaviours acquired.

● As a rule of thumb it must be remembered that the large, high-profile consultancies despite their undoubted resource capabilities are not the sole depositories of training and development expertise. Independent consultants may have more specific skill contributions to make, relative to purpose.
● Utilizing managers as contributors in direct and indirect training and development activities is often overlooked as a valuable extension to resources. Not only are there possibilities in providing first-hand knowledge, which is information based and motivational, but such managers may be the primary depositories of technical knowledge. The managerial role in coaching and counselling is central.

There are arguments against such involvement, such as time restrictions and reluctance to present or carry out such processes. Managers clearly do need appropriate development in basic skills and the encouragement that engaging in such activities generates is integral to their own development. This is one example where training and development needs to be clearly tied into performance evaluation and arguably reward provision.

Revisiting commitment

It is questionable if there are many texts on training and development which, at some point or another, fail to acknowledge the relevance of management commitment as being essential to the success of T&D! However, it is important to go a little beyond general acceptance and ask what it is that really provides evidence of the existence of genuine management commitment in the context of training and development.

There is much practical evidence to show that when there are downturns in a particular organization's performance, training is the first activity to be cut. This was certainly true in the past and may well have significant currency now. The question that could well be asked is whether such cuts are due to management's shortcomings or to the failure of those involved with T&D to prove their worth.

The first piece of evidence that would be relevant to determining the degree of management commitment would be how learning is being managed! What evidence is there of how personal development and learning contribute to maintaining leadership within an industry sector and of the existence of a high-performance culture? What supports the contention that there is a clear and coherent message on training and development and shared learning, focused on core competencies; that visible support at all levels of management for innovative approaches that encourage collaborative learning; that knowledge is managed as an independent asset in its own right, and that active contributions from all employees to this are fostered?

Obviously there are other more mechanistic pieces of evidence that can be tested, such as budget allocations. However important, it is worth keeping in mind that the challenge to the effective deployment of allocated resources, by all levels of management interest, may provide more helpful indications of management awareness and commitment to T&D, as a critical strategic response factor. The key guides to positive commitment could be regarded as follows:

- The existence of clear processes of corporate thinking on what is sought from organizational learning.
- Evidence of consistency in communication of learning philosophies and on individual responsibilities, throughout the organization.
- Selected personnel who are perceived to have the power to diffuse and operationalize management demands from T&D investment and clearly communicate the linkage with the core competencies of the business.
- Generating a skills culture which promotes skills rather than training and development, as good things in 'themselves': that is, 'training for training's sake'.
- Creating paths to role excellence.
- Acknowledging the need for effective knowledge management as a critical contribution to the development of a learning organization.
- Fostering the idea of knowledge dissemination and shared learning.
- Creating the conditions for comprehensive learning with active promotion of accessible technology.

In companies which are seen to promote an active learning culture there is evidence of proactive management involvement. This is in the sense of integrating systems thinking about people development, integration into corporate decision making, as opposed to delegating training and development as relatively low-priority tasks to lower levels in their organization. The following are illustrations of the consistency of approaches in a disparate sample of companies, of high-level commitment and involvement in T&D.

Example: NCC is the leading construction and real estate company in the Baltic Sea Region. It has operations in Sweden, Finland, Norway, Denmark and Poland, but has ambitions for wider globalization.

Learning is particularly focused on IT, the environment, sales and quality. Corporate focus is on attracting and retaining young people. Training is for the most specialized categories and runs through the various divisions. A key addition to the provision of specialist skills is the emphasis on developing competencies related to dealing with change. Development takes place within a coherent framework referred to as the 'skills ladder' which provides an integrating mechanism with corporate aims (http//www.ncc.se).

Example: SKF is well known for its pioneering inventions in rolling bearer technology and its continuing image for technical innovation in this and other special steel applications. The strategic aspirations focus on maintaining and developing this position with the emphasis on customer and shareholder value and on the third critical strand of employee development.

Management has significantly intensified focus on organzational learning through establishment of a 'Learning Centre', at corporate level. Its remit is to continually monitor the changing business environment and to ensure that people are the focus for sustaining competitive advantage. Responsibility is placed on the Learning Centre to provide innovative approaches to leadership development and to ensure competency in non-technical subjects. The specific area of developing competencies for global adaptiveness is covered in their Global Leadership Programme.

In addition, the investment in skills development extends to the work of the SKF College, concentrating on technical skills development. It is, however, the way in which management seeks to ensure coordination and synergy, from their various strands of concentrated T&D, that marks the significant extent of management recognition of the expected contribution from their investment (http.//www.skf.com).

Example: Deutsche Bank is well known as one of Europe's leading financial institutions. Strategically it sees its focus primarily as Europe but has aspirations to develop its profile while maintaining a presence in Asia.

Learning in Deutsche Bank utilizes a centralized training department. The investment in people development is divided almost equally between consultants engaged on IT systems for the divisions and on the development of a global learning platform, referred to as the DB University. The other 50 per cent of training and development investment is concerned with moving towards a coherent learning culture, the main streams of which are:

- utilizing the resources of the DB University brand for the entire Bank;
- focusing on the quality of learning opportunities;
- promoting a common learning platform;
- finding or leading the development of innovative learning solutions.

A key aspect of the guiding philosophy is that divisions are free to select their own suppliers and this means that the internal resource has to compete. Prior consultation with Corporate Centre is mandatory, with the proviso that they:

- ensure that appropriate arrangements are in place for tracking, costing and delivery of any agreed training initiative;
- ensure coordination with other HR applications such as Peoplesoft, providing the necessary structure for measuring Web training utilization.

The Corporate Centre is only granted funding for a few strategic projects and is obliged to generate income through provision of services to other divisions, in competition with the market (http://www.public.deutsche-bank.d).

Example: Lloyds TSB is typical of the traditional bank with a broad product line. It is globally represented in Europe, the Americas, New Zealand and in the off-shore business through international banking, insurance and investment divisions. As in the case of the other examples, the strategic drive is to be 'leader in their chosen markets' and 'the preferred first choice' for some 15 million customers. This focus is the belief in the need for increased effectiveness driven by cost reduction.

Learning in Lloyds TSB is very much in the hands of the Board of Governing Directors who decide on the focus areas. HR has the delegated responsibility to operationalize these strategic choices. The main medium is the Lloyds TSB University, born out of surveys which indicated employee perceptions of training deficiencies. The key aims are:

- Making learning more accessible to employees – 'learning where they are'; no employee, it is asserted, should have more than ten minutes to walk to any learning resource. Such resources are in the form of some 2000 PCs installed in branch offices, for training purposes.
- Tailoring training and development opportunities to individual needs, while keeping alignment with the changing needs of the business. This is achieved through access to an Internet site, where training can be followed, irrespective of geography or time.

The 'University' is accountable for appropriate application of funds, directly to the 'Committee of Business Partners' constituted primarily of heads of divisions. The University also has a Strategy Board which oversees the strategic mix of formal classroom and Internet learning. The process for identifying deficiencies and designing curricula actively involves senior line managers. Additionally, support is integrated in ongoing line manager involvement, with key-word online access to information on training and development. Managers can call and discuss needs and approaches to delivery with assigned professionals (http://www.lloydstsb.co.uk).

These examples provide an indication of the increasing involvement in very different types of organizations by top managers, who are seeking to integrate training and development initiatives into strategic thinking and who are prepared to continually monitor their investment. It may well be argued that the examples are related to substantial enterprises who are well able to afford to go to such lengths. It could equally well be argued that if such well-resourced organizations see it in their interests to exercise such prudence, smaller businesses could be served by testing what they do and how they do it, in the context of meeting training and development needs.

Trends in responsibilities for training and development

The preceding section has been concerned with providing an indication of the extent of management involvement in the direction of training and development, with the strategic aims of the business in mind. The purpose here is to examine the process of managerial involvement more fully, by looking at some significant empirical studies.

As an overall view of the status of training and development, a study by Millward and Stevens (1992) states that the number of designated personnel specialists, with specific responsibility for training, fell from 78 to 67 per cent between 1984 and 1992. This needs to be qualified in that it is not possible to conclude whether it represents a shift of emphasis towards line manager accountability or a contracting out from the training function.

A study, conducted for the IPD (Hutchinson and Wood, 1995) in 25 UK organizations, provides data on personnel vs. line management involvement in training and development (Table 2.1).

The summary to this IPD Report asserts acknowledgement, by personnel managers, that line managers are 'best placed to determine the training needs of individuals'. In some of the organizations, line managers saw T&D as the weakest area in responsibilities delegated to them, seeing it as not deserving immediate attention: a view represented by the statement 'managers only think about training if a problem occurs'. There is clarity in the view that line managers receive inadequate development for taking on T&D responsibilities. Often there is lack of clarity in the shared responsibilities of personnel and line managers. The consequence is that a valuable resource, in the form of line management contribution to training and development processes, can be lost. This refers to the comments made in the context of resourcing the implementation of T&D.

Another IPD survey, 'The Impact of People Management Practices on Business Performance', conducted in 1997, states, with specific reference to training, that only 52 per cent of respondents claimed to have a formal strategy. Only in 20 out

Table 2.1   Personnel (PD) versus Line Management Responsibility for T&D

	LM	LM/PM	PM/LM	PD
Analysis of training needs	5	4	13	3
Allocation of training Budget	5	4	10	5
Decision of participants	9	10	6	0
Administration of courses	2	2	5	16
Running of internal courses	1	3	9	12
Evaluating training effects	4	6	9	6

Source: S. Hutchinson and S. Wood, IPD, London, 1995.

of the 111 companies responding was there evidence of systematic planning. In only 13 per cent of those companies responding was there any indication of effective needs assessment. There was general agreement by managers that the approach to training and development was unplanned – only 6 per cent reported a planned and organized approach.

The views emanating from these significant surveys are reinforced by a Leading Edge Forum Consortium study (Hope-Hailey *et al.*, 1997) which concluded that evidence of devolution to line management remained 'problematic' and that strategic decision making was still essentially dependent on the persuasive skills of senior HR managers and directors. There is, concludes the report, evidence of a shift towards recognition of the strategic importance of HRM generally as a contributor to business performance. From this it could be inferred that T&D would be regarded as a key factor.

A very up-to date survey, 'Training and Development in Britain 1999' (IPD, January 1999), covering 800 training managers and/or the most senior person in the organization responsible for training, provided feedback on the current status of training and development as follows:

- **Expenditure on training**: 22% of respondents said they did not have a training budget. Of those that did, only 63.7% have budgets which include fixed costs, with a further 29.5% only providing cover for external courses. Salaries for trainers and trainees were found to be almost 'universally excluded', together with costs relating to on-the-job training – this being the type of training most extensively used.
- **Nature of the link between training policies and workplace practices**: The most important strategic concerns were stated as 'making the most effective use of staff' (97.4%), followed by 'an attempt' to meet quality standards (89.9%) and the need for 'organizational development' (88.9%). The implications of these responses reinforces previous comments on the need to place training and development in a holistic context which endorses the systems approach and the need for effective interaction with key HRM activities.

Conclusions

According to Ulrich (1998), 'in the new economy winning will spring from organisational capabilities such as speed, responsiveness, agility, learning capacity and employee competence'. The emphasis on core competencies in this chapter is deliberate, as businesses organized around them is a growing trend. Some writers on the topic interpret core competencies as a portfolio of skills rather than as a portfolio of business units. Prahalad and Hamel (1990) bring this concept closer to the need for strategic thinking on the approach to people development, in the part of their definition of core competency which asserts the concept as 'the collective learning in an organization, especially how to coordinate diverse production skills and integrate multiple streams of technology'. This brings the emphasis on skills, knowledge and learning to the heart of strategic thinking.

This more positive move towards strategic orientation is further evidenced by

Barney (1991) and Hall (1992), in relation to the resource-based theory of the firm, asserting that competitive advantage results from the firm's internal resources. Quinn (1992) talks about 'intelligent enterprises' and Stalk (1992) identifies the concept of 'competing on capabilities'. All of this moves to complete the argument, presented in this chapter, of the need to stress the focus on core competencies as a positive link between training and development contributions and the strategic needs of the business, regardless of size.

Glyn Macken of The Institute of Management is quoted as saying ' a community where an atmosphere of continual learning and development delivers benefit to all stakeholders and to create in our people a desire to improve themselves no matter which stage they are at in their career. Therefore 'lifelong' learning is the key to both individual and organisational success'. Put another way, the need is for organizations to learn faster than competitors to sustain competitive advantage. The conditions for developing such a beneficial process of shared learning revolve around the creation of a conducive culture. As Kent A. Greenes , BP Virtual Teamwork, Project Director, is quoted as saying, 'if it is easy for people to connect, communicate and share knowledge, they will do it' (*HBR*, October, 1997). There are good examples which are working hard to create such conducive conditions and culture, as the following profiles suggest.

Bovis Construction has in operation a distance learning programme aimed at ensuring the transfer of best practice, knowledge and management skills across the Group. This process provides the opportunity for those who wish to gain a postgraduate qualification. As stated by the Bovis Chief Executive, Luther Cochrane, in the *Professional Manager* in 1999, 'ours is very much a people's business ... giving both new trainees and seasoned managers the opportunity to broaden their understanding of Bovis and enhance their own career prospects [has] to be beneficial to everyone concerned'.

Bradford and Bingley Building Society is engaged in radical change, according to its Training and Development Manager, Margaret Johnson, who states 'we needed to do something quite radical – we needed to develop and modernise our management thinking and the way we operate', which required challenging existing assumptions, through use of external involvement, focusing on development of leadership skills within a changing organization. This involved 260 middle managers on a three-day Henley workshop and 76 senior managers on a five-day programme with similar objectives. This approach is reported as being integrated through a focused communication process, with wide employee involvement.

IBM has approached the need for flexible responses to skills development by combining the best features of company-wide and local approaches in the development of a skills database. This has the aim of overcoming the highly centralized and complex worldwide skills inventories maintained by Corporate HR. The driving force is to equip line managers to define the range of skills relevant to their part of the organization, while maintaining the link through inputting the data into the main HR database. This allows more effective incorporation into strategic level planning.

In 1998, the UK **Post Office** introduced a significant change in their procedures using computerized processes. This included integrated skills planning and training. The focus on training and development is emphasized in a quote by one senior manager: 'one of the important things for us to keep in strong focus is the development of people as the change takes place . . . which will be driven by our line managers, and this will certainly be true of how we approach the development of individuals'.

The UK food retailer **Sainsbury's,** too have been concerned with culture change aimed at helping staff to work together more effectively, encouraging release of their talents. The process emphasizes continuous improvement and is supported by the involvement of no fewer than five board members.

The question is, what can be drawn from the profiles? Essentially it could be suggested that there is clear evidence of more active devolvement of responsibility for training and development to line managers; indications of closer interest at board level in ensuring that the T&D contribution is integrated into strategic thinking and that the investment is monitored. The other important point is that the growing concern is with flexible responses, although there is a need to balance this with an obvious interest, on the part of global enterprises, with consistency in supporting core competencies. It is also apparent that demarkation lines between what has been traditionally defined as training and development and broader organizational developments are becoming increasingly blurred. In the light of the prognostications of acknowledged thinkers this close interaction between how organizations approach the development of people and their businesses would seem to be inevitable. Professor Richard Scase of Kent University advances the view on the probability of increased mobility not only of people but of organizations in the twenty-first century (*The Money Programme*, BBC 2, Sunday, 12 December 1999). This mobility needs to be supported by demonstration of flexibility in individual competencies and with emphasis on how to access and manage knowledge. The implication would seem to be that although frameworks, such as those embodying competencies or Investor in People principles for integrating training and development with business strategies, may have value in stimulating processes aimed at improving training, they may be inadequate in responding to the dynamics of knowledge-driven enterprises in the twenty-first century.

There is little doubt that recognition of human resource management, as a contributor to organizational response capabilities, is currently a high-profile area in the mission statement rhetoric of many organizations. Of the six global capabilities that the World Economic Forum see as essential to effectiveness, human resources seems to animate chief executives most (Steward, 1999). The implicit importance of innovative organizational learning here is evident. The blending of diverse national practices into global 'best' practice and converting this to local levels of consistent good practice is one example. For instance, no one could doubt the determination of Ford's Jacques Nasser in promoting clearly stated values throughout the Corporation, yet the difficulties of doing this are evident in the recent ethnic problems that Ford has experienced in its UK operations.

It is, however, evident that top international managers like Nasser recognize the interrelationships between sub-systems in trying to promote learning. It is here that the contributions of systems thinking derived from Senge and others such as Argyris (1994) have value in the promotion of organizational learning and where managers can engage in the learning process which can utilize experience. This view recognizes that much of the learning that takes place within an organization is experimental – that is to say that organizations tend to manage by doing and do not experience the challenges they face until they experience them. This revives the notion of the 'Reflective Practitioner' model suggested by Donald Schon (1990), summarized by Cheetham and Chivers (1996) thus:

> [Schon] has offered a new epistemology of professional practice based on 'knowing in action' (a form of acquired tacit knowledge) and 'reflection' (the ability to learn through and within practice). Schon believes that professionals apply what he calls 'artistry', in reframing and resolving many day-to-day problems which defy the simple application of scientific principles. He argues that reflection (both 'reflection-in-action' and 'reflection-about-action') is a vital part of the process.

Frameworks such as Investors in People, which Plath adequately describes in the first edition (pp. 86–7) and which was noted at the outset of this chapter, have a contribution to make in developing an integration process with business needs. They remain unconvincing, however, if they cannot promote the level of reflective thinking by managers which the writings of Senge, Schon, Argyris and others advocate as the fundamentals of effective organizational learning.

There can be no doubt that comparisons on training and development show significant expenditures. Australian figures from 1993 show the training spend, as a percentage of gross employee emoluments, as 2.9 per cent (*Australian 1995 Yearbook*). South African statistics for the same period and criteria show a 3.74 per cent expenditure (Molin and Harrod, 1996). However, perhaps some insights into perspectives on training and development's positioning in managerial thinking is an appropriate contribution to complete a chapter aimed at providing managers with a basis for understanding and challenge.

According to the 1999 ASTD State of the Industry Report – USA, the twin forces of technological change and globalization have created a knowledge era. Possession and development of an organization's intellectual property is regarded as the main sustainable source of competitive advantage. There is a union here between an organization's attention to creating the conditions for continuous learning and its economic success. This indicates the need for an executive shift from superficially subscribing to the notion of the training and development contribution to seeing it as an investment rather than as a cost.

The ASTD survey generally asserts that increases in training and education investment are followed by improved performance and that cutting out such investment puts performance at risk. But the balance still appears to need addressing more convincingly, for corporate America spends ten times more on information technologies than on training! The ASTD survey covers some 754 organizations. Using cluster analysis 55 leading-edge organizations were identified, scoring highly on the following criteria:

- percentage of employees trained;
- training expenditures per employee;
- use of innovative practices;
- use of high-performance work practices.

It is perhaps not too surprising that the typical leading-edge organization employs fewer than 500 staff and is likely to be located in the IT sector.

What insights can be derived from this significant study of North American interest in planned development of people and top management's commitment to this?

- First, leading-edge firms tend to outsource at a significant level and have a greater mix in the types of providers employed.
- Executive spend is higher in organizations using learning technologies than in those firms using more conventional approaches to training. The former also tended to be characterized by a greater training staff provision.
- Learning technologies are on the increase, signifying a move away from the classroom. The emphasis is moving towards facilitation of learning processes which does not exclude even very small companies, providing managerial interest is engaged. The ASTD survey indicates that, in 2000, use of learning technologies will accelerate, the average US firm expecting that 22.5% of training will be delivered via multimedia technologies. This is followed by text computer-based training (CBT) applications at 48% of all training taking place. The figures for leading-edge business suggest as high a level as 75% engagement in this kind of delivery.

Summary

It is interesting to conclude that more esoteric application of technology such as virtual reality is still not regarded as a forerunner in practical delivery, nor are conventional methods of delivery, such as classroom and on-the-job training, likely to disappear. In the learning organization there is room for many combinations providing they are accommodated within a clear strategic framework (Bassi and Van Buren, 1999).

Perhaps, with the rate of globalization of enterprise and the diversity this implies, the need is greater than ever for effective business–educational collaboration. In spite of the belief that this takes place, it is more questionable if either business or educational institution emerge with depth understanding of needs or the development process for meeting them. Mintzberg's indictment of educational establishments' MBA programmes as 'teaching the wrong things, the wrong way, to the wrong people' is not simply provocative – it needs to be considered seriously in strategic thinking about how best to develop resources to meet fast-changing and widely diversified challenges. The proposals for an appropriate response are evident in the curriculum for a 'new-generation' management degree involving collaboration between five business schools worldwide. Mintzberg, the main inspirational source, calls the programme 'next generation' because it deems to break out of the mould of functional teaching, focusing instead on managerial 'mindsets'. Each campus devotes itself to projecting a different mindset, or local approach to business. This is illustrated by Japan's Hitosubashi University devoting itself to a 'collaborative' approach, the UK's Lancaster University emphasizing a 'reflective' approach to business strategy, and INSEAD an 'action' perspective. The shift is on developing managers instead of teaching management. The postscript from Mintzberg is not by any means new, in the sense that many trainers have been wholly conscious of its essential message for the past half-century, but it is worth repeating: 'you can't train managers in the classroom'. Such a view is in accord with many of the insights conveyed in this chapter. The opportunity is reflected in inputs such as those of Mintzberg and others for more imaginative partnerships between institutions and business organizations to balance concept and practice and return responsibility for strategic use of learning to where it should be, at the heart of the organization.

Questions

1 Training and development can only be of value if it is integrated into overall business strategy! What are the options open to management and how can you convince top management of the need to do this?
2 Training and development initiatives are unlikely to be effective in the absence of clear top management commitment! What do you see as the characteristics of commitment and how can senior management interest in training be promoted?
3 Current organizational need is for learning specialists not conventional trainers?
4 Global markets require new educational technologies?
5 'You can't train managers in the classroom!' What are your thoughts on this?
6 Consider each of the preceding questions from an ethical perspective. Using the ethical reasoning framework suggested in the introductory chapter, assess your answers to the above questions.

MINI-CASE

You have been employed as a training specialist in a medium sized manufacturing firm which has not engaged in a planned approach to training operatives. Training is on the job and, because of the pressure to meet bonus, allows little time for experienced workers to give instruction, even if they were disposed to do so!

Your manager is the Financial Director whom the firm's owner manager sees as the most appropriate person to deal with 'non-core' people issues. He has asked you to carry out an assessment of needs for operatives and report to him within two weeks!

What approach would you adopt to enlisting the support of all concerned?

What would your approach to analysis include?

How would you sell your recommendations to all concerned and engage the interest of all key management interests? Here you should demonstrate awareness of the key constraints which a firm with limited resources is likely to present in the implementation of training.

References

Argyris, C (1994) *On Organisational Learning*, Blackwell, Oxford.
Australian 1995 Yearbook.
Barney, JB (1991) Firm resources and sustained competitive advantage. *Journal of Management*, March.
Bassi, LJ and Van Buren, ME (1999) *State of the Industry Report*. USA.

Cheetham, G and Chivers, G (1996) Towards a holistic model of professional competence. *Journal of European Industrial Training*, **20** (5).

Coopers and Lybrand (1986) A Challenge to Complacency. Report for Manpower Commission and National Economic Development Council.

Cornford, I and Athanason, J (1995) Developing expertise through training. *Industrial and Commercial Training*, **27** (2).

French, D and Saward, H (1975) *Dictionary of Management*, Gower Press, Hants.

Hall, R (1992) The strategic analysis of intangible resources. *Strategic Management Journal*.

Higson, M and Wilson, JP (1995) Implementing personal development plans: a model for trainers, managers and supervisors. *Industrial and Commercial Training*, **27** (6).

Hope-Hailey, V, Grattan, L, McGovern, P, Stiles, P and Truss, C (1997) A chameleon function? HRM in the 1990s. *Human Resource Management Journal*, **7** (3).

Hutchinson, S and Wood, S (1995) *Personnel v Line Management Responsibility for T&D*, IPD, London.

Institute of Personnel Development (1997) *The Impact of People Management Practices on Business Performance*.

Institute of Personnel Development (1999) *Training and Development in Britain 1999*, January.

Kirkpatrick, D (1994) *Evaluating Training Programmes: the Four 'Levels'*, Berret-Koehler Publishers, San Francisco, CA.

Millward, N and Stevens, M (1992) *Workplace Relations in Transition*, Dartmouth Press, MA.

Molin, K and Harrod, J (1996) *Issues Management, Education and Training and Development in business – a Training Perspective*, Business Monitor International.

Opinion Research Centre (1978) *A Survey of the Motivation of Top British Management*.

Plath, AR (1999) Training and Development in N Cornelius (ed.) *Human Resource Management: a Managerial Perspective*, International Thomson Business Press, London.

Porter, ME (1990) *The Competitive Advantage of Nations*, Free Press, New York.

Prahalad, CK and Hamel, G (1990) The Core Competencies of the Corporation. *Harvard Business Review*, May/June.

Quinn, JB (1980) *Strategies for Change*, Irwin, Holmwood, Il.

Robertson, C (1995) NVQs: the impact of competence approaches. *Management Development Review*, **9** (5).

Schon, D (1990) *Educating the Reflective Practitioner*, Jossey-Bass, San Francisco, CA.

Senge, PM (1990) *The Fifth Discipline: The Art and Practice of the Learning Organisation*, Century Business, London.

Seymour, WD (1966) *Industrial Skills*, Pitman, London.

Stalk, G, Jr. and Webber, AM (1993) Japan's dark side of time. *Harvard Business Review*, July/August.

Stewart, R (1976) *Contrasts in Management*, McGraw-Hill, UK

Ulrich, D (1998) A new mandate for Human Resources. *Harvard Business Review*, January/February.

Suggested Reading

Radcliffe, P (1994) Investing in managers. *Management Development Review*, **7** (5).

Mindell, N (1995) Devolving training and development to line managers. *Management Development Review*, **8** (2).

Journals

Industrial and Commercial Training.
Journal of European Industrial Training.

Legal briefing

Opportunities for training and development must be offered to all relevant employees in a manner that does not offend against the anti-discrimination laws. Please refer to the legal briefing for Chapter 1 for more detail.

An exception is provided by the Sex Discrimination Act, 1975, where a special programme of 'single sex' training is permissible to correct a discrepancy which has appeared in the previous 12 months in the number of women, or men, who appear to be qualified to carry out a particular job. In other words, if it becomes apparent that fewer women than men are capable of carrying out a particular job due to lack of suitable training in the past, this may be corrected by the employer putting on a special course available to women only.

There does not seem to be an equivalent provision in the Race Relations Act.

In line with the enhanced status of independent, recognized trades unions (please see the legal briefing to Chapter 3), such organizations now have the right to be consulted about training policy, and to have access to the appropriate information.

Generating commitment through involvement and participation processes

3

Alan Blackburn

Learning objectives

After studying this chapter you should be able to:

- explain the influences on, and developments of, present-day involvement and participation processes;
- distinguish between the different forms of involvement and participation processes;
- assess the strengths and limitations of common forms of involvement and participation processes within an organization;
- explain how such processes contribute towards gaining employee commitment.

Introduction

This chapter explores the development of participation and involvement processes used in organizations. These issues will be discussed through a sociological framework normally used to explain the relationship between individuals, groups, the state and society. For our purpose the unitarist, pluralist and to a lesser extent the radical perspectives will predominantly be used and before proceeding further the terms are explained here.

From a unitarist perspective, an enterprise is viewed as a unified whole; all staff who work there have a sense of common purpose within an overarching paternalistic style of management. In such an organization conflict is seen as unhelpful, caused by troublemakers.

By way of contrast the pluralist perspective views organizations as coalitions of separate interest groups presided over by a top management which serves the long-term needs of the organization (Fox, 1975). In such an organization conflicts of interest are seen as inevitable, but can be used creatively for the overall good of the organization.

The radical perspective views the employment relationship as conflictual where management have more power than employees. A worker's ability to work is a commodity that can be bought and sold by managers. Individual employees who rely on managers for employment are relatively powerless to influence working arrangements, but such a relationship generates cynicism and mistrust which is never far below the surface (Fox, 1975).

It must be said that involvement and participation processes are not new, but have received increased attention as to their potential use to minimize conflict and are central to human resource management practice because:

1   they emphasize a unitarist approach to managing people;
2   they contribute towards the overall management of a company, by encouraging people to take an active part in enhancing effective service provision;
3   they contain elements of a powerful system of social control which may help reduce management costs.

Participation and involvement processes are noted by Storey in his 27 points of difference between traditional personnel management and a human resource management approach to managing organizations (Storey, 1992; see Chapter 1). They may be said to play an essential part in the development of an organization's managerial climate and style. Retaining the commitment of staff and taking account of their views is important when increasing environmental pressures force rapid change, or innovation. Participation and involvement processes can help managers achieve commitment, while releasing the talent of staff to help organizations become more effective. Participation processes can encourage the alignment of staff attitudes in an appropriate way, while creating a vehicle for a mutual exchange of obligations between managers and their work teams. Effective employee involvement is not just a matter of good employer practice . . . it is above all a prerequisite for business growth in a modem economy (Employment Department, 1994).

Involvement and participation processes are not new. For example, the Second World War brought Government into direct discussions with the Trades Union Congress, on a wide variety of work and wider public issues. Moreover, trade unions over many years had, as one of their central concerns, the desire to extend the involvement of employees in the decision-making processes in industry. This introduction will discuss some of the reasons why there has been continued interest in participation processes. Then we examine participation theory, which perhaps reveals its rise in popularity as a means to improve employee relations management, within an overall human resource management process.

The changing environment and organization of work

The business environment has become increasingly competitive during the past decade. European companies are facing competition from a wider range of countries which often have lower wage costs. Markets for goods may be thought of as global, rather than local. Technologies used in business promote speed in decision making and economies in production of goods and services. The emergence of human resource management and labour flexibility, where labour is treated as a relatively expensive commodity, has altered approaches to managing people. These features have contributed to complexity for managers, of how best to organize working arrangements and people, to maximize the economic advantage for their organization.

At the heart of these organizational issues there remains a fundamental problem for managers, which is the lack of clarity in the normal contract of employment. This is because a contract of employment fails to specify with any degree of accuracy the duties of an employee, or the amount of effort employees are required to put into their day-to-day activities. This ambiguity was highlighted by Liebenstien (1978) who described the discretion within an employment contract as an APQT Bundle, where workers, to some extent, have the discretion to choose the **A**ctivity they engage in; the **P**ace, or speed at which they choose to work, the **Q**uality standards to achieve in their work and the amount of **T**ime to spend on their chosen set of preferred activities. Put simply, workers can choose different activity bundles to use during their working day, i.e. how much energy they put into working for the organization and how much energy they spend on other displacement activities. People adopting such an approach and attitude to their work would be able to externalize work issues within their minds. Here, organizational problems of work would be viewed by staff as someone else's responsibility to resolve. Workers adopting this attitude would simply go to work to do a job and no more.

Under this model an organization purchased a worker's labour, but failed to harness workers abilities to contribute to the organization of their work. In this context workers were free to provide labour only and allow others, usually managers, to solve problems. This process created pluralist organizations where groups of people with their own interests could flourish, often at the expense of organizational effectiveness. This model highlights flaws in the supervision process and the control of work activities which may also contain imperfections. For Cole (1920), the major objection to this type of job design was that labour was treated as just another commodity and so the humanity of labour was denied. These attitudes were created by organization design based on scientific management, which relied on labour compliance and subservience while emphasizing imbalances in the power and status of each respective group. By producing detailed sets of rules and regulations to supplement the contract of employment, managers attempted to limit worker discretion, which created a fertile ground on which conflicts of interest could develop. This dominant form of work design created a basic contradiction in the management process. Managers needed to organize working arrangements to limit worker discretion, however informal arrangements were developed incrementally in the vacuum between the management/worker divide. This was done by employees, or their representatives, often in collaboration with management which added to organizational control problems (Batstone *et al.*, 1979).

This mode of organization design became out of step with current business needs; however, the problem of how to create a committed workforce remained. Furthermore, uncertainty and competition in the business environment mean that organizations must respond quickly to prosper. This in turn creates a need for a flexible yet committed workforce, who respond positively to changes in their duties and responsibilities. To continue to use traditional control systems in new emerging circumstances will incur high overhead costs relative to competitors. Participation and involvement schemes can emerge as a flexible control system which can help managers to contain conflict and adjust staff attitudes by involving them in the decision-making processes of an organization. The strength of these processes is that they are flexible enough to remain effective as organizations change their shape and form. Furthermore, once working, they can become self-sustaining at manageable cost.

There are a wide variety of views as to what involvement and participation mean. The two terms are used interchangeably in the literature. Definitions offered tend to be rather indistinct. Involvement in an organizational context can mean, for example, that people take part in organizational activity which will allow them to influence or take part in decision making. The main issue for managers and employees is, how much involvement and how powerful is the exerted influence? What issues are influenced? At what levels in the organization does influencing take place and what mechanisms are used to facilitate the influencing process?

Failure of established management systems to achieve organizational aims will stimulate activity to develop replacements. This chapter will argue that involvement and participation processes can provide an alternative system of control while avoiding traditional proceduralization. We will argue that participation processes can provide an effective system of social control which can generate employee commitment and form the basis on which psychological contracts can be developed. We start by considering some theory of the participation process.

Who should participate and how should they do it?

To more fully understand the participation process, we discuss here participation theory which will raise some issues about the process. For Rousseau (1913), 'participation hinges on the individual participation of each individual citizen in political decision making'. Pateman (1970) adds, 'this process also has a psychological effect on the participants, ensuring that there is a continuing interrelationship between the working of institutions, the psychological qualities and the attitudes of individuals interacting with them'. If we accept these views then for people at work to be fully involved in the process of participation everyone must contribute individually within the participation process. The byproduct of this will be for individuals to enter into a mindset of open cooperation with their fellows within an overall unitarist environment.

For work organizations, this presents certain problems, in that workers are often grouped into work teams to perform similar and complementary functions. This, for Rousseau (1913), would be unacceptable. As he points out, 'the ideal situation for decision making is where no organised groups are present, just individual ones, as the former may be able to make their "particular wills" prevail' (Rousseau, 1913) thus reinforcing pluralist attitudes. Participation then, is for people to take part in the decision-making processes in a workplace. For participation to be fully effective, everyone must take an active part which allows individuals to protect their private interests and ensure sound government, or management of the workplace.

The most appropriate system of participation for Rousseau, then, is direct individual participation, for which a definition is provided later in this chapter. A problem here, however, is the inherent imbalance in power between managers and the managed which may limit the influence that individual workers have in the decision-making processes of the organization. As Hyman (1975) suggests, a power relationship is thus central to industrial relations. An alternative is suggested by Mill, who believed an acceptable method of participation may be achieved through representatives, who look after the interests of their constituents. In an organization, employee representatives perform this role and have the support of a collective group, either a trade union or staff association; it is through the collective organization of a trade union that employee representatives may be able to counter the power of management through participation processes (Hyman, 1985). This may be described as indirect, representative participation, for which a definition is also provided later. This issue apart, a major difference between the approaches of Rousseau and Mill is that for Rousseau, participation was between people of equal status, as such 'people were open to its psychological effects' (Pateman, 1970). But for Mill, representatives taking part in such a participatory process were inferior and may not be able to resist the implementation of policies that would disadvantage them; it was essential that work people had a voice in management, 'as some form of co-operation is inevitable in industry . . . without it the employer/employee relationship, would not be maintainable in the long run and some form of co-operation must take its place' (Mill, 1910). Hyman would see this cooperation taking place through trade unions and elected representatives, enabling collective employee power to counteract the power of management. On the other hand, Mill would argue, the way to achieve this, while accommodating status differentiation, was by having managers elected by the workforce who could be removed if their performance was not satisfactory (Mill, 1910). In modern industry this is unlikely. For example, British Gas shareholders failed to exercise sanction over the salary increase of their Chief Executive in the mid 1990s. Additional evidence regarding the limitations of this view was shown through an Open University video case study featuring 'Suma', a workers cooperative. In this study, theoretically, all workers irrespective of their role, had equal say in the decision-making processes of the company. In reality, however, because of organizational processes, the commonly understood and accepted hierarchy and information availability, people in managerial roles could exert greater influence over higher-level decisions within the company. Through greater knowledge and experience, they could also manipulate the organizational technology to achieve their own ends. Any real 'say' in decision making by rank and file members of the cooperative was severely limited (Open University). The example highlights the interdependence of the manager/worker relationship. Within an organizational context each needs the other for the organization process to work.

The implications of participation processes

In a workplace once a participation system is established, the system should become self-sustaining. This is because the qualities required of the individuals, for the system to continue to work successfully, are those that the process of participation develops and fosters within itself (Pateman, 1970).

The implications of this for managers are that once a system is in place and people are given the opportunity to contribute and work within it, it may be difficult to re-establish a traditional control regime. 'Within such a system, work people who were once shackled within their jobs, are "forced to be free"' (Rousseau, 1913). This, in turn, may produce a challenge to the ways in which managers manage, if indeed they continue to be required, once the participation system is working. Full participation in decision making must lead the organization towards industrial democracy. The advantage to the organization is, however, that by forcing people through a process of adjustment, they are forced into socially responsible actions. Assuming the participation process is aligned to organizational needs, it will improve attitudes of employees, while containing conflicts of interest within the system. Employees then may limit the amount of discretion they display within their jobs, by choosing an activity bundle oriented towards the organization, without managerial intervention. This in turn will provide individuals with a sense of freedom. By participating in decision making, individuals will be given a very real degree of control over the course of their (working) life and the structure of their (working) environment (Pateman, 1970). Traditional organizations with heavily regulated work regimes posed a direct threat to a worker's individual freedom; they make freedom impossible – workers everywhere are in chains (Rousseau, 1913).

For Rousseau the ideal organization was where a worker's freedom was guaranteed, where everyone was able to participate in decision making. Providing an organization where people feel able to participate helps people to buy into and share ownership of decisions, which may in turn affect how, where and what an individual's organizational role is. Collective decisions are more likely to be accepted by people, if they have had a say in them. For example, allowing workers to be involved in 'law making' in the organization may make the laws more acceptable and less likely to be broken. In a work situation, jointly drafted procedural agreements, by management and employee representatives, of say a performance and conduct procedure, are likely to assist the use of such in practice. The main departure here from Rousseau is that for him the application of sanction would be by the 'law makers', i.e. by a joint panel of managers and employee representatives. In practice such sanctions are applied by managers and usually defended by employee representatives.

Rousseau went on to suggest that participation has another, additional function. This is an integrative function, which increases the feeling among individual citizens (workers) that they 'belong' in their community. This process of integration is derived from the functions of participation which have already been mentioned here. In organizational terms, however, economic inequality will prevent participation from developing fully in an organizational setting, as for Rousseau 'economic equality will create a disruptive divide between rich and poor', which within itself will create unequal status and prevent full participation from taking place. This was endorsed by Mill (1910) who also contends that 'organisations' economic equality will create a disruptive divide between rich and poor'.

As with any system, the whole process of participation needs to be held together to make it sustainable. For Cole (1920), when such a system was fully installed and working, 'it would be held together by the will of the members' (participants). To build a system of participation Cole suggested the 'workshop' as the basic building block and the unit of participation should be small enough to allow everyone to take part. He went on to outline a sophisticated system through which elected representatives would fully represent the whole society (company) to maximize participation in decision making (Cole, 1910).

Summary of main points

This section has set the scene and provided two views of participation. The first, emerging from discussions by Rousseau, is that everyone in an organization should have the opportunity to take part in the process of influencing decision making. Workers should elect managers, who could be voted out of office. Rousseau also believed that participation in decision making should be full and direct. An example of such a system could be viewed as a workers' cooperative, although we have already suggested that this process too may be problematic. For Mill, Cole and Hyman, participation could be achieved through a process of representation, where elected representatives represent the interests of their constituency through appropriate forums. The problem of this approach, for Rousseau, is that alliances of representatives would defend sectional interests, which would fragment the process. In organizations, however, people tend to work in teams rather than as individuals, hence the development of sectional interests may be inevitable. The reconciliation of sectional interests could, however, be built into the process and become self-sustaining.

From the above we can extract the key features of participation processes:

1   Participation hinges on either individual participation in decision making or participation through elected representatives.
2   The ideal place for this activity is seen as the workplace level, but others suggest that because of the inherent power imbalances at the workplace level, collective organization will be needed to ensure the process works (Hyman, 1975).
3   Economic inequality will create a disruptive divide between rich and poor.
4   Within such a system, work people who were once shackled within their jobs are 'forced to be free'.
5   In a workplace, once a participation system is established, the system should become self-sustaining.
6   To maintain the employment relationship it is essential that work people have a voice in management.

A useful by-product is that the participation process has a psychological influence on those taking part. This influence may be positive or negative and it is up to management to ensure a positive influence, by appropriate use of the process. This could include careful design of the system which may include the extent to which people can influence management by taking part in the process. Pateman (1970) suggested that the degree of participation could be measured horizontally and vertically to assess the true extent of the process. These measures are explained and discussed later in this chapter. Next we consider some definitions of participation and involvement.

Definitions of involvement and participation

Employee involvement is defined by the Institute of Personnel and Development as 'a range of processes designed to engage the support, understanding, optimum contribution of all employees in an organisation and their commitment to its objectives' (IPD, 1990).

Participation consists basically in creating opportunities, under suitable conditions, for people to influence decisions affecting them. That influence can vary from a little to a lot. Participation is a special case of delegation, in which the subordinate gains greater control and greater freedom of choice, with respect to his or her own responsibilities. The term participation is usually applied to the subordinate's greater influence over matters within the superior's responsibilities (McGregor, 1960). For McGregor, participation seems to be a process of delegation where workers can influence the work mix which is delegated to them and the freedom subordinates have to choose their own preferred methods of achieving the agreed objectives. A key part, however, is the distinction made over the amount of influence exerted, from a little to a lot. In relation to this, a useful distinction was made by Pateman who differentiated between full, partial and pseudo-participation.

Employee participation may be defined as 'a process of employee involvement designed to provide employees with the opportunity to influence and where appropriate, take part in decision making on matters which affect them' (IPD, 1990).

Participation itself may be subdivided into two forms: direct participation and indirect participation.

Direct participation for the IPD is defined as 'structured methods, which provide opportunities for each employee to influence, or contribute to the decisions on the task he or she is performing and on its relationship to the organisational structure' (IPD, 1990). Rousseau (1913) called this 'full participation' but it would largely depend upon the range of issues open to discussion. For example, it could include what people do, how they do it and how the rewards are divided, or a limited range of these.

Indirect participation is where representatives of employees meet with representatives of management, within a predetermined and agreed forum, to discuss matters of mutual interest to both groups. Representatives of employees may be elected, or appointed by a membership constituency to undertake this function. Rousseau (1913) called this 'pseudo-participation'. This will also be influenced by the range of issues open to discussion, which could be narrow or broad.

A more recent definition is provided by a European Union publication as follows: 'Opportunities which management provide, or initiatives to which they lend their support, at workplace level for consultation with and/or delegation of responsibilities and authority for decision making to their subordinates either as individuals, or as groups of employees relating to their immediate work task, work organisation and/or working conditions' (Geary and Sisson, 1994). It is this last definition that is the most persuasive in that it contains key elements which may be found in all earlier attempts. Although it does not make a distinction between direct and indirect participation, the definition is generic and enables coverage of both. More importantly, however, it locates the level at which participation takes place in organizations.

Salamon (1992) makes a further distinction between forms of participation: ascending participation, which seeks to protect the interests of workers and extend their influence into a wider range of decisions, and descending participation, which is initiated by management for its own purposes, which may transfer authority and responsibility to workers.

The definitions of participation may change over time, depending upon the context in which the process takes place. The next section will review developments in participation and involvement processes from a British perspective. For convenience of analysis, these developments are discussed in the context of the 1970s, 1980s and 1990s. It is important to note, however, that at the end of each decade, the processes discussed did not simply cease to exist, but can usefully be thought of as developing as waves which ebb and flow into the next context, the processes of which emerge into revised forms of participation to suit developing organizational needs (Ramsey, 1977). To illustrate this, a diagram showing the comparative importance of the main processes is shown at the end of the next section (Figure 3.1, page 121).

Background to developments in involvement and participation processes

The development of large, complex and centralized organizations with remote management led workers increasingly to question the unilateral decision making often used by managers. Early processes of participation normally developed in the form of joint consultation committees at workplace level. Employees were represented indirectly, by elected representatives, to provide workers with some means of influencing managerial decision making. These forums expanded rapidly in the late 1940s and into the 1950s, particularly as a result of nationalization and an expanding public sector. The priorities of trades unions for these representatives were to develop organization, communication and negotiation processes with management (Clegg *et al.* 1961).

The priority for many workplace representatives of 'blue collar' unions was to safeguard the earnings of union members, which led to the rapid expansion of formal and informal collective bargaining over remuneration and working arrangements. Organization (recruitment of new members) and negotiation (formal and informal productivity bargaining) took precedence over communication to the membership on matters that concerned them over and above these issues. Later, Jenkins (1958) identified five employee rights which unions sought to obtain on behalf of their members. Included here were demands that workers should have a say both in workshop management and in higher-level policy making, and he further suggested that workers' representatives should sit on the board of an enterprise.

During this period there was a rapid expansion of trade union organization and membership, but also that of the labour movement more generally, with corresponding increases in influence. For example, in 1948 there were 735 unions with 9.4 million members and a density of 45 per cent. By 1975 this changed to 470 unions with 12 million members and a density of 51 per cent. This led to a corresponding expansion in the functions of personnel departments; personnel officers emerged as custodians of the rules and regulations which surrounded the employment relationship.

The 1970s – consultation and collective bargaining

The furtherance of the aims identified by Jenkins largely remained unfulfilled until the 1970s. Two issues were of concern. Firstly, the UK joined the European Economic Community (now European Union) whose draft Fifth Directive proposed that employee representatives were appointed to represent workers on the boards of companies. Secondly there was a recognition by trade unionists that union organization and representation arrangements had not extended employee influence to decisions at boardroom level. In response to these pressures the then Labour government set up a committee of enquiry to make recommendations which would promote employee involvement in decision making.

The Bullock Committee Report (1977) made recommendations for employee representatives and shareholders to sit on a company board of directors to encourage what was viewed as industrial democracy. Decision making on the board would be shared so that all board members including employee representatives would take ultimate responsibility for company decisions. This approach recommended by Bullock saw trades unions as central to a representative, indirect participation process, where employee representatives received their privilege from statute. The implication of this approach was that existing arrangements of managing employee relations through participation processes of collective bargaining and joint consultation were unsatisfactory. However, concerns were expressed by trade unionists, employers and others about the Bullock recommendations. It was suggested that:

● Trade unions could become incorporated into the managerial decision making process, which would make it difficult for them to resist decisions at a later date. Unions, it was argued, should remain independent.
● Confidentiality may hinder the effectiveness of worker representatives, i.e. commercial in-confidence information.
● There might be conflicts of interest between the management and union role of worker representatives.
● The representatives would lack training and business experience and therefore would not understand the issues they were asked to consider.

In 1979 an incoming Conservative government decided not to enact the legislation. The predominant organization and job design of the time, coupled with industrial unrest, amplified into a climate of mistrust. 'Us and them' attitudes prevailed, with a consequent reduction in formal cooperation between managers on the one hand and employees on the other. Meanwhile, informal cooperation at workplace level would continue, provided it was in the interests of both parties to do so. Overall, however, organizations were pluralist in outlook where sectional interests prevailed.

The 1980s – team briefing, quality circles and gain sharing

The 1980s saw a change in approach. The conservative government provided a climate which was hostile to industrial unrest. Trades union power was reduced by the decline of traditional industries, rising unemployment and restrictive labour laws. Where industrial action was taken, a number of significant defeats led to a depressed labour movement and contracting trade union influence. The relative decline in trade union power saw a corresponding rise in the influence of management. Macho management and increasing turbulence in the business environment meant a retreat for trade union organization and union-centred participation processes.

Developments in technologies and the influence of Japanese management techniques filled a communication vacuum created by the inadequacies and diminishment of previous practices. The quality circle and problem-solving group arrived to create new forms of participation. Harmonization of terms and conditions of employment for all employees reduced barriers between management and workers. There was also a growing recognition by management that previous modes of job design were unlikely to sustain industry in the face of increasing business competition (Purcell, 1995; Sisson *et al.*, 1992). To prosper, organizations would need a committed workforce, who would work to company objectives in a partnership with managers. The need to challenge traditional pluralist organizations and create a more unitarist approach, a sense of teamwork, to managing people was therefore at the heart of this sea change.

The 1980s saw initiatives for involvement and participation processes move from trade union/management-sponsored processes, to processes which were more managerially controlled. The decentralization of organizations and their management damaged bargaining arrangements and union-sponsored communication channels. There was a decline in trade union membership and influence. For example, in 1985, trade union membership had fallen to 10.7 million members with a density of 41 per cent. Significant defeats for the National Union of Mine Workers during the mid-1980s created a different outlook for employee relations. The language changed from that of militancy, shop steward representation, employment rights and productivity bargaining to that of moderation, team briefing, quality circles and profit sharing. Reporting on Quality Circles, a survey by Bradley and Hill (1987), reported that the initiatives tended to be short lived and the processes collapsed early. It was also reported that quality circles increased a worker's job satisfaction, improved team working and team spirit. There were also improvements noted to productivity and product quality (Dale *et al.*, 1992). It was also reported, however, that there failed to be any changes to the overall attitude of workers who were part of a quality circle (Bradley and Hill, 1987).

These new approaches provided forums where employees were more directly involved in the dissemination of information and in providing feedback into the managerial system. These processes were not without their managerial critics. For example, middle managers complained that they were unwelcome burdens in an already taxing job and that circle meetings could jeopardize departmental production targets (*ibid*). In team briefings, managers would typically pass onto their work groups information with which they themselves had been provided by a senior. The cascade system of team briefing bypassed the traditional communication channel of trades unions through shop stewards whose influence was reduced further. At the same time, the legitimacy of the manager's role as an authority figure was reinforced through positional and informational power. At the same time the loyalty of employees to the company could be enhanced through the regular meetings of work groups to discuss common issues of concern. Finally, financial involvement through share option purchase schemes or profit-sharing arrangements created added interest for employees. Such processes created notions of an organization as one team rather than us and them. It was during the late 1980s that the American term human resource management began appearing in the UK amid suggestions that organizations needed to become innovative in their approach to managing people if they were to survive in an increasingly competitive product market.

The 1990s – involvement and participation processes

Deregulation and decentralization of collective bargaining arrangements have continued and attention has been given by government to developing an enterprise culture (Sisson *et al.* in Hyman and Feriler, 1992). An ACAS survey in 1990 concluded that:

- there had been an increase in the extent of consultation in recent years;
- many employers and workers shared a belief that consultation brings rewards to both;
- formal techniques of consultation and communication are more likely to be used in large organizations than small ones;
- unionized establishments are likely to discuss a wider range of issues than non-unionized ones, especially where the company was foreign owned.

The report also highlighted overlaps between those issues handled by consultation and those handled through negotiation.

With the encouragement of an enterprise culture has come a range of initiatives to improve the efficiency of organizations. For example, variations on the quality circle concept became common, business process re-engineering or revamped work study is in vogue, and hearts and minds campaigns, company conferences and sophisticated communications systems are linked with packages to provide individual recognition for outstanding service to the team and the organization.

The decline in trade union membership continued and in 1994 membership had fallen to 8.3 million. In addition, unions were continuing to merge into larger alliances and in 1994 the number of trades unions had also fallen to 243, a reduction of 492 since 1948.

In 1993 a survey of organizations identified four distinct groups of participation processes (Marchington *et al.*, 1993):

1   Direct communications. Face-to-face communications by managers, including regular briefing sessions, company newspapers and employee reports.
2   Problem-solving groups, designed to tap employee knowledge and opinion either in a group situation or as individuals.
3   Financial employee involvement, attempts to link specific areas of the reward package to the performance of the unit or enterprise.
4   Representative participation on joint consultative committees.

The survey noted that forms of participation with the same name would operate differently in different organizations and concluded that just because one type of participation process worked well in one organization, it did not mean it would have the same effect in another (Marchington *et al.*, 1993). To the above list and in accordance with McGregor's definition presented earlier, we can add the process of empowerment, a 1990s buzzword, which will be discussed later. Furthermore, a 1996 survey highlighted that organizations generally use more than one method of communication, one process of participation, or one method of employee representation. The survey concluded that the most common methods used are team briefing, company journals and collective bargaining. Moreover, all organizations believed that communications in the surveyed companies had improved with the introduction of these processes (Employment Trends, 1996).

Involvement and participation in Europe

To date discussions have reviewed developments in employee involvement processes in the UK. Throughout Europe, countries have developed their own patterns of involvement processes, in response to the industrial traditions of their country. A recent report concluded, however, that participation in the UK was worse on average than in other European countries (IBM and London Business School, 1996). The EPOC project on direct participation found that there were many differences in the level of interest and forms of participation process used in member states of the European Union. The project does not examine, however, the types of process used in European organizations but extracts information at a higher level, to assess the likelihood of direct processes being extended. For example, in Austria, Finland, Greece, Luxembourg, Portugal, Spain and Sweden, both employers and trades unions thought that direct participation was of low relevance and importance. In Denmark, Germany, Great Britain, Ireland, Italy and the Netherlands, both employers' organizations and trades unions thought that direct participation processes were of increasing importance to industrial relations processes. In France and Belgium, there was decreasing interest in the process from employers' organizations, but increased interest from trade unions (Geary and Sissons, 1994).

In 1996 the European Works Council Directive came into force, which places obligations on organizations which operate in more than one member state of the European Union. Large companies with more than 1000 employees overall, including at least 150 employees in two or more member states, must comply with the directive to disclose information to employee representatives and to establish a forum where an exchange of views and the establishment of dialogue between employee representatives and central management can take place. According to the European trade union confederation, 'the councils provide a major opportunity for the establishment of social dialogue in multi-national companies. Once mutual trust has been established and once the preconditions for dialogue have been fulfilled . . . then agreements on topical subjects, such as vocational training, equal opportunities, job protection and so forth can be made' (ETUC, 1995). The point of the directive is to ensure that the views of employees are taken into account and included in the decision-making process of the company. For example, a report in 1995 showed that 185 American-owned multinational companies would be affected by the European Works Council Directive. The organizations themselves must also bear the costs of setting up the arrangements for the council.

The Conservative party view of the works council proposals can be gleaned from the following statements reported in the press. 'The proposed European works council directive embodies a concept which is alien to the UK tradition and would be incompatible with British information and consultation practice' (M. Howard). This was echoed by Mr Portillo who said, 'they (works councils) are irrelevant and likely to stifle job creation . . . it is putting a pistol to the heads of business' (reported in the *Guardian*, 1995). The present Labour administration is likely to adopt a more sympathetic approach and made a manifesto commitment to sign up to the Social Chapter. This would mean the government would commit themselves to agreeing to all existing and future directives. Finally, the European Union has indicated its desire to extend the Works Council Directive to establish works councils at national level. This could prove problematic for the UK, as there are no obvious mechanisms which could facilitate the process.

Summary of main points

From the above discussion it would seem that in spite of mixed reviews about the benefits, there is a continued interest in maintaining participation processes in organizations. The processes have moved from worker directors as full members of a company board to works councils which are more of a consultative process. The next section will examine how participative these processes are, to assess their worth in involving employees in decision making and the extent to which workers have real influence over decisions. Direct processes such as company journals, suggestion schemes and promotional videos have been excluded as they are predominantly one-way communications aimed at passive employees. Financial participation has been excluded from discussions too, owing to the remoteness and individualization of the process.

For employees, how participative are participation processes?

This section will attempt to 'measure' the amount of participation that takes place in certain processes, by making an assessment of the extent to which employees can influence decision making. To do this, Pateman's model will be used, in that the length, depth and breadth of each process will be measured, where:

● Length is the number and range of people involved in the process.
● Breadth is the range of issues which are discussed or information disclosed in the process. Breadth may range from issues within a single workplace to issues at the same level from a different part of the organization.
● Depth is the extent to which workers can influence decisions. This will consider the level of decision making which may range from workplace level (low) at one end of the scale to boardroom level (high) at the other end of the scale.

The processes taken are as follows: joint consultation, collective bargaining, team briefing, quality circles, empowerment and works councils. The comparative importance of these processes is shown in Figure 3.1.

Joint consultation committees (JCC)

This is an indirect, descending form of participation. A process where employee representatives meet with management representatives to discuss issues of mutual interest. The agenda is set jointly by the nominees and is normally chaired by a manager. Managers make the final decisions on issues discussed and take responsibility for the decisions they make. In terms of length, the number of people directly involved is relatively small, although all workers have an opportunity to be represented, as both union-affiliated and non-union representatives may be delegates to the meeting. The breadth of information disclosed may be narrow or wide; it would depend upon the level of trust and management style of the organization. As previously discussed, there is an indistinct boundary around

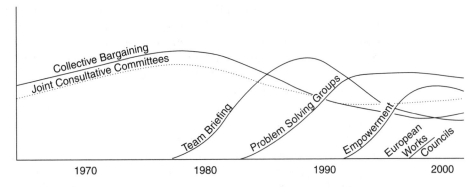

Figure 3.1 The comparative importance of different employee involvement and participation schemes. *Source:* Adapted from Marchington *et al.*, 1993.

the issues covered by a JCC and, say, collective bargaining. Issues dealt with in JCC meetings tend to be those which are not considered important enough to be handled through collective bargaining processes. Finally, for depth, employees can use influencing power only; the forum is not for negotiations and managers have the final say in making decisions.

Collective bargaining

This is also an indirect, ascending form of participation, but is limited in participation to recognized unions and/or associations. Elected worker representatives negotiate with representatives of management to reach agreement on a wide range of issues. The process of negotiation and agreement may take place formally through meetings arranged for the purpose, at work site, division, company or national level. Formal meetings will produce a formal written outcome, which may affect both working arrangements and terms and conditions of employment. If reaching an agreement is in the interests of the parties, the process may also take place informally, within individual workplaces. The outcome of these encounters may not produce written agreements, but may in some way affect the behaviour of the parties within a workplace. Change in behaviour may be temporary or permanent, depending upon the will of the parties. Parties to the agreement are jointly responsible for implementation of agreements, which once finalized, will affect the whole workforce, not just those directly involved with the negotiations, but the precise coverage will depend upon bargaining structure and scope. For enforcement, all agreements reached are voluntary.

In terms of length, there are relatively few people involved in the process of formal negotiation. At the informal level, more people may become involved in reaching agreements, therefore the process becomes more meaningful to them. For workers, once a proposed agreement is made, all of their constituents may have a voice in its acceptance, hence in this case there is considerable length; however, this may be achieved impersonally through a ballot, which may make the process seem distant and the role of individuals unimportant to the overall outcome. Considering breadth, there seems little. Decisions about company policy, plans and their implementation are taken elsewhere. Questions about the business more generally, for example site closure, transfer or expansion, are not normally considered within this forum, albeit there are rules laid down about information disclosure in the event of redundancy. It is employment conditions only that are at issue. As for depth, there may be some depth in that the outcome of decisions are agreed jointly; real decisions are made between the parties but this may be over a limited range of issues. The process would suggest that it encourages employee input into decision making and decisions made are jointly agreed between the parties. Central to the process is the uncertain environmental context in which decisions are made, which will affect the influence which managers or employee representatives bring to the process. Ability to negotiate is also dependent on the information available to the negotiators. The balance of influence must remain on the side of managers.

Team briefing

Team briefing is a direct form of descending participation, which managers initiate for their own purposes. It is essentially a cascade system, where information is passed down the hierarchy of the organization by managers to subordinates at team meetings. Employees discuss with their managers the proposals or decisions and their implications for their part of the organization. Managers can then pass back to their seniors employee comments about proposed initiatives, which may or may not be taken into account when final decisions are made. In terms of length, the number of people involved in the team briefing process is high. All employees receive information as it affects them, as all work teams will be involved in the process. For breadth, the information disclosed may be narrow or wide, depending on the organizational climate and the issue involved. Considering depth, it is difficult to gauge the impact that employee feedback would have on decision making. The nature of the system would suggest that it is managerial influence that dominates decision making in this process.

Problem-solving groups (quality circles) and their derivatives

A direct, ascending form of participation. Originally developed to encourage workers to resolve product quality issues at the point of production. Teams of workers would meet to discuss how to improve quality, which by implication would involve them in discussions about the ways in which work was organized. Circles could be either instigated by management or set up voluntarily by workers. Meetings may be held in paid working time or outside of normal working time, with or without payment. The meetings relied on the product knowledge and ingenuity of workers to improve organizational efficiency.

Many companies have derived their own systems, based upon the quality circle idea, but under a different name. The length of participation may be great as the processes could involve everyone in an organization. The nature of the system, however, means that it is essentially small groups of workers who meet in isolation from other groups. This can add an element of competition into the workplace, as groups strive to make changes which have the greatest impact. Problem-solving groups have an artificial life, which may end once a problem issue is resolved, but may recommence if other issues arise.

This discontinuous process can affect the coherence and effectiveness of the participation process overall. For breadth, discussions are limited to a team's own workplace, and issues of concern to them. There would seem to be little influence over the policy, plans, or macro issues of job design. For depth, workers do make decisions about micro issues of job design, but these may or may not have an impact on the overall system of work. Decisions taken by the work group to make improvements need the agreement of managers before implementation. Once agreed, the decision is arguably a joint one between the work group and manager; however, managers may reserve the power of veto.

Empowerment

Empowerment is a process of participating in the management of an organization, rather than the administration of routine tasks. The purpose of empowerment is to free people from rigorous control by instructions and orders and give them freedom to take responsibility for their ideas and actions. This is intended to release intellectual and organizational resources that would otherwise remain inaccessible (Whipp, 1993). Where empowerment has proved successful is in delayered organizations. People willingly take on additional duties and responsibilities for which they may or may not receive additional financial rewards. People are provided with broad policy guidelines to work within and overall objectives of performance to be achieved. The achievement of these objectives is then left to the work group responsible for them. Managers monitor the situation from a distance, through regular reviews and management information systems. The work group gradually takes ownership of the service they provide, which can generate tremendous loyalty to the service and their colleagues.

In terms of length, if empowerment is associated with delayering, then everyone in the organization is likely to be involved. The potential for length is high, but it would also mean a radical change to a traditional management style. For breadth, the issues may be as narrow or wide as the whole group responsibility. For depth, decisions within limits are taken by the work group over a wide range of work or service delivery issues.

European works councils

An indirect, descending form of participation based upon the process of consultation originating in Germany and the Comitée de Groupe of France. The process will only affect large multinational companies with operations in more than one member state of the European Community and subject to certain qualifying conditions. The objectives of works councils are to improve the right to information and consultation of employees in Community-scale undertakings. The aims of the works council directive are to ensure that the point of view of the employees is taken into account and included in the decision-making procedures of the central management of a company.

The councils are not negotiating bodies, although in Germany they may perform this function. The works council is made up of representatives of both management and employees from all parts of the company across Europe. The size of the council may vary, for example in 1995 the Elf Aquitaine council had 54 members while Bull had 29 members. Employee membership of the council will be through elections and the frequency of their meetings will vary, according to rules agreed between the parties. It is too early to say how councils will develop; theoretically we can, however, take a view of their impact.

In length, there is indirect representation of employees' views across the European organization to senior management, hence there is wide indirect participation. For breadth, the issues discussed are intended to be a full exchange of views on a wide range of issues, including company policy, finances, future plans and market trends, expansion and closure plans, employment issues and relocation and redundancy (this is not an exhaustive list but provides an indication of the issues) (EIRI, 1995). The discussions are clearly about a wide range of issues which affect the whole company, hence there is considerable breadth. In terms of depth, it is unclear to what extent the council will exert influence over managerial decision making, concerning the issues identified above. It may depend upon the organized reaction by workers to managerial proposals, to test the situation regarding depth.

Summary of main points; How involved and how participative?

The discussion here has questioned the amount of influence over decision making that employees obtain from some common forms of involvement and participation processes. The processes of participation discussed here bear passing resemblance to the theoretical models of Rousseau, Mill and Cole in that some are direct processes and others are indirect.

The involvement of employees, to undertake what amounts to special problem-solving projects (quality circles) in their workplace, may give a sense of freedom and some measure of control over their actions. The members of problem-solving groups may have little economic differences between them, but the amount of influence exerted by team members may vary according to personal skills and perceived seniority.

Empowerment is associated with devolved management, in lean organizations, where there may be few alternatives other than to give people low in the hierarchy the opportunity to undertake activities from which they would normally be excluded. The process of empowerment individualizes employees. During the empowering process, which it may be argued is an extended form of delegation, they may feel unable to resist or be carried along if everyone else accepts the opportunity to become empowered.

For briefing sessions the process is essentially top down. There may be individual attendance at briefings, but the level of participation is questionable. There may also be considerable economic difference between the briefer and the briefed, which will detract from the process of providing open feedback. There will be little sense of freedom for staff as the agenda is set by managers. Control remains on management's side. These processes are nevertheless managerially sponsored structures.

Of the trade union/employer-sponsored processes discussed here, for ability to influence, joint consultation lies at the 'low influence' end of the spectrum and collective bargaining towards the other. The agenda coverage of each overlaps. With the expected greater information disclosure through the works council process, this may prove to influence decisions most. In these processes there may exist economic differences between representatives of management and employees, but the roles taken are different. Employees taking the role of trade union representative may feel a degree of freedom to put a case more effectively and exert greater influence over the process.

Table 3.1 Summary of the process of participation in relation to the theory and key aspects of definitions

	Type of participation scheme in use					
	Collective bargaining	Joint consultation	Team briefing	Problem-solving groups	Empowerment	European Works council
Direct individual participation			✓	✓	✓	
Indirect representative participation	✓	✓				✓
People are forced to be free				✓	✓	
The system becomes self-sustaining	✓	✓	✓	✓	✓	✓
Workers have a voice in management	✓			✓		
Organized groups present	✓	✓	✓	✓	✓	✓
Ascending (A)/ descending (D) form of participation	A	D	D	D	D	D
Length high/low	L	L	H	H/L	H	L
Depth high/low	H	L	L	H	H	H/L
Breadth high/low	H/L	L	H/L	L	L	H/L

Indirect forms of participation, because of the nature of the system, remove the majority of people from the centre of the process, i.e. the meeting. Participation at its best takes place by mandating representatives, which is participation by proxy. The process may allow apathy to creep into place and it therefore relies on the employee representatives continuing to generate and maintain interest in the process themselves and in the constituents they represent. Next, we turn to the links between participation processes and psychological contracts. A matrix which summarizes the process of participation in relation to theory and key aspects of definitions is shown in Table 3.1.

Involvement, participation and psychological contracts

In many organizations, for example Rover, a range of communication, involvement and participation processes are used alongside one another. Ascending, employee-oriented and descending, management-sponsored processes operate side by side. Rover therefore operates traditional collective bargaining processes alongside problem-solving groups. The process of direct involvement through company-sponsored schemes may have a more powerful influence than indirect involvement in employee-oriented schemes. In the literature, each system tends to be discussed as a separate issue, but when these processes are used in parallel, a cumulative effect may occur. This may encourage workers to identify more closely with their organization.

As with other behavioural issues, a situation which has a positive behavioural effect on one person may not have a positive outcome for another. Perhaps the beauty of a 'scatter gun' approach to the use of participation systems is that the process an individual chooses to buy into is a matter for that individual. The operation of these processes, however, is not without its problems. They may, for example, have a shelf life, and need to be periodically reviewed to retain their appeal. Nevertheless, we cannot ignore the combined effects of environmental

CASE STUDY
Unipart Ltd

Unipart is the former parts division of British Leyland Motor Corporation. It was subject to a management buy-out in 1990 and, led by the vision of its Chief Executive, has transformed itself into a highly successful organization. At the heart of this transformation was a change to employee attitudes and organization culture, created by a revised management process which included the use of involvement and participation processes.

In 1992, the company ended the long-standing trade union recognition agreement which they had inherited as part of British Leyland and moved the company from a predominantly pluralist outlook to one of unitarism. The company generated a mission statement and introduced a suite of sophisticated participation processes including:

- In place of the union-oriented structures, an employee forum was created for consultation purposes.
- In addition, the company conference, an annual event held off site, allows the directors of divisions to review achievements of the last financial year and present plans for the future. It is normal for all employees to attend this event.
- A company video is produced bi-annually, which may be borrowed by any employee. The video contains a collection of key initiatives in the form of a news and current affairs programme, to update staff on achievements.
- A company journal, *The Update*, is regularly published and circulated to all employees. Any

employee can write an article for publication. The journal gives profiles of staff and their achievements too.
- 'Our Contribution Counts Circles', a process where employees form themselves voluntarily into problem-solving groups to improve operations. Groups are open for all staff to take part. Presentations of findings are made to the Chief Executive or senior board member. Successful groups are presented with an 'Our Contribution Counts Award' at the end of the project.
- 'Mark in Action' awards, where employees nominate another member of staff for the award for providing an outstanding example of customer service.
- More recently, the company has opened its own fitness centre, the 'Lean Machine' which employees and their families can use.
- The completion of the Unipart 'U', the company university, which provides a library, open learning materials and interactive on-site facilities for staff to improve their skills. This can range from numeracy and literacy to high-level management skills.
- The company slogan, which can be seen on the sides of its larger vehicles, is 'Yesability'.

Here, a whole range of both indirect and direct participation processes have been used to transform a company once held in the shadow of British Leyland into a well-respected organization in its own right.

uncertainty and managerial processes designed to draw an employee's mindset into identifying more with his or her employing organization than with employee-sponsored bodies who offer only limited resistance and influence.

Turning back to Rousseau, perhaps it is the psychological effects of descending participation processes, the by-product identified earlier, which places a set of obligations in the minds of both manager and employee, that accounts for the continued interest in using them. The development of a psychological contract relates to an employer's need to have an enthusiastic and motivated labour force and the employees' wish for psychological rewards such as a sense of achievement, responsibility, recognition and opportunities for advancement (Herzberg, 1966).

Direct forms of involvement, especially empowerment and problem-solving groups, can expose a large number of employees, who may undertake humdrum routine activities, to opportunities where they can gain a sense of achievement from improving their lot at work. It is through direct and personal involvement, where employees see they can influence decisions, that the psychological influence takes place. In such circumstances, managers encourage their staff to take responsibility for generating ideas and implementing solutions, for which they receive recognition in their own workplace, among colleagues and, through internal publicity, the whole organization. Participation processes, Rousseau contends, reinforce themselves and generate a sophisticated set of expectations and rules, which forms the psychological basis for the continuing commitment of an employee to an employer (Rousseau, 1989). Both the employer's and the employees' expectations help form the contract; for example, problem-solving groups may decide to meet after working hours for which staff are not paid nor obliged to attend.

The whole notion of participation is that managers give up some control on their own terms and hand it over to their work team and individuals. Enhanced perceptions of distributive justice are likely, due to choice based on the attraction of outcomes, and enhanced perceptions of procedural equity result, due to increased individual choice. The reciprocal extension of trust and discretion creates a social exchange of obligations extending beyond those in the economic exchange of the employment contract. Furthermore, Blauner noted that the amount of control that an individual has over his or her work and environment is crucial to a worker's psychological orientations. The notion of employee control, however, may be illusory, but the psychological effects of this illusion may help develop employee commitment to the company cause (Blauner, 1960). As Dale identified, it is not so much the economic benefits which accrue to an organization from the quality circle but more the social aspect, which is why they continue to be sponsored (Dale and Plunkett, 1992).

Three ways of viewing participation processes

The continued popularity of participation processes suggests they are perceived as adding value to workplace organization. This can be viewed in three ways:

- *As a means of generating commitment.* This perspective emphasizes the joint problem-solving approach which runs through many of the participation processes discussed here. This tends to incorporate employees into the management process of the organization, which in turn encourages them to identify more with their employing organization than, say, a trade union. When coupled with other techniques such as an overall unitarist style of managing, development of a high trust relationship and open communication systems can create a positive effect on workplace relations.

- *As exploitation of workers by management.* This perspective emphasizes labour as a commodity to be bought by management as agents of the organization. A manager's role is therefore to extract as much surplus value from the labour process as possible by encouraging workers through various means to work harder. Participation schemes contain an element of supervision, they encourage workers to solve problems that were once the domain of managers and supervisors, and permit more senior managers to reorganize work, often cutting out tiers of supervisors as a cost saving to the organization. Problem-solving groups create competition between workteams to produce solutions to organizational issues. These tensions encourage participation by introducing new group norms that in turn create innovation, at little cost to the organization, from which potential benfits are derived. Additional surplus value is extracted through the labour process at little or no cost to management.

- *As a means of encouraging workplace learning.* Participation processes tend to be centred at workplace level, involving groups of workers in problem-solving activities. Generating solutions to ongoing workplace problems encourages dialogue over issues known to workers within a particular context. In many cases, resolving workplace problems requires creative thinking and generation of new ideas from a common starting point. To create new ways of working, have ideas accepted and then implemented through collaborative working involves workers learning more about their workplace, their organization and collaborative working skills. In time, this creates a Community of Practice at a workplace which is responsible for generating and utilizing of new knowledge which is located within the workplace (practice community) (Lave and Wenger, 1995).

Conclusion

Employee involvement and participation appear in many forms and each of these has its own particular strengths and weaknesses: the need to locate various approaches within the context of developments in employee relations within a local and national context and the resolution of the tensions between the need to be 'heard' of employees against the desire for control of managers and employers. Decisions about the degree of individual and collective contributions to involvement and participation have, in many organizations, been the result of bargaining between employers and their representatives and employees and theirs (often for the latter, via the trades unions or staff representations), reinforced or weakened by employment law. However, there are a range of involvement and participation processes that lie outside of this 'representative participation' approach, such as briefing sessions, problem solving groups and financial employee involvement, which is less collective and pluralistic and more individualistic and unitary in nature. The success of any approach in large measure depends upon the organization and those managing the processes.

Moves within the European Union to increase worker democracy and social dialogue through for example, works councils, may challenge some of the long held employee relations traditions in countries such as the United Kingdom. However, such proposals not only highlight the options available to organizations, but also the need to take into account the culture, traditions and expectations of organizations as a factor that may aid or undermine the likely success of any particular approach.

CASE STUDY
Oxford Radcliffe Hospital

The Oxford Radcliffe Hospital is a District General Hospital which provides a range of acute and specialist services. The trust employs a total of 5000 staff on two sites which are about two miles apart. The trust has the largest accident and emergency department in the country, which is open for admissions through the year. In response to the resource management initiative, the trust has introduced a devolved management structure. Organizationally the trust has divided operations into 76 service delivery units (SDUs) where multidisciplinary teams of staff provide patient services. Each SDU is headed by a senior professional or consultant called a clinical director who is responsible for all aspects of service delivery. The clinical director takes responsibility for medical matters. Each clinical director is supported by an SDU manager, normally a nurse, who takes responsibility for the day-to-day management of all nursing, administrative and clerical staff. A number of SDUs that deliver complementary services form a clinical centre which is headed by a consultant called a clinical centre chair. Clinical centre directors are supported by a clinical centre manager, an accountant and a personnel manager. There are 12 clinical centres in the trust. Management of the trust overall is through a series of committees, which are: a trust board made up of clinical centre chairs, chief executive and directors of finance, personnel, business development, medical and nursing directors; a clinical centre board made up of clinical directors of SDUs,

SDU managers, clinical centre manager, accountant and personnel manager.

Each clinical centre operates semi-autonomously in that it decides its own development plans and manages within broad trust guidelines. Each SDU also decides its own development plans and manages personnel and finance issues within guidelines set by the trust. Development plans are proposed by staff in SDUs and form proposals which are considered by the trust for implementation. All staff are given opportunities to contribute to this process. Decisions concerning expenditure are taken at SDU level, as are decisions concerning all aspects of patient care. Twice each year all staff are given the opportunity to question the chief executive about future plans of the trust. An in-house newspaper keeps staff informed about current issues. Directors in the trust operate an open door policy and any member of staff can see any director about issues that concern them.

The trust has a joint consultative committee and recognizes trades unions to consult and negotiate on behalf of staff. Recently, under increased financial pressure, the trust issued a directive that only cost-saving or cost-neutral development plans would be considered for future developments. This has had a restrictive effect on staff at SDU level who are unhappy with the trust's stance on expenditure. In addition to this, the accident and emergency policy creates extra pressure and makes it difficult to control expenditure. It also interferes with planned episodes of patient care.

Summary

This chapter has argued that participation processes used in organizations have limited effect in providing employees with real opportunities to influence high-level managerial decision making. The processes that provide such access seem in decline. Decisions that employees are able to influence tend to be at a (workplace) level low in the organization and centred around an employee's immediate job role. If organizations receive a variable, economic benefit from the process, then we must search for other reasons for their continued popularity. Looking to the by-products of participation processes, it was noted that the processes are self-sustaining and have a psychological effect on those who take part. The processes can therefore form the basis of a powerful control system. They can contain conflict, by diverting the attention of workers from agitating about imperfections in the work process by channelling their skill and energy for the common good of a company. Participation processes therefore are predominantly top-down, managerial-oriented systems, which support the development of a psychological exchange of obligations between the company and the employee, which will encourage employees to become committed to organizational goals.

Questions

1 What are the key differences in the involvement and participation policies of Unipart and the Oxford Radcliffe Hospital?
2 Identify any problems with the present involvement and participation processes at
   (a) Unipart
   (b) The Oxford Radcliffe Hospital.
3 What changes would you make to the participation process at these companies to improve their effectiveness?
4 What are the advantages and disadvantages of manning a company which uses participation processes and
   (a) recognizes trade unions for consultation and bargaining purposes;
   (b) does not recognize trades unions for consultation and bargaining purposes.
5 Examine each of the following participation processes from a unitarist, pluralist and radical perspective.
   (a) Collective bargaining
   (b) Industrial democracy
   (c) Problem-solving groups
6 Develop a rationale to support a unitarist approach to participation and involvement, using ethical theory to support your assignments. Do the same for a pluralist approach.

References

ACAS (1990) *Communication and Consultation*. Occasional Paper No 49.

Batstone, E, Boraston, I and Frenkel, S (1979) *Shop Stewards in Action*, Blackwell.

Blauner, R (1960) Work Satisfaction and Industrial Trends in Modern Society. In *Labour and Trade Unionism* (eds Galenson, W and Lipset, SM), Wiley, New York.

Board of Trade Report of the Committee of Enquiry on Industrial Democracy (Bullock Committee) HMSO, 1977.

Bradley, K and Hill, S (1987) Quality circles and management interests. *Industrial Relations*, **26**(1).

Dale, BG *et al.* (1992) The process of total quality management. In *Managing Quality* (eds Dale, BG and Plunkett, JJ), Phillip Allen, London.

Clegg, HA, Killick, AJ and Adams, R (1961) *Trade Union Officers*, Blackwell, Oxford, p. 181.

Cole, GDH (1920) *Guild Socialism Restated*, Leonard Parsons, London.

EIRI (1995) European Works Council Report, July, Dublin.

Employment Department (1994) *The Competitive Edge; Employee Involvement in Britain*, London Employment Development Group.

Employment Gazette, Various issues for statistics.

Employment Trends (1996) *Assessing employee involvement strategies*. Industrial Relations Services, 614, August.

ETUC (1995) Guidelines on Implementing the EWC Directive.

Fox, A (1975) *Man Mismanagement*, Hutchinson.

Geary, J and Sisson, K (1994) Conceptualising Direct Participation in Organisational Change. The EPOC Project. Dublin. European Foundation for the Improvement of Living and Working Conditions.

Hertzberg, F (1966) *Work and the Nature of Man*, World Publishing.

Hyman, R (1975) *Industrial Relations, A Marxist Introduction*, Macmillan.

IBM Consulting Group and the London Business School (1996) Made in Europe: A Four Nations Best Practice Study.

Institute of Personnel and Development (1990) *Employee Involvement and Participation in the United Kingdom, The IPM Code*.

Jenkins, C (1958) The insiders. A supplement of *Universities and Left Review*, 3, Winter, 59–60.

Lave, J and Wenger, E (1995) Situated Learning: Legitimate peripheral participation, OUP.

Liebenstien, H (1978) *General X Inefficiency Theory and Economic Development*, OUP, New York.

McGregor, D (1960) *Human Side of the Enterprise*, McGraw Hill.

Marchington, M, Wilkinson, A and Ackers, P (1993) Waving or drowning in participation. *Personnel Management*, March, IPM, London.

Mill, JS (1910) *Representative Government*, Everyman.

Open University, Case Study Video featuring 'Suma' Healthfoods of Leeds. OUP.

Pateman, C (1970) *Participation and Democratic Theory*, Cambridge University Press.

Purcell, J (1995) *Corporate Strategy and its Link with Human Resource Management*. A critical text. Ed J. Storey, Routledge.

Ramsey, H (1977) Guides to Control, Worker Participation in Sociological and Historical Perspective. *Sociology*, Vol. 11, No 3.

Rousseau, JJ (1913) *A Discourse on Political Economy*, Everyman

Rousseau, DM (1989) Psychological and implied contracts in organisations. *Employee Responsibilities and Rights Journal*, 2.

Salamon, M (1992) *Industrial Relations*, 2nd Edition, Prentice-Hall.

Sisson, K, Waddington, J and Whitson, C (1992) *The Structure of Capital in the European*

Community and the Implications of Industrial Relations. Warwick Papers in Industrial Relations, No. 38, University of Warwick.

Sisson, K *et al.* (1993) in *Industrial Relations in the New Europe* (eds Hyman, R and Ferner, A), Blackwell.

Storey, J (1992) *Human Resource Management: Still Marching on or Marching Out in Human Resource Management.* A critical text ed. J. Storey.

Whipp, R (1993) Reported in The Real Meaning of Empowerment. *Personnel Management,* November.

Legal briefing

A. Employees' rights to information and participation

The traditional UK preference **for** voluntary negotiation (and therefore **against** statutory compulsion) is one of the more striking differences between the industrial relations regime in the UK and that in other EU member states. This cultural difference with its deep historical roots explains, at least in part, the initial opposition in the UK to extensions of employee rights by legal compulsion.

The present state of the law is dealt with under two heads.

(i) Rights of independent, recognized trades unions.
Independent, recognized unions are free of financial or other dependence upon the employer and are recognized by the employer for purposes of negotiation. Such TUs have a limited statutory right, granted under the Trade Union and Labour Relations (Consolidation) Act, 1992, to certain information from the employer. The purpose of the information is to extend and enhance collective bargaining. The right to information is not unlimited; the union must show that the disclosure required is 'in accordance with good industrial relations practice' and that, without it, its power to negotiate effectively in the collective bargaining process will be 'seriously impeded'. Employers are not obliged to give union representatives access to original documents, or even copies, but can prepare a package of information of their own devising. Information can be withheld completely if disclosure would involve a breach of confidence to a third party, or would involve risk to commercial or national security. Remedies for non-compliance by the employer are very weak, and do not involve any order to provide the information required.

A union may report an employer's failure to disclose the required information to the Central Arbitration Committee. This is almost the last function remaining to that body. The complaint may be referred on to ACAS, if there is a realistic chance of a settlement being reached. In the last resort, CAC may make an award relating to the terms and conditions of employment of relevant employees of the employer concerned, and these terms will become enforceable as part of their individual contracts.

It is interesting to consider why the late Conservative administration left this provision on the statute book; it was thought that giving TUs access to relevant financial information would result in more 'realistic' wage demands.

A great boost has been given to the role of independent trades unions by the Employment Rights Act, 1999. These provisions came into force on 6 June 2000. For the first time in 20 years, such unions may, in certain circumstances, **require** recognition by the employer for the purposes of collective bargaining. This will be limited to the topics of pay, hours and holidays, unless the parties agree otherwise.

Any independent trade union can apply for recognition from any employer employing 21 or more employees. (Please also see the legal briefing to Chapter 8 on small businesses.) Clearly, such a trade union must command the support of the majority of appropriate employees, to be known as the 'bargaining unit'. If the employer refuses recognition, the union can apply to the Central Arbitration Committee (CAC) for a declaration. The role of the CAC, which has been dwindling over the years, has received a great boost by this legislation. If the CAC is satisfied that the majority of workers in the 'bargaining unit' are members of the union making the request, then a declaration will be made

Continued on page 134

that the union is entitled to recognition by the employer for the purposes of collective bargaining on the topics specified above. If the CAC is not satisfied as to the percentage of union members involved, it will require a secret ballot of the appropriate workforce before a declaration is made.

Once a declaration has been made that a trade union has been recognized to conduct bargaining on behalf of the bargaining unit, the parties must agree a procedure, failing which, the CAC has power to impose a procedure which will be legally enforceable against the parties.

There are complicated provisions relating to derecognition by the employer. If the agreement is voluntary, the employer can terminate it after three years from its implementation. Presumably, this will only be a practical proposition on the part of the employer if the trade union membership of the employees in the 'bargaining unit' has demonstrably fallen below the threshold number. Where the agreement has been imposed by declaration of the CAC, de-recognition can only take place with the consent of the union involved or after an application to the CAC to hold a ballot on the question.

The collectively bargained terms will become, as is usual, incorporated into the individual contracts of workers comprising the 'bargaining unit'. These waters have been somewhat muddied, however, by the incorporation of a new provision by the House of Lords late on in the Employment Relations Bill's passage through Parliament. It allows employers and individual employees to agree 'individual contracts'. This would have the effect of taking the employees involved out of the collectively bargained terms and allowing them to negotiate better ones. There is already a law in place disallowing discrimination against employees on the ground of trade union membership: could this new provision be seen as a contradiction? One must await the outcome of future challenges before the courts. Another uncertainty is whether such 'exempted' employees will be counted as part of the 'bargaining unit' in the 'numbers game' that will inevitably accompany the fight for compulsory recognition.

(ii) Information to, and consultation with, employees
In this context, 'employees' includes their 'representatives'. There is a provision in the Companies Act, 1985, that in all companies employing more than 250 persons there is an obligation placed on the directors to disclose in the directors' annual report the steps taken during

the preceding year to provide information to the employees 'on matters of concern to them'; to consult the employees, or their representatives so that their views may be taken into account in decision making; to encourage the participation of employees in company performance through employee share schemes and the like; and to bring about a 'common awareness' on the part of the workforce of the financial and economic factors affecting the performance of the company. It should be noted that the obligation put upon the directors is to report what has been done; it would be in strict accordance with the present law if it were stated in the annual report that nothing of this sort had been done. This state of affairs is likely to change in the future, with the present administration expressing greater sympathy with European ideals of worker participation – but see comments in the next section on EU Works Councils.

The Companies Act also requires directors to have regard to the interests of employees as well as those of shareholders when taking decisions. This is a 'toothless' provision, because there is no right conferred upon employees or their representatives to enforce this obligation.

The 'enforcement authority', as with the bulk of the Companies Act, consists of the shareholders at a general meeting. In the absence of a sizeable number of employees with voting rights, or a sizeable number of 'employee directors' on the board, the chances of enforcing this obligation are thin. The question of employees on boards of directors will be expanded upon below.

B. The EU works councils directive

This is the successor to the 'Vredeling' proposals relating to information to be supplied to employees in multinational companies. It provides for a European Works Council in Community-scale enterprises (not necessarily companies) for the purposes of informing and consulting employees. It applies to large-scale enterprises with at least 1000 employees within the Community, and at least 150 employees in each of at least two member states. The previous UK government preferred the more traditional, informal approach, and negotiated an 'opt-out' from implementing this Directive. This optout is purely territorial in its effect. Holding companies registered in the UK and UK subsidiaries of European holding companies are exempt; European subsidiaries of UK holding companies are, however, caught by the

Directive. Given the multinational character of these enterprises, it would be strange if the management were to implement a regime of information and consultation for employees in their establishments in continental Europe, and exclude establishments in the UK. Indeed, there is evidence of European-style Works Councils established, albeit on a voluntary basis, in a number of UK companies, including United Biscuits and Coats Viyella.

In keeping with the philosophy of the new Labour administration, the 'opt-out' has now been overturned, and the European Works Councils Directive will be implemented within the UK. There is a certain degree of discretion allowed regarding the 'special negotiating body' which must be set up, and the Directive does not apply at all where there are, at the date for its implementation, procedures already in place for information and consultation covering all employees.

In a new development, reported in *The Times* newspaper of 5 June 1997, the EU Commissioner for Social Affairs proposed the extension of European Works Councils to all establishments with more than 50 employees. The indications are that if this idea is developed, it will be opposed by the UK government.

C. The fate of the 5th Draft Company Law Directive

It seems generally agreed that this Draft Directive, which has been going the rounds for more than 20 years, is unlikely to see the light of day. Too many governments, not only that of the UK, have found at least some of its measures objectionable. Despite this, it is worthwhile to mention its existence because its original proposal – that of employee representation **as of right** on boards of directors of large companies – may surface again in a different form some time in the future.

D. Health and safety – involvement of the workforce

The Health and Safety at Work etc. Act, 1974, introduced a a number of important new features into the law of health and safety at work. One aspect that has remained unchanged is the employer's implied obligation under the contract of employment to provide a 'safe system of work'. This obligation is not absolute, but is based on the taking of reasonable care. It is for breach of this implied legal duty that employees injured

at work claim compensation from their employers. The 1974 Act is a 'penal' statute – that is, it provides for criminal penalties, in the form of fines and imprisonment, to be inflicted for failure to take care to provide a 'safe system'. Again the obligation is not absolute; running through the Act like a refrain are the words '. . . as far as is reasonably practicable'.

The main changes in approach which mark this statute out from, for example, the Factories Act, 1961, and the Offices, Shops and Railway Premises Act, 1963 (both of which, incidentally, remain in force), are the following:

- **all workers**, except those working in domestic premises, are covered by the Act;
- the establishment of a Health and Safety Commission to integrate the administation of the various Inspectorates;
- cooperation with, rather than coercion of, employers is seen as conducive to greater health and safety in the workplace;
- involvement of the workforce in these matters by the appointment of safety representatives and safety committees.

This last point will be expanded upon later in this section.

The Act is very wide-ranging. It covers:

- the employer's general duty towards those in his or her employment;
- the employer's general duties towards those who are not in his or her employment, including contractors on his or her premises and members of the general public;
- pollution of the atmosphere;
- a duty imposed upon those who design, manufacture, import, supply or install any article or substance for use at work;
- an individual employee's duty to take care for his or her own safety and that of others;
- a duty on all persons not, intentionally or recklessly, to interfere with or misuse any safety equipment.

Obligations are placed upon responsible individuals as well as upon the employer.

All employers are obliged to publicize, in writing, a safety policy.

Involvement of the workforce in health and safety
Health and Safety Inspectors have the right of entry and

Continued on page 136

inspection of premises, other than domestic premises, where they reasonably expect that people are at work. They have the right to arrive unannounced, but in line with the 'cooperative' approach referred to above, the 'dawn raid' is a rarity, and generally confined to employers with a history of breaches of the law, or where confidential information has been received.

Where an accident that must be reported under the Act has occurred, the inspectors attend as a matter of course. In other cases premises will be routinely inspected, and if unsafe practices are found, an improvement notice or prohibition notice will be issued (depending upon the perceived danger to those working) which gives the employer a limited time in which to put matters right.

The Act has provided machinery for health and safety matters to be monitored by employees. Originally independent, recognized trades unions had the sole statutory right to appoint safety representatives from among the workforce. Employers have a duty to consult with these representatives about matters of health and safety, and to allow them reasonable time off with pay to attend training sessions. Since 1996, however, as a result of a judgement of the European Court of Justice, the consultation process in health and safety matters (and, indeed, in any other matter) may no longer be confined exclusively to representatives of trades unions. The wider workforce is entitled to be involved. The employer is obliged to establish a safety committee if requested to do so by the representatives. The representatives may carry out inspections of the workplace at least every three months. It is an interesting legal point to consider for whom the representative is working while carrying out his or her health and safety duties. This becomes important if the representative is injured in these circumstances; if it could be argued that as he or she was not engaged upon the employer's business at this time, he or she may not be covered by the **employer's** obligation to provide a safe system of work and hence not by the employer's liability insurance policy. It is a wise precaution for a safety representative to enter into an agreement with the employer which states that inspections are carried out on behalf of **both** the union **and** the company's safety officer.

Dismissal of safety representatives in connection with their carrying out of their duties, or, indeed, of anyone who refuses to work in dangerous premises, is regarded as 'automatically unfair'. This is discussed in the legal briefing to Chapter 1.

E. The European dimension

Article 118A of the Treaty of Rome now renumbered Article 137, lays down a general policy that member states should pay particular attention to the improvement of the working environment, especially in the matter of health and safety. This Article paves the way for specific laws to be framed in this area, and it has, in fact, given rise to a number of Directives on the subject which have been incorporated into UK law. Of these, the most important has been the 'framework' Directive and its five 'daughter' Directives. In response to these, six Regulations came into force in the UK on 1 January 1993. The most important are listed below.

● *Management of Health and Safety at Work.* These Regulations are wider and more detailed than the general duty imposed by Health and Safety at Work Act, 1974. Amongst other things, they require a 'risk assessment' exercise to be carried out in certain situations, information to be given to workers, and the appointment of competent and suitably trained persons to implement the health and safety laws. These Regulations were updated in 1994 in order to implement the Protection of Pregnant Workers Directive. They now require, in appropriate circumstances, the assessment of risk to the health and safety of new or expectant mothers. Further, in line with this last mentioned Directive, the Maternity (Compulsory Leave) Regulations, 1994, prohibit the employment of any woman entitled to maternity leave to return to work within two weeks of giving birth.

● *Personal Protective Equipment Regulations.* Employers must ensure that protective equipment is provided for employees where they may be exposed to a risk to health and safety while at work. The same obligation extends to the self-employed. This provision is not enforced where there are in place effective alternative means of protection. Since 1995, the EU has harmonized the standards of safety equipment put on the market, and it should now carry the 'CE' mark, or equivalent.

● *Manual Handling Operations Regulations.* As far as is reasonably practicable, an employer is obliged to avoid the need for employees to undertake manual handling operations at work which involve a risk of injury. Where some risk is unavoidable, the employer is required to reduce it to the lowest reasonably practicable in the circumstances. The same obligations are imposed with regard to the self-employed.

- *Health and Safety (Display Screen Equipment) Regulations*. The employer is required to assess the risks to the health and safety of VDU operators and to reduce them to the lowest extent that is reasonably practicable. This will include adequate training and the offering of eye-sight tests.

F. The EU Working Time Directive

Among the extraordinary features of the EU legislation is the following: while changes to 'employee rights' require the unanimous consent of all the governmental representatives in the Council of Ministers (hence the 'opt-out' negotiated by the late Conservative administration), health and safety law can be introduced on the basis of 'qualified majority voting'. That means that reforms can be imposed on any national government against its will. This was not considered a problem, as the UK government has a good record of introducing EU health and safety measures. However, the Working Time Directive was issued, not as 'employee rights', but as 'health and safety'. The ECJ refused to allow the appeal by the UK government against this classification, and so it had to be implemented. It came into force 1 October 1998.

Restricting hours worked, particularly by adult male employees, has been rare in UK law. Miners working at the coalface and drivers of public service vehicles are examples. The Directive requires a maximum average working week of 48 hours, including overtime, a minimum daily 'rest period' of 11 consecutive hours, and rest periods during the working day to be agreed by collective bargaining, or to be imposed by legislation. There must be at least one whole day's rest during the week which would normally include Sunday. There are controls on the amount of night work that can be done. In general, the Directive requires that the organization of shift work and monotonous assembly-line work should take into account the affect such work may have on the health of the employee. The legal briefing for chapter 9 will discuss the effect of stress at work on the health of employees.

Each employee has a right to four weeks paid holiday a year which may not be commuted to payment in lieu. This requirement may be reduced to three weeks as a transitional measure during the first three years of the operation of the Directive.

There are exclusions from the operation of the Directive. There is a complete exemption for air, rail, road, sea, inland waterway, fishing and other work at sea, and doctors in training*. In addition, individual states can enact their own exceptions, or 'derogations', in 5 areas:

(i)   workers with a degree of control over their own time, such as managers;
(ii)   where strict controls are inappropriate to the type of work, such as those in emergency services, the media, research and development;
(iii) shift-workers – but under regulations or collective bargaining, and with compensatory rest periods;
(iv) exceptions can be agreed by collective bargaining, regardless of the type of work;
(v)   for a limited period of seven years from 23 November 1996, when the Directive was passed, it will be permissible for individual exceptions to be granted where an employer has obtained the employee's agreement to work longer than the permitted maximum. This exception will be reviewed after seven years. In the first case to be brought on the Directive, five pit deputies working for RJB Mining alleged that pressure had been applied by the employer to get them to agree to longer working hours. The judge gave a strong judgement in favour of the employees.

* There is a move to *include* trainee doctors.

G. Breach of confidence and covenants in restraint of trade

Employees owe a duty of confidence to the employer. They may not use for their own gain, or pass on to another person, confidential information that has come into their possession in the course of their employment. Information that is truly confidential exclusively belongs to the employer, and misuse will automatically put the employee in breach of the employment contract. It is sometimes unclear precisely what information exhibits these characteristics, and so it is often advisable for the employer to protect his business by means of a covenant in restraint of trade. This involves a term in the employment contract restricting the commercial and employment opportunities available to the employee after he or she has terminated his or her contract with the employer. These have to be used with great care as will be explained below.

Continued on page 138

Breach of confidence

Information obtained in circumstances of confidentiality cannot be used by the recipient without the authority of the 'owner' of the information. The situation arises in a number of ways in the commercial or industrial context.

Certain industrial processes, for example, are operated without an application for a patent, relying instead on secret working and the trust reposed in the employees; in other cases, an employee's work may give him access to his employer's customer list and pricing policies. In all of the above instances, there is a contract between the parties, and while the contract is still in existence, there is a duty upon the employee not to disclose the information to any unauthorized person or to use it for his own gain. This will include, as in the 19th century case of *Robb* v. *Green*, the copying-out of names and addresses of customers which the employee proposes to use for his own gain after terminating his employment.

This leaves the problem of the employee who terminates his employment to take up another post, or to set up in business on his own account, who carries away confidential information **in his head**. The problems raised by former employees in this position were discussed in the 1987 case of *Faccenda Chicken Ltd*. v. *Fowler*. The defendant had been a sales manager for the plaintiffs, setting up a door-to-door delivery service delivering chickens to customers. After he had been dismissed, he set up his own business, delivering chickens to customers' premises. He targeted his former employer's customers, recruited its staff and used his knowledge of customers' requirements, pricing policy, etc. The trial judge, upheld by the Court of Appeal, divided information held by employees into three categories.

(i) information that is in the public domain and which can be freely disclosed; this would include information already published in the press, a specialist journal or on the register at the Patent Office;

(ii) information which is confidential during the course of the employment, but which the employee is free to use after the employment is terminated, for example, *basic* manufacturing processes or customer information that he carries in his head;

(iii) trade secrets properly so-called which the ex-employee is not free to make use of and which are regarded as confidential even after the employment is terminated.

Fowler had only used information in category (ii) and for his own commercial purposes. He was not, therefore, in breach of duty towards his former employer. The Court left open the question of what the result might have been if Fowler had composed the customer list from memory, and sold it on.

The main lesson from the *Fowler* case is that employers should make more use of covenants in restraint of trade. These are dealt with in the next section of this 'briefing'.

Not only employees and former employees find themselves subject to the law of confidentiality. Recipients of such information, either knowingly or innocently, may find themselves subject to legal sanctions if they attempt to use it for their own benefit or disclose it for any other purpose. This will include the former employee's new employer.

There is the 'safety-net' of the 'public interest exception'. This operates to protect employees, former employees and third party recipients of confidential information where disclosure is made in the interests of the public. An example would be where the confidential information reveals that a serious breach of the law has taken place, or is about to take place, or a serious threat is posed to public safety. Disclosure 'in the public interest' is not confined to the extreme cases cited above, and each case will be decided upon its own facts. In a number of instances, the 'informer' has taken the information to the press instead of to the 'proper' authorities for dealing with such matters. There does not seem to be, at present, any official discouragement for this kind of revelation.

Please refer to the legal briefing to Chapter 1 with reference to the Public Interest Disclosure Act, 1998.

Covenants in restraint of trade

A term in a contract of employment prohibiting an employee from working for another employer (not necessarily a competitor) during the currency of his present contract is normally enforceable by the employer. Even where there is no such specific term, an employer may be able to restrain an employee from working for another employer during the notice period laid down by the contract, even where the employee has been allowed to give shorter notice or has taken payment in lieu. This is what is quaintly termed 'garden leave'.

What is meant, however, by the term 'covenant in restraint of trade' is the right of the employer to place restrictions upon the employment opportunities of employees after they have left. Such clauses are basically anti-competitive and therefore regarded as contrary to public policy and potentially void. Similar clauses restraining business opportunities are also to be found in a wide variety of commercial contracts.

These clauses, if challenged, are subjected to a 'reasonableness' test before they can be declared valid and operable. Courts are particularly vigilant in this regard in the case of employment contracts where it is recognized that the parties are not normally on an equal footing when the contract is made, and where it is considered to be in the public interest for workers to be free to exercise their skills for remuneration wherever, and for whomsoever, they wish.

For such a covenant to be upheld, the employer must demonstrate that he has a 'proprietory interest' to protect. This might consist of secret working, or special lists of customers who might be wooed away by an employee who had personal dealings with them. An employer may not insert such a clause simply to protect himself or herself against competition from a former employee, or to discourage skilled staff from leaving. Faccenda Chicken Ltd., in the case quoted above,

could have protected itself from the erosion of its business at the hands of a former employee by putting such a clause in his contract. It would normally be the case that such a clause was in the contract at the outset of the employment, but there has certainly been one case where a court upheld the imposition of a covenant in restraint of trade some time after the employment had commenced: *R.S. Components* v. *Irwin* [1974], where the court held that in the special circumstances of the case, the employer had a 'substantial reason' for dismissing an employee who refused to accept this change to his contract terms.

In addition to establishing the existence of a 'proprietory interest' and the fact that the employee in question can inflict substantial damage to the business, the employer must also ensure that the actual restraint imposed is not too wide in terms of time or area to protect his legitimate interests. If a former employee is found to be breaching his covenant, and successfully claims in his own defence that it was drawn too widely, the employer will be left with no protection whatever. The court has the power to strike down such a clause on the grounds of public policy; it has no power to rewrite it so that it can be legally enforced.

Performance management: strategy, systems and rewards

4

Nelarine Cornelius and Larraine Gooch

Learning objectives

After studying this chapter you should be able to:

- understand how managing employee performance can be tackled from a strategic perspective;
- understand the importance of developing holistic, coherent perfomance management systems;
- identify ways in which line managers can effectively manage performance in a number of ways, including the use of performance appraisal systems;
- understand how remuneration and reward strategies should be developed, and how such strategies can help or hinder other HRM activities;
- outline a range of approaches for the effective management of individual reward;
- outline a range of approaches for the effective management of team reward.

Introduction

Effective performance management can make a major contribution towards the achievement of business objectives while maximizing the contribution of employees. Moreover, appropriate use of performance appraisal systems within a performance management system can provide valuable assistance in supervising and developing staff within work teams also.

Too often, there is a gap between what organizations preach and what they practice. The result of this gap is not only that it is often difficult to find 'hard' evidence of a demonstrable link between employee performance and organizational performance in 'measurable' terms, but also what it is claimed is happening according to the policy breaks down once the policy is put into operational practice. The latter may be due to a variety of factors, including lack of training, poor guidelines, apprehension or cynicism about the organization's motivation for evaluating performance.

In spite of these possible difficulties, there are potential benefits of effective performance management that it would be unwise to overlook. The first is that it can lead to better information exchange, more open communication between employee and manager, can help greatly to clarify organizational, managerial and employee expectations and highlight actual and potential shortfalls in performance. This not only allows all involved to have a clearer picture of where they stand but, if managed well, can also exert a positive impact on employee motivation. Secondly, one of the reasons for the abundance of company guidelines in this field is that specific aspects of performance management fall under the remit of employment law, and it is easy for the line manager to get it wrong. Furthermore, there are many examples of employees who feel that they have been differently and unfairly treated relative to their peers and have sought legal redress.

We will cover some of the key objectives of, and terminology used to describe, performance management systems, consider how to establish performance aims, objectives and targets, and how to monitor performance at all levels in the organization. The focus will then move towards approaches to appraisal, before moving on to consider briefly employee development needs as an outcome of the appraisal process. Throughout, attention is paid to the design, administration and management of such procedures. The management of poor performance and unacceptable behaviour is considered in chapter 5.

A key aspect in relation to performance, that of **reward management**, is addressed. We will explore ways in which effective strategies for managing reward can and should be developed, and outline the misconceptions and limitations of what manipulation of these strategies can yield for the organization and employees.

Therefore, in this chapter, performance management is considered *within an overall organizational context* which extends beyond staff appraisals and paying employees. Attention is paid to aspects of practice which, irrespective of the system of performance management, need to be understood.

Performance management in context

An increasing number of companies have installed performance management systems. In a survey by the Institute of Personnel and Development in 1987 (cited in IPD, 1992) it was discovered that 97 per cent of organizations utilized such a system. Unfortunately, many systems fall into disuse once implemented. To retain the effectiveness of the system it is important that the aims of the system are clear to everyone who is asked to use it. The system needs to be visibly owned and used as a management tool by all managers in their day-to-day activities and not be seen as an annual performance review cycle only. Moreover, employees need to be clear about the potential benefits for them.

Clearly, collecting and communicating the information generated within performance management systems is a cost for any organization. However, if used correctly, the expense will be offset by the benefits to the organization in terms of the contributions the information generated can make to business planning, managers will be helped in their day-to-day jobs through monitoring arrangements and individuals will feel they also buy into the process through increased development and reward opportunities. The more open a performance management system is, the more successful it is likely to be in the long term. For staff this means fairness and consistency of operation across the company with equal access to development opportunities.

Performance management provides a means of getting improved results from the organization, departments, work teams and individuals by understanding and managing performance within an agreed overall framework. Performance management is a broader approach than staff appraisal in that it consists of a systematic approach to the achievement of organizational objectives by providing an interconnected set of goals which link at organizational, departmental, work team and individual levels.

The performance management process normally encourages continuous and regular informal and formal feedback to individuals, work teams and departments. Moreover, the resulting organization-wide findings are an important source of **management information**. Monitoring performance enables any corrective managerial decisions and action to be taken. The system also enables managers at all levels to identify the performance of work groups and individuals for which they have a direct responsibility, which in turn provides the potential for **recognition of group and individual achievement as motivational and developmental** and improves relations between managers and staff at all levels also.

This is achieved by increasing levels of clarity about what is expected of groups, individuals and managers in relation to each other's role, duties and responsibilities, which is an inherent part of the system. As a by-product of this, communication and problem-solving processes can also be improved. This in turn can generate positive and constructive relationships across the organization as people become focused on how to perform their roles more effectively, to their mutual benefit.

Figure 4.1 shows how corporate, departmental, work team and individual objectives are linked through a hierarchy of objectives to strategic plans. The system operates as a loop with objectives and targets being distributed from corporate level to departments and people. These objectives and targets are structured to enable everyone in the organization to contribute effectively towards the achievement of corporate objectives. Information to monitor progress against plans is provided via monitoring arrangements and interim targets which are fed back up the organization to enable any corrective decisions to be made. The accuracy of goals and monitoring arrangements are important as they help to maintain the effectiveness of the system at all levels. The performance management process should not be a bolt-on system, but an integral part of managing employees and producing more rounded management information systems.

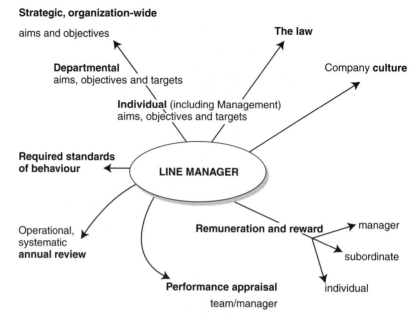

Figure 4.1 Performance management: line manager considerations.

Managing performance at different levels in the organization

There are different levels at which evaluating employee performance can be undertaken. These include the following:

● **Performance of the entire 'HR system'** and the interrelations between specific systems and sub-systems. For example, how effective is an organization's HR strategy and what is the contribution being made by it to securing general corporate strategic objectives? The primary concern is **how these strategies will influence employee effectiveness in the organization as a whole**. The aim here is to establish an *overview* of the effectiveness of employee performance and the organization-wide management of human resources within a strategic framework.

● **Performance of specific HR sub-systems**. Here, the focus of attention is on specific HR sub-systems, such as staff development or recruitment and selection policy and practice: what are the strengths and weaknesses of these? For example, how effective are recruitment and selection procedures and practice, and what are the implications of the strategy for training and development for new and existing employees?

● **Performance of specific departments**. One way of gauging the strengths and weaknesses in the management of employee performance in an organization is by comparing and contrasting the performance of specific departments. Inter-departmental comparisons for common performance criteria may reveal not only employee effectiveness but also indicate how effectively or ineffectively employee performance is being addressed by line managers.

- **Team performance**. Specific teams may have tasks for which they have a permanent or a short-term responsibility. One needs to consider how best to evaluate and reward team performance.
- **Individual performance**. Most of us will have had some experience of being appraised or having to conduct an appraisal. How appropriate, fair and well managed are appraisals and how can their reliability and relevance be improved?

In the broadest sense, performance management in human resource management involves **the establishment of minimum standards of work performance and required standards of behaviour**. 'Performance' is concerned with the achievement of specified outcomes. It is the organization's role, facilitated via the HRM department and the line manager (sometimes in collaboration with employees), to identify the means by which an organization can facilitate the achievement of desired outcomes. Ideally, performance management should help to facilitate *improvements* in performance also. Central to effective performance management is the **long-term perspective** (beyond the annual cycle of staff appraisal or pay review) which should centre around **proactive strategy** setting and the development of a range of activities which will assist in the achievement of acceptable performance (including such demonstrably developmental line manager activities as mentoring and coaching).

In Figure 4.2 a broad outline is provided of the territory that is encompassed by the term performance management. In this chapter, there is a brief discussion of HR system and sub-system aspects of performance management, as this provides a useful framework in which to locate more local, operational aspects.

The downside of performance management

A number of criticisms have been made against the practice of performance management. It could be argued that some of the ideas underpinning performance management are grounded in very manipulative views of employees. Specifically, the employee is viewed as merely an 'economic animal' who can be motivated largely through the manipulation of rewards systems. Others are concerned that too many organizations have performance management systems which are out of touch with reality (e.g. Fletcher, 1993). For example, appraisal schemes are often designed, driven and policed by the HR department in a mechanical fashion. This may work modestly well in stable bureacracies. However, they are less well suited to flatter organizational structures and more dynamic business environments in which cross-functional management, team working and flexible working are increasingly the norm. Another anecdotal criticism is that schemes can be used to manipulate employees in a negative sense, where power plays and the manipulation of appraisal and associated rewards are misused carrots and sticks to make employees do what the manager wants them to do, whether or not it is reasonable or desirable, with little attention paid to the views of employees.

However, to downplay the vital role that effective performance management can hold in not only improving but, indeed, turning around employee performance would be to throw the baby out with the bath water. As mentioned earlier, there is an increasing awareness that organizations should attempt to monitor

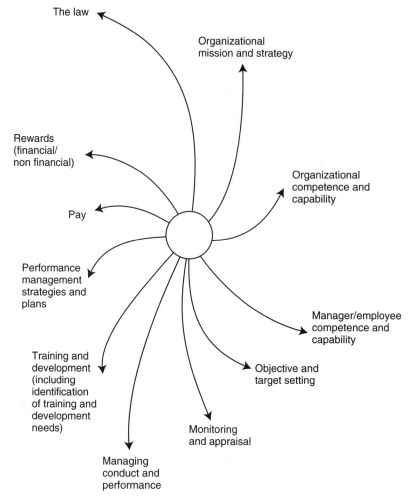

Figure 4.2 The terrain of performance management.

routinely the link between employee performance and strategic performance, and also that employee communication and motivational gains can be made. Furthermore, line managers are increasingly expected not only to take *direct* responsibility for the appraisal of their staff and the improvement of staff performance but also may have the freedom to determine levels of pay and bonuses. Irrespective of the criticisms rightly made of the manner in which performance management is sometimes viewed and administered, the reality is that it is an area of management in which line managers are often *expected* to take a lead.

Performance management and strategy: developing measures of performance

An **organizational strategy** details the direction pursued in the long to medium term, against a desired future state. The strategy may be deliberate or emergent in nature. It is achieved through major resource mobilization and organization-wide, cross-functional coordination of activities, often outlined in a plan of action to make the vision a reality. Commonly, strategic decisions often affect the product market (or in the case of non-profit organizations, the client–activity mix) of an organization.

One of the ways in which strategic effectiveness can be assessed is through the development of **corporate performance indicators**, which form part of the basis for **corporate performance assessment**. From this, there is the idea that organizations need to present a 'balanced scorecard' in which softer measures such as customer satisfaction are seen as important in the evaluation of the performance management of an organization, along with the traditional financially driven performance indicators. Increasingly, annual reports include information on non-financial performance indicators to complement traditional company performance measures, especially around employee costs, the HR aspects of quality management, and innovative activities.

Therefore, **HR-based corporate performance indicators** are increasingly being recognized as valuable by management accountants as one of the ways in which an organization's strategic performance can be assessed. Performance management in this context is concerned primarily with the manner in which human resources are contributing to the improvement of organization-wide performance so that strategic objectives can be pursued and specific strategic outcomes secured. So, for example, it may be that an organization's service delivery systems are being revitalized in order to remain at the forefront of customer care practice amongst its competitors and, importantly, to be seen as an organization for which customer care is important by the customers buying its goods and services. It is the HR component of this that is securing new attention.

Beyond the corporate-wide performance indicators that might appear in the annual report, how well are an organization's human resources being managed and to what extent can improvements be made to this management in order to secure or improve results organization-wide? A review of the HR strategy *per se*, over and above set performance indicators, is likely to provide an indication of this.

Within an HRM context, determining how over time the HR organization-wide strategy fits with other functional strategies, such as the marketing and financial strategies, is also an important measure of performance. At its most basic, this might entail determining whether specific plans for succession, recruitment and retirements have been effectively outlined and addressed, the sorts of activities that lie in the traditional remit of manpower or **human resource planning** (HRP). We can define HRP as securing a workforce (from labour markets outside and within the organization) with the appropriate skills, knowledge and expertise, while maintaining adequate levels of staffing in the short and longer term in the light of internal promotions and increases or decreases in employee numbers associated with, for example, expansion, downsizing or retirements. However, it is equally important to assess the contribution made by HR inputs of one kind or another directly to the achievement of strategic objectives. For example, how did employee performance on the shop floor contribute to increase in sales and what were the HR policies and practice that made this a reality?

Most importantly, a strategic perspective can provide a framework in which more operational but equally vital systems performance management can be developed and evaluated (Figure 4.3). Therefore, an effective performance management strategy can provide a means of getting improved results from the organization, departments, work teams and individuals by creating an **overall framework** across the organization of planned targets, objectives and standards of performance. Within this, a systematic approach to the achievement of organizational objectives is more viable, as an interconnected set of goals which link at the organizational, departmental, work team and individual levels is provided. This is not to suggest that these goals never come into conflict, but it does imply that much can be gained from a common understanding of what an organization aspires to. If teams or individuals do not have accurate guidance on the required performance to aim for, it can lead to inappropriate decisions being made at higher levels of the company, ambiguity about what people are expected to achieve and staff demotivation because of anxiety over the lack of clarity about what they should achieve.

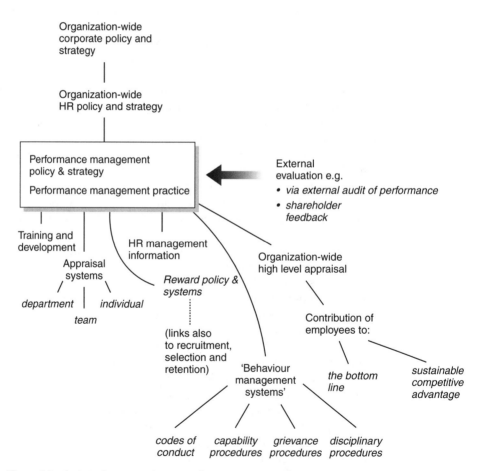

Figure 4.3 A strategic perspective on performance management.

Overall, confusion over what is expected may create dissatisfaction and frustration among staff, which in turn may lead to a loss of trust and confidence in management. The responsibility to contribute effectively within a performance management system therefore results in everyone who works within the framework being under the scrutiny of others (directly or indirectly), both managers and the managed. Responsibility and accountability can be increased for all staff by concentrating people's efforts on those activities most important for the achievement of strategic plans.

Performance appraisal: the balance between employee and management inputs

Organizational and management culture and climate play an important role in determining the approach to performance appraisal that is developed, deemed acceptable, or both. One aspect of managerial culture which is likely to be particularly influential is the degree of managerial control that is considered desirable, be it officially or unofficially. The range of options loosely mirrors that of the kind of **communication style** that is viewed as appropriate given the culture, and broadly encompasses and reflects **different degrees of manager and employee contribution and control of the process**.

- **Top-down** approaches where there is a high degree of managerial control and limited employee inputs to the assessment of their performance. Employees are essentially **told** what assessment their line managers have made and do not make any contribution to their assessment.
- **Tell and listen** approaches in which line managers still maintain primary control of the assessment process but during a formal meeting such as an appraisal interview, employees are able to comment on the findings. Employee comments are taken on board as part of the assessment.
- **Joint assessment** approaches in which managers and employees assess employee performance independently, which usually includes completing pre-appraisal meeting forms and then comparing and contrasting the findings. This may be through exchanging manager and appraisal assessment forms prior to an appraisal meeting or by discussing the findings during the meeting itself. This process centres around a **joint problem-solving approach**.

Our exploration of performance management will now centre around **tell and listen** and **joint assessment** approaches.

Performance management: overall design and issues further down the line

At the highest level one needs to consider the **design of the system as a whole**: do the elements hang together and are they appropriate given the strategy, climate and culture of the organization? However, there are a number of related operational issues that need to be considered as an integral part of the design phase also:

- **Evaluation and measures**. How defensible are the evaluation techniques within the system? What is the balance between qualitative and quantitative assessment and feedback? How valid and reliable are the assessment items, given the type of staff for whom they have been developed (for example, are you using criteria which would be suitable for managers but not for non-managerial employees)?
- **Documentation**. Are the policies and procedures written up clearly for both managers and employees?
- **Briefing and training**. Have employees and managers received adequate briefing about the performance management system? What training has been given to managers, for example, in interview skills?
- **Contingencies**. What procedures are in place for disagreements, complaints and managing poor performers?
- **Review**. How regularly should your system be reviewed, how and by whom?
- **Implementation strategy**. If you are developing a new or revised system, how are you going to manage its introduction? For example, has it been arranged to pilot the scheme? Are you going to introduce the scheme gradually or across the whole organization immediately?

There are a range of performance management systems available, but it is particularly helpful to start by considering one system in detail. The system selected is one in which there is formal collection of data for which objective setting and the development of key results areas and performance indicators are core. Systems are developed with direct connections to the corporate strategic framework and evaluation of performance is against what contributions individuals or groups have made towards taking the strategy forward. We can refer to such a system as a **strategy-driven performance management system**.

Strategy-driven performance management systems – general characteristics and controls

An important principle of strategy-centred performance management systems should be that they need to be **forward looking** and regarded as a shared responsibility between individuals and the organization. Such performance management systems often contain:

- A clear definition of what they aim to achieve.
- A shared understanding of how performance management systems operate, supported by appropriate training for those involved.

They are typically but not exclusively operated by line managers with top management support.

Factors to be measured within the system, i.e. to uphold core values and to develop staff, should be determined.

The key aims of such approaches to managing performance are to:

- provide a means which allows the company to encourage an appropriate culture of continuous improvement;

- encourage continuous review of current activities against business plans;
- provide specific links between corporate aims and individuals jobs;
- provide people with organizational 'headroom' which allows managers to identify high performing individuals.

The key to success is regular reinforcement of the aims of the process and its consistent application across the company.

The Performance Management Control Cycle

Figure 4.4 shows how performance management ensures that both the individual activities and goals of staff contribute towards the achievement of corporate objectives. Working towards the achievement of individual goals improves motivation of staff, but also monitoring progress towards goals helps management make more accurate predictions of business unit performance and more accurate and informed decisions. Performance management acts as an enabling process in motivating staff by providing

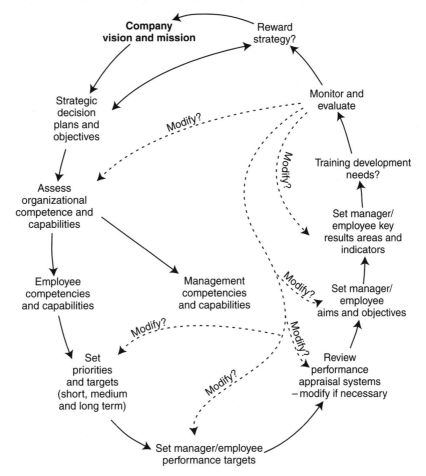

Figure 4.4   An idealized performance management cycle.

staff with opportunities to undertake specific tasks within broad parameters. Elements of supervision are therefore built into the way in which the process operates.

Managerial control is achieved using the cycle shown in Figure 4.5 which operates both informally on an ad hoc basis and formally on an annual basis in the context of performance appraisal.

A key result area is an activity or activities within a person's job where particular actions must be taken to ensure that goods are produced according to set criteria or service delivery to customers achieved to the required standards. **Key performance indicators** are quantitative and/or qualitative measures which indicate to what extent a key result area has been achieved and provide an indication of how stretching future targets or job goals should be undertaken. A key performance indicator acts like the instruments on the dashboard of a car – they provide signals to the driver about how well the engine and ancillary equipment are performing.

Key result areas and strategy centred performance management systems

Key result areas are linked directly to departmental business plans. This means that key result areas (KRAs) could include a range of activities and dimensions, for example:

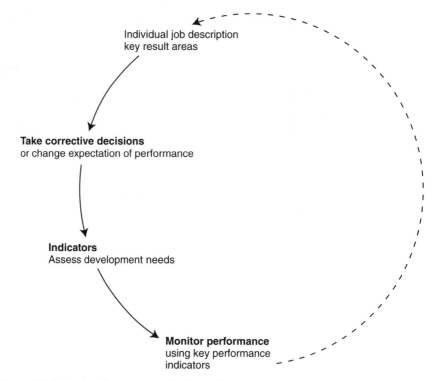

Figure 4.5   Typical performance monitoring cycle.

- Business performance targets
- Step-by-step change improvements
- Implementing self-development plans
- Development or maintenance of management practices

In isolation, KRAs are of limited use. To become meaningful KRAs need to be linked to goals which the department or individuals aim to achieve during a review period. A key performance indicator (KPI) is a description of a situation which a manager and their team aims to achieve within a given time scale and other appropriate constraints. Furthermore, the goals set should be achievable and reasonable in their complexity. Prioritization is also necessary to ensure achievement of the most important goals at the expense of others. The role of KPIs is to identify the business outputs which must be achieved in order to achieve the business plan. These outputs should be included in a manager's KRA and provide the business performance target of the KRA. It is also appropriate to include other components in a manager's KRA which may come about as a result of, say, the company's mission as an equal opportunities employer or other associated departmental goals. The advantage to managers of learning to use the key performance indicator approach is that by monitoring trends in performance it can be seen at a glance if operations are going according to plan or going awry. Management time and effort can then be targeted at the key areas of activity. Key performance indicators can be used:

- to report progress against objectives throughout the company;
- to help diagnose any causes of shortfalls in performance;
- to provide feedback loops to aid continuous improvement in business operations;
- as a basis on which to appraise the performance of individual managers.

The combination of key result areas (KRAs) and key performance indicators (KPIs) within performance management systems helps provide the means of accurately allocating responsibility for operational activities and monitoring progress towards their achievement.

- KPIs should be **Specific** in terms of the aspect of work performance to which they relate.
- KPIs should be **Measurable** in terms of quantity and quality.
- KPIs should be **Achievable** within other work constraints.
- KPIs should be **Relevant** to the aims and objectives of the department.
- KPIs should be **Time constrained**.

(In other words, they should be **SMART**). With the increasing complexity of business, however, it may not always be possible to allocate responsibility for an area of service delivery to one person in isolation from others and the balance between individual and shared responsibilities should be identified.

Goal setting and monitoring performance

Within a department the first step for setting KPIs is to establish the KRAs of the department. These will be based upon the reasons for the existence of the department in the company. The job descriptions of staff can be established in relation to the departmental objectives. Sometimes a job will have more than one distinct purpose and it will not be possible to capture it in one headline or statement. In these cases it is convenient to break down the job description of an employee into functions which may be considered as key result areas within the overall job. The job description of each person should directly contribute towards the department's KRAs.

Delegation and performance management

In Figure 4.6, it is obvious from the range of duties outlined in which the transport manager would become involved that it is unlikely that the manager could carry out all of these duties and some would be delegated to staff within the manager's work group. Some KRAs within the transport team may be allocated in their entirety to particular individuals. For example, assume that a supervisor is responsible for operations in the dispatch bay. The transport manager's KRA 'Providing effective dispatch of goods' would become the overall job role of this supervisor. The transport manager and supervisor would discuss and agree areas of performance by breaking down the dispatch bay supervisor's job of 'Providing effective dispatch of goods' into functions and develop KPIs in support of the overall job role. In this way **performance management provides *interlocking objectives* across an organization in support of corporate aims**.

Employee development-centred performance management systems

To date, we have paid attention to a strategic management-driven performance management and the characteristics of such systems. However, there are examples of performance appraisal for which the primary consideration is individual performance and development of employees. This is often encountered in organizations for which tight managerial controls on performance are less viable, such as those dominated by professionals who are likely to have greater freedom of action and expect a greater say about how they are to be assessed. As with more strategy-centred performance management systems, an assessment of performance and interventions to improve key performance areas remain, but the basis on which the dialogue between management and subordinate takes place is more likely to centre around joint problem-solving and the securing of resources on the part of the employee, not only to improve work performance but also to keep abreast of professional developments.

Case study: Westshires Transport Depot

The case consists of a company which operates warehousing and transportation activities on the site of Westshires Road Haulage Company. The reason for the existence of the operation is to 'provide an excellent internal and external transportation service to support the operation of the warehouse'. The responsibility for these activities rests with the transport manager whose job description contains the following:

Westshires Transport Depot Manager

Job Description – Duties and Responsibilities

Ensure provision of an efficient network of internal and external transport services to the warehouse complex.
Manage the effective dispatch of goods.
Maintenance and repair of the whole vehicle fleet.
Supervision of pallet control, collection and reclamation of scrap to ensure control of wastage.
Manage and control all staff within the remit of the Transport Manager post.
Maintain transport operations within budget.
Maintaining a safe working environment within these given areas of responsibility.
Any other duties falling within the scope of the grade of transport manager which from time to time may be demanded by the company.

Key Result Areas

1. Provide effective dispatch of goods.
2. Ensure maximum vehicle utilization of the delivery vehicle fleet.
3. Ensure effective internal transport services.
4. Minimize pallet loss.
5. Ensure requirements of supervision and management control are maintained while promoting and maintaining good employee relations.
6. Maximize reclaims for scrap and faulty goods.
7. Maintain operations within budget.

Key Performance Indicators for each KRA

Goals for the manager to achieve during the next review cycle. These can either be added as amendments to existing KPIs, by adding another key task to a person's existing portfolio of work, or by giving specific targets to achieve in relation to the KPIs above. Whichever method is used it is important that the KRAs to be achieved by staff are clear to themselves and their line manager to avoid subsequent confusion.

1. KRA. Provide effective dispatch of goods.

KPIs:
- Goods to be dispatched within 8 hrs of receipt of order reducing to 6 hrs in time for the next review.
- Lost consignments not to exceed 6 per annum.
- Costs not to exceed budget by more than 3 per cent/tonne/kilo reducing to 2 per cent in time for the next review.

2. KRA. Ensure maximum vehicle utilization of the delivery vehicle fleet.

KPIs:
- Fleet utilization to exceed 70 per cent/annum increasing by 5 per cent per review period to 85 per cent during the next three years.
- Maintain 95 per cent availability of vehicles/annum.

Figure 4.6   KRAs and KPIs in action.

3. *KRA. Ensure effective internal transport services.*

KPIs:
- Forklift fleet utilization to exceed 85 per cent/annum.
- Minimize goods damaged to 2 per cent of average stock holding.

4. *KRA. Minimize pallet loss.*

KPI:
- Pallet loss to be retained within 5 per cent of current stock/annum.

5. *KRA. Ensure requirements of supervision and management control are maintained while promoting and maintaining good employee relations.*

KPI:
- Production lost by industrial disputes retained at 0 days per annum.

6. *KRA. Maximize reclaims for scrap and faulty goods.*

KPI:
- All losses accountable reclaimed within warranty period.

7. *KRA. Maintain operations within budget.*

KPI:
- Operating costs retained within current budget working towards a 5 per cent budget saving over-all during the next review period.

In setting a target KPI for a manager to improve the service offered by a department, it would seem unreasonable to expect immediate improvement as certain arrangements may need to be made such as embedding into operation changes in working practices. It would seem appropriate to set interim KPIs within the overall target time to encourage gradual improvement within the department's overall target.

Figure 4.6 Continued.

Furthermore, the areas concentrated on in such **employee development-centred performance appraisal systems** highlight a limitation of strategy-driven performance management systems. Specifically, the focus on business objectives allows for coherence between strategic and individual objectives but may potentially provide limited opportunities for long-term development plans outside of this immediate remit: potentially, this could make organizations *less* flexible in the long run. Therefore, some strategy-driven schemes will also incorporate longer-term development plans in which skills and knowledge levels overall are improved, which may link only indirectly to the strategic plan but also provide for development in areas which are relevant to the job but are not necessarily immediately exploitable. Moreover, many employees are now encouraged to develop **self-development plans**, containing job-relevant but personal aims and objectives, in order that they can maintain a generic and flexible, rather than only strategy-driven, programme of development (employee development issues are discussed in more detail in Chapter 2 on training and development).

More specific approaches to appraisal

360 degree appraisal

The range of options for appraisal systems can incorporate a number of approaches within which employee feedback on management performance, upward appraisal, review by peers and ultimately, employee choice regarding how and by whom they are appraised may be incorporated, thus affecting the degree of employee influence on, and contribution to, the appraisal process.

360 degree appraisal involves the assessment of employees' but usually managers' performance by the people who work with them, including peers, subordinates and superiors in addition to self-assessment.

This can be a tricky though particularly informative form of assessment, and careful decisions need to be taken about the following:

- the **likelihood of acceptance** of such an approach (with the necessary training), given the organizational culture;
- the **design of the data collection methods**, which should allow for a complementary mix of information to be collected from the different assessors;
- **guidance for assessors** regarding completion of forms, through the use of published guidelines within a clear code of practice and **assessor training** in how to provide constructive feedback;
- **clear guidelines** regarding how the data should be analysed and presented;
- a **structured forum** such as an appraisal feedback meeting in which the results of the 360 degree appraisal are communicated to the appraisee verbally but also in writing;
- a **clear policy** regarding how to develop action plans based on feedback from such appraisals.

Many line managers may be anxious about receiving feedback on their performance from peers and subordinates. Coping with criticism is difficult at the best of times, and is likely to be particularly so if opportunities for open communication between line managers and their subordinates are not the norm. One way in which feedback can be managed is through the use of a 'neutral intermediary'; an individual who is skilled in providing such feedback but who is not a close acquaintance of either the line manager or his or her assessors. Also, the feedback can be put into context by collecting the 360 degree appraisal results for *all* managers in key areas, and then comparing individual performance against the common findings within that department or across the entire organization.

Mary Vinsom (1996) has produced a list of the difficulties that can be associated with 360 degree appraisal.

- Feedback can hurt – it needs to be carefully managed.
- Survey fatigue – appraisees may tire of having to complete large numbers of forms for all of the peers, subordinates and subordinates with whom they are associated.
- Friends of appraisees may present a flattering but unrealistic assessment in order to avoid hurt feelings.

- Evaluators are not always nice or positive and may use 360 degree appraisal as an opportunity to criticize others.
- Unless training and briefing are adequate, feedback may not be accurate, reliable or truthful.
- Managers receive the feedback – but they ignore it and nothing changes.

Vinsom has identified a number of ways in which the process of 360 degree appraisal stands a better chance of producing a change:

- Anonymous and confidential feedback, often using a specialist external consultant.
- Consideration of the length of time the appraisee has spent in the position: if it is less than six months, consider using the first appraisal as a benchmark only for a follow-up appraisal.
- A feedback expert should 'interpret' the feedback and remove all the jargon and unnecessary statistics so that it can be easily understood by the appraisee: make the feedback report 'user friendly'.
- Follow-up is an essential part of the process and action plans should be developed for 'low scoring' areas and improvements should be assessed six months to a year later.
- Written descriptions are as important as numerical ratings as feedback because they are likely to be more meaningful to the appraisee.
- Ensure that the feedback data collection method is reliable, valid and based on sound statistical methods.
- Avoid survey fatigue by not using 360 degree appraisal on too many employees at the same time.

Pick and mix appraisal

The issue of who decides upon the nature of the appraisal has been taken a step further in some organizations with the introduction of **pick and mix appraisal** (IRS 570, 1994). With pick and mix appraisal, employees are able to choose how they wish their performance to be assessed, from a range of options. For example, Mercury Communications (in IRS, 1994) introduced such an approach on the basis of survey feedback in which they found that managers and employees considered their current appraisal scheme too inflexible to cope with the rate and scale of change in the company.

A precursor to pick and mix appraisal is the **'performance contract'** in which employees have to jointly agree with their line managers:

- what the employee is to contribute on a range of work activities;
- how the employee is to achieve these contributions;
- what the company will contribute in return to the employee, in terms of training, development, support and resources.

Employees are then able to choose how their performance against the contract is assessed. The selection is made from an **appraisal portfolio** of options. Within the portfolio are **core and optional assessment tools**. At Mercury, the core tools include:

- a work objectives review (especially for higher level jobs and senior managers);
- key performance indicators;
- job-specific appraisal (with a focus on job-related factors such as complaints handling);
- a blank sheet of paper for those employees who feel constrained by forms and prefer face-to-face discussions with managers who are then required to make detailed notes.

Supplementary tools include:

- competence review;
- virtual team member review, used particularly for employees who are members of cross-functional teams, so for example a project manager review may be included in addition to a line manager review;
- a blank sheet of paper (assuming this option was not selected as a core option);
- 360 degree review.

As employees may not be familiar with some of the appraisal methods available, employee choice is assisted by providing guidance, so that it is clearer which types of assessment are likely to be the most meaningful. So, for example, it is argued that junior jobs are less amenable to assessment using key performance indicators as the main appraisal method.

Accuracy of subordinate performance rating

How accurate are the ratings that are made by employees of themselves? John Lane and Peter Herriot (Lane and Herriot, 1990) have conducted a study in which they found that self-rating appeared to predict future performance reasonably well. Indeed, they found that self-ratings predicted subsequent performance over six months as well as did supervisor ratings. Lane and Herriot acknowledge that previous experience of self-rating, even in a different job or capacity, may improve rating reliability. This suggests that preparation through appropriate training and development is likely to improve the effectiveness of the process.

Team appraisal and peer review

It may be more likely that a **team** of people may be involved in the completion of tasks. In some cases, therefore, performance indicators may measure behavioural cooperation of people within a work team too. However, it should not be assumed that team working is appropriate: it may be for quality circles but not for work which is more individualistically designed. Team working is most likely to be accepted and effective when the production of goods or the delivery of services is dependent upon a strong mutual dependence between employees, and team coherence and a strong *esprit de corps* are desirable for reinforcing this dependence.

Furthermore, if one is switching from more individualistic working to team working, there is a need to 'convert' (both manager and employee) performance management systems to accommodate this; the balance between individual and team contributions must be carefully thought through.

In a case study of self-managed groups in the Digital Equipment Corporation at Colorado Springs in the USA, Carol Norman and Robert Zwacki (1991) found that team appraisal appeared to improve participation, commitment and productivity. The need to participate is reinforced by the requirement for all team members to take specific roles and responsibilities for performance appraisals. As with 360 degree feedback, the use of a neutral outsider is vital to the feedback process.

Integral to effective team appraisal is effective **peer review**. Bader and Bloom (1992) cite the work of Eric Trist and Fred Emery of the Tavistock Institute who observed peer review being practised in the coal mines of South Yorkshire in their research on mineworkers some 45 years ago. Bader and Bloom have also outlined what they see as the pitfalls and the options that should be considered in relation to peer review. These include:

- not ensuring that the time allocated is adequate for the task;
- not keeping performance appraisal input anonymous, especially in small departments;
- inappropriate use of peer review in order to instigate 'corrective action'; not informing peers as to the kinds of decisions their inputs may be used to support;
- a tendency for reviewers' judgment to be coloured by recent events, be they positive or negative.

Those planning to develop peer review appraisal systems need to consider the following:

- What aspects of performance are to be assessed?
- Will participation in peer review be compulsory or optional?
- What are the safeguards that will need to be built into the procedures?
- What training and orientation do employees need?
- What tools are required? For example, will mission statements, job descriptions, performance standards be linked to the assessment process? Will the feedback be verbal, written or both?

An integral part of the management of performance appraisal is effective management and execution of **appraisal interviewing**, irrespective of whether this is within the context of individual or team performance. Core to the intervention process are the skills and competencies of data collection, problem analysis and decision making, and clear communications, on the part of both the interviewer and the inteviewee. A more detailed account of appraisal interviewing is provided in Chapter 5 on managing performance and conduct.

Rewarding performance

Raising productivity performance has always been a challenge for line managers. The UK, for example, has poor unit labour cost competitiveness, particularly in comparison to the USA and Japan. The CBI (1996) identified that raising productivity performance is a key challenge for organizations and that improved training and employee involvement initiatives might be the levers to achieve this. Involving employees in their reward is an employee involvement initiative which organizations are now increasingly seeking to employ.

If organizations are to improve productivity then the means to achieve this is through increase in performance. Rewarding for performance is concerned with rewarding those who have made a contribution to taking the business forward and, conversely, not rewarding those who have not done so. Reward management, then, is managing the reward that employees receive so that they can see a direct relationship between reward and effort; it is managing performance through reward.

Reward management is concerned with identifying those strategies, policies and systems that enable an organization to achieve its objectives by obtaining and keeping the people it needs and by increasing their motivation and commitment (Armstrong and Murlis, 1994).

Reward strategy cannot be 'bolted on' to organizations; it must be integral to and contribute to the achievement of corporate goals. It needs to drive and support desired behaviour, provide the competitive edge to attract and retain the 'right' people and give value for money from reward practices. Reward is concerned not just with the weekly or monthly pay packet, but with all the elements that make up the financial reward that employees receive. Reward is therefore concerned with total remuneration – this includes basic pay rates, performance-related pay and fringe benefits (see Figure 4.7).

Payment structures

The purpose of payment structures (Armstrong and Murlis, *op. cit.*) has been identified as:

- providing a fair and consistent basis for motivating and rewarding employees;
- managing pay relativities between different jobs and levels;
- rewarding individuals according to their job/role size, their performance, their contribution, their skill and their competence.

Problems with traditional payment structures

Traditional payment structures are often based on a job evaluation system which assessed the relative size of jobs in the organization and then placed them in rank order. Typical criteria for assessment for position in the rank order would include:

- 'know how' required to achieve the job;
- problem-solving requirements;
- accountability;
- working conditions.

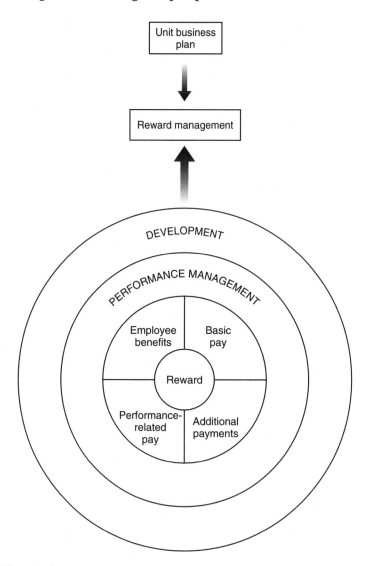

Figure 4.7   The reward management process.

Many organizations had, and still have, separate job evaluation systems for different categories of employees, in particular for 'wage earners' and 'salaried employees'. Traditionally, 'wage earners' receive a fixed level of pay based on skill level, determined by management or by collective bargaining. The emphasis is on differentiating between skill levels and maintaining those differentials.

Pay structures for 'salaried employees' often allow career progression through a series of grades which focus on the job and not the person, the middle point of each grade being linked to market rate (see Figure 4.6). The concept behind such pay structures is that an employee enters an organization at the lower end of an appropriate grade band for the job they are doing and progresses through the grade structure throughout their career as they take on more tasks and responsi-

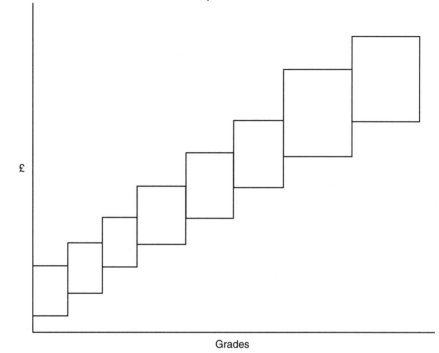

- Focus on the job not the person
- High link between grade status and job – pressure on regrading
- Middle point linked to market rate

Figure 4.8 Traditional graded structure (white collar).

bilities. These structures emphasize the link between grade status and the job and allow little room for individual reward – the reward is for being in the grade. The link between effort and reward is not clear.

Traditional pay structures underpinned a philosophy which separated 'wage earners' and 'salaried employees'. They were separated not only by different job evaluation systems but by different pay and fringe benefit systems. The pay structures for 'salaried employees' emphasized hierarchies of grade which would be climbed during the employee's career.

Organizations use a range of different pay structures to those described above. A number of systems emphasize recruiting at the market rate. For example, individuals can be recruited at market rate for a job or role and then negotiate for pay increases by showing their market rate has increased. In such organizations it can be a disciplinary offence to discuss rates of pay. There can be 'ethical' and legal problems with such a pay system. Other organizations recruit individuals at market rate but attach individual job ranges to their pay rate through which the individual progresses. The public sector tends to favour pay spines which include a number of incremental points, progression through which is often determined by length of service rather than performance. Figure 4.9 shows changes in payment structures.

These structures worked well in a different era with different social values. They

- Need to focus on person not job
- 'Broad banding' pay structures

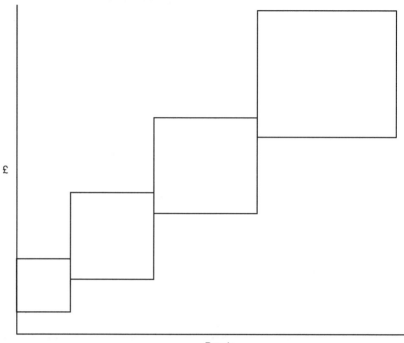

Figure 4.9   Broad banding payment structures.

worked well in an economically stable environment in which the future was predictable, but they work much less well with current social values and with the current unstable, competitive, global environments which organizations face today.

Changing social values, increased education and increased diversity in the workforce have changed the expectations of employees in respect of how organizations treat them and how organizations reward them. These changes can be summarized (Murlis, 1996) as shown in Table 4.1.

As organizations seek to increase productivity, to increase flexible working, to look for competitive edge, to increase multi-skilling, the inflexibility of traditional pay structures becomes more apparent.

These changes in organizational and individual needs have also coincided with increased involvement in 'reward' management for line managers. It is the line managers' responsibility to manage their teams to achieve their objectives. Reward is no longer owned and driven by the Personnel or Human Resources department; it is a line management tool, enabling line managers to use reward to increase motivation and commitment and reward those who have contributed to the achievement of objectives.

Armstrong (1996) identifies some key issues in reward philosophy. These include the need for organizations to determine:

Table 4.1 Changing expectations

	Past	*Present*
Changing career patterns	From 'womb' to 'tomb'	To flexible working
Employee profile	Male bread winners	Diverse bread winners Increase in flexible workforce
Expectations	Grateful/compliant	Demanding Financially literate 'Aware' through global communication systems
Reward focus	Security; conformity; retention	Performance emphasis Recognition of contribution
Tax	Minimalization was key	Largely neutral impact

- how reward underpins the organization's values regarding innovation, team-work, flexibility and quality;
- the need to achieve fairness, equity and consistency in reward structures;
- the balance between internal equity and external competitiveness;
- the importance attached to relating pay to individual versus team reward;
- the extent to which employees and managers are regarded as 'partners' in developing and managing the reward process.

The changing environment in which organizations operate and key issues in reward philosophy underpin the way in which organizations operate and question their reward policies.

Broad banding payment structures

Many of the changes in reward management have developed from the changes outlined above. Organizations have increasingly moved away from separate structures for 'wage earners' and 'salaried employees' which emphasized differences and differentials and from pay structures which emphasize job differences to those which focus on flexibility and on the individual.

The movement is towards pay structures which allow for maximum flexibility for individuals, for maximum potential to reward the individual for performance and to enable progression within flattened hierarchies.

'Broad banding' pay structures provide a better basis for modern organizations to reward their employees. These are based on job families and not on individual jobs. Pay structures are made up of a few (possibly four or five only) wide pay bands – up to 300 per cent from minimum to maximum levels which are often divided into pay zones. Progression through each broad band is possible for the individual by the achievement of objectives and competencies (see Figure 4.7).These pay structures blur the link between status and pay and are based on the premise that it is possible to be rewarded within a band rather than having to be rewarded by moving up a band; promotion and reward are not necessarily linked.

The example given in Box 4.1 shows how such a pay structure works at Nissan.

The involvement of the line manager in such a system can be clearly seen in that if progression through the band is by achievement of objectives and competencies then the line manager has a key role to play in the assessment of that achievement of objectives and of levels of competence.

Employee benefits and reward management

When Hoechst Roussel calculated that their employee benefits were costing them £6.5m per annum, they realized that employee benefits were a very expensive cost to the business. They also realized that their employee benefits were not part of a carefully thought out reward strategy which linked reward to meeting individual and business needs but rather that their employee benefits were based on a concept that individuals would work for them from 'cradle to grave'. The Personnel Director also saw that their employee benefits policy was one of 'employees receiving what was best for them' rather than receiving what they wanted.

With the changing demographic patterns which have been observed in earlier chapters and the increasing diversity of the workforce and with increasingly flexible working patterns, Hoechst Roussel realized that the employee benefits needed by different individuals should be linked to their individual needs and that different groups had different needs and expectations.

The result of this was the introduction of flexible or 'cafeteria' benefits. Woodley (1993) defines flexible benefits as meaning anything from choices in one or two benefits to offering a wide range of permutations from a sophisticated menu of benefits. The IDS (1994) identified a typical 'cafeteria menu' as including:

- Car
- Pension
- Life assurance
- Holiday
- Medical insurance
- Disability cover

Involving employees by asking them to identify employee benefits they value can be a good way to start drawing up a list of benefits to be offered.

Box 4.1 Broad pay banding at Nissan

Features of the Nissan system are:

- No job descriptions
- Generic job titles, e.g. engineer, supervisor, manager
- Band divisions are based on management responsibility, not job complexity
- 'Single status' (one pay and benefits structure) for the organization

The main problem is identifying the cost of benefits, which has to be done by careful actuarial calculation. Additionally, you need to decide what 'core' benefits are essential for your team members to have – do you want them not to have any additional holiday, for example?

The main advantage of flexible benefit systems is that they ensure that benefits are costed and that decisions about them are properly considered. Employees begin to recognize their value and to think carefully about choices. In this way, benefits play a full role in the objectives of the organization's reward strategy.

The phase of market development

Reward structures cannot be developed in isolation from business needs.

The phase of market development (see Figure 4.10) is often overlooked when critically evaluating an organization's reward philosophies. This is a key consideration when deciding relevant pay structures.

Performance-related pay

From Figure 4.10 it is clear that the phase of market development is a key consideration when identifying appropriate reward systems. Having determined the appropriate reward system for the phase of market development, the line manager needs to determine how best to reward those who have contributed the most to the achievement of organizational objectives.

As organizations seek to increase performance, to improve quality and to retain valuable people, they also need to achieve best value from their pay bill; payroll costs form a significant proportion of an employer's costs; in the public sector they may be as much as 70–80 per cent of all costs. However, the link between

The emergent business:	Low to medium base pay (low overheads) Moderate short-term incentives (annual bonus) Stake in the business (to encourage employees to stay)
High growth business:	Competitive base salary (to recruit and retain) High annual bonus (to reward contribution)
The mature business:	High base rate (to recruit and retain) High long-term bonus (to encourage employees to continue success)
Decline/renewal:	High and competitive base rate (to attract and retain) Low to moderate annual and long-term bonus plan (retain and encourage growth when immediate bonus unlikely)

Figure 4.10   Market development.

performance and pay is to some extent a controversial one and it is a link in which the line manager plays an important role.

What, then, is performance related pay?

Performance-related pay (PRP) links pay progression to a performance and/or competence rating (Armstrong and Murlis, 1994).

An Institute of Personnel Management survey (1992) identified that the main methods of performance-related pay were:

- Profit sharing: a percentage of annual profit paid as a bonus.
- Merit pay: an increase on basic pay determined by an assessment of individual performance at work (see Box 4.2 for an example of merit reviews at Pizza Hut).
- Individual bonuses: based on assessment of individual performance.
- Team bonuses: based on assessment of team performance.
- Share options: awarding shares in the business with tax-free advantages on their sale.

The survey also found that nearly three-quarters of the organizations they surveyed used performance-related pay; of those, the majority found that performance-related pay improved organizational performance, and nearly all who used it found that it improved organizational performance if it was part of a performance management system rather than being used in isolation as a stand-alone policy.

Organizations with performance-related pay are more likely to have devolved decision making over pay as this is an essential element if performance measures and assessment are linked to pay. For this reason, the line manager has an important part to play in performance-related pay and its linkages to performance management. The objectives of performance-related pay (Armstrong, 1994) are to:

Box 4.2 Merit reviews at Pizza Hut

Merit reviews for hourly-paid employees take place at six-monthly interludes, while management and head office staff are reviewed on an annual basis. A notional company-wide minimum underpins hourly rates for some catering staff. There is no recognized trade union or staff association.

Employees are assessed against two sets of equally weighted factors by line managers:

- Key results areas: pre-set performance targets
- Key competencies: the most important skills, attributes and areas of knowledge related to each occupation

The company's five-point merit rating system ranging from 'below target' to 'significantly above target' is applied to each factor, and then to the employee's overall appraisal.

Annual pay rises for field management and head office staff are linked to merit ratings and the individual's position within the salary range for that grade. The company aims to keep salaries at or near the mid-point of the range to ensure rates are competitive.

Merit payments for this group accounted for 3.5 per cent of the pay bill in 1995.

Source: IDS Survey, July 1995.

- motivate employees;
- deliver a positive message about performance expectations;
- focus attention and drive on key performance issues;
- differentiate rewards to people according to their competence and contribution;
- reinforce a culture of high levels of performance innovation, quality and teamwork;
- improve retention and recruitment;
- link the pay bill to organizational performance.

Performance-related pay and motivation

The basis for performance-related pay is the rather controversial view that money is a motivator. Over the years, researchers have differed in their view of this, and some of the key positions are presented in Figure 4.11.

It is clear from these views of motivation that motivation is not simply about money. Indeed, performance-related pay often becomes linked to performance management, yet the whole process of performance-related pay assessment can distort the developmental aspects of performance management. Bevan and Thompson (1992) concluded that 'remuneration forms only one part of the reward package and a simplistic carrot and stick approach is likely to give rise to difficulties'. They also make the point that the majority of employees do not necessarily receive a high percentage of their pay under performance-related pay systems, which again pours doubt on the role of the reward as a motivator. This is particularly true in the public sector. There is evidence of wide variation in the percentage of salary linked to performance. An Industrial Society survey (1994) found wide variations in the proportion of pay which was dependent upon performance, ranging from under 10 per cent to 100 per cent. Lawler (1988) believes that an increase of 3–4 per cent is not sufficient to improve motivation, and that 10–15 per cent is probably required to increase motivation.

Kohn (1993) believes that money as a reward only achieves 'temporary compliance', not lasting commitment, and that the 'surest way to destroy co-operation and therefore, organisational excellence, is to force people to compete for rewards or recognition or to rank them against each other'. Rewards discourage risk-taking and ignore the fact that exceptional work is done for interest, not reward. This view was reinforced by Marc Thompson (1995b) of the Institute of Manpower Studies who believes that:

- appraisal may be more effective than PRP;
- the process of setting goals may be the key to improving performance;
- PRP can undermine the psychological contract in the workplace.

Kohn (1993) believes that managers often use incentive schemes as a substitute for giving workers what they need to do a good job:

- treating workers well;
- providing useful feedback;

Throughout the past 100 years, many theories of motivation have been developed. Some of the most widely known are listed below.

Taylor (1911): Taylor's research suggested '**economic man**' was driven by money alone, thus work needed to be concentrated around economic outcomes – payment for quantity. With the rise of the Human Relations school in the 1940s and 1950s and more recent moves to 'Japanized' management systems such as Total Quality Management, this theory has lost popularity.

Maslow (1954): When defining his '**hierarchy of needs**' Maslow identified that until the bottom level of the hierarchy is satisfied – basic needs such as food, water and shelter – higher motivators cannot come into force. As each level is satisfied, so the higher level pushes the individual towards the highest level – self-actualization.

Maslow viewed money as a security need – essential to life, but once satisfied other needs in the hierarchy became more important.

Herzberg *et al.* (1957): His research showed that **money was a hygiene factor**, a source of dissatisfaction if inadequate, and important, but not a motivator. In his famous expression 'jumping for jelly beans' he saw that people would jump if given money, but needed to be given more money to jump again. Herzberg saw **motivators as those things that gave inner satisfaction**; these included achievement, the nature of the job, ability to control one's own destiny and personal growth.

Manager's need to ensure that basic monetary needs are met in their teams but to understand that other factors are important to motivate individuals and to meet intrinsic needs.

Adams (1965) and Jacques (1961): They observed that the ratio between outcomes and inputs compared to others is important – **individuals are concerned with 'equity' and 'fairness' in the reward they receive**. They need to feel that the reward for effort is fair and that what others receive in relation to them is also 'fair' and 'equitable'.

The impact of comparison with others in the workplace needs to be recognized by managers. Equity is also about employee involvement; do all employees have the opportunity to participate, does the scheme encourage competition among employees at the expense of cooperation, are some being rewarded at the expense of others. Is reward based on objective performance criteria?

Porter and Lawler (1968) and Vroom (1964): Their research suggested that it is **the expectation of achieving a reward that motivates, not the actual achievement**. There does, however, have to be an expectation that the effort will result in the reward and that the reward is worth striving for, i.e. it is something the individual values.

The ability to achieve a task can depend on the perception an individual has of his or her ability and role.

Managers need to ask whether the reward scheme they have introduced is appropriate for the employees it is to cover, taking into account the fact that different people are motivated by different things. Managers need to understand what motivates the different individuals in their team.

Latham and Locke (1979): Motivation and performance are higher when individuals are set specific goals, when the goals are stretching and mutually agreed and when there is feedback on performance to ensure satisfaction from achievement. Managers also need to ensure that team members have the training and development to enable them to achieve their goals and that the goals they are set are seen by the individual to be fair, reasonable and achievable and the reward for doing so is one that is valued by that individual.

Figure 4.11 Theories of motivation.

- social support;
- room for self-determination.

Where does this leave the manager then, who has a reward system to manage and who seeks to reward those who contribute to the business?

The answer is that reward management is not just about pay, it is also about understanding motivation theory. Performance-related pay works if it is within a framework of performance-management.

Rewarding individual performance

Setting objectives and measuring achievement are the critical factors in establishing any performance related structure

(IDS, 1995).

Key considerations when introducing performance-related pay are (Armstrong and Murlis, 1994):

- A clear and strong link between performance and contribution and reward;
- A fair and consistent basis for measuring performance and contribution;
- A worthwhile reward in line with employee expectations;
- Value for money – gains to the company in terms of improved organizational performance should exceed the cost of the scheme.

Some organizations, e.g. Mobil, measure against objectives and achievement of core competencies (see Box 4.3).

Rating performance

Rating performance can be particularly difficult for a manager unless a proper procedure is established at the outset. In order to rate performance fairly it is important to:

- identify corporate strategies and objectives and translate them into departmental objectives and plans;
- jointly identify with the individual his or her own SMART objectives (see p. 153) from departmental objectives and plans;
- jointly identify outputs, accountabilities, task achievement, knowledge, skill and competence requirements;
- jointly agree performance measures;
- jointly agree training and development needs to achieve objectives;
- explain the method by which performance will be measured;
- use performance level definitions that are positive, e.g. not 'outstanding . . . unacceptable' but 'very effective . . . improvable';
- get joint agreement of an individual's performance rating;

Box 4.3 Mobil – assessment against objectives and competencies

Assessment is against:

- Effective communication
- Concern for effectiveness
- Enthusiasm for work
- Self-confidence

- Building consensus
- Forward thinking
- Improving the organization
- Flexibility
- Innovation
- Setting high standards

- avoid a 'middle' rating tendency, e.g. 3 in a scale of 1 to 5;
- be aware of the problems of a forced distribution – it can mean that a good performer is ranked poorly;
- agree training and development needs where performance is below standard.

Rewarding team performance

Recent research by the Institute for Employment Studies (Thompson, 1995b) suggests a growth in team working arrangements with 40 per cent of employers introducing initiatives to encourage team working. With flatter hierarchies in organizations, self-managed teams fit well with a line management structure where spans of control are wider and managers find it more difficult to monitor and control the tasks of subordinates. Team incentives can also be a means of focusing on income targets and encouraging team performance. Team working also has the benefit of encouraging collaboration and sharing of information to achieve quality. Team working, allied with multi-skilling, has also been identified as a means of increasing flexibility, the ability to respond to changing organizational needs and to increase individual job satisfaction. In turn, these factors have the benefits of reducing absenteeism and labour turnover. Effective teams have a number of features as cited by Thompson (1995b):

- The ideal team size has been identified as 15 (Hackman, 1990), as teams over this size have difficulties in terms of information sharing, coordination of work and tasks and agreeing specific and measurable goals.
- For teams to be cohesive, the work must require group efforts rather than individual efforts. This involves employees in the group seeing themselves as part of a team and having a task that involves interacting frequently as a team.
- For teams to share a common goal or purpose, specific performance goals are necessary. Objectives should define an output that is the product of teamwork, not the aggregation of individual outputs. Outputs need to be measurable and team members should understand these measures and their contribution in relation to them.
- Teams can be both permanent and temporary.
- Temporary teams are often set up for specific projects and they have specific short-term objectives.
- Permanent teams may be organized around a function, a process used by Nissan or Rover or a product market or geographical region.

Team payments

Temporary teams need to have clear objectives and a time period for the achievement of performance. Bonus payments are frequently used to reward team performance; these payments are not consolidated into basic pay, but clearly reward the output of the team against agreed objectives.

Permanent teams

Thompson (1995b) identified that organizations often seek to change behaviours and attitudes. One way in which this can be achieved is through the introduction of team-based measures into the assessment process. The most widely used approach is to introduce 'team working' as an assessment criterion into the performance appraisal process for individuals. This builds a team dimension into the individual pay determination process.

Alternative methods of rewarding permanent teams are through bonus schemes or through skills- or competence-based pay, whereby pay progression depends on the acquisition of skills by the employee. Skills which support or reinforce team working can thus be rewarded.

Allocating team reward can be divisive if differential payments are made based on individual contribution to team performance.

A gainsharing method of rewarding team performance is used by BP Exploration (see Box 4.4).

Conclusion

Performance management in organizations

Any system of performance management should be developed in a coherent structure in which the relationship between the various performance management-related activities is clear. The reasons for developing such systems might be either to make more explicit the relationship between employee performance in

---

Box 4.4 Gainsharing in BP exploration

At BP Exploration teams were identified as 150 people.

Gainsharing: the balance between costs and income. Gains over targets are shared out. The incentive is to reduce costs and to increase output.

Gainsharing was used as a tool for

- team involvement
- team recognition
- team reward

Bonus payments from the gainsharing were self-funded from *STRETCH* performance identified at the beginning of the financial year.

Gainsharing provides a way of rewarding teams and of saving costs.

The manager who wishes to reward teams needs to:

- be committed to team reward;
- ensure the team has high trust with the manager and themselves;
- agree SMART objectives with the team which link to the business plan;
- agree with the team how the achievement of objectives is to be measured;
- encourage the team to identify what success will look like;
- determine how the team reward is to be allocated and ensure that the team understands this;
- ensure that the team has the resources, training and development to achieve their objectives;
- identify the role the team expects you, as manager, to play in their performance.

meeting strategic objectives or to identify long-term plans for employee development, or some mixture of the two.

Irrespective of the system, performance management requires commitment from the top which is clear and communicated effectively. Ideally, it should be an organization-wide position as the restriction of performance management to particular categories of employees such as managers may lead to a dual culture, within which attention to employee performance issues is highly focused or largely absent. Performance management systems have the potential to be divisive, particularly if they are developed alongside performance-related pay schemes. Performance management schemes with a substantive employee development element are likely to be accepted, particularly in organizations dominated by professional groups. This is not to downplay the impact or effectiveness of well-designed strategy-driven performance management systems, but the latter, though popular and potentially powerful, do have their drawbacks: in particular, it can be difficult to strike the right balance between the demands of the organization and the aspirations of the employee. Over and above this, too sharp a focus on strategy may mean that employee and ultimately organizational flexibility is reduced.

The impact of culture and climate on the likely success of any performance management system should not be underestimated. There are many considerations that need to be made when designing a system according to your organization's needs, but it would be foolhardy to introduce a system which had no chance of success, even if it is envisaged that, in part, performance management may be used as an HRM lever for change.

Moreover, any system of performance management requires that attention is paid to the skills and expertise of those with primary responsibilities within the system. In most systems, line managers have a central role and it is vital that they are given the necessary training and development inputs in order to be able to manage employment performance issues effectively. This should include adequate briefing about the scheme but also training in aspects that require specialist knowledge such as coaching, mentoring, line (rather than specialist) counselling, and the identification of training and development needs. Often, performance-management related roles require some sensitivity in and around employee support as well as dealing with difficult and sensitive situations such as capability, grievance and disciplinary activities. Therefore, training in interpersonal behaviour and skills training should be available.

However, many forms of performance management require substantial inputs from all, as there may be substantial peer review or upward appraisal, such as for team or 360 degree appraisal. All employees should receive adequate briefing and it is also as important that they receive the appropriate training as it is for their line managers.

The manager's role in rewarding performance

The manager has a key role to play in managing the reward of performance of individuals and teams within the organization. As managers take responsibility for the performance of those who work for them, so they are increasingly involved in rewarding those who perform well. This means that the manager needs to understand the relationship between performance management and reward. In addition, managers need to understand that reward management is intrinsically linked to understanding the needs of their organization and the needs of the individuals who form part of their work team. This applies to not-for-profit organizations as well as profit-making enterprises.

Rewarding for performance is not just about rating an individual or a team for a percentage pay increase, it is about recognizing that individuals and teams have needs and that those needs are not just about monetary reward. The manager needs therefore to understand the need for flexible pay structures and employee benefits that match the phase of market development of the business. Managers need to recognize the need for clearly defined policies and procedures for measuring performance, jointly agreed with the individuals concerned, and to also recognize the need to reward teams as well as individuals in the organization. When all this has been successfully achieved, then the manager will have understood the role of reward in performance management.

Performance management is a dynamic process and the system should be monitored and evaluated using a combination of hard data and sound judgement, in order to continually adjust, upgrade and revise policy and practice.

Summary

In the chapter, we have outlined the reasons why effective performance management should be strategic, holistic and proactive. Potentially, the outputs from performance management systems can provide important information for managers and employees alike. Deciding on the systems that will work in any specific organization requires throrough evaluation, including an honest appraisal of what is not worth pursuing, given factors such as the organization's culture and predominant management style, particularly as there will be an impact on the employer–employee relationship via the psychological contract (discussed in more detail in Chapter 3 on Generating Commitment Through Involvement and Participation Processes and Chapter 9 Change in Organizations).

The challenge is to strike a balance between the immediate needs of the organization and those of the employee, so that employee performance objectives, development opportunities and rewards are not too narrowly focused on strategy to the point that long-term flexibility, goodwill and motivation are lost from the organization as a whole.

Questions

1   Identify ways in which the manager plays a role in performance management. Compare your research to your own experience in an organization with which you are familiar.

2   List the factors that motivate you in your job. Research those factors that researchers have identified as motivating and check them against your list.

3   Relate the factors that motivate you and that researchers say motivate others to the way in which performance is managed in an organization with which you are familiar. What conclusions can you draw about the link between performance management and motivation in that organization?

4   What role does performance-related pay play in performance management?

5   How might you evaluate the effectiveness of a performance management system?

6   How might you evaluate the likely viability of a performance management scheme in an organization with which you are familiar? What criteria could be usefully employed?

7   Assess the relative strengths of team appraisal and peer review from an ethical perspective.

8   What ethical issues might arise from paying people based upon some measure of their individual performance?

References

Adams, J (1965) Injustice in social exchange. In *Advances in Experimental Psychology*, (ed.) Berkowitz, L, Academic Press, New York.

Armstrong, M (1996) *Reward Management*, IPD.

Armstrong, M and Murlis, H (1994) *Reward Management*, IPM.

Bader, GE and Bloom, AE (1992) How to do peer review. *Training and Development*, June, 61–62.

Bevan, S and Thompson, M (1992) *Performance Management in the UK*, IMS.

CBI (1996) Human Resource Brief, CBI.

Fletcher, C (1993) Appraisal: an idea whose time has gone? *Personnel Management*, September, 34–37.

Hackman, JR (1990) in Thompson, M (1995b) Team Working and Pay, IES Report 281.

Herzberg *et al.* (1957) *The Motivation to Work*, Wiley, New York.

IDS (1995) *Performance and Objectives*, July, IDS.

IDS (1994) *Flexible Benefits*, October, IDS.

Industrial Society (1994) Performance Management – Managing Best Practice No. 2, June, 11.

Institute of Personnel Management (1992) *Performance Management*, IPM Publications.

IPD (1992) *Incentive Pay: Impact and Evolution*, IPD.

IRS Employment Trends 570 (1994) Pick and mix appraisal: individual choice of performance reviews at Mercury, October, 18–20.

IRS Employment Trends 592 (1995) Discipline at Work 2: the procedures, September, 5–16.

IRS Employment Trends 636 (1997) Handling employee grievance part 1, July, 5–12.

Jacques, E (1961) *Equitable Payment*, Heinemann.

Kohn, A (1993) Why incentive plans cannot work. *HBR*, Sep–Oct.

Lane, J and Herriot, P (1990) Self-ratings, supervisor ratings, positions and performance. *Journal of Occupational Psychology*, **63**, 77–88.

Latham, G and Locke, R (1979) Goal setting – a motivational technique that works. *Organisational Dynamics*, Autumn 68–80.

Lawler, E (1988) Pay for Performance: making it work. *Personnel Management*, October.

Maslow, A (1954) *Motivation and Personality*, Harper & Row, New York.
Murlis, H (1996) Reward management. Lecture at Oxford Brookes University, unpublished.
Norman, CA and Zwacki, RA (1991) Team appraisals – team approach. *Personnel Journal*, September, 101–104.
Porter, L and Lawler, E (1968) *Management Attitudes and Behaviour*, Irwin-Dorsey, Homewood, IL.
Taylor, FW (1964) *Work and Motivation*, Wiley, New York.
Thompson, M (1995a) BBC broadcast, unpublished.
Thompson, M (1995b) Team Working and Pay. IES Report 281.
Torrington, D and Hall, L (1995) *Personnel Management in Action*, Prentice-Hall, London.
Vinsom, MN (1996) The pros and cons of 360–degree feedback: making it work. *Training and Development*, April, 11–12.
Vroom, V (1964) *Work and Motivation*, Wiley, New York.
Woodley, C (1993) The benefits of flexibility. *People Management*, IPM.

Further Reading

Armstrong, M and Murlis, H (1994) *Reward Management*, 3rd edn, IPD, is a thorough text on reward and reward management. Another useful text is Armstrong's (1996) book *Employee Reward*. ACAS leaflets on job evaluation and appraisal-related pay are also valuable.

Legal briefing

The main legal issues contained within this chapter relate to employee pay and its determination. Decisions about how pay is designated need to be fair, and challenges may be made if this appears not to be the case.

It is a major source of industrial action and a source of employee challenge to the company view, either through internal mechanisms or through the law courts (including industrial tribunals).

Most of the legal issues relating to these areas have been discussed in detail in the legal briefings for the Introduction and overview and Chapter 1.

Reference should also be made to the enhanced rights of trades unions discussed in Chapter 3. The increased rights to statutory recognition will result in far more employees having their pay determined by collective bargaining. The right of employees to enter into 'individual contracts' (the result of a late Conservative amendment in the Lords) may prove to be short-lived if Parliamentary time is found for amending legislation.

Managing performance and conduct 5

Alan Blackburn and Nelarine Cornelius

Learning Objectives

After studying this chapter you should be able to:

- understand the importance of using a vigilant and consistent approach to managing performance and conduct;
- identify areas of potential weakness in the systems and rules used by you and your organization to manage performance issues;
- manage issues of performance and conduct in your part of your organization more effectively;
- diagnose when performance issues are likely to escalate, know when to seek help and who to seek it from.

Introduction

At the heart of organizational performance management systems lies the use of power by managers on behalf of the company to control employee behaviour. For employees to comply with an organization's wishes on standards of behaviour and conduct, individuals give up some of their personal freedoms to comply with the way their employing organization wants them to behave. To control behaviour organizations develop rules and regulations to which they expect people to conform. These rules and regulations may be thought of as push or pull systems. For example, in a pull system, organizations offer these rewards to staff to perform in certain ways. These rewards may take a number of forms, the most common of which will be payments on top of salary or promises of rewards to come. By way of contrast, in a push system organizations also use 'sticks' to punish people who do not perform appropriately or who break rules, but may then coach people to help them perform more effectively.

Organizational rules appear in different forms. Perhaps the most obvious is the use of legitimate instructions by managers. Some organizations back this up using job descriptions and staff handbooks, others choose not to. In certain instances people are controlled through technology; for example, in building society call centres managers monitor call rates and the way employees interact with customers by eavesdropping. The nature of an employer's business and organizational culture will drive the way rules and regulations are applied within a workplace. This process will be handled differently by departments as people are likely to be controlled in different ways depending upon the specific work environment, the job itself and the category of employee in terms of skill and expertise.

The regulation of employee behaviour is illustrated in Figure 5.1. The histogram shows that the behaviour of all employees will fall between the left-and right-hand limits of the graph. Towards the right-hand end of the graph, a number of employees are performing highly, displaying behaviour which may be rewarded by performance payments and/or promotion. Towards the centre of the graph a larger number of employees are displaying slightly above or below average conduct and performance. At the left-hand end of the graph a small number of employees are displaying behaviour which is well below that expected by the organization. The purpose of managing performance and conduct is to minimize the number of people who fall into this category by encouraging them to improve their performance and conduct, or to manage their exit from the organization. When managing an employee's performance and conduct, managers must proceed with care to ensure the process at least meets with external requirements.

From an employee's point of view, there must also be a system in place which can look after an employee's interests. This may be needed where people feel they have been treated unfairly, inconsistently and inappropriately by their manager. This process is referred to as a grievance procedure, the intention of which is to prevent arbitrary and unfair use of managerial power. This chapter will examine approaches to managing performance and conduct. This commences with the process of individual performance review through the appraisal interview. In this context, the appraisal interview may be thought of as a process of retaining

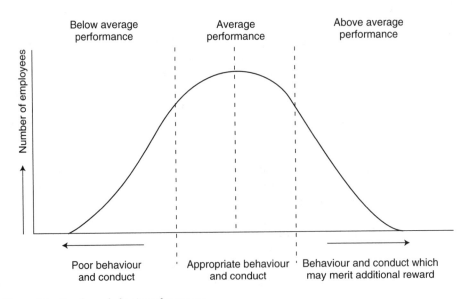

Figure 5.1   Employee behavioural patterns.

employee behaviour in terms of performance and conduct within acceptable limits. Should this prove unsuccessful, then progressively more serious approaches are adopted by organizations. Each of these will be covered in turn. We start with the appraisal interview.

The appraisal interview

Typically, during the **appraisal interview**, job role performance is discussed and agreements reached regarding any staff development issues that may arise. The term interview may be considered unfortunate, as although it adds a degree of formality to the proceedings it also suggests an imbalance of input to the process, the emphasis is often placed on the manager who conducts the discussion.

The interview process itself is valuable as it potentially provides a forum for an exchange of information between a supervisor and subordinate. The way in which the interview is conducted is crucial to the success of performance management. Handled appropriately, the interview can provide motivation and encouragement which will facilitate staff being able to identify with the performance management system. However, if the interview is handled inappropriately it may alienate staff from the process and have a demotivating effect, whatever the original intention. Staff may be appraised by a number of people, including their immediate supervisor, their supervisor's boss, a member of a human resources department, their peers and in some cases their subordinates. Often, it is a person's direct supervisor who undertakes the appraisal interview. Whoever carries out the process, the following problems may present themselves and steps should be taken to ensure the performance appraisal is as objective as possible. Potential problems that can arise around the interview process include the following:

- **Poor preparation** on the part of the interviewer and interviewee
- **Prejudice** arising from hearsay or previous unrelated experiences with the person
- **The 'halo' effect** where the generally good relationship with the person can influence the overall assessment of performance in a positive way irrespective of actual performance
- **The 'horns' effect** with the generally bad relationship with the person influencing the overall assessment of performance in a negative way, irrespective of actual performance
- A **reluctance to communicate** by either the interviewer or the interviewee
- **Poor record keeping** before, during and after the interview
- **No follow-up** or **clear plan of action**

Maier (1958) identified three styles of appraisal interviewing almost 40 years ago. The styles identified are outlined below:

- **The tell and sell style.** This approach is 'boss centred'; the manager tells the employee what he or she thinks and then attempts to sell his or her ideas to the employee in order to make progress. Development plans are based upon subordinate weaknesses perceived by the boss and there is little input to the process by the subordinate except to agree the outcomes of the interview.

- **The tell and listen style**. This approach is also 'boss centred'; the manager presents the picture he or she has built up about a person's performance to the subordinate. The manager then listens to what the employee has to say about the manager's evaluation. The manager then attempts to justify his or her evaluation and offers a development plan to the subordinate. This style is really consultation by the manager with the subordinate. At the end of the interview the boss may or may not change his or her initial evaluation.
- **The joint problem–solving style**. This approach advocates a style where the manager and subordinate have equal input to the process and joint responsibility for the agreed outcomes from the meeting. The appraiser normally starts the meeting by encouraging the employee to identify and discuss problem areas and then consider solutions. The employee therefore plays an active part in analysing problems and suggesting solutions. The evaluation of performance emerges from the discussion at the end of the meeting rather than being imposed in any way by the manager (Anderson, 1987).

Of the three approaches offered above, it is the joint problem-solving method that has been advocated by Anderson as the most appropriate. Figure 5.2 shows a suggested structure for appraisal interviewing.

Managing poor performance

From time to time every manager will be faced with a subordinate who for one reason or another is not performing satisfactorily. This will be a major concern as, if not addressed, the situation can have a demotivational effect on others within a work team. In addition, problems can become bigger and take up a disproportionate amount of managerial time. The employee may not be aware that his or her performance is below standard and therefore continues in blissful ignorance. Alternatively, the employee is aware that things are not up to scratch but hopes that it will go unnoticed, or at least, nobody will make too much of a fuss.

Often employees are aware that their performance is lacking in some way but do not know how to bring it up to standard. It is vital that the manager gathers evidence to substantiate that there is a clear gap between what is required and what has actually been delivered.

Hidden effects on performance

Before dealing with the issue as a performance problem, it is worth considering if the problem is in reality a performance issue, or if the lack of performance is caused by factors outside an employee's control. For example, poor performance could be caused by the following issues which may be a result of work, or personal matters outside work (Stuart, 1992):

- Stress
- Medical conditions
- Psychiatric or personal or domestic problems

Some common causes of poor performance are shown in figure 5.3.

Approaches to appraisal interviewing	
1. Purpose and rapport building	Agree purpose with subordinate Agree structure for the meeting Check preparation is adequate
2. Factual review	Review known facts about performance Check for unknown facts
3. Subordinate views	Get comments on performance What has gone well and less well What could be improved Work preferences and reasons Possible new Key Result Areas (KRAs) and Key Performance Indicators (KPIs)
4. Manager's views	Manager adds own perspective Disagreements discussed
5. Joint problem solving	Discussion of differences and how they can be resolved Development needs: how the boss can help
6. Goal setting	Agreement of revised KRAs, KPIs and goals Development plan with allocated responsibility

Figure 5.2 Suggested structure: appraisal interviewing. *Source:* adapted from Torrington and Hall, 1995.

There are a range of a factors that can result in poor employee performance. Some of these may relate to the predisposition, attitude or motivation of an individual, but may just as easily be as a result of work-based factors beyond the employee's control, or indeed, the reasons may lie outside the workplace altogether.

Employee-centred factors

- Lack of effort (motivational and attitudinal causes)
- Lack of ability (lack of the necessary skills or knowledge)

Workplace-centred factors

Lack of clarity about job requirements. This may be due to a lack of employee ability but is just as likely to be due to poor instructions from line managers or supervisors, poor written policies or procedures, or a lack of training.

Excessive workload

Employee workloads may become unmanageable. Under such circumstances, it becomes increasingly difficult and eventually impossible for employees to do their job well. The reason why workloads become unmanageable include reduced headcount, increasing customer demands, or a change to the manner in which work needs to be completed. Whatever the reason, good employees should raise their concerns and good managers should ensure that employees do not have to struggle in the first place.

Non-work factors

The cause of poor performance may arise outside the workplace. Major life events such as births, divorce, bereavements, moving house, serious illness or changing domestic responsibilities may all have a negative impact on work performance. Employees may be reluctant to raise these issues with their managers, so it is down to the line manager to recognize when things seem to be going awry. Not all of these problems can be addressed by managers. Nonetheless, the manager may need to seek professional advice or encourage the employee to do so.

Figure 5.3 Common causes of poor performance.

Alcohol in the workplace

In a survey of 450 employers, 53 per cent were found to have policies on the restriction of consumption of alcohol during working hours, perhaps unsurprising given that it is estimated that eight million days a year are lost due to alcohol misuse, three times the number of days associated with industrial action (IRS Employment Trends, 1992). The nature of the policies included the following:

- A total ban during working hours
- Restriction of alcohol consumption to specific times and places
- Specific restrictions for certain employees (for example, those using machinery or driving)
- A restriction to workplace social events and entertaining

Enforcement tended to be primarily through two means: management or supervisor observation and disciplinary procedures, although a small number of organizations did carry out random checks. Most of the alcohol policies centred around line management procedures for dealing with the 'problem drinker' at work, in which managerial responsibility for bringing individuals' attention to the existence of help and support, such as counselling, is outlined. Clearly, line managers are not professional counsellors, nor are they qualified to identify clinical alcoholism. These policies usually require managers to identify whether a problem *might* exist, or whether poor work performance could be due to some other factor, such as work stress arising from poor job design. Such problems are complex, and beyond the skill of an individual manager to deal with.

The manager's role here is often to introduce the idea of professional help to the person concerned and to provide as much help as appropriate in the circumstances of the case. The company may be able to help too, for example through occupational health services or the employee assistance programme. Also, sensitive decisions may need to be made as to whether an individual is entitled to return to work if intervention to address the drink problem is an integral part of the organization's policy (although in some occupations, the dangers of drinking on the job are so high that instant dismissal is the likely outcome). Ironically, only 38.3 per cent of those companies that had an alcohol policy actually provided training for managers. Other causes of poor performance could be:

- **Lack of effort** is often a symptom of a more deeply rooted problem, perhaps one of the others listed above, or some lack of clarity about the way in which work is organized.
- **Lack of training** is sometimes regarded cynically as the universal panacea to all performance problems. In many instances this solution does not resolve the problem, can prove expensive and simply delays dealing more directly with the heart of the issue. Care is needed when diagnosing a training intervention to improve performance. The diagnosis of an employee's skills gaps must generate specific suggestions which may help improve performance.
- Labelling the performance problem as **lack of ability** takes the issue away from the person concerned and their manager, as it presents the case as an impossible problem to solve unless the person is removed from the work

situation. Employees who once performed well do not simply lose their abilities overnight. The perceived lack of ability may be outside of an employee's control to deal with, whereas some timely investigation by managers may be able to alleviate the problem.

However, it is worth re-emphasizing that it is the line manager who is expected to take a lead in dealing with these issues both in terms of gathering evidence and making interim suggestions for dealing with the problem, and it is usual for it to be stated in company policies that such actions are a line management responsibility, not an activity which is optional.

In dealing with issues of poor performance, managers should always expect the unexpected. It is important to stay calm, stick to the facts of the case and maintain a positive attitude throughout. Such meetings can in many instances be avoided if early action is taken by managers by monitoring and providing feedback on performance regularly in addition to formal appraisal interviews. In a few cases where performance or behaviour does not improve or where inappropriate action is taken by employees, it may prove necessary to use a formal disciplinary hearing to encourage employees to improve. It is important to note, however, that the processes of performance appraisal and disciplinary procedures are not linked in any way; they simply both contribute towards the overall approach to managing employee performance within organizations.

If below-standard performance is serious it is not appropriate to leave it to the next appraisal interview to discuss the matter. Such situations need to be addressed promptly. Dealing with the matter promptly can be beneficial for the person involved by removing pressure. It can be equally rewarding for the manager and the organization too. The aim of the process is to bring the standard of work undertaken by the person up to an acceptable level.

Capability procedures

Capability procedures may be used when an employee has consistently performed below standard. It is assumed that:

- for some reason the employee finds the application of the skills and knowledge required to undertake the task too demanding for their abilities;
- there is a persistent problem with the willingness or motivation of the employee to undertake their work to the required standard;
- the standards required for the job have changed and while the employee believed that he or she knew what is required, their performance actually remains below what is required.

Capability procedures are an early formal opportunity to get employee performance back on track, if informal approaches have failed. They are important because if they are not present, the first port of call may be the disciplinary procedures which are likely to be inappropriate given the nature of the problems being dealt with. Capability is normally dealt with at the line manager level, with support from a senior manager and a HRM or personnel specialist.

Within a capability procedure, the manager needs to collect evidence to substantiate the claim that performance is consistently below the required standard, and that the cause of the below standard performance is not 'hidden' problems or more serious breaches that would merit the use of a disciplinary procedure. There needs to be a shared belief between the employee and the manager that performance can be improved and the required standard met. It is important that a clear action plan and short-term targets are developed so that progress can be facilitated and monitored. Also, the following should be made clear:

- the details of the organization's capability procedures;
- how long performance will be closely monitored as part of the capability plan;
- what courses of action will be taken if the plan is met, especially concerning how long the incident will remain on personnel records;
- what course of action will be taken if capability targets are not met;
- to whom the employee may appeal if he or she feels unfairly treated.

Figure 5.4 gives guidelines on managing performance assessment meetings.

Required standards of behaviour

Work organizations are concerned with the production and delivery of goods and services but they are social systems also. There are a range of interactions between members of an organization, their customers, the community as a whole, and other influential agencies such as the government, the media, and potential competitors or strategic allies. As with any social system, there are certain attitudes and behaviours that are likely to cause problems and that need to be discouraged. This is not to suggest that organizations need to act like totalitarian states with draconian controls over what employees are or are not able to do or express among their colleagues and with other individuals or groups external to the organization. However, safeguards need to be in place to protect the interests of the organization and, equally importantly, the integrity and well-being of the organization's social system as a whole. Within this context, there is a need to formally define **unacceptable behaviour**, which can be laid out in **codes of conduct**.

Where codes of conduct are broken, most organizations also have **disciplinary codes and practices** as a form of corrective mechanism for the individual and a symbolic gesture of the type of behaviour that is or is not acceptable.

Discipline: the organizational context

At first glance the term discipline can be considered part of 'Old Management' involving formal regulation of behaviour and punishment.

Another way of looking at the term is to take a dictionary definition which, although including the terms correction, chastisement and mortification of the flesh through penance, also includes words such as instruction, having as its aim 'to reform the pupil to proper courses of action' and 'instruction, imparted to disciples

Below is a list of general guidelines on managing performance.

Prepare and collect evidence

The manager will need to collect evidence about the person's performance. This should be obtained from a number of different sources as corroboration. A meeting should be arranged to discuss the problem and an agenda prepared to ensure that all topics relating to the problem are covered. The meeting should take place away from disturbances. To help the meeting to go smoothly, it may be useful to plan out some initial questions to ask.

The meeting

The purpose of the meeting should be made clear to the person, i.e. to discuss the performance of the person in relation to his or her duties and responsibilities. The scope of discussions should be made clear in relation to the person's duties. For example, does the poor performance of the person extend across the whole range of duties or is it only a limited part of the whole job? This is important as it puts the scope of the poor performance into an overall context. For example, it may be that the person performs adequately across 80 per cent of job activities, and it is only the remaining 20 per cent of the job where unsatisfactory performance is being displayed that will be covered in depth at the meeting. The structure of the meeting may be:

State your case

- Go through the evidence collected, using specific examples.
- Be clear, concise and direct; do not apologize.
- Keep discussions impersonal.

For example: 'You can be rather brusque with customers at the enquiry desk.'
                        'There have been formal complaints made in writing dated . . .'
                        'This is against company policy and impairs the image of the company.'

Ask the person to state his or her case

Are there any reasons for the poor performance?

What are the person's views?

Were there any mitigating circumstances to explain the poor performance?

Ask for solutions: what suggestions does the person offer to remedy the situation?

It is better if the poor performer can own the solution, because then he or she is more likely to stick to it. If difficulties are perceived, offer suggestions; this shows you are interested in resolving the issue.

Agree solutions and actions

Finally both parties should come to an agreement on the remedial steps to be taken. In setting standards you will need to be as specific as possible to ensure the agreed actions are understood. The SMART approach to goal setting may be useful here (see page 153).

Summarize the meeting

Briefly go over what was discussed, the problem, the plan of action and the agreed solution. Agree a review date to discuss implementation of the solution.

Follow up

Make sure that some review dates are agreed to discuss the action plan and progress made towards it.

Figure 5.4   Managing performance assessment meetings.

or scholars, teaching, learning, education and schooling'. There is therefore more than one view as to the purpose of a disciplinary hearing, inevitably affected by the circumstances surrounding its application. Maintaining discipline, however, does not start by applying the procedure. Procedures only become active once other levels of discipline have broken down. These levels of discipline may be considered as:

- **Self-discipline**: self-control stemming from the personal values, skill, training and strength of character or pride of an individual.
- **Team discipline**: peer control arising from the mutual dependence, trust and respect of each team member. This is based upon the notion that cohesive teams will regulate the behaviour of members without any outside interference; indeed outside interference may be resisted by the whole team.
- **Managerial discipline**: managerial control where a team is responsible and answerable to a team leader who may stand apart from the team. The leader is directive and responsible for the behaviour and performance of the team.

The imposition of managerial discipline in this model can be seen as a last resort used only when the other levels of discipline have failed to have the desired effect, by regulating or bringing back into line the inappropriate performance or behaviour. The intention of formal procedures is to make an employee 'pull back' from an infringement of company rules, improve performance and so bring his or her behaviour back into line. From the employee's point of view, the experience of discipline should reduce the chances of any reoccurrence.

Dealing with disciplinary cases

The application of a disciplinary procedure must follow the rules of natural justice which are derived from common law. There are seven rules and these are set out here.

- A person should know and understand the standards of performance he or she is expected to achieve and the rules to which his or her behaviour is expected to conform. Merely providing a copy of the procedure may not be sufficient.
- Except for cases of gross misconduct, employees should be given an opportunity to improve *before* disciplinary action is taken.
- The person should be given an opportunity to appeal against a disciplinary decision.
- The person should know the nature of the accusation against him or her.
- The person should be given an opportunity to state his or her case.
- The disciplinary panel should act in good faith.
- The person should be given a clear indication of where they are failing or the rules they have broken.

These principles are put into practice within the context of a **disciplinary procedure** and within a reasonable time frame.

An exception to this may be for a persistent offender when it may be appropriate to have a fixed time frame specified in order to review improvements in performance.

The application of discipline at work

The application of discipline can be divided into five parts:

- Company rules
- Disciplinary rules
- Disciplinary procedures
- Disciplinary practice
- Contingencies if things go wrong

Company rules

Company rules are set out in staff handbooks and standards of performance are contained within other systems which regulate the behaviour of staff. These rules set out the basic parameters within which staff are expected to comply. For example, they establish starting and finishing times of work, the criteria for claiming expenses and the myriad of other issues with which people become so familiar that they can become pushed to the background of working life and can seem of relatively little importance. It is at this basic level that managers can address basic performance improvement issues by encouraging staff to comply with these requirements. If matters of basic performance issues are not addressed they can lead to more serious offences, because by not acting, managers may be deemed to have condoned the basic offence. It is unlikely that company rules will cover all circumstances or areas of operation as there needs to be sufficient flexibility within the rules to allow the safe performance of work activities within different work contexts.

The responsibility is clearly on managers to remedy the situation. Failure to act promptly can affect the morale and motivation of other staff in a work team. Should an 'informal warning' fail to work then managers may be forced to use formal procedure. In these circumstances it may be construed that the offending employee has forced managers into applying formal sanction.

Disciplinary rules

The rules should, however, not be so general as to be meaningless in their application. The **rules of discipline** should be stated clearly, and the people and place to which the rules apply should be clear too. Organizations often apply sanctions to people who are found consuming alcohol while at work. For some employees the consumption of alcohol, in moderation, may be part of a person's job. Sales people who entertain potential clients, or senior managers who discuss policy matters over a working lunch, may be legitimate exceptions to this rule.

Another example in terms of 'place': in a munitions factory, eating a sweet was stated as being gross misconduct. This fortunately did not apply to the whole of the factory, but only to one particular part where explosive was loaded into munitions. The explosive was highly toxic and the rule was enforced in this way for safety reasons. People who did not poison themselves to death were obviously disciplined!

Disciplinary rules need to keep abreast of business and social developments. The implications of this are that all staff must be made aware of any rule change and understand the application of the rules for themselves and their conduct and performance at work.

Disciplinary procedures

The purpose of a disciplinary procedure is to ensure an employee is treated fairly, that each situation is investigated thoroughly and sanctions for punishment are imposed consistently. The procedure forms an agreement between managers and employees, which sets out in a progressive manner, the way in which sanctions leading to a termination of the contract of employment can take place for continued breaches of company rules. In a unionized company the procedure is often agreed between management and trade union representatives. To encourage a degree of consistency a disciplinary procedure developed by ACAS (The Advisory Conciliation and Arbitration Service) has been accepted in the UK as a **Code of Practice**. This means the procedure is the standard against which the disciplinary procedures used by companies are compared. Although the ACAS Code of Practice (1999) is not in itself legally binding, the degree to which a company's disciplinary procedure differs from the ACAS code may have a bearing on any claims for unfair dismissal at an industrial tribunal. The ACAS code is therefore used in evidence as representing 'best practice' for disciplinary procedural agreements.

To be regarded as appropriate the ACAS code of practice sets out minimum standards as far as a **disciplinary procedure** is concerned. The procedure should

- be in writing;
- specify to whom it applies;
- specify the types of sanction which may be applied;
- specify the levels of management who can make decisions;
- provide an opportunity for a person to appeal;
- make clear the representational rights of employees at a disciplinary hearing; for example a trade union representative or colleague may be acceptable, even if the organization does not recognize a trade union, but a solicitor or an employee's mother may be unacceptable. The role of the person in attendance should also be made clear, for example whether the attendees are representatives or observers;
- list specific examples of offences constituting gross misconduct.

Except for a case of gross misconduct, a person should not be dismissed for a first offence. All employees should understand the application of the procedure. Alleged lack of awareness of company rules or those contained within a disciplinary procedure may be used as a defence by an employee. In overall terms, the procedure should encourage people to improve their performance and conduct.

Examples of unacceptable behaviour may differ somewhat according to industry, sector or profession but there are some examples which are likely to apply irrespective of the organization. Disciplinary action is pursued when some form of **misconduct** or **offence** is alleged to have taken place.

Typical examples are:

- **Minor offences**: one-off, first occurrences which affect only the employee, for example lateness, sub-standard performance, issues which do not involve the safety and security of colleagues.
- **Misconduct**: unauthorized or uncertificated absenteeism, persistent poor time keeping, continued failure to carry out duties to a satisfactory standard, failure to carry out reasonable instructions, failure to comply with Health and Safety rules.
- **Gross misconduct**: typical examples of gross misconduct include:
  - theft of company property,
  - fraudulent claims or falsification of records,
  - assault of another employee,
  - criminal damage to property,
  - serious incapability due to alcohol or drugs,
  - serious acts of insubordination,
  - repeated actions of misconduct.

Penalties applied will depend upon the seriousness of the offence. For example, reductions in grade, withholding or withdrawing increments, withholding company concessions and suspension without pay may be applied for misconduct. If found guilty, dismissal may be the penalty for gross misconduct.

Fairness and consistency

When deciding if a disciplinary penalty is appropriate, consider the employee's general performance and disciplinary record and whether or not the disciplinary procedure points to a particular remedy. Consider also if the penalty is reasonable in the circumstances.

Consideration should be given to:

- penalties imposed in similar cases in the past;
- any circumstances which may mitigate to reduce the penalty;
- whether the penalty is reasonable in the circumstances.

Disciplinary procedures are not necessarily sequential in operation; the stage at which the procedure starts will depend upon the severity of the offence. For example, in a case of misconduct it may be appropriate to issue a written or final written warning straight away, depending upon the offence. Furthermore, in certain cases, special arrangements may need to be made to handle a disciplinary matter. Some examples are provided here.

- **Discipline of trade union officials**: Normal rules should be applied to a shop steward's conduct or behaviour. Care is needed, however, as disciplinary action taken against a shop steward may be misconstrued as victimization or an attack on the union. In these circumstances, it is advisable to discuss the issues involved with a full-time official of the union at the earliest opportunity and to ask the official to attend any hearings.

- **Employees who work shifts**: Many employees work away from main work areas and may not have access to the full disciplinary procedures. They should be given paid time off to attend hearings on the main site during normal working hours. If witnesses need to be called, an alternative is to hold the hearing during the employee's normal working time.
- **Criminal offences**: Employees should not be disciplined or dismissed simply because they have committed a criminal offence. A disciplinary investigation should be conducted in the normal way and a decision reached at the end of the process. The disciplinary process may be held before the end of a prosecution and if necessary in the absence of the employee.

The outcomes of disciplinary hearings are recorded and filed on an employee's personal file. In cases where an employee does not re-offend and continues to show improved behaviour and performance over an extended period of time, the employee can ask to have records of the offence removed from their file. The normal time scale involved is three years, but this action may not be appropriate in all circumstances.

Disciplinary practice

To avoid potential pitfalls, it is essential that the disciplinary procedure is followed every time. In times of doubt it is advisable to consult a personnel professional before action is taken. It is very difficult to recover the situation if an inadvertent mistake is made and there can be serious and expensive consequences for organizations, if an aggrieved employee decides to complain to an industrial tribunal. A suggested process for handling discipline is considered here.

If a full disciplinary process is gone through, it is likely to include the following stages:

- Preliminary investigation
- Disciplinary hearing
- First-stage appeal
- Final-stage appeal

Throughout these stages, there is a need to:

- decide if the employee should remain at work or be suspended;
- decide how precisely to conduct a preliminary investigation;
- convene a disciplinary hearing (if appropriate);
- on the balance of evidence make a decision to discipline or not;
- apply appropriate sanction;
- advise on right of appeal;
- record the outcome.

In addition, it may be desirable that the employee does not remain at work, either from the employer's or the employee's point of view. In such circumstances, a manager can suspend an employee from work while the incident is investigated. During the suspension the employee should receive basic pay, which need not include shift-working enhancements. If later in the process the disciplinary matter is dropped, the employee will be entitled to financial reimbursement.

The preliminary investigation

The purpose of the preliminary investigation is to establish all the likely facts of the case and to decide if there is a case to answer and if a disciplinary hearing should be convened. The investigation should be held soon after the alleged offence, typically within 14 days and investigated by an employee who is not connected with the offence. The investigation will involve collection of any documentary evidence (corroboratory evidence is important here), talking to other employees, looking through personal records and talking to the person who committed the alleged breach of rules to enable them to explain their involvement. The issues arising from a preliminary investigation will depend on circumstances pertaining to the individual case; each is likely to differ.

The first matter is likely to be **the seriousness of the offence**, whether the offence is the first and whether the person should remain at work or be suspended. This will also determine the level of manager that must be involved in the process. One of the rules of natural justice is that no one should act as judge and jury when someone's livelihood is at risk. The manager who carries out an investigation should not be involved in deciding the outcome of a disciplinary hearing. Bearing this in mind, the investigating manager should be chosen with some care.

Particular problems are caused if the alleged offender is a trade union representative when involvement of a full-time trade union official is required. Shift workers too cause particular problems for investigation and interview arrangements. All such matters need to be considered as well as the investigation process itself. This will involve collecting evidence from a variety of sources, which are directly related to and surround the work of the alleged offender. **Corroboratory evidence** is important here. It is important that managers investigating an offence should keep an open mind and not pre-judge the outcome of an investigation before all circumstances of the incident are known. The investigation should be completed within a reasonable time scale and as soon as practicable within the operational constraints and the time scale laid down in the procedure.

Once the preliminary investigation has been concluded, a decision will be made as to whether there is a case to answer. The offending employee should be notified of this decision as soon as possible and informed of their right to be accompanied. This can be done face to face if the employee is still working, or in writing if the employee is suspended. The allegations, and reasons for dropping the matter or pursuing the issue, should be made clear to the employee in relation to company rules. If the matter is dropped, then all evidence should be destroyed. If the matter is pursued to the hearing stage, then reasonable notice should be given to the employee to enable him or her to arrange representation by, say, a colleague or trade union official. The investigation must not be merged or connected in any way with the disciplinary hearing.

The disciplinary hearing

The intention to convene a hearing must be made clear to the employee. The purpose of the disciplinary hearing is to enable a fair, consistent and reasonable decision to be made regarding disciplinary action. The hearing should be held quickly, typically within seven days of the conclusion of the preliminary investigation and extended only by mutual agreement. The hearing will take into account all the facts of the case and the employee's views before reaching a decision on any sanction.

Both parties to the hearing can submit evidence, call witnesses and ask questions of the people present. Copies of all documentation to be used as evidence will be copied and circulated in advance of the hearing to all those who will be present. The people who will normally attend are: for management, a personnel officer, a senior manager of the employee (the level of seniority will be decided by the nature of the alleged offence) and the employee's line manager; for the employee, an appropriate companion or representative chosen by the employee, and the employee himself/herself. Entitlement of the employee to a companion is now embodied legally even if the employer does not recognize a trade union; however, the right to be accompanied does not extend to representation hence the colleague or trade union representative is not entitled to speak and restrictions can also be placed on the companion by the employing organization. For example, entitlement to be accompanied by a trade union representative in an organization that does not recognize trade unions may be restricted to more serious cases. Witnesses for each side can be called and will be allowed time off to attend the hearing. Specific arrangements for time off should be facilitated by the 'side' calling the witnesses. If during the hearing it becomes apparent that the offence committed is beyond the powers of the attending managers to deal with, then the hearing should be adjourned. A new hearing can then be arranged with managers of appropriate authority in attendance. The preparation for and structure of the hearing would normally take the format suggested here.

The interview. Preparation by the manager

A manager should have all the facts. It is better to over-prepare and collect too much information that may not be used than to risk not preparing sufficiently. If the problem is misconduct, evidence is needed about what happened. If the problem is one of performance, the standards of expected performance will need to be available, as well as evidence of the performance displayed by the employee. In such cases neither hearsay nor opinion is sufficient in isolation. As manager, you should approach the hearing expecting to be challenged on the facts or their interpretation.

If the facts are incorrect, or sufficient doubt can be cast upon them by the employee and his or her representative, then the case may become untenable irrespective of innocence or guilt. Where the employee is represented by a trade union official, managers need to be aware that it is likely that the official may handle substantially more disciplinary hearings than a manager, is likely to be more skilled at handling the hearing and may, in fact, have more in-depth knowledge of procedures. In such cases, extra care is needed and the advice of HRM specialists is recommended. During the hearing it is essential that management retain control of the process at all times.

The interview. Preparation by the employee

The employee, too, needs adequate time to prepare. Too much delay in the process will build up an undue amount of tension and subsequent resentment. If the employee continues to work, performance is likely to suffer.

Structure of the hearing

- **Introduction**: The objective of the hearing should be made clear to everyone present. People at the hearing should be introduced and the role of each person clarified. This is particularly important where a representative is in attendance. The nature of the complaint should be outlined. The order of business must be set out and the opportunity for each side to ask questions made. The stage in the procedure that the hearing represents should also be clarified.
- **Explore the problem**: The case is opened by management. As clearly and concisely as possible, a manager should explain precisely why there is a problem. Evidence should be presented which supports the existence of a problem. Check with the employee that he or she agrees with the evidence presented. To date, most of the talking, and the tone of setting out the case, must be impartial, non-emotional and impersonal.
- **Exploring the performance gap**: During the hearing a picture should be built up, backed by evidence about the expected and actual levels of performance of the employee and the displayed performance difference between the two levels which is considered to be a 'performance gap'. Any mitigating circumstances should be brought to light. The extent to which circumstances have a bearing on the case should be carefully checked. Once the extent of the performance gap and the circumstances for it have been 'agreed', the next stage is to look for ways (if possible) of eliminating the gap.
- **Finding a solution**: Once all evidence is presented, management must make a decision on what action to take. The action must be decided based on the evidence presented. In some cases more evidence may be needed before a decision can be made. Before reaching a decision it is good practice for an adjournment in proceedings to be made. The employee can be called back to the room to hear the decision. Depending on the circumstances, the meeting may turn into an action planning process to eliminate the performance gap. If a disciplinary sanction is to be applied, then reasons for the punishment should be made clear to the employee. Implications for future misconduct and performance of the employee in their job role must be discussed. Finally, the employee must be advised of their right to appeal against the disciplinary decision.
- **Summarize the hearing**: At the end of the hearing the whole process should be summarized by management. Afterwards, relevant written records are produced, filed and communicated to all parties involved in the process.

Disciplinary hearings: the need for control

The skill of controlling a disciplinary interview should not be under-estimated. An employee may be highly emotional, rude and unruly, not stop talking, rush in with excuses before the facts have been established, or not turn up at all!

Similarly, to retain control of a hearing, managers should themselves remain calm and be prepared for the unexpected. Under the pressure of the hearing managers and employees can occasionally act irrationally and time should be allowed for people to calm down. To retain control, managers must have a clear mindset of how the hearing is to be conducted, stick to it and think about the most effective way to keep the hearing on track. Retaining control is also helped by building a clear picture of the evidence regarding the offence, knowing the likely reaction of the person involved and being prepared for it.

This requires a certain amount of flexibility, being able to manage the pace of the hearing and being able to 'think on your feet'. Keeping the objective of the hearing and the structure of the process in mind can help with control, and making some notes in advance about the structure you wish to follow may be useful for emergencies.

Briefing the others involved in the hearing to come to an agreed understanding of how the hearing is to be conducted can also prevent embarrassment. Skills of listening and questioning are also key to the process of examining the validity of any contra-evidence presented. Every hearing is different, because of the personalities involved; this is why preparation is the key to conducting a successful hearing. Effective preparation allows managers to remain one step ahead and in control of the situation.

Copies of all written material will be given to all who are due to attend the hearing, often at least 72 hours beforehand.

Outcomes and time scales

The decision of the hearing will be notified in writing, commonly within seven days of the conclusion, and a copy placed on the employee's personal file.

Appeals

First-stage appeals must be submitted in writing, commonly within seven days after the decision has been notified to the employee. The reason for the appeal must be stated, and the result of the appeal will be notified within seven days of the conclusion of the hearing. This level of appeal is normally dealt with by a manager. The time constraints for final-stage appeals are the same as for first-stage appeals. This level of appeal is normally dealt with by a manager one level of seniority above the manager who handled the first-level appeal. In respect of dismissal, the final appeal is to senior management.

Figure 5.5 lists reasons for disciplinary action and dismissal, and figure 5.6 gives a review of procedures.

In one survey (IRS, 1995), the most commonly listed minor misconduct offences included:

- Absenteeism
- Lateness
- Poor time keeping
- Unacceptable performance
- Aggression

Among the offences most commonly listed as gross misconduct, the following were included:

- Assault
- Theft
- Fraud/serious financial irregularities
- Sex/race harassment
- Indecent assault
- Serious infringements of health and safety regulations
- Alcohol/drug misuse
- Helping competitors / unauthorized disclosure of information
- Time recording offences
- Criminal conviction

(IDS Brief 570, 1996)

In another survey of 50 organizations, it was found that in 10 per cent of the companies surveyed, line managers spent between 5–20 per cent of their time on dealing with disciplinary issues (IRS 591 1995).

Primarily, disciplinary action fell short of dismissal although this varied according to sector and industry. For example, dismissal was more common in manufacturing, finance and retail. Furthermore, it was found that:

- 64 per cent of companies surveyed had been to an Industrial Tribunal
- 26 per cent admitted to losing their cases
- 19 per cent were still in progress

Clearly such action is costly in terms of time, company and managerial reputation. It was argued also that vital to the successful management of discipline in the organizations surveyed were:

- training in disciplinary management;
- clear written guidelines;
- intermediate courses of action before final written warnings and dismissal.

Figure 5.5   Reasons for disciplinary action and dismissal.

Grievance

Grievances are raised when there are issues about which any employee feels dissatisfied. Usually, it is thought of as an action taken against a fellow employee or, more commonly, against management, be it the line manager or a company policy.

The causes of grievance are numerous. One study suggests that the most common causes are the introduction of new work practices and disciplinary action (IRS 591, 1995). Other causes of grievance include the following:

- Disagreements about the interpretation of terms and conditions
- Staffing levels
- Personal issues
- Discrimination

(1) Purpose and scope

This procedure is designed to help and encourage all employees to achieve and maintain standards of conduct, attendance and job performance. The company rules (a copy of which is displayed in the office) and this procedure applies to all employees. The aim is to ensure consistent and fair treatment for all.

(2) Principles

a) No disciplinary action will be taken against an employee until the case has been fully investigated.
b) At every stage in the procedure the employee will be advised of the nature of the complaint against him or her and will be given the opportunity to state his or her case before any decision is made.
c) At all stages the employee will have the right to be accompanied by a shop steward, employee representative or work colleague during the disciplinary interview.
d) No employee will be dismissed for a first breach of discipline except in the case of gross misconduct when the penalty will be dismissal without notice or payment in lieu of notice.
e) An employee will have the right to appeal against any disciplinary penalty imposed.
f) The procedure may be implemented at any stage if the employee's alleged misconduct warrants such action.

(3) The procedure

Minor faults will be dealt with informally but where the matter is more serious the following procedure will be used.

Stage 1 – Oral warning

If conduct or performance does not meet acceptable standards the employee will normally be given a formal oral warning. He or she will be advised of the reason for the warning, that it is the first stage of the disciplinary procedure and of his or her right to appeal. A brief note of the oral warning will be kept but it will be spent after . . . months, subject to satisfactory conduct and performance.

Stage 2 – Written warning

If the offence is a serious one, or if further offence occurs, a written warning will be given to the employee by the supervisor. This will give details of the complaint, the improvement required and the timescale. It will warn that action under Stage 3 will be considered if there is no satisfactory improvement and will advise of the right of appeal. A copy of this written warning will be kept by the supervisor but it will be disregarded for disciplinary purposes after . . . months subject to satisfactory conduct and performance.

Stage 3 – Final written warning or disciplinary suspension

If there is a failure to improve and conduct or performance is still unsatisfactory, or if the misconduct is sufficiently serious to warrant only one written warning but insufficiently serious to justify dismissal (in effect both first and final written warning), a final written warning will normally be given to the employee. This will give details of the complaint, will warn that dismissal will result if there is no satisfactory improvement and will advise of the right to appeal. A copy of this final written warning will be kept by the supervisor but it will be spent after . . . months (in exceptional cases the period may be longer) subject to satisfactory conduct and performance. Alternatively, consideration will be given to imposing a penalty of a disciplinary suspension without pay for up to a maximum of five working days.

Stage 4 – Dismissal

If conduct or performance is still unsatisfactory and the employee still fails to reach the prescribed standards, dismissal will normally result. Only the appropriate senior manager can take the decision to dismiss. The employee will be provided, as soon as reasonably practicable, with written reasons for dismissal, the date on which employment will terminate and the right of appeal.

(4) Gross misconduct

The following list provides examples of offences which are normally regarded as gross misconduct: theft, fraud, deliberate falsification of records, fighting, assault on another person, deliberate damage to company property, serious incapability through alcohol or being under the influence of illegal drugs, serious negligence which causes unacceptable loss, damage or injury, serious acts of insubordination.

If you are accused of an act of gross misconduct, you may be suspended from work on full pay, normally for no more than five working days, while the company investigates the alleged offence. If on completion of the investigation and the full disciplinary procedure, the company is satisfied that gross misconduct has occurred, the result will normally be summary dismissal without notice or payment in lieu of notice.

(5) Appeals

An employee who wishes to appeal against a disciplinary decision should inform . . . within two working days. The senior manager will hear all appeals and his/her decision is final. At the appeal any disciplinary penalty imposed will be reviewed but it cannot be increased.

Figure 5.6 Review of procedures: ACAS guidelines. *Source:* ACAS code of practice 1: disciplinary procedures and practice in employment.

- Bullying
- Health and safety
- Harassment

As with disciplinary procedures, there are ACAS recommendations for how grievances should be dealt with. This includes making sure that there are clear levels through which the grievance can be pursued, specifically:

- departmental head
- works manager
- personnel manager
- managing director and then finally,
- national level.

ACAS recommend representation at all bar the first stage (by a trade union official or another employee) as good employment relations practice. Furthermore, in reality, the number of stages is likely to vary between three and five, and the vast majority of companies have reasonable time limits for each stage (IRS 636, 1997). The management of the process very much mirrors that of the informal and formal stages of disciplinary procedures.

Dismissal

For most organizations, **dismissal** is still a fact of organizational life. Dismissals can be categorized as **fair or unfair**. **Fair dismissal** is where an employee's contract is terminated fairly as a result of the contract coming to an end, i.e. fixed-term or temporary contract, or as a result of a reasonable and properly conducted series of disciplinary hearings. It may also be for other reasons discussed below. Potentially fair reasons for dismissal are:

- **'Misconduct'**: Where behaviour consistently falls below the required standard. Gross misconduct also falls under this heading, although this is a more serious offence which results in a more stringent disciplinary sanction.
- **Capability**: Where performance falls consistently below standard.
- **Legal disqualification**: In these circumstances the contract of employment

becomes frustrated because it may be impossible for the employee to perform the duties expected of them. Take the case of a delivery driver who is banned from driving due to drinking: the contract would be impossible for the employee to carry out. Frustration of contract, however, is technically not dismissal. If, for example, a person is imprisoned, the situation makes it impossible for them to undertake their normal duties due to changed circumstances of the employee. If frustration of contract can be proven, then an employee cannot claim for unfair dismissal as no dismissal has taken place.

- **Redundancy**: Genuine needs of the business. In redundancy it is the post or job that disappears. In these circumstances there is no job for the person to do.
- **Any other substantial reason**: For example, actions carried out by the employee which can reflect badly on the nature of his or her employment. In these cases the employee is deemed not to be a suitable person to hold the job. Examples could be criminal offences of indecency, fundamental breach of confidence, telling lies to an employer, or misrepresentation of qualifications when applying for a job.

Unfair dismissal is where an employee is dismissed using unfair reasons or means or not following procedure. Potentially unfair reasons for dismissal are:

- **Pregnancy**: Typically, dismissal on the grounds of pregnancy or any reason connected to the pregnancy is automatically unfair.
- **Business transfer**: Dismissal on the grounds of business transfer, unless there is an economic, technical or organizational reason for the dismissal which results necessarily in a change to the workforce composition.
- **Trade union membership**: Dismissal of an employee simply for being a member of a trade union or taking part in its activities is typically an offence, unless it is held to be 'in the national interest'.
- **Health and safety** and dismissal in connection with Health and Safety regulations.
- **Denial of statutory rights**: Dismissal of an employee because he or she asserts statutory rights.
- **Instant dismissal**: Dismissal with appropriate notice, and all pay entitlements.
- **Summary dismissal**: Dismissal without notice or any pay entitlements. Only used where the term and action are specifically included in the disciplinary procedure, normally for specific cases of gross misconduct that are so serious as to render the employment contract as being fundamentally breached.
- **Wrongful dismissal**: Dismissal process undertaken in the same way as summary dismissal, which is in breach of the disciplinary procedure and therefore unfair.
- **Constructive dismissal**: Alterations to an existing contract of employment or working practice with which it is extremely difficult or impossible for an employee to comply, which makes remaining employed untenable.

Contingencies if things go wrong

If in doubt seek advice. This will help to reduce the likelihood of the process going wrong. However, if the process goes wrong and it results in an employee being dismissed unfairly it may be too late to avoid a claim. Such cases are sometimes taken to an industrial tribunal, where legal redress and financial compensation are sought.

The tribunal will look at the question of whether the employer followed the agreed procedure, i.e. was the process of the dismissal reasonable and were the reasons for the dismissal reasonable? Care is needed because a potentially fair reason for dismissal may not be upheld at tribunal if the process of the dismissal was not conducted in accordance with procedure. Let us look at some examples. Decisions can be found at the end of this section.

- **Loss arising from the manner of the dismissal**: If as a result of the dismissal the employee has suffered illness which makes it more difficult to find work.
- **Loss of statutory rights**: The loss of rights within a new employment context. A dismissed employee will need to re-qualify under the unfair dismissal legislation. In calculating an award the industrial tribunal takes into account the extent to which the employee contributed towards his or her own downfall.

Conclusion

This chapter has discussed the ways in which the conduct and performance of employees are controlled and managed by organizations. On behalf of an organization, managers draft rules and regulations to produce controlled conduct and performance. As a backup to this process, the organization develops a systematic process to manage people who cannot or will not conform to the norms of behaviour laid down. The responsibility for implementing these processes lies with individual managers and is regarded by many as the most challenging part of a manager's role.

Formally disciplining an employee may be seen as the last resort of a performance management process. The imposition of discipline can reinforce 'us' and 'them' attitudes in organizations. In many cases appropriate and timely managerial action in managing poor performance may reduce the need to use the formal procedures. Encouraging appropriate performance and behaviour in a work team, by all staff, can in time build into shared, accepted behavioural and performance patterns. The manager's role in achieving this is through timely interventions and reinforcement of organizational values.

Such behaviour can be reinforced by peer group pressure, obviating the need for managerial interventions. On the other hand, organizational demands on workers do seem to have increased in recent years. The boundary between acceptable and unacceptable employee behaviour may have become narrowed. This increases the need for employee self-discipline to encourage employee performance to comply with organizational demands. Personal skills of organizing oneself within the organization are therefore more important now than ever before. The key challenge for managers is to continue to manage effectively the balance between controlling employees at work, while motivating and encouraging high performance and commitment to organizational activities. Handled effectively, the personal credibility of a manager can be enhanced with commensurate gains in productivity and performance.

Summary

In this chapter, we have considered the ways in which managers are required to address the performance needs of organizations through the management of individual performance and ensuring that required standards of behaviour, as set out in codes of conduct or contracts of employment, are adhered to. The importance of developing clear policies and procedures in order to reinforce policy and practice is outlined. In particular, attention is paid to the operational roles and responsiblities that managers are often expected to undertake in relation to appraisal, capability, disciplinary, grievance and dismissal activities, and the importance of ensuring that managers provide opportunities for improved performance or the making good of poor performance is emphasized.

Questions

1   How does your company lay down standards of conduct and performance in different parts of your organization? How does your organization communicate these to employees? What are the potential pitfalls of these approaches?
2   Managing conduct, performance and unacceptable behaviour – case examples.

Your portfolio of companies has had to deal with a spate of industrial tribunal appearances. You have been appointed as a senior manager with responsibility to appraise these cases.

Case 1

Your security firm delivers and collects cash from high street banks.

Each morning at the depot of a security firm the '10 Golden Rules' were broadcast through a tannoy system to all staff. One rule was that no more than one bag of cash should be carried between a bank and the van at one time. The second was that no more than £2000 should be carried at once. Breach of any one of the Golden Rules may result in an employee being dismissed. During the last collection of the day, two bags containing £3000 in change were to be collected from a bank. The collector decided to carry both bags at once, breaking two Golden Rules.

The collector was spotted by a supervisor, who immediately took disciplinary action and as a result the collector was dismissed.

Was the dismissal fair? Give reasons for your decision.

Case 2

Three employees were entrusted with keys to a safe. A large sum of money went missing from the safe. None of the employees would admit to taking the money. A disciplinary hearing was held and all three employees were dismissed. After the event, one of the employees confessed to the manager that he had taken the money, therefore proving the innocence of the other two employees. What courses of action are open to the company and the employees?

Case 3

One of your porters assaults a supervisor during working hours. The assault was witnessed by other workers and a manager. Assault is considered as gross misconduct by the company. The employee was immediately dismissed, with all pay and entitlements. The employee complained to a tribunal that the dismissal was unfair.

   As this employee's line manager, you have been asked to justify your actions by the tribunal. Give reasons for your response.

3   In criminal law, the burden of proof lies with the Crown Prosecution Service to prove beyond reasonable doubt that a person is guilty. In what ways does the application of discipline in a company differ from this?
4   For your work team, think about and list the norms which produce controlled performance under the headings of self-discipline, team discipline. What actions can you take as a manager to reinforce these norms?
5   How might ethical analysis assist in answering the above questions?

References

Advisory, Conciliation and Arbitration Service (ACAS) (1999) *Discipline at work: the ACAS advisory handbook*, UK ACAS.

Anderson, G, and Burnell, J (1987) The characteristics of effective interviews, *Personnel Review*, Vol 16 No 4.

Fletcher, C (1993) Appraisal: an idea whose time has gone? *Personnel Management*, September, 34–7.

IDS (1995) *Performance and Objectives*, July, IDS.

Industrial Society (1994) *Performance Management – Managing Best Practice No. 2*, June, p. 11.

IRS Employment Trends 518 (1992) Alcoholism awareness at work 2: alcohol policy provisions, August, pp. 5–10.

IRS Employment Trends 591 (1995) Discipline at Work: The Practice, September 1995.

IRS Employment Trends 592 (1995) Discipline at Work 2: the procedures, September, pp. 5–16.

IRS Employment Trends 636 (1997) Handling employee grievance part 1, July, pp. 5–12.

Maier NRF (1958) *The Appraisal Interview, Objectives Methods and Skills*, Wiley, New York.

Stuart, P (1992) Tracing workplace problems to hidden disorders *Personnel Journal*, June, pp. 82–95.

Torrington, D and Hall, L (1995) *Personnel Management in Action* Prentice-Hall, London.

Legal briefing

A. Appraisal

It is to state the obvious that individual staff appraisal should be carried out in the fairest possible manner, both as regards the method of appraisal adopted and the choice of appraiser. Failure to do either could result in a legal challenge by an employee whose promotion is blocked or who, in an extreme case, is dismissed for incapacity as a result.

Continued on page 204

Employees are entitled to know what information relating to them is stored on an electronic system. (Please see legal briefing to Chapter 7.) An employer must also be circumspect in the use that is made of this information, for example in giving references. A duty is owed both to the employee and to the prospective new employer. A poor reference that is false or misleading could involve the employer in an action for damages on the part of the employee for negligence or defamation; an unjustified glowing reference (sometimes given to be rid of an unsatisfactory employee) would entitle the new employer to damages for negligence or even fraud. A negotiated severance package for an 'under-performing' employee that includes providing a reference should be drawn up very carefully and, if possible, with legal advice.

B. Grievance procedures

The 'section 1 statement' (please see legal briefing to Chapter 1) requires the employer to specify, by name or description, the person to whom the employee can apply if he or she is dissatisfied with any disciplinary decision, or for the redress of any grievance in relation to his or her work. The necessary information can be conveyed in another document ('works rules', for example) to which the employee is referred and to which he or she has reasonable access. Enterprises with fewer than 20 employees are exempt.

C. Disciplinary procedures

As with grievance procedures (above), the employer must inform the employee of the disciplinary procedures that have been put in place. In a unionized workplace, these will have been agreed with the recognized trades unions. There is the same exemption for enterprises with 20, or fewer, employees. Please refer to the legal briefing to Chapter 8.

Procedures will vary from company to company, and as employees have a statutory right to know the procedures to be followed by their employer, and will, impliedly, have agreed to them as part of their contract, they will have virtually no chance of challenging disciplinary sanctions applied to them where the procedure has been followed to the letter. The only possible exception might arise in the unlikely event of the rules, as laid down, being found to be unreasonable, and in breach of what is termed 'natural justice'.

The rules of 'natural justice' as applied to disciplinary procedures are as follows:

- The employee must be informed of the nature of the complaint made against him or her.
- The employee must have the opportunity to be heard in his or her own defence; this need not necessarily be in person – it could be by a representative, which would normally be a union official or fellow employee; in more serious cases the employee may wish to be legally represented.
- While it is not possible in these 'domestic tribunals' to select a panel that is totally divorced from the matters to be determined (it is not a court of law, and the employer is both bringing the complaint and sitting in judgement), the procedures have to be as fair as circumstances allow; the manager most involved in the dispute should in no way be part of the panel, and any appeal should be to an appeal panel composed of persons different from those involved in the first hearing. The ideal of a truly independent arbiter cannot, realistically, be achieved in the majority of workplaces.

Allegations of a serious character, such as theft, must be supported by such evidence as can be obtained by a reasonable investigation by the employer.

After a disciplinary tribunal has found against the employee, sanctions available to the employer have to be applied with some care. Monetary sanctions, such as fines and deductions from pay, must comply with the Employment Rights Act, 1996 (which now includes the provisions of the former Wages Act, 1986). There is no inherent right recognized in English law to suspend an employee without pay; if an employer wishes to exercise such a right, it must be incorporated into the contract of employment. Other sanctions include warnings (which are usually included in the formal disciplinary procedures), demotion or transfer to another job.

The most serious sanction of all is dismissal for misconduct or incapacity. (Please refer to the legal briefing to Chapter 1 for the law relating to dismissal.) Any sanction short of dismissal which is found to have breached the law, or to have contravened the terms of the contract of employment, may entitle the employee to claim that he or she has been constructively dismissed.

Another change in the law strengthening the role of trades unions is the provision that an employee involved in a disciplinary or grievance procedure now has a statutory right to be accompanied at the hearing. Such a 'companion' must be either a trade union employee or a suitably experienced or trained trade union official or a co-worker. Both the worker who is the subject of the hearing and the 'accompanying person' have statutory protection against victimization, including dismissal, for exercising their rights under this provision.

D. ACAS Code of Practice relating to disciplinary procedures

This contains good advice relating to the need for clear rules, communicated to the employees. The recommended procedure consists of an oral warning, or, if the conduct is sufficiently serious, a first written warning, to be followed in either case by a final written warning. Employers need not stick slavishly to the ACAS formula, but the procedures adopted should be at least as fair as the ACAS Code. The advantage to the employer is that strict observance of the rules will save, in an extreme case, a finding of unfair dismissal on procedural grounds. (Please see the legal briefing to Chapter 1.)

Dismissal without a formal disciplinary hearing, and without the employer incurring a sanction for unfair dismissal, is, in theory, possible. This would be where the employer could demonstrate that, in all the circumstances of the case, the disciplinary procedures would be 'utterly useless'. The conduct of the employee would have to be so extreme that summary dismissal would be the response of any reasonable employer. Such circumstances would be so rare that an employer would be well advised to initiate the formal procedures however expensive and time-consuming. In any case, the employee may well, against all predictions to the contrary, have a rational explanation for his conduct.

International human resource management within the context of the global economy

6

Clive Wildish

Learning objectives

After studying this chapter you should be able to:

- understand the impact of internationalization and globalization on aspects of work organization and HR processes;
- appreciate the significance of international management development to the success of international operations;
- be clear about the importance of understanding diversity management in an international context, in particular for the management of multinational teams;
- understand the significance of effective international human resource management for the management of international strategic alliances and joint ventures;
- be aware of the importance of addressing compensation, employment conditions and performance management policy and practice for 'locals' and 'expatriate' employees.

Introduction

It would be very easy to refer to international human resource management as little more than HRM on a national scale with some additional features that relate to people management issues in different parts of the world. There are indeed similarities in the role of human resource management within national and international organizations; however, there are also some significant differences, not least of which is the development and deployment of staff in different national and regional locations around the world. The somewhat overused maxim encouraging the imperative to 'think globally and act locally', if nothing else, illustrates the importance of looking at the management of the global organization at two, sometimes distinct, levels. The first of these may take the form of a management strategy based upon the concepts of *standardization* and *universalism* where the principal aim is to create a management culture that is recognizable to a specific organization wherever it operates around the globe. The second level of strategy may involve taking different approaches to management in different locations around the world. This second approach may be particularly important where there are significant cultural differences, brought about by national and organizational culture, between one location and another. The role of the international human resource manager is, therefore, that of setting the *tone* of management for the organization as it conducts business across the globe, dependent upon cultural variation and variety and market needs from one region to another. Put perhaps more theatrically, the international human resource manager is the *conscience* of the international firm.

International human resource management and the injunction to 'go global'

To understand the role of the international human resource manager within the global firm, it would be helpful if we tried, at least, to provide a definition of 'globalization'. A number of varying definitions of the term 'globalization' have been put forward by writers and practitioners alike over the years. This, in turn, has led to confusion and indeed misconception as to the true or most accurate meaning of the term. As a result, some leading management theorists now doubt its very existence, while others are still searching for what they consider to be the most comprehensive analysis of the phenomenon.

'Globalization' has been defined as the process by which the development of a 'global ideology' has begun to transcend national boundaries, with far-reaching consequences for both the conduct of business transactions and the theory and practice of management (Vernon-Wortzel *et al.*, 1990). Following Levitt's (1983) definition, the process of globalization is expressed simplistically as a growing similarity in what citizens of different countries want to buy.

A more appropriate definition might be that the term 'globalization' encompasses the concept of a world economy based upon the increasing interdependencies and transactions between 'national' economies and between *sub* and *inter*national corporate actors. The terms 'integration', 'federation', and 'transnationality' come, perhaps, closest to an understanding of the dynamics of globalization. The degree to which these terms contribute to an understanding of the process may, of course, vary from one organization, or indeed from one sector, to another.

The lowering of trade barriers and the revolution in international transport and communications (notably the impact of containerization, international air travel and worldwide telecommunications linkages) have enabled companies to treat the world in a much more integrated manner. A further *trigger* of globalization is the emergence of a new wave of competitors, particularly from Asia, who have capitalized on falling tariffs and efficient global distribution to leverage their country-specific comparative advantages. New global market segments have appeared as technology has been imitated and diffused worldwide, almost simultaneously. Progressively, the key management requirement has been for global integration and cross-market coordination. The strategic mentality and organizational capability have shifted to a mode that Perlmutter (1969) terms 'geocentric'. In so doing, international managers, particularly in the United States and Europe, have been challenged to develop an entirely new approach to managing their worldwide operations.

There appears to be a common view among contemporary writers, such as Hedlund and Rolander (1990), Kogut (1990), Nonaka (1990) and White and Poynter (1990), that the modern multinational corporation (MNC) has outgrown the stage in which managers at the centre coordinate a set of peripheral subsidiaries, largely independent of each other. The utilization of the multinational network as an integrated and interdependent whole is presented as the basis for successful global business.

Hedlund and Rolander (1990) suggest that a genuine global MNC can better be thought of as what they term a 'heterarchy' rather than a classic 'hierarchy'. They define this new form as a set of reciprocally interdependent and geographically dispersed centres, held together largely by shared strategies, norms and information.

Kogut (1990) introduces the concept of sequential advantages of the MNC to indicate the shift of competitive advantage subsequent to the initial penetration of foreign markets. In his view it is the management of a company's global network that eventually becomes the source of advantage, allowing it to achieve economies of scale and scope, to learn about foreign conditions, and to achieve the operating flexibility inherent in such a network.

Nonaka (1990) argues that a shift from an information process to an information creation paradigm is necessary to understand the globalization of Japanese firms. He emphasizes the interplay between corporate-level articulated information and local tacit information, and the important intermediating role of entrepreneurial middle management.

White and Poynter (1990) focus on the horizontal organization of an MNC. They describe how lateral processes with widely distributed and shared responsibilities replace groupings of sets of functional activities under strict hierarchies with unity of command.

The concept of transnationality

Bartlett and Ghoshal (1989) distinguish between multinational, global and international companies. Each of these definitions, depending upon how the organization perceives itself, has implications for the role of international human resource management.

● **Multinational companies**: This term refers to companies that have developed a strategic posture and organizational capability that allow them to be very sensitive and responsive to differences in national environments around the world. In effect these corporations manage a portfolio of multiple national entities.

Box 6.1 The transnational company

The *transnational company* is described as possessing the following characteristics:
- Many centres
- Utilization of networks
- Organic structure

- Process oriented
- Interactive
- Many channels of communication
- Information = an important resource
- *Thinks globally and acts locally*

- **Global companies**: This term refers to companies that have developed international operations that are much more driven by the need for global efficiency, and are much more centralized in their strategic and operational decisions. These companies treat the world as an operational whole to whom the global operating environment and worldwide consumer demand are the dominant units of analysis, not the nation-state or local market.
- **International companies**: The strategy of this third group is based primarily on transferring and adapting the parent company's knowledge or expertise to foreign markets. The parent retains considerable influence and control, but less than in a classic global company; national units can adapt products and ideas coming from the centre, but have less independence and autonomy than multinational subsidiaries.

Bartlett and Ghoshal (1989) maintain that environmental forces have dramatically changed the nature of the strategic demands in a wide range of businesses, and the traditional approaches of multinational, global and international companies can no longer yield an adequate response. This has given rise to the development of a thesis which Bartlett and Ghoshal refer to as the 'transnational solution'.

The concept of *transnationality* has since been developed at Ashridge Management Centre by Barham *et al.* (Barham and Devine, 1991), who define globalization as the 'art of being local worldwide'.

International HRM and the Euromanager

Calori and Lawrence (1991) point out that there still remain a number of national and local differences between organizations within Europe, particularly in the way in which they invest in technology and market their goods. However, this does not mean that there cannot be a 'marriage' between the forces of global integration and local adaptation.

Forces of global integration might include: capital intensity, the ratio optimal scale/size of the world market, pressures from clients and/or suppliers, the ratio value added cost of transport and communication, economies of scale, international strategies of some competitors.

Forces influencing local adaptation of a business might include: differences between customer preferences (by country), physical proximity being a key success factor, differences in technical norms between countries, protectionist policies, differences in distribution channels between countries, attractiveness of a single domestic market.

The impact of the above forces will vary from one segment and indeed from one country to another.

For instance, across industries, French managers have a tendency to classify and segment, and they consider products and innovation as more important than British managers do. On the other hand, British managers are more concerned with control of mergers and monopolies and with the financial performance of their companies, being in growth segments and creating shareholder value.

Managers' thoughts influence their decisions and acts which, in turn, transform the competitive system. According to this logic, the homogenization of managers' understanding and the homogenization of competitive systems across Europe could take a long time.

Box 6.2 Characteristics of the multinational company

Research undertaken by Kevin Barham *et al.* was concerned with the integration of the following areas:

- Strategy and culture
- Culture (engendering an international spirit – the role of international HRM?)
- International management and the expertise produced through a rolling management development programme

The multinational company was described as possessing the following characteristics:

- One-centred
- Hierarchical
- Rigid
- Boss/subordinate relationships
- Clear chain of command

Organizations possessing the above characteristics were seen to be suffering from 'power hug', i.e. strategy was developed at the centre but information was held at the operating units.

Cracking the 'power hug' was seen by Barham as the key to developing the international manager within a globalized industry.

Box 6.3 Competitive activity in Europe

Roland Calori and Peter Lawrence, in their study of European Managers (Calori and Lawrence 1991, 1992), arrived at a number of common themes from their research:

- The increasing segmentation of markets
- The increasing duality of industries between major international multi-segments on the one hand and smaller competitors focused on one segment on the other hand
- A continuation of the concentration of industries, exits, mergers and acquisitions but with alliances and agreement becoming a more frequent form of quasi-concentration

- The increase in international competition, at different levels of intensity between segments in a given industry
- Investment in former Eastern Europe
- The belief that high diversity across European countries will not be rubbed off quickly
- The perception of the single European market as a 'non-event' or as a secondary force in the dynamics of the market
- A concern that the development of managers and training the workforce will be crucial sources of competitive advantage

There is also a high diversity between the behaviour of European customers:

> ... the German consumers are chauvinistic, the British are price sensitive, the Dutch are critical and thrifty, the Spanish are extremist, the French are impulsive and like novelty, the Italians are impulsive and take care of how they look, the Scandinavians are quality minded and consumerists. These stereotypes are caricatures but they express the feeling of strong diversity.
>
> (Calori and Lawrence, 1991)

Differences between regions of a country are sometimes also very strong; for instance, the Catalans, the Andalusians, the Basques and the Castilians speak different languages in Spain.

Considering the whole value chain, the alchemy between integration and differentiation will depend on the balance between globalization and localization forces in each segment of the market. So the resulting organization will be asymmetrical; it will also be specific to each company, for instance depending on the growth strategy. A few international firms will deal with this issue by building a more international executive committee.

When the development of the process of global integration and local adaptation was looked at from a specifically human resource perspective, most of the European manufacturers were seen to have started intensive training programmes of the workforce to exploit process technologies fully. For lower-level managers, it was considered that training will be more a mix of technical and management skills and teamwork, where cross-fertilization between functions will be more and more emphasized.

International management development

Preparing international managers for overseas assignments in the late 1990s is no easy task. The role of the international manager, as indicated in the foregoing paragraphs, is largely dependent upon the task that he or she has to perform, the culture of the local national and business environment and the period that the manager is expected to remain in that locality.

The consultancy role, in this regard, may be performed by either an internal or external consultant, or perhaps both! What international organizations require is a high degree of specialization in selecting and developing staff for overseas assignments. The role of line management in association with the international human resource specialist is to facilitate that process.

The cultural imperative

Developing managers for overseas assignments is not simply a matter of developing an acceptable proficiency in relevant hard skills such as linguistic ability and an appreciation of the social, economic and political infrastructure of the region to which they are being sent. It is, in other words, far more than a classroom activity. International management development is, rather, a continuous process that facilitates management exposure to different ways of managing and conducting business relationships around the world. This is facilitated in some organizations, for example in the publishing and media sector, through project teams, bringing together managers not only with different skills and competencies but also from varied cultural experiences. Exposure to cultural difference, with time, will build an acceptance and appreciation of the significance of sensitivity to different ways of conducting business relationships in different geographical locations. This is relevant not only to companies wishing to expand their overseas interests via new start-up operations but also through joint ventures and strategic alliances. It is worth mentioning here that what for many companies appears to be the right strategic decision in terms of operational 'fit' may ultimately run into difficulties where cultural 'fit' has either been glossed over or ignored altogether. We will explore this dilemma in greater detail when discussing the role of international human resource management in joint ventures and strategic alliances.

The creation of an appropriate managerial mindset

International management development plays an important role in building competitive advantage within the global economy and should, therefore, be seen as one of the core elements of any international business strategy. The actual contribution that it makes, however, is largely dependent upon how IMD is viewed by senior management and the executive board. It should be seen, therefore, not only as the responsibility of line management and HR specialists but also as that of the Chief Executive and the Board of Directors, wherever they may be located.

Companies may adopt different approaches dependent upon different philosophies to training. For example, some companies may seek to develop younger executives with perceived potential by immersing them in a risk-taking and innovative environment. They quickly learn from their mistakes and develop an instinct for creativity, adaptability and flexibility. Other companies may require young executives to demonstrate proven ability before exposing them to the rigours of the global business environment. Whichever approach is adopted, the overarching philosophy should be one where managers with perceived potential are actively encouraged to participate in the strategic decision-making process from a very early stage in their careers. In an important developmental sense this will pave the way for a sense of commitment to the organization and the assumption of essential skills for preferment in the corporate hierarchy. At the same time, international management development can assist in: the creation of a cadre of highly skilled and qualified international managers who, ideally, have the facility to work within any region of the global economy; the development of healthy competition among managers who seek to be challenged by the rigours of globalization; and most importantly, perhaps, the demonstration of the company's commitment to internationalization.

International management development is no longer an 'option' that companies may or may not wish to follow. It is an 'imperative'. Increasingly, companies of whatever size or sector find that to survive and compete they must either

Box 6.4 Preparing managers for overseas assignments

A typical international management development programme might include the following:

- Visits to host countries where the organization has
  subsidiary operations
- The development of linguistic ability and multilin-
  gualism

- Cross-cultural training for managers and their
  families
- General Management courses at business schools
- Training in negotiating across a variety of organizational and cultural norms

Box 6.5 Some of the key characteristics of the international manager

- Strategic awareness
- Adaptability to new situations
- Sensitivity to different cultures
- The ability to work in international teams
- Language skills
- An understanding of international marketing
- Relationship skills

- International negotiation skills
- Self-reliance
- High task-orientation
- Open, non-judgemental personality
- Awareness of own cultural background

(*Source:* Barham and Devine, 1991)

develop or extend overseas operations. In that sense, international management
development is, increasingly, a process through which all managers within the
organization and at whatever level should be put.

Creating an international learning organization

To develop and sustain the above characteristics requires a continuous commitment to learning. It is important that development is not seen as a peripheral or
cosmetic phenomenon. Where this is likely to be the case, improvements in performance are either fortuitous or short-lived. As mentioned earlier in this chapter,
one of the global company's key resources is information and knowledge. The
willingness to share information and learn from the successes and failures of one's
colleagues operating in different parts of the world with, perhaps, very different
responsibilities is an organizational cultural norm that should be fostered and
developed within the international management development process. What is
required of the organization, in a very practical sense, is not high philosophy and
grand themes with spurious references to the importance of organizational learning, for which some of the more scholarly references to this topic are, perhaps, to
blame, but specific details and clear processes that will enable managers to communicate with one another. There need to be clear guidelines for practice accompanied by operational advice.

David Garvin (1993) believes that learning organizations are skilled at five main
activities: systematic problem solving, experimentation with new approaches,

learning from their own experience and past history, learning from the experiences and best practices of others, and transferring knowledge quickly and efficiently throughout the organization. He goes on further to say that:

> By creating systems and processes that support these activities and integrate them into the fabric of daily operations, companies can manage their learning more effectively. (p. 81)

This is particularly important for the global company. International management development programmes are not sufficient, on their own, to instil this culture of sharing and networking. Organizational designs and systems should be there to ensure that the cultural norms fostered within the development process become a reality. The ultimate focus should not be solely on the development of individual competencies but also on the collective competence of the organization, where a worldwide view of management resources is taken.

The role of consultants

As the concept of the 'flexible firm' comes increasingly to characterize the management of international organizations, so the role of the 'consultant' offering specialist skills becomes more important to those organizations. This situation arises where there is a core workforce operating at the centre on a fully employed and permanent basis and a peripheral workforce operating at the edges of the organization on a part-time or subcontract basis. Consultants act as subcontractors, in possession of specialist skills, who are paid fees and not salaries for results. The role of the consultant in international firms relates to the management of cultural difference and variety in social, economic and political infrastructure. The term 'consultant' applies not only to expert strangers who come into the organization to share their specialist or technical knowledge but may also be found within the organization, such as human resource specialists or training specialists who tender for business on an intrapreneurial basis. HR specialist are often the first to make contact with external consultants, having applied their specialist skills in identifying the issues that must be addressed and the specialist consultants from whom to draw advice.

The role of the consultant in international human resource management is a relatively recent phenomenon. In a survey conducted by Torrington and Mackay in 1986 of 350 personnel specialists, it was found that not one of the respondents mentioned the use of consultancy advice with particular reference to international business.

Box 6.6 Choosing an independent consultant

Derek Torrington (1994) provides a six-point checklist for the selection and appointment of independent consultants:

1   Check the experience of previous clients.
2   Describe what you want done.
3   Formulate an approach.
4   Work out how you could do it without an external consultant.
5   Obtain proposals from consultants.
6   Decide between the alternatives.

Torrington then makes the highly relevant point that there is absolutely no point in hiring the services of an independent specialist unless the organization has the resources to implement the recommendations, whether they be human or financial.

Specific roles for external consultants in international firms

It is not easy to divorce the role of the external or indeed internal consultant in imparting advice to the purely domestic organization from the same role in the international organization. Consultants may be brought into the organization to look at, among other things, recruitment and selection issues, management development issues, human resource planning issues, compensation issues and employee relations issues. However, for the international firm there is an added dimension brought about by a number of *cultural* unknowns. For example, a staffing strategy for international management appointments will require specialist knowledge of business culture, markets and national culture, in addition to specific skills such as negotiating with host country partners, governments and other competitive players in the targeted region. The role of the independent consultant may be particularly important in establishing and managing joint ventures and strategic alliances, in negotiating deals relating to import/export issues and distribution and in making foreign direct investment decisions. The consultant has the ability to see the wood for the trees. He or she can raise questions that those employed by the organization cannot recognize or have never thought about.

Cultural diversity and the management of multinational teams

In the international context the term 'culture' refers to at least two different determinants, **organizational culture**, namely the traditions, beliefs, norms of behaviour and management style that characterize a particular organization, and **national culture**, the language, codes of conduct, attitudes to human rights, ethical standards and historical influences that characterize behaviour in a particular country or region of the world. These two different cultural determinants will often overlap, for example when we look at the influence of German or Japanese national culture on the way in which German and Japanese organizations are structured and managed. The issue of cultural diversity arises where organizations from disparate cultural backgrounds, whose cultural make-up represents a blend of national and organizational cultural influences, engage in business relationships. The issue may also arise where, within the international organization itself, there exists a blend of national cultural influences which must be managed within the context of project teams or matrix structures.

As Derek Torrington (1994) points out:

> Managers who deliberately or unwittingly work counter-culturally will constantly be frustrated by failing to get a response from colleagues, by being

misunderstood or by being bypassed. Managers who try to work out the nature of the culture in which they are operating can at least begin the process of change and influence the direction of the cultural evolution. (p. 31)

A classic example, perhaps, of the mismanagement or misunderstanding of cultural diversity is the attitude of British companies conducting business within the international arena. For many it is a cruel accident of birth that English is used as an official language in over 60 countries (Crystal, 1987). Indeed, English is commonly regarded as the 'lingua franca' of the global business world. As a result, there appears to be no injunction for the British manager to learn other languages or become multilingual. The problem is that although British managers may be able to converse at the formal level with overseas business partners and competitors, they are often unable to converse at, perhaps, the more important informal level where the appreciation of cultural nuance may be critical to striking a deal or to negotiating terms. In fairness, however, this may be more of a phenomenon of the period up to the 1980s rather than the 1990s and beyond.

Geert Hofstede (1993) contends that there is no such thing as universality in management. This provides further support for the view that global management in the 1990s has as much to do with the appreciation of difference as it does with a focus on similarity, often contextualized in terms of standardization and universalism. He illustrates this by pointing to the origins of the word 'management' itself:

... The linguistic origin of management is from Latin 'manus', via the Italian 'maneggiare' which is the training of horses in the 'manège' ... the word also became associated with the French 'ménage' ... the art of running a household. The theatre of present day management contains elements of both 'manège' and 'ménage' and different managers and cultures may use different accents. (p. 82)

Hofstede (1993) further points, interestingly, to the origins of management theory as deriving from such, largely European, writers as Adam Smith, John Stuart Mill, Leo Tolstoy, Max Weber, Henri Fayol, Sigmund Freud and Kurt Lewin. The contentions of these writers have been adapted and condensed in a number of varied ways across the business world, largely as a result of cultural determinants and intepretation.

In his seminal work on culture and the relationship between organizational and national culture, Hofstede (1980) defines culture as the 'collective programming of the mind', distinguishing the members of one group or category of people from another. In the late 1960s Hofstede analysed 116 000 questionnaires administered to employees of IBM in 70 countries.

Hofstede argued (1991: 140–6) that in societies stating a preference for power distance and uncertainty avoidance, there is likely to be a reliance upon hierarchy and bureaucratic organizational structure. In societies with small power distance and strong uncertainty avoidance, there is more likely to be an implicit acceptance of a clear structure, rules and set procedures. In countries where relatively small power distance exists and there is limited uncertainty avoidance, there tends to be more of an ad hoc approach to decision making and problem solving based upon a contingency approach to management in organizational terms.

Box 6.7 Hofstede's cultural dimensions

Hofstede maintains that national culture may be viewed principally with reference to four key factors:

● **Power distance**: This characterizes societies where there is an acceptance of the fact that power in institutions and organizations is distributed unequally. In organizations this may be apparent where there is a centralization of authority and a tendency to an autocratic management style.
● **Masculinity**: Here the dominant values in society are associated with assertiveness and lack of compassion, interestingly regarded by Hofstede as equating to male values.
● **Individuality**: This represents the opposite of col-

lectivism, where the predominant value is that of independence. People expect to look after only themselves and their immediate families. In collectivist societies there exists a strong sense of community and social responsibility.
● **Uncertainty avoidance**: This dimension is associated with those societies where structure and control are regarded as essential values and where risk taking and uncertainty are assiduously avoided.

To this list was later added the fifth dimension of 'Confucian dynamism' (Hofstede, 1991) which in practical terms related to the long-term versus short-term perspectives on life.

Managing cultural diversity

Managing cultural diversity is a complex and often bewildering task; however, those organizations that have been able to manage it successfully have, at the same time, created a distinct competitive advantage in individual and organizational competence. Cox and Blake (1991), for example, argue that the organization's ability to attract, retain and motivate staff from diverse cultural backgrounds provides distinct competitive advantage in cost structures, creativity, problem solving and the ability to respond and adapt to changing circumstances. Mixed groups apparently (Mead, 1994) provide greater opportunities for synergy:

> Members contribute a wider range of educational, professional, and cultural experiences than they would to a single-culture group. (p. 14)

Mead (1994) points to Shaw (1983), who found that mixed groups outperform homogenous groups on complex problem-solving tasks, and Watson *et al.* (1993) who discovered that when groups are newly formed, diversity constrained processes and performance, but that in the end heterogeneous groups caught up and outperformed homogeneous groups.

The alternative is to ignore the important role that diversity can play in enhancing organizational performance and losing the opportunity of developing a valuable competitive advantage.

IHRM and managing strategic alliances and joint ventures

International joint ventures (IJV) have become an increasingly popular vehicle for overseas expansion in recent years. Anderson (1990) maintains that between the years 1981 and 1990, more joint ventures were announced than in all previous

Box 6.8 Cultural dimensions: national profiles

Examples of countries that relate to each of the four dimensions can be illustrated as follows:

Dimension	High	Low
Individualism	United States	Peru
	United Kingdom	Venezuela
	Canada	Pakistan
	Australia	Colombia
Uncertainty avoidance	Portugal	Hong Kong
	Greece	Singapore
	Belgium	Sweden
	Japan	Denmark
Power distance	Former Yugoslavia	New Zealand
	Venezuela	Austria
	Mexico	Denmark
	Philippines	Israel
Masculinity	Venezuela	Norway
	Japan	Sweden
	Italy	Former Yugoslavia
	Austria	Denmark

Box 6.9 Creating synergy

Mead (1994) identifies, with reference to the work of Anderson (1983) and Kanter and Mirvis (1989), a list of variables that help to provide synergy within culturally diverse groups. This occurs when members:

- value the exchange of alternative points of view;
- tolerate uncertainty in group processes;
- cooperate to build group decisions;
- respect each other's experiences and share their own;
- use the exposure to others' cultural values as a positive opportunity for cross- cultural learning;
- can overcome the misunderstandings and inefficiencies that result from members of different cultures working together.

Box 6.10 Creating synergy: organizational factors

Management can increase the likelihood of synergy in a diverse group, maintains Mead (1994), by adjusting the cultural mix. This alone may not be sufficient, however, and the following factors must also be taken into account:

- Support from top management
- Setting tasks that demand a creative and non-routine response
- Providing the group with time to overcome process difficulties
- Investing in diversity training
- Providing administrative support (facilities, opportunity to meet in office hours etc.)
- Rewarding commitment and working to overcome problems

Box 6.11 Reasons for entering an international joint venture

- The benefit of economies of scale by combining resources
- The sharing of risk
- The sharing of research and development costs and information technology

- The avoidance of competition
- Opportunities to invest in management development activities and training
- Opportunity to generate hard currency
- The attraction of foreign direct investment

years in total. With its popularity, however, the IJV brings with it a number of issues that impact upon the role of human resource management, not least of which is the creation of a framework for the management of staff across the parties to the joint venture and the development of a strategy that will cope with any issues of cultural diversity that may arise.

The human resource implications of setting up and managing an international joint venture

From a purely operational point of view, setting up a joint venture can appear to be strategically the right thing to do, particularly where there appears to be a *fit* between the operational requirements of both parties to the joint venture. In human resource terms, however, there may be wider and previously unforeseen human relations issues.

Ideally, as a means of avoiding any possible conflict of interest in the early stages of partnership, the cultural values of the partners should coincide in terms of shared experiences, related interests etc. It is likely that staff will be recruited from more than one source and will include a mixture of staff recruited from the local parent, the foreign parent, and local nationals. It is also likely that employees will be drawn from different levels within their respective organizations, i.e. top, middle and junior management including the recruitment of non-managerial staff and specialists or professionals.

Possible conflict of interest may occur where the interests of the parent are placed above those of the project and where contradictory loyalties are complicated by professional, hierarchical and cultural differences. This situation may be compounded where the parents come not only from different cultures but also from different sectors.

There are, therefore, a number of issues here for line management within the respective parents and within the partnership to consider.

One of the key issues here that plays an important part in facilitating the most effective management of an international joint venture is *trust*. There must be an atmosphere of trust at two levels: between the managers in the parent organizations and between the managers and staff operating in the partnership.

Box 6.12 Developing trust

Mead (1994) refers to certain prerequisites that must be followed if trust is to be developed:

- Senior managers of the two parents are recruited to policy groups in which they work jointly on planning.
- There is an exchange of data between professional staff.
- Staff who are to be posted to work on the project are brought together in social events.

Box 6.13 Securing managerial agreement

Additionally, Mead (1994) points to a range of cultural factors that can influence the likelihood of different groups of managers agreeing upon a range of issues. These include:

- Structured priorities
- Management style

- Systems for communicating
- Systems for motivating, rewarding and punishing
- Relationships across management and non-management levels and professionals and generalists
- Ongoing assessment of how the project is progressing – following a contingency approach

These structural priorities need to be clarified at the early stage of the negotiation process so that they form the essential ingredients of any agreement.

International joint ventures can provide their parents with a raft of new and fresh approaches to management and internationalization. Some of the advantages that they can bring include:

- New ideas and technologies
- A paradigm shift in the way in which the modus operandi of the organization is viewed

At the same time IJVs can bring disadvantages, such as:

- The inflow of new personnel and the outflow of established personnel can have a culturally destabilizing effect;
- Staff may feel threatened and respond negatively to the possibility of new challenges.

The degree to which partners to an international joint venture communicate with one another on a regular basis may make a significant contribution to its success or failure.

Communication should, ideally, take place:

- between partners;
- between partners and the IJV;
- between the partners, the IJV and the immediate business environment in which the IJV is located.

Box 6.14 Developing communication plans

To ensure that this takes place a communication plan should be set in place at an early stage of the project. This plan will make it clear:

● who has responsibilities for communicating with whom;

● what the content of the communication might be, to whom by whom;

● how the content should be communicated;

● when the content should be communicated.

Compensation and employment conditions abroad

Compensation

The level of compensation that the employer will have to provide for expatriate managers will vary according to where they are placed within the organizational hierarchy and their level of skill and experience. 'Cosmopolitans', a term used by Torrington (1994) to refer to a cadre of international managers who have the facility to work anywhere in the world and who represent, in a sense, a global business elite or diplomatic corps, will expect compensation that 'transcends by a large margin what they would receive by staying put . . .' (Torrington, 1994: 17). The terms of the compensation package will have to be calculated with reference to fluctuating currencies, problems of hyperinflation, political uncertainty, and social and economic conditions at the local level. The focus of comment in this chapter will be the typical, middle ranking international manager, if there is such a phenomenon!

Compensation issues will be broken down between:

● salary,
● allowances, and
● taxation.

Salary

Salary levels may vary considerably from one part of the world to another. They may be fixed to the home country or host country, depending upon the relative prosperity of each. In the main, the expatriate is unlikely to earn less while working overseas than he or she earns in the home country.

> Few people, whatever their nationality and . . . circumstances, are willing to take a drop in salary. In theory several major companies do move salaries downwards to reflect local levels but in practice various cushions are often built in to compensate.

(Pinder, 1990)

Box 6.15 Criteria for hardship funds

Some of the criteria upon which the hardship fund might be based include:

- Health hazards
- Geographical isolation
- Social and political conditions

- Food shortage
- Lack of cultural and recreational facilities

They may also include educational allowances for expatriates with children and home leave and travel allowances.

Allowances

One of the main functions of allowances is to maintain parity between expenditures likely to be incurred at home and abroad. The key issue here will be to ensure relativity with home country colleagues.

Reynolds (1986) refers to this approach as the 'balance sheet method'. It is based on the assumption that home pay supports four principal areas: savings, goods and services, housing and tax. The likely expectation of the expatriate is that the employer will compensate for the last three of these.

A hardship allowance (Box 6.15) may, on occasion, be paid to expatriate employees on the basis of either real or assumed hardship in the host country. These may vary considerably, depending upon the location, from 5 per cent in Australasia, North America and Western Europe to 30 per cent in developing countries.

Income tax

For a UK expatriate manager, residence outside the UK for 12 months or more will ensure that no tax liablility is incurred under UK law. However, there will be a liability to local tax at the place of residence. This will vary enormously from one country to another (e.g. Luxembourg 60 per cent, Denmark 50 per cent, Belgium up to 70 per cent, Hong Kong 16 per cent).

Managers who travel overseas on frequent trips for relatively short periods are unlikely to have their domestic tax arrangements altered in any way.

Box 6.16 Trade unions and international operations

Kennedy (1978) identified seven key areas of concern for trade unions in this regard:

1 Formidable financial resources, including the ability to absorb losses in foreign subsidiaries where there has been a dispute with national unions
2 Alternative sources of supply, in the form of explicit 'dual sourcing' policy to reduce the vulnerability of the organization to a strike by any national union

3 Ability to move production facilities to other cheap labour countries
4 Superior knowledge and expertise in labour relations
5 Remote locus of authority
6 Production facilities in many industries
7 Capacity to stage an 'investment strike' in which the organization refuses to invest any additional funds in a plant, thus ensuring that the plant will soon become obsolete and non-competitive

---

Box 6.17 International trade unions: lack of success

Sparrow and Hiltrop (1994) identify five reasons for the lack of success of international trade unions. These are as follows:

1 Good wages and working conditions provided by MNCs in Western Europe
2 Strong resistance from multinational managements to transnational bargaining and consultations
3 Significant ideological, political and structural differences between national unions
4 Differing national laws and regulation in labour relations
5 Conflicting national economic interests when dealing with MNCs

---

Employment conditions abroad

In recent years the emergence of global organizations has intensified the pressure on trade unions to equalize the balance of power and influence often exerted by large multinational corporations.

Foremost among the problems that international trade unions face in attempting to achieve consistency across a range of policies and practices is cultural differentiation. Issues such as *trust* and *good faith* are particularly relevant here and are subject to a variety of different interpretations. Brown and Sisson (1984) and Baglioni (1991) cite three different approaches to European labour relations. These are:

- **The consultative approach**: Here the strong involvement of employees with the organization's goals and culture through direct worker–management communication is seen as being paramount. Country examples include Germany and the Scandinavian countries.
- **The constitutional approach**: Here concepts such as collective bargaining and dealing indirectly with employees via trade unions is looked upon unfavourably. Country examples include Belgium, Spain, Portugal and the Netherlands where labour organizations have a close relationship with government.
- **The deregulatory and laissez faire approach**: Here management attempts to maximize discretion and flexibility. In some regards this is typical of labour relations in France.

Performance management in the international arena

Performance management can and should be related to competitive advantage. Pressure for change in the systems of management, the perception of quality and value, and increasing competition for customers make some form of organizational appraisal an imperative for the international organization. The rationalization of business and the delayering of management have placed increasing pressures on line management to take responsibility for the performance of their staff or teams. For the global organization there may be a number of varied social, economic and cultural pressures that necessitate the creation of complex project teams and strategic alliances. Additionally there may be a number of marked differences in national culture and differences in manager–subordinate relationships that shape and determine the way in which organizations respond to change, appraise and reward their staff, consider the relationship between performance appraisal and remuneration and, in particular, tackle the problem of performance-related pay.

In many ways performance management is a transatlantic strategic management technique that is based upon the concept of linking business objectives with individual goals, actions, performance appraisal and rewards through a clearly defined process. If used effectively, it can be a powerful tool for driving change through an organization. Performance management is a system or habit. It introduces the concept of continuous improvement at the individual, group and organizational level.

While there is limited available research evidence of the role of performance management within an international context, Sparrow and Hiltrop (1994) point to some recent studies on the management of performance within the European context. The work of Bournois and Chauchat (1990) is cited. Their studies have tended to show that managers in certain countries are less effective than others in leading and motivating their subordinates. According to Saias (1989), the efficiency of the manager–subordinate relationship is at its lowest in Portugal, Spain and Greece,

---

Box 6.18 Performance management within the international environment

Sparrow and Hiltrop (1994) view performance management within the international environment at the macro and the micro level.

Factors influencing change in performance at the macro level include:

- Social pressures
- National culture
- Foreign direct investment
- Transnationalism
- Competitive pressures

Box 6.19 Pressure for change in performance management within the international environment

At the micro level, pressure for change in performance includes:

- Differences in management–subordinate relationships
- Differences in the desire and need for individual rewards
- Complex performance relationships, for example international projects, teams, strategic alliances etc.
- Adapted structures and control systems

- International competition and privatization creating new productivity pressures
- Rationalization of business reducing vertical levels and increasing spans of control
- Shorter product and development cycles requiring faster performance
- Changes in business processes redefining measures of effective performance
- Changing values and career expectations

making these countries clear targets for improved performance management techniques. The UK and Italy have relatively inefficient relationships, followed by France and Ireland. The demand for performance management techniques appears to be lowest in countries such as Switzerland, Germany, Belgium and Denmark.

Sparrow and Hiltrop (1994) interestingly point to two specific dimensions within the Hofstede (1980) framework: power distance and uncertainty avoidance. For example, French managers have a higher power distance score of 68 than UK managers with 35. This is to some extent reflected in the greater differences in formal power across a hierarchy in France and the observation that French managers are more tolerant of inequalities of power.

CASE STUDY
Developing the global manager

In the following extract taken from an interview with the Director of Personnel and Organization of a leading scientific publishing house, the significance of 'worldwide' strategic 'networks' and the necessity for managers to gain 'experience of dealing with different countries' is made apparent. It is also clear from this account that this respondent makes direct recourse to a language of 'global management', and that from his perspective a 'global manager' is categorically different from a 'Euromanager'. In this extract, elements of the text have been highlighted which are particularly relevant to the interpretation of global management presented in the foregoing pages.

What I believe a Euromanager should be is someone who has got experience of dealing with different countries, being in different countries and who might gradually grow to a global manager rather than a Euromanager, because we are a global company. We are not in a position to transfer many people from one location to another, perhaps some transfers between the UK and the Netherlands and limited transfers over the ocean, but the kind of business that we are in requires a lot of travel, it is a worldwide responsibility for a publishing editor. So wherever you are located doesn't matter really, you've got a worldwide network of contacts.

The idea that it is possible to be 'worldwide' without transferring staff from one country to another is illustrative of Roland Robertson's definition of globalization (1992), namely, what is important is the consciousness of treating the world as an operational whole. Managing by travelling the globe, working with other nationalities, in many ways obviates the necessity of having staff live overseas for any length of time. The fact that a publish-

ing editor should have a worldwide network of contacts is clearly indicative of a concern for 'global networking'.

The same Personnel Director helped to develop this thesis with reference to the development of global management 'competencies'. There is an explicitly 'international flavour' to the programmes that he mentions, it being 'essential' that managers are comfortable working with 'all kinds of nationalities'. Managers are said to be 'recruited internationally' with a view to being 'internationally mobile':

We've got a trainee programme and that is meant to be for the high potential graduates. The programme itself is an introduction of one year into the publishing industry, followed by two-to-three month assignments abroad to get that international flavour. Recruitment for that programme is carried out internationally. We are looking for internationally mobile and adaptive individuals whom we feel will be able to work with all kinds of nationalities, which is an essential part of our business and which is essential also for our future management.

Very important in the selection process is social skills. If you've got that academic degree, that's a given, so we're not talking about that anymore, we're talking about behaviour within the company environment, influencing skills, we are also talking about leadership (as far as we can). Those kinds of aspects are very important in our selection process.

The Corporate Business Director in the same company gives voice to the importance of key management 'competencies' that will complement and facilitate the management of new technology brought about by what he apprehends as a significant 'paradigm shift' faced by his business. He makes mention of what we might call 'harder' specialist skills needs in order to negotiate the boundaries between 'information producer' and 'information consumer'.

... we are talking here about paradigm shifts, that is a shift that is of such a structural nature that it might be that the competencies that our business is based on today might not have any correlation with the business competencies of tomorrow. We are saying that society changes with technology causing paradigm shifts in our business.

He goes on to categorize what he regards as some of the key competencies that global managers of the future should possess. These include:

- Information handling
- Quality and selection
- Marketing
- Network specialists
- Software specialists

These skills will, of course, vary from one sector and from one organization to another but there are some common competencies that cut across sectors and organizational boundaries.

There is considerable food for thought here for international human resource specialists and general international managers alike, whether they be concerned with human resource development, human resource planning or facilitating the 'fit' between the IHRM function and corporate strategy.

Conclusion

The importance of effective management in the international arena is probably best illustrated by the example of international strategic joint ventures or alliances. Not only are the initial viability assessment and tendering costs high, but so are the coordination of effort and the visibility of your failures is across international borders. The need for a strategic approach towards human resource management is more clearly an imperative, and the effort needed to maintain effectiveness also.

The pressures to globalize in many industries has already taken hold. Moreover, in those where it is less immediately an imperative, the globalization of labour markets means that keeping an eye on what is happening matters. In the international arena, it is important for the local as well as the global player who wishes to maintain competitiveness or, indeed, keep in the game at all; within certain industries whole sector activities have relocated to low-wage, high-skill labour markets.

There are an increasing number of companies who are actively adopting 'international development' programmes to enable their staff to undertake international assignments. For line managers, there is a need to ensure that they and their subordinates acquire the skills needed to operate in this international arena. Too often, there is an assumption that what works here will work 'over there'. The proactive line manager will ensure that much of the necessary skills and knowledge are gained *before* 'that important assignment'.

Summary

Managing the firm in the global business environment is seen in some quarters as partaking in a risk-laden and thoroughly dynamic process. The role, therefore, of the international manager with responsibility for the design, development and implementation of human resource strategy should become increasingly fraught. In reality, however, different organizations and different sectors react and contribute to the process of globalization in varied ways. The role, therefore, of the international human resource specialist and the international manager will vary also.

The essence of this chapter is to capture the variety and significance of international human resource management in its contribution to the process of globalization. This has included an overview of the various facets of the global business consciousness that make up international human resource management, including:

- the significance of globalization itself;
- the role of the global manager, the impact of culture (in particular the overlay of national and organizational culture) on international human resource planning and employee development;
- cultural diversity and the management of multicultural teams;
- strategies for international management development;
- the management of strategic alliances and international joint ventures;
- creating an international learning organization;
- the role of human resource consultants in aiding international managers and IHRM specialists;
- compensation and employment issues for staff operating in countries other than the home country;
- the creation and application of performance management systems for staff operating in a variety of disparate global locations.

This list should by no means be seen as exhaustive. Indeed, there are probably as many different interpretations of international human resource management as there are of globalization itself. What has been attempted in the foregoing chapter is a hands-on guide to the management of international human resources with a focus on the role and responsibility of the international manager for human resources.

Appendix: International human resource management – the future

In many ways the future of international human resource management is bound up with the changing nature and characteristics of the global economy itself. As mentioned in the summary to the chapter, it is not possible to be prescriptive, nor should writers attempt to be so, about the role that management with responsibility for international human resources should take. Different organizations and different sectors will develop in varied ways, each requiring an approach to international human resource management that best reflects their industry or organization practice. The future of international human resource management does, however, appear to be developing around a number of common themes and determinants, each of which may be applied to different organizations in a way which suits them best.

These common themes include:

- The increasingly important role of international management development in developing core skills and competencies
- The interdependence of decision making within the transnational corporation
- The role of technology as an important aid to the production process, management information systems and general communication processes
- The demise of the expatriate manager
- The development of cross-cultural teams
- A situation where all human resource management is international human resource management

I will address each of these in turn, albeit briefly.

The increasingly important role of international management development in developing core skills and competencies

International management development has an important role to play in the development of a 'cadre' of international managers, managers who fit most closely into Howard Perlmutter's (1969) 'geocentric' category relevant to staffing strategy. Here, the ideal is to develop managers who can operate effectively anywhere in the world, without being weighed down by the cultural baggage of their home country. Managers will possess the important competence of cross-cultural sensitivity, the facility to readily appreciate both the hard (social, economic and political infrastructure) and soft (language, attitudes and behaviours) cultural issues from one region to another.

The interdependence of decision making within the transnational corporation

In the future, decisions affecting international human resource management issues may be taken as a result of a consultation process involving the sharing of information, views, experiences etc. across subsidiaries. The IHRM strategy will draw heavily upon a range of expertise and will no longer be the prerogative of management operating from a centralized position. Indeed, many subsidiaries may have their own IHRM specialists who assist in the design and implementation of strategy at the local level.

The role of technology as an important aid to the production process, management information systems and general communication processes

Technology enhances production processes, bringing with it the imperative to secure appropriate skills levels at different production plants around the world, and communication processes that aid management decision-making processes across national and cultural borders. IHRM, operating in an increasingly integrative way, will draw upon this facility in respect of skills development for staff and management alike and international human resource planning.

The demise of the expatriate manager

The expatriate manager, if not already a phenomenon of the past, is unlikely to last in his or her current state much beyond the millennium. Where the emphasis is on the development of a *cadre* of international managers who possess a 'kit bag' of transferrable multicultural skills that they carry with them from one location to another, the company compound and the expat on a two to three year 'posting' may no longer be a viable proposition.

The development of cross-cultural teams

An essential part of international management development will be the acquisition of cross-cultural skills by exposure to different national and business cultures through cross-cultural teams. This 'action learning' approach to international management development will obviate the necessity for extensive travel and relocation from one subsidiary to another for any lengthy period of time.

A situation where all human resource management is international human resource management

As the world becomes even more of a 'global village', in a sense all human resource management will become international. Global companies are now comprised of small, medium-sized and large enterprises. Companies operating previously in exclusively domestic markets now find themselves competing with a variety and complexity of international operators. The HRM issues that pertain to the global company become, in time, the same issues for the local operation conducting business at the national level.

Questions

1   How does the role of the human resources manager operating within a purely domestic business environment differ from that of the international human resources manager operating within a global remit?

2   What are the essential differences between the international, Euro and global manager? What are the implications of the differences between these three different 'types' for the international human resource development manager?

3   How important is an understanding of the role of 'culture' to the international manager when devising staffing strategies for overseas assignments?

4   Is it still necessary, in a global managerial environment where the concept of a 'posting' may no longer be relevant, to think in terms of compensation packages for international managers?

5   How would you devise an appraisal process for staff operating in disparate locations around the world? How would you ensure that whatever process you selected maintained the essential criterion of equity or at least the perception among those exposed to the process that equity was a paramount consideration?

6   What different staffing strategies are available to the international manager in conjunction with an international human resource specialist (where they exist) when:
   - staffing established overseas operations?
   - setting up strategic alliances and joint ventures?
   - building a project team for an assignment not due to last for more than six months?
   - setting up a greenfield site operation without any form of partnership?
   - considering the foreign direct investment prospects of a developing region of the world?

7   Consider the importance of 'language' in its broadest sense for the global manager when communicating with colleagues, business partners and competitors within the global business environment. Identify at least three different situations where the failure to communicate can be attributed to a dearth of appropriate skills and competencies in managing a particular situation.

8   With reference to Question 7, what can the international manager, with line responsibility for overseas staff, do to overcome the problems that you have identified?

9   Differences in definitions of acceptable, 'ethical' business behaviour among countries and cultures are often raised as possible barriers to successful interaction of businesspeople at the global level. How might international HR management assist in lowering these barriers in the international firm?

References

Anderson, E (1990) Two firms, one frontier: on assessing joint venture performance, *Sloane Management Review*, **31**(2), 19–30.

Anderson, LR (1983) Management of the mixed cultural work group. *Organisation Behaviour and Human Performance*, **31**(3), 303–30.

Baglioni, G (1991) Industrial relations in Europe in the 1990's. In *European Industrial Relations: The Challenge of Flexibility* (eds G Baglioni and C Crouch), Sage, London.

Barham, K and Devine, M (1991) *The Quest for the International Manager*, Ashridge Management Research Group, Special Report No 2098, Economist Intelligence Unit, London.

Bartlett, CA and Ghoshal, S (1989) *Managing Across Borders – The Transnational Solution*, Hutchinson Books, London.

Bournois, F and Chauchat, JH (1990) Managing managers in Europe. *European Management Journal*, **8**(1), 3–18.

Brown, W and Sisson, K (1984) Current trends and future possibilities. In *Industrial Relations in the Future* (eds M Poole *et al.*), Routledge and Kegan Paul, London.

Calori, R and Lawrence, P (eds) (1991) *The Business of Europe – Managing Change*, Sage, London.

Calori, R and Lawrence, P (1992) Diversity still remains – views of European managers. *Journal of Long Range Planning*, **25**(2), 33–43.

Cox, TH and Blake, S (1991) Managing cultural diversity: Implications for organisational competitiveness. *Academy of Management Executive*, **5**(2), 45–56.

Crystal, D (1987) *The Cambridge Encyclopaedia of Language*, Cambridge University Press, Cambridge.

Garvin, D (1993) *The Learning Organization*, HBR.

Hedlund, G and Rolander, D (1990) Action in Heterarchies – New Approaches to Managing the Multinational Corporation. In *Managing the Global Firm* (eds CA Bartlett, Y Doz and G Hedlund), Routledge, London and New York.

Hofstede, G (1993) Cultural constraints in management theories. *Academy of Management Executive*, **7**(1), 81–93.

Hofstede, G (1991) *Cultures and Organisations: Software of the Mind*, McGraw-Hill, London.

Hofstede, G (1980) *Culture's consequences: International differences in work related values*, Sage Publications, Beverly Hills.

Kanter, DL and Mirvis, PH (1989) *The Cynical Americans*, Jossey-Ball, San Francisco.

Kennedy, T (1978) *European labour relations*, Associated Business Programmes: London.

Kogut, B (1990) International Sequential Advantages and Network Flexibility. In *Managing the Global Firm* (eds CA Bartlett, Y Doz and G Hedlund), Routledge, London and New York.

Levitt, T (1983) The globalization of markets. *Harvard Business Review*, May–June, 92–102.

Mead, R (1994) *International Management – Cross Cultural Dimensions*, Blackwells, Oxford.

Nonaka, I (1990) Managing Globalization as a self renewal process: experiences of Japanese MNC's. In *Managing the Global Firm* (eds CA Bartlett, Y Doz and G Hedlund) Routledge, London and New York.

Perlmutter, HV (1969) The tortuous evolution of the multinational corporation. *Columbia Journal of World Business*, January–February, 9–18.

Pinder, M (1990) *Personnel Management for the Single European Market*, Pitman: London.

Reynolds, C (1986), Compensation of Overseas Personnel. In Famularo, JJ (ed), *Handbook of Human Resources Administration*, 2nd edition, McGraw-Hill, New York.

Robertson, R (1992) *Globalization: Social Theory and Global Culture*, Sage, London.

Saias, M (1989) Compétitivité et stratégies des enterprises face a l'horizon 93. *Revue française de gestion*, May.

Shaw, ME (1983) *Group dynamics, the psychology of small group behaviour*, McGraw-Hill, New York.

Smith, A (1990) Towards a Global Culture. In *Global Culture, Nationalism and Modernity* (ed M Featherstone), Sage, London.

Sparrow, P and Hiltrop, J-M (1994) *European Human Resource Management in Transition*, Prentice-Hall, Hemel Henpstead.

Torrington, D (1994) *International Human Resource Management*, Prentice-Hall, Hemel Hempstead.

Torrington, DP and Mackay, LE (1986) *The Changing Nature of Personnel Management*, Institute of Personnel Management, London.

Vernon-Wortzel, H and Wortzel, L (1990) *Global Strategic Management – the Essentials*, John Wiley and Sons, New York.

Watson, WE, Kumar, K and Michaelson, L (1993) Cultural diversity's impact on interaction process and performance: Comparing homogeneous and diverse task groups. *Academy of Management Journal*, **36**(3), 590–602.

White, RE and Poynter, TA (1990) Organizing for Worldwide Advantage. In *Managing the Global Firm* (eds CA Bartlett, Y Doz and G Hedlund), Routledge, London and New York.

Wildish, C and Case, P (1993) *Managing Globalization in the Publishing Industry: An Interpretative Investigation*, unpublished paper presented at Associate Section III of the Association of Social Anthropologists IV Decennial Conference, 'Anthropology on the Profit Margin', July

Legal briefing

A. Allowable exceptions to the anti-discrimination laws

The legal briefing to Chapter 1 dealt with the law governing discrimination in employment and referred to allowable exceptions known as 'genuine occupational qualifications'. One example of this allows employers to reserve employment for men where it involves work overseas in a country where the culture or, indeed the law, forbids women to work or carry out commercial negotiations on an equal footing with men. The commercial difficulties must be real. For example, a travel company was held liable under the Sex Discrimination Act, 1975, for refusing to consider a woman to drive a tour coach, on the grounds that she would be driving in Turkey, and women were not permitted to drive in Muslim countries. While this may have been true of some Muslim countries, it was patently untrue of Turkey.

B. Employment protection laws and work overseas

The UK employment protection laws, including discrimination on various grounds, unfair dismissal, rights to time off with or without pay, minimum periods of notice etc., are excluded even in a contract governed by English law, where the employee 'ordinarily works outside Great Britain'. The redundancy payments law is also excluded, unless the employee is present within Great Britain at the request of the employer when the dismissal takes place. In cases where it is doubtful as to whether the employee 'ordinarily works' inside or outside Great Britain, the principal source of information will be the terms of the employee's contract. The latest update of requirements for 'written particulars' includes a statement of any period of time, more than a month, during which the employee is required to work outside the United Kingdom; the currency in which he is to be paid during this time; any additional remuneration to be paid to him and any additional benefits to be provided by reason of him working abroad; any terms and conditions relating to his return to the UK. This may not give the essential information as to whether the work is ordinarily situated in Great Britain where the work seems to be split between home and abroad. Another test adopted by the court is to look at where the employee's 'base', or centre of control, is situated. Hence, merchant seamen, airline pilots and other crew, long-distance lorry drivers and others whose work necessarily takes them overseas most of the time, but whose 'base' is in Great Britain, will retain all their rights under the employment protection laws. In any event, the legislation simply excludes the automatic application of these laws; there is no reason why these laws should not be explicitly included in the employment contract by agreement between the parties. Such a solution could well avoid costly litigation at a later stage.

Continued on page 234

Offshore employment is defined as employment in connection within the territorial waters of the UK, or the exploration of the seabed or subsoil or natural resources in the UK sector of the continental shelf, or connected with the exploration or exploitation, in a foreign sector of the continental shelf, of a cross-boundary petroleum field. The employment protection legislation has been extended to cover such offshore employment. More detailed discussion on the employment protection law will be found in the legal briefing to Chapter 1.

C. The law governing an overseas employment contract

The preceding section dealt with the situation where the employment contract was undoubtedly governed by English law, but the employee might be deprived of statutory employment protection. The problem to be considered here is how the law to be applied to the employment contract is to be determined. This area is known as private international law, and the 'proper law' of contracts is governed in the UK by the Contracts (Applicable Law) Act, 1990 for all contracts made after 1 July 1991. This is of importance in the employment field where an employee is recruited to work overseas, or largely overseas, by a company based in the UK, or by a multinational whose headquarters could be anywhere.

In default of a choice of law being made by the parties (to be dealt with in more detail shortly), the 1990 Act provides that the law governing the contract will be the law of the country where the employee 'habitually works'. This will not be affected by occasional, temporary periods of employment in another country. Where it is not possible, because of the nature of the job, to ascertain with certainty where a particular employee 'habitually works', the applicable law will be the law of the country where the organization through which the employee was employed is situated. The applicable law will govern pay, hours, and all other conditions of work, including health and safety. An employee whose contract is governed by a law which has already incorporated the 'Social Chapter' will be entitled to such benefits as that entails.

As indicated above, it is open to the parties to express a 'choice of law' in the contract, and this will, with two important exceptions, be upheld. The parties are free to choose any law, and it does not necessarily have to have any connection with the contract. For example, multinational companies sometimes draw up standard-form employment contracts to be used anywhere in the world, where the applicable law is stated to be that of the country where the central administration of the company is situated.

As mentioned above, there are two exceptional cases where a choice of law by the parties will not be upheld. One is where, apart from the choice of law, the contract is connected in all respects with one law system; where both parties, employer and employee, and the workplace are all situated in England, a term in the contract choosing Norwegian law to govern the contract will effectively be ignored, unless there is a clear demonstration that the employee will not suffer any disadvantage. The courts are realistic enough to realize that apparent 'choices' by both parties are in fact dictated by the employer. The other exception, based on similar principles to the first, is that in a contract where there is an international dimension, the choice of a law other than the law of the country where the employee 'habitually works' will not be applied so as to deprive the employee of any overriding (mandatory) rights provided by that law. If, for example, a company based in the UK, where there is at present no law relating to paid parental leave, were to recruit employees to work on construction projects in Germany, where, for argument's sake, it will be supposed that such a law applies, the place of 'habitual employment' will be Germany, and the choice of English law to govern the contract will not relieve the English employer from the obligation to pay in such circumstances.

In connection with the laws relating to taxation, employees contemplating work overseas should check to ascertain whether there is in place an agreement at governmental level regarding double taxation.

D. EU laws on the right to work and to establish businesses

Freedom of movement of workers throughout the EU, provided that they are nationals of a member state, is one of the pillars upon which the single market is based. This is enshrined in the Treaty of Rome, and is reinforced by a prohibition against discrimination in employment, as far as EU nationals are concerned, on the ground of nationality.

Nationals of one member state are permitted to enter another state to take up employment, or merely to seek employment opportunities. Rights of residence for the worker and his or her family are guaranteed together with other 'social advantages', including social security, that are accorded to workers of the host state. One who is merely a 'job seeker' does not have an indefinite right to remain in the host country, which is not expected to shoulder an unfair social security burden. There are no hard and fast rules as to how long a person may remain while still seeking work, but in one case it was held that the UK Home Office could require a citizen of another member state, with no independent means of support, to leave the UK six months after failing to obtain work.

There is a generous interpretation of 'work', which relates to any economic activity, even that which does not pay enough to support the worker and his or her family. A right of residence remains where the worker loses his or her job through illness, redundancy, or any other cause without his or her fault.

There are exceptions to the right to work, and these include reasons of public policy, public security and public health. A Directive is in force expanding upon these rather vague principles, and taken together with cases on the subject heard in front of the European Court of Justice, it is clear that an excluded worker must pose a substantial threat. For example, a criminal record on its own would not provide a reason for exclusion.

The Treaty of Rome itself provides a 'public service' exception. Again, the ECJ has made it clear that this exception is not to be used as a mere excuse to reserve employment to nationals of the state. The exception is allowed only for employment at the heart of government; the employees involved must be 'safeguarding the national interests of the state'. Among the examples where it has been held that the 'public service' exception does not apply are city council workers, unskilled workers in general, plumbers, nurses, architects, merchant seamen and the like.

An EU national is also free to provide and receive services anywhere in the Community. This includes the provision of professional services – law, medicine, engineering, etc. – and this freedom, predictably, came up against the problem of very different requirements of education and training in the member states. A process was begun of trying to 'harmonize' requirements for each profession, so that personnel trained in one country could practise in another without having to requalify. Progress was very slow; it was not unusual for 16 or 17 years to elapse before substantial agreement was reached on acceptable standards. There are now in existence a number of Directives covering the EU requirements in various professions. In addition, a new policy has been implemented where separate Directives have not been issued, but 'mutual recognition' is accorded to national qualifications. The host state is not precluded from requiring a period of adaptation, or an aptitude test, where very different conditions apply in the state where the applicant received his or her training.

E. The Posted Workers Directive

This Directive seeks to give posted workers within the EU the same employment rights as workers in the host country. It was adopted on 24 September 1996, and must be implemented by the member states within three years.

F. International Labour Organization

It might be pertinent to mention the International Labour Organization at this point. The ILO is a United Nations Agency, and is the most important source of international standards in employment. It issues Conventions on a number of topics which national governments are free to ratify. One of its major policies is to guarantee freedom of association, a matter of great importance to trades unions. There is no legal sanction upon governments for failure to observe ILO standards.

Under the previous Conservative administration, the opinions of the ILO were virtually ignored. Since 1997, however, the new Labour administration has emphasized that its policy is to implement international labour standards and, indeed, has already restored the right to trade union membership to workers at Government Communication Headquarters (GCHQ). Please refer also to the legal briefing to Chapter 3 relating to the new enhanced rights of trades unions.

Other standards have been implemented by the adoption of EU Directives.

Some ILO policies may well prove to be too controversial to be implemented, and, indeed, do not appear in the Employment Relations Act, 1999. These include giving trades unions immunity when calling upon their members to take secondary industrial action (that is, against an employer or industry other than their own) or restoring their right to discipline their members who refuse to obey an official call to take industrial action. To restore these rights would undoubtedly provoke a public outcry, particularly among 'New Labour' supporters, and the present administration would not be willing to take such a risk.

Further reading

Smith, R and Cromack, V International Employment Contracts – the Applicable Law (1993). *Industrial Law Journal*, 1.
Steiner, J (1998) *Textbook of EC Law*, 6th edition, Blackstone Press.

Information technology – transformer of organizations and enhancer of the HRM approach

7

David Wilson

Learning objectives

After studying this chapter you should be able to:

- develop a better view of the effects of computers and networks on the business environment and our working lives;
- understand why 'command-and-control' organizations are unlikely to flourish in today's business environment;
- review the advantages and problems of flatter organizational structures;
- see that the success of flatter structures and the HRM culture can be enhanced by appropriate support from computer networks.

Although your particular background is unique, I hope you will see this chapter as building on a foundation of your own observations and experience.

Introduction

When the files go digital in the Personnel Department, the lid comes off and there is no putting it back. Few people anticipate the changes that will inevitably follow sooner or later. Have you any idea of how your job will change as a result?

In many organizations today, computers in personnel tend to be used for routine tasks such as salary and wage administration, and monitoring sickness and absence. In other words, computers are often being used simply to automate the day-to-day, internal routines of the Personnel Department. This first stage in computerization cuts costs and boosts efficiency – indeed the purchase of a CPIS (computerized personnel information system) is often justified purely on the immediate savings that will arise from higher individual productivity in the department.

The next stage, however, is to connect the personnel department computers to the company network, which then makes it possible to completely re-engineer the personnel function. Routine paper-shuffling and administration will mostly disappear, and the roles of those left will be to develop the full potential of the human resource, which is the organization's most important strategic resource in the era of the knowledge worker.

The HRM approach can only take root when computers have automated the chores that fill 80 per cent of the day, and networks have opened up strategic information on human resources to the rest of the organization. Computers are the enabling technology for the metamorphosis of Personnel professionals into Human Resource professionals.

The Personnel Department was the last outpost of staff specialism, and it has been one of the last departments to make full use of computers. The events that happen when computers come to the Personnel Department will follow a similar pattern to what has happened in most other staff departments. We know that computers have always eliminated jobs through automating existing processes, but it is the networking of computer-held information that allows the roles of departments to be fundamentally re-engineered. In the banking sector, for instance, High Street hole-in-the-wall cash machines automate the jobs of clerks, but this network of machines then makes telephone banking possible. Of course direct banking is much cheaper to operate with no High Street branches to support, and the easy, instant, paperwork-free, 24–hour availability is more popular with customers too. Computers are thus reshaping the whole sector. In 1990, banks employed about half a million clerks and middle managers, but the trends suggest that ten years on, about 200 000 will have left, and many of the rest will be doing jobs that bear scant resemblance to what they did before.

This ability of computer networks to redefine how a service is delivered is also happening within organizations. We can therefore expect big changes in the way that personnel departments deliver services to their organizations. When computers are brought in to the department to automate the sorting and filing tasks, it is inevitable that they will eventually be networked to the rest of the organization. Indeed, where this has happened, line managers now have the benefit of a direct service. In some leading organizations, end users are authorized to download certain types of personnel data to their own computers without having to request it through their line managers or the personnel department staff. This 'disintermediation' cuts out middle managers, allowing the information needs of internal customers to be met faster and more precisely. It is absolutely in line with current HRM thinking: it fits perfectly with the notion of empowered, multi-skilled, proactive, self-managing teams of employees. And of course it hastens the metamorphosis of the personnel function. The personnel manager is dead: long live the human resource manager.

It seems clear that computer networks are essential for a thorough implementation of the HRM approach, or is it the other way round? The HRM approach is essential for a full payback from an investment in computer networks. Either way, computers and networks are central to a full understanding of the whole Personnel Management versus Human Resource Management debate.

Change, challenges and choices

Box 7.1 Need to change?

Brrr – brrr . . . brrr – brrr . . . click.

'Human Resources, Gillian Brown here.'

'Oh, hi Gillian. James Shepherd from Dispatch here again. I've been trying to get you all morning.'

'Sorry James, I was helping shoot a training video. How can I help?'

'Well, you know I asked you for statistics on staff turnover in my department?'

'Yes . . . '

'Well, I didn't just want the overall annual percentage. I really need more detail, to see if I'm losing my best people quickest. It certainly feels that way, and I need some hard evidence for a report I'm putting together.'

'Ah . . . I can do that for you James if you tell me what you mean by "best people". But I'm afraid it'll have to wait till tomorrow, as I'm already late for a meeting. Did you know you can get the information for yourself? It's very easy . . . just go to the HR page on our intranet. There's a list of ready-made queries you can run, or you can create your own query and run it.'

'That may be so Gillian, but I haven't time to mess with computers . . .'

'Well, it's up to you, James. Either wait till tomorrow, or . . . I tell you what. Haven't you got that work-experience student in your department this week? She told me she's a Net surfer. Get her to help you . . . '

The business world is going through a period of unprecedented change, and to survive we must try to understand and adjust. Five hundred years ago change was barely perceptible. In the Middle Ages, your lifestyle, that of your grandparents, and that of your grandchildren would all have been similar. Had you been born 250 years ago, however, in the middle of the Industrial Revolution when people were moving from field to factory, lifestyles then were changing from generation to generation. Then, as today, those who could understand what was happening were able to benefit from, and not fall victim to, the changing environment. But today's information revolution is happening faster, with big changes within a generation, and it is therefore more difficult for us to adjust.

Our first task in this chapter is to review the changes we see taking place, to build a coherent picture and try to draw conclusions which will be useful to us as managers. Computers and communications networks require new skills and new ways of working, and so we will see how technology not only brings about change, but offers ways to cope with it. We are hooked: the more we get, the more we seem to need. It is fundamentally restructuring the business environment, demanding new methods and new skills.

Our second task, therefore, is to look inside organizations to see how they are responding to the current business environment of rapid change, intense competition and global markets. The new buyers' markets are forcing organizations to respond faster, with better quality at lower cost, just to hold on to their existing customers. Product life-cycles are shortening, quality standards constantly rising, and successful organizations are having to learn how to continually improve their products and services. So much change is needed that everyone must be capable of making – and be empowered to make – good decisions quickly. The old command-and-control hierarchies with their decision-making bottlenecks at the top are just too ponderous, and are being replaced by more nimble, team-based structures.

Our final task, a theme running throughout this chapter, is to bring these strands together through case studies and practical examples. Computers can, of course, be used to enforce a rigid command-and-control regime, by controlling access to centrally held data and monitoring the output of keyboard operators. This approach, used in some call centres for instance, may work in the short term, but it denies the organization access to the combined brainpower of the workforce – a resource more versatile than the most powerful computer. The other more appropriate way of using computers today is in support of the HRM approach, in which technology is used in a less control-oriented way. Computers can just as easily free people from repetitive tasks and dependent, passive roles, and support them in finding imaginative, creative solutions to problems. Computer networks can provide self-managing teams with the information and tools they need to make decisions, and to stay focused on shifting organizational objectives.

In this new era of the knowledge worker, technology can thus deliver the key to business success. Computer networks can release time and provide opportunities for people to interact and develop their critical, creative and imaginative abilities to ask the right questions as well as find the right answers.

How closely does theory fit with practice? What do real managers say about the new technology? What is technically possible, and what is worthwhile in practice? We will try to sort out the hype from the reality.

Making sense of a changing business environment

You could argue that the information age began in 1946 when ENIAC, the first electronic computer, was built, or in the 1960s with the first business use of computers, but the new age did not gain much momentum until about 1980 when the microchip became more widely available. Before, computers were complicated and unreliable machines. They were incredibly expensive to build, and required teams of engineers to maintain and operate them. The raw data for these old machines was stacks of punched cards, and the finished output was tons of concertina-fold print-out. These machines belonged more to the industrial age than to the information age.

The revolution really began with the microchip, a tiny slice of silicon with microscopic circuitry etched onto it. This magic component, made from sand and reproduced by a process closer to printing than to conventional manufacturing, has become a commodity of the information age. But unlike pork bellies or orange juice, it owes nothing for its existence to the toil and sweat of labourers: it is a product of knowledge workers, and its value arises from its ability to store information and carry out instructions. It is used of course in personal computers (PCs), but also to control factory machinery, domestic appliances, car engines, mobile phones, military weapons, consumer electronics, cash machines, surveillance and security equipment – in effect, a tiny computer is being installed in every device. And the result is that many unskilled and semi-skilled manual and clerical jobs are simply disappearing. The microchip continues to double in power every two years and the consequences are difficult to predict, but already the

Box 7.2 Tax a bit or lose a lot

Electronic commerce has taken root on the Internet for a range of products and services available from electronic malls despite worries about security and payment. This burgeoning new market is especially appropriate for information products and services, which can be ordered, delivered and paid for over the Net, and opens up new possibilities for international trade. For example, you can already use your home PC to buy and instantly take delivery of software, music recordings, computer games and voice messaging services from another country – which is thus currently free of Value Added Tax (VAT).

This of course presents a threat to the tax revenues of nation states, who may eventually respond with a 'cybertax'. One possibility being investigated by Prof. Luc Soete for the European Commission is a 'bit tax', to be levied on every bit (binary digit) of information passing across communications networks. However, at present the UK and US governments take the view that a duty-free Internet will encourage sufficient growth in the economy and subsequent income tax revenues to more than compensate for losses in VAT.

Meanwhile, at the London School of Economics Prof. Ian Angell believes the growing deluge of information flowing though the Net will simply overwhelm any attempts to tax it, with obvious long-term consequences. 'The last death knell of the nation state has been sounded,' he says.

(You can find up-to-date opinions on the bit tax by searching the Internet. One address to try is http://www.ispo.cec.be)

effects are so far-reaching that we are being forced to revise our existing theories of economics, business and management.

Technology and efficient markets

The microchip has made possible a new generation of products which are far smaller, much cheaper and hugely more powerful than before. It is scarcely remarkable any longer that you can receive the National Lottery numbers on your pager, or see the wicket keeper's view of a test match from a TV camera in the cricket stumps. However, these are simple examples of another effect the microchip is causing, which is the opening up of communications and information. It is a global effect. On satellite TV CNN transmits news from around the world live as it breaks. Over the Internet we can buy opera tickets from Verona and Microsoft shares from New York. We can roam most of the developed world and still be in touch by mobile phone.

This opening up of global communications is a major factor in the globalization of markets and the intensely competitive business environment we are now experiencing. Markets can only operate efficiently when information on products, prices and availability is freely available. Whether you are buying for your organization or just as a retail consumer, you can only choose from the range of options you can find out about, and until fairly recently, that meant the options on offer nearby, in your own country. But increasingly now you can select from the best value on offer anywhere in the world.

These are fundamental, probably irreversible changes which the microchip is bringing about. You and I as consumers enjoy the new range of choice, and being able to decide for ourselves. In this new marketing environment, we will no longer tolerate organizations that offer poor value and limited choice: we will

Box 7.3 Arthur Andersen – a senior partner's view

'Hot damn! What now?' I'd sliced the shot just off the fairway. 'You've played this course before ... can I reach the green from there?'

'You might,' said Mary, 'but it's a risky shot. I think I'd chip across to the dog-leg. Then you'll have an easy five-iron onto the green.'

'OK.' We picked up our clubs and set off down the fairway. 'So Mary, what's this I hear about you taking early retirement? I thought you'd be really enjoying your work now. Isn't this senior partnership what you've been working for all these years?'

'Yeah ... ironic, isn't it? You know, I started work at 16 as a bank clerk, and did night school for five years to get into Arthur Andersen. And the work schedule was gruelling in the early years. One thing which kept me going, though, was seeing the easy lifestyle of the senior partners. I gave up the best years of my life and the chance of starting a family for this job.'

I took my seven iron for the chip shot. 'So what's the problem, then? Are you being leaned on?' I asked.

'Well, the juicy contracts are certainly harder to come by, but no, nothing like that. It's just that ... the goal posts seem to have moved. I'm working as hard now as I was 30 years ago, and there's a whole pack of smart and hungry computer whiz-kids snapping at my heels. I'm not as young as I was, and I feel kind of cheated.' Mary played just onto the green, but her ball rolled away from the pin. 'Typical . . .'

My chip shot had left me well placed for the green. I played the five iron, still slicing a bit. The ball landed in a bunker to the right of the green.

'It's a bummer, isn't it. The end-game never works out the way you planned it.'

(Based on a real conversation with Mary – not the senior partner's real name)

walk away from them and instead vote with our pound, dollar and euro for the organizations which offer the best value, wherever they are in the world. The old bureaucratic hierarchies and state monopolies cannot survive in this environment, and neither, it seems, can totalitarian states. The fall of the Iron Curtain and the demise of the Soviet Union were due in part to the free availability of satellite TVs and video recorders. The Kremlin could no longer keep their people in the dark. Once the Soviet people saw the abundance and choice in Western supermarkets, they simply wouldn't tolerate any longer the food queues and shortages they had endured for decades.

In our global village on the verge of the twenty-first century, ordinary citizens of the networked world vote with their money, empowered by the microchip. The poor and unemployed, however, are being disenfranchised.

Economics and society

As with any revolution, the information revolution is changing the basis on which money and power are distributed. In the western world Bill Gates and his company Microsoft is an obvious winner, while others such as the ship building and steel bosses have lost out. But the new, more open global markets are also affecting all of us as individuals. Of course, as consumers we like the lower prices and better value that these markets bring, but as workers our jobs are more difficult and less secure, exposed to the fiercest competition from the lowest labour costs and the smartest brains anywhere in the world. And for some, the heat is too much: they are walking out – or being forced out – of the kitchen.

Of course, our capacity to adjust varies from person to person, and it depends on our ability to observe, interpret and acquire skills to cope with the changed environment – in other words, our ability to learn. The idea is summed up in the formula $L > C$, the formula for survival. It states that for an organism to survive, its rate of Learning must be greater than the rate of Change in the environment. The theory was used by Reg Revans (1980), the Cambridge professor and management educator who developed Action Learning in the 1970s. The formula applies both to individuals and to organizations – hence the current interest in the so-called learning organization. Computer networks can enhance organizational learning by enabling self-management, thus uniting in one role the function of 'doing' with the functions of reflecting, thinking and deciding what should be done next. The benefit to the organization is that it speeds up learning by closing the learning cycle described by David Kolb (1984). People see directly the results of their own decisions.

Not everyone in society will benefit from the increasing use of computer networks. Which groups of workers in the economy do you think are the winners and losers as a result of the new global markets? According to the newspapers, there are some big winners in the City, but most of us are having to work harder while accommodating continual changes in work practices, and feel less secure in our jobs. Robert Reich (1991), Harvard professor and advisor to the Clinton administration, analyses similar effects in the USA. As a political economist, he chose not to use the usual employment categories (managerial, manual, service, etc), but devised his own categories which he thinks give a better picture of the situation. The categories he uses are 'repetitive producers' (e.g. assembly line workers, etc.), 'in-person servers' (e.g. bank clerks, etc.), 'symbolic analysers' (e.g. information workers, designers, etc.) and 'agricultural and government employees' (those sheltered from the effects of global competition). His analysis shows that it is the symbolic analysers – those who use knowledge and ingenuity to create new products, software, persuasive cases etc. – who are the big winners. Meanwhile, the repetitive producers are losing heavily as their jobs are either automated or exported to the developing world where labour rates can be as low as one fortieth of those in the USA. The rest – about half the working population – are maintaining their income as their roles are re-engineered and outsourced, but only at the expense of harder work, longer hours and reduced job security. Figure 7.1 summarizes Reich's view of growing inequality in America at the start of the 1990s.

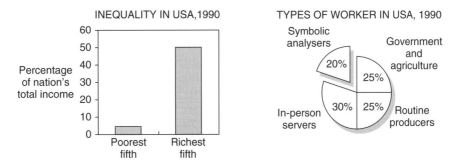

Figure 7.1   Reich's view of growing inequality at the start of the 1990s in America. The pie chart and bar chart were constructed using data quoted by Reich (1991).

In the UK we often follow trends set in the USA, and indeed the 30/30/40 breakdown used by Will Hutton (1995) to describe UK society in 1995 is similar to Reich's view of inequality in the USA. According to Hutton, two-thirds of wage earners earn less than the average income, resulting in growing insecurity for the majority. He believes that in the UK now, people's incomes leave 30 per cent disadvantaged (the unemployed), 30 per cent marginalized (part-time and short-term contract workers) and only 40 per cent privileged (permanent full-time workers) to earn enough to feel reasonably secure.

These figures, and other commentaries, such as that by William Bridges (1995) predicting the end of the 'job', show that major changes are taking place in how work is shared out in society. This is bound to affect people's expectations and attitudes to work, and the way they feel towards employers. Clearly there are important implications for all managers, concerning for instance recruitment, placement, job design, training and reward packages. And the technology that created the problem also plays a key role in the solution, which we will turn to shortly. For now, it is important to remember that we cannot discuss computers in isolation. For beautiful music, a Stradivarius by itself is useless: we must also have a violinist and a score.

New attitudes and expectations

In the developed world it is paradoxical that many people should feel less secure at a time when most commodities are in surplus. Throughout the Western world we have food surpluses and over-capacity in many raw materials, including oil and steel, and most manufactured products, from ball-point pens to passenger jets. All the traditional factors of production are in over-supply, including labour, the result of automation and technology. But the flip side, of course, is that jobs are disappearing, and the few that are left require higher levels of skill. We now have a generation of workers who grew up in a land of plenty, but in which jobs are scarce and insecure. Their attitudes to work are quite different from the attitudes of those whose formative experience was product scarcity and full employment. In America this phenomenon started in the 1960s when Generation X was being born. American author Douglas Coupland (1991) gave this label to the thirteenth generation since the founding of his country because those belonging to it are often stereotyped as cynical, pessimistic, disillusioned, nihilistic slackers with no respect for authority – in short, no longer buying into the American dream.

In the UK too, the children of the information age now as adults have attitudes and expectations quite different from those of their parents. But on both sides of the Atlantic they are perhaps more realistic than nihilistic. They see people devoting their lives to jobs, then losing those jobs through re-engineering, despite obediently having done as they were told – indeed perhaps *because* they did as they were told instead of being more proactive. The new generations are simply responding to the new environment. The old loyalties to company, union, craft or profession are no longer any guarantee of security. When competing for jobs in the global employment market, employability is the key: increasingly it is sought by job-seekers and offered by employers as a substitute for security of employment.

And employability means maintaining up-to-date skills, and being able to work unsupervised as a member of a team.

So how are organizations responding to this new environment, and what should they be doing to maintain competitive edge?

Organizational strategies for the information age

The industrial age was an age of expansion and growth, and most markets were sellers' markets with unsatisfied demand. Many households still looked forward to acquiring their first refrigerator, car or telephone. There were few suppliers and little competition from abroad, and our home suppliers could sell all they could produce. With captive and uncomplaining markets it is not surprising that suppliers concentrated on volume at the expense of choice and quality, and in many Western countries these attitudes persisted into the 1960s. Then we began to wake up to the threat of foreign competition when we began to lose whole industries, starting with motor cycles and television tubes, to the Japanese who despite having to ship their products halfway round the world could still offer higher quality and lower costs in our markets.

At first our manufacturers could not accept we were being beaten in fair competition, and called for protection against dumping. This politicking lost us at least a decade before we began tackling the real problems, which of course were our own wasteful methods and poor quality products. We began to copy the Japanese kanban and kaizen methods, initially in a top-down piecemeal way, but later during the 1980s in a more comprehensive fashion which came to be known as Total Quality Management (Oakland, 1989).

Total quality management (TQM)

TQM should be more than a 'flavour of the month' quick fix for product quality. It can be more fundamental representing a real challenge to the old bureaucratic command-and-control management model which evolved in the industrial age. In its fullest form, TQM should be concerned with continually improving the quality of everything in the organization, not just the product or service delivered. The kaizen philosophy from which TQM is derived takes for granted that product and service quality depends on the quality of the whole organization. In other words, if you want to improve the product, improve the process. As the people learn, and the methods and processes of the organization improve, the quality of the product or service will permanently improve. Thus, the success of the organization does not depend on the commands of a few key people at the top, and their ability to control. It depends – as the Japanese have shown – on the deploying, co-ordinating and improving of resources, including the intellectual abilities of the whole workforce.

TQM brought empowerment and the flatter organization. Teams of workers called Quality Improvement Teams were set up at every level in the organization. They learned how to make decisions of real consequence, instead of just being told what to do by managers as before. For the first time in Western countries, ordinary workers were expected to make a contribution with their brains as well as their hands, but middle managers, whose role was diminished, felt threatened and took every opportunity to reassert their authority. Perhaps that is why in most organizations TQM failed to gain any momentum of its own, and without constant championing at the highest level, tended to stall after a couple of years.

TQM was a step in the right direction for the information age, but as applied in many organizations was not enough on its own: often its focus on quality, teamwork and a scientific approach described by Brian Joiner (1994) ignored the hierarchy and the way information is formally disseminated within an organization. How could Quality Improvement Teams make sensible decisions if the information they needed was not freely available to them? And freely available information is only possible when a suitable information system is in place, and a culture of openness rather than secrecy prevails and the teams have access to management information. The norm in most hierarchies is for information to be held centrally, with access determined by seniority. Information is power, and ambitious people working in hierarchies were therefore reluctant to release information freely. Hierarchies tend to foster cultures of secrecy and mistrust – which was exactly the wrong environment for Quality Improvement Teams to flourish. It was perhaps senior mangers' disappointment with the results of TQM which opened the door for the next miracle cure to emerge in 1990 – Business Process Re-engineering (BPR).

Business Process Re-engineering (BPR)

Mike Hammer and James Champy (1990) launched BPR in the *Harvard Business Review* with a paper titled 'Re-engineering work: Don't automate, obliterate'. In it they suggested that computers and communications had advanced so much that it was no longer appropriate just to use them to automate existing processes and support existing functional departments in the organization. They admitted it was still possible to gain 10 per cent improvements like that, but promised nearer tenfold improvements by redesigning the whole organization to take full advantage of modern technology. And indeed there were some dramatically successful examples quoted, but Hammer (1993) later admitted that as many as seven out of ten so-called business process re-engineering projects failed. A common oversight was that hard-pressed chief executives often pushed ahead without taking sufficient account of the people whose jobs were to be re-engineered or obliterated. Radical change on such a wide front cannot succeed without the full support and cooperation of everyone, which is unlikely to be forthcoming where there has been a history of secrecy and mistrust. As the saying goes, turkeys don't vote for Christmas.

So again for most organizations BPR, the latest miracle cure, failed to deliver the promised returns. Like TQM, BPR is proposed as a complete solution when in fact both are only partial solutions. The techniques as implemented in practice give insufficient attention to the human resource implications of such radical change; in particular the mistrust that persists when people have worked in overly hierarchical organizations.

Box 7.4 BPR offers ten times, not 10 per cent improvement

Business process redesign (BPR) does for office work what just-in-time (JIT) does for factory work – it cuts out the queues of work waiting to be processed at each stage of production, thus dramatically reducing the time a job takes to pass through the system. Pre-JIT, one job in a batch might spend six weeks in the factory, yet might only be worked on for a total of ten hours. The rest of the time it was just being stored and moved around. And pre-BPR it was the same with office work: for each new job a paperwork file was generated which moved intermittently through the system as part of a batch.

BPR is transforming the loans and insurance industry by delivering big savings and huge improvements in customer service. One case quoted by David Davidson of PA Consulting Group was a building society which typically took six weeks to offer a mortgage but the file was only open for 7.5 minutes in total. After BPR the turnaround time was reduced to two weeks. And of course the telephone direct line motor and house insurance companies routinely turn around the whole deal from initial inquiry through offer and acceptance to card payment in the space of a single phone call.

How is it done? By supporting the core process with the latest computer technology. Where possible, one person with the relevant information and the rules for decision making handles the whole job immediately, so there is no need for jobs to hang around in in-trays. Also, all paperwork is scanned into the network so that files no longer have to pass sequentially from one person to the next. All staff can work on copies of the file at the same time. The key technologies are document image processing, and workflow software, the digital equivalent of the conveyor belt.

By now you can probably put the pieces of the jigsaw together for yourself. In retrospect, TQM and BPR now appear as worthy but incomplete attempts to adjust to the demands of the information age. Both have made invaluable contributions, but the problem now is that of low trust – and yet high trust is one of the benefits promised by the HRM approach described in this book. Taken together, TQM, BPR and HRM point to a new style of management, an alternative to the Taylorist style of the industrial age, one more appropriate for the information age, and more likely to succeed. Instead of aiming for the biggest possible profit by managing the money, the new style requires us to manage the knowledge in the organization, to the benefit of all stakeholders, not just the shareholders.

Managing knowledge, through networks and teams

The critical factors for managing successfully really have changed in the information age. We don't have time here to go into detail, though if you are interested you can read about it elsewhere (Wilson, 1996). Here we will just identify some of the more important changes occurring as we move from the industrial age into the information age, and examine their implications.

The shift from tangible to intangible products

The manufacturing sector is no longer the big provider of jobs and employment it once was, but we are left with a legacy of the management approach developed for ranks of manual workers. One of the functions of managers in the profit-motivated industrial age was to monitor throughput and quality by counting and measuring a tangible product. There were departments responsible for production planning and control, and for quality control – which were only possible because the product was tangible. A broad raft of middle managers were routinely employed to do the headwork for the manual workers. This was the legacy of FW Taylor's (1911) Scientific Management in which managers decided what was to be done, and then supervised the workers to see they got on and did it. This management approach persisted into the middle of the twentieth century, way beyond the time when ordinary workers had little education and couldn't be expected to think for themselves. It persisted because it was still just possible to manage (though not very well) assembly line production, for instance, in that way.

With information products and services, however, the product is intangible and it is not possible for a manager to count and measure work in progress. Throughput and quality are impossible for a middle manager to monitor while the work is being done. For example, monitoring the quality and progress of writing a program or repairing a copier, if possible at all, can only be done by the worker herself or himself.

The shift from visible to invisible processes

With information workers, not only is the product intangible, but the process is mostly invisible too, going on inside the worker's head. There may be a manual element to the work, but it is the headwork and knowledge that add value. A supervisor cannot come along and instantly see problems, advise on methods or judge how well the work is being done. Thus method study – the most developed form of Taylor's scientific management, in which an industrial engineer with a stop-watch studies the work of a worker before developing an improved method – is out of the question.

It is possible that some Western companies may have restructured as flatter organizations because it was the latest fad and other companies had shown savings that way, but middle managers would be dispensed with sooner or later anyway. When the value-adding processes have become invisible to managers, it does not take long to realize that the previous role of the middle manager – that of monitoring and controlling those processes – is quite impossible. The middle manager is no longer needed. The self-managing team is the best way, perhaps the only way, of organizing knowledge workers.

The shift from physical resources to the knowledge resource

Earlier in this chapter we noted that buyers' markets have superseded the sellers' markets of the industrial age. Shortages and unsatisfied demand no longer exist in the Western world because of automation and an inexhaustible global supply of cheap manual labour. We have surplus capacity in most materials and manufactured goods. Also, the traditional factors of production: land, labour, machines, materials and money are all easy to acquire in global markets, and so it is unlikely that a competitive edge can be sustained for long through unique access to one of the traditional factors of production. In the information age, it is the ability of an organization to deploy knowledge resources that creates competitive advantage.

Although knowledge is that which is known by people, managing the knowledge resource is not quite the same as managing human resources. There are many organizations that have knowledgeable people on the payroll, yet their knowledge remains unused by the organization. For example, business schools on both sides of the Atlantic have people with all the skills needed to run a successful business, but some schools still perform poorly at managing their own affairs. Often there are simple reasons for this paradox, arising from secrecy, mistrust and lack of mutual respect, all of which can be put right through better, more open communications.

The shift from hierarchical to networked organization

The very earliest organizations were military hierarchies with a few educated people at the top telling the masses below what to do. This command-and-control model worked well in business too, during the industrial age when the business environment was changing only slowly and therefore did not overwhelm the decision-making capacity of the few at the top. But today, as we have noted, too much change is occurring on too many fronts for a command-and-control organization to respond quickly enough: it takes too long for information to be relayed up the chain of command, and decisions to be made and sent back down again. People on the spot must have the knowledge to assess situations and be empowered to do what is necessary. The global corporations which just a few years ago had up to 14 layers in their hierarchies have been scrambling to restructure with far fewer levels. And in the most progressive organizations, nearly everyone works in small teams essentially in the same level, with just a small headquarters team providing strategic direction and support.

Obtaining the right quality of people to work unsupervised in a network organization can be achieved by recruitment and training, but other problems arise when the hierarchy is removed and centralized control is no longer possible. How

Box 7.5 Smartly structured

The professional service organizations have never organized hierarchically. The big consulting and accounting groups like McKinsey and Peat Marwick survive by selling up-to-date knowledge, and their global practices with tens of thousands of partners are deployed as small teams in offices around the world. They operate at the leading edge of change, and their success depends on bringing the right brains to bear on their clients' problems. Their headquarters provide central support, not central control.

And this approach works in industry and commerce too. IBM (UK) with 10 000 people organizes sales as a federation of 32 small self-managing businesses, accountable to a UK board of four people. Rolls Royce Motors with 2 500 people operates as 16 sub-businesses organized as multi-skilled teams of six to ten members. Asea Brown Boveri, an industrial giant with 200 000 staff worldwide and revenues of $30 billion, operates with just three levels of management.

So who needs hierarchy?

should the efforts of individuals be coordinated? And should the organization as a whole be controlled, and if so, by whom? A very general answer to these questions is that the network organization operates according to democratic rather than autocratic principles, with individuals and teams who share the same values exercising self-control in pursuit of agreed goals. Fine words, but all this is only possible among people engaged in regular, free and open communication, dialogue and debate.

The shift from delayed and constrained, to instant and open communication

The need for good communications keeps cropping up. It is a big topic in its own right, and very important to the network organization. Once again, we only have time to skim the surface, but clearly there are many different types of communication. For instance, there are internal communications to do with work flow and scheduling; to do with knowledge acquisition, training and research; and to do with raising involvement, commitment and trust. Also, there are external communications to do with orders, sales, purchases, invoices and payments; and to do

---

Box 7.6 Remote working and virtual teams

If your idea of remote working is sitting at home with your PC and a cup of coffee, try the North Sea. Imagine being aboard a BP Exploration vessel with drilling operations halted by equipment failure and with no one to diagnose the problem. It happened in 1995, and the engineers on board faced the prospect of taking the ship – leased for $150,000 a day – back to port. In fact, thanks to a new computer fitted with a tiny video camera, the downtime lasted only a few hours. The engineers put the faulty hardware in front of the camera and dialled up a BP drilling equipment expert, who was able to guide them through the repair.

The computer was there as part of a 'Virtual Teamwork' project being piloted, to support collaboration between the 42 separate business units created when MD John Browne reorganized BP Exploration. He had transformed the company into a 'federation of assets', each with the freedom to develop their own processes and solutions. The aim was for BP to gain from the variety and creativity of 42 companies sharing their experiences.

The 18-month, $13 million VT (Virtual Teamwork) pilot was not led by Information Technologies, but by Kent Greenes from Human Resources, who had a background in Operations. His team decided on five different communities to be equipped with VT computers for the pilot. Mature and emerging oilfield groups, existing and new expert groups, and a business centre network of key BP offices around the world were networked with VT computers. The network allowed video conferencing, multimedia e-mail, application sharing, shared chalkboards, Web browsing, document scanning and data storage. The purpose was to achieve business goals such as making better decisions, controlling costs and schedules, and solving problems creatively.

Two important findings emerged. First, coaching is very important, not so much on how to use the VT system, but more in challenging users to exploit it to serve their business needs. And second, VT did not eliminate the need for meetings. Though meetings were significantly reduced, they were still needed to maintain trust, and to resolve important issues involving large groups. The ultimate objective is now to make continuous learning and knowledge-sharing the company norm.

This short description of virtual teamwork is based upon an article, 'Knowing the Drill: Virtual Teamwork at BP', by Don J. Cohen. The article appeared in Issue 1 of the Ernst & Young journal *Innovation in Action*, found at the Ernst & Young Web site *www.businessinovation. ey.com*

with customer, supplier, shareholder and community relations. In fact the dynamics of the network organization operating in a changing business environment generate such a volume of communication that it can become a serious overhead cost, diverting people's time and attention from the main task of delivering the product or service.

The answer, however, is not to cut down on communication – that road leads to poor coordination, misdirection and mistrust. Instead, we should seek to eliminate the transaction cost for each message – in other words, avoid the high costs of writing memos and playing telephone tag, and seek instead to make each exchange as quick and easy as asking someone the time. New technology has a major role to play here, in the form of e-mail, voice mail, the Internet and intranet, but it will never entirely replace older technology and the need for face-to-face meetings. For building trust, there's no substitute for a smile or a handshake.

When you compare these shifts with your experience of organizations you may find examples to support the claims, though perhaps feel they are being exaggerated. Of course, progress is patchy and inconsistent. We do still have manufacturing companies in the UK managed traditionally. We also have companies at the

Box 7.7 The latest 'RP' – business software for the knowledge economy

Recently something called ERP has been the fastest-growing money tree in the corporate computing garden. It is the third in a series of RPs offered to companies by the computing industry. In the 1960s we were offered MRP, in the 1980s came MRP-2, and now we have ERP.

MRP or materials requirement planning was the first complex business application to be run on the new generation of more reliable computers (using transistors instead of valves) which were becoming available at the time. Before that, the only business applications for computers were simple highly repetitive routines needed in the finance department for calculating payrolls – which of course required a list of employees to be held on computer.

MRP, however, was used to handle the detailed logistics required to ensure that the right amounts of raw materials and parts were available to mass-produce complex products. It was important for products such as cars, where a shortage of one small component could stop the main assembly track and all the flows of materials supplying it. The three main inputs for the software were the master production schedule for the product, the parts list for the product, and the current stocks of parts and their delivery lead-times. The software would work backwards from the finished product requirements and calculate when orders for parts and materials should be released so as to keep the assembly track and all the sub-assembly lines flowing smoothly.

MRP-2 or manufacturing resource planning was an even more complex application, which did everything that MRP could do, but could also plan resources such as finance, production machinery and operators for the machinery. This was at a time when long-term business forecasts and corporate plans were credible options for keeping big business on track. Today of course, the emphasis is on getting the organization into shape, staying nimble and grabbing opportunities as and when they arise.

ERP or enterprise resource planning is designed to do just this. It is an integrated package of modules to serve all the needs of the organization from supply chain through to customer care. The employee list that languished first in the Finance and the Personnel Departments is now being recognized as a most important resource – not just a cost. It is now an important database at the heart of the system. It holds details of the knowledge, skills and experience available in the organization, and makes it available not just in the Personnel Department, but online wherever it is needed by the organization.

'Our people are our most important asset.' Organizations are not saying it so much now. They're acting on it.

leading edge, but most organizations are somewhere in between, having made some changes along these lines in their attempts to remain competitive. We are trying to understand a dynamic, changing situation.

Let us now turn to hardware and software. What functionality is available, and how appropriate is it in practice?

Technology in support of HRM

There are two stages in the implementation of technology for the HRM approach:

- initially, stand-alone computer-based personnel information systems to automate work in the HR Department, and then
- networked systems, such as ERP (enterprise resource planning) systems which include a personnel database to support the HRM philosophy throughout the organization.

But first, a word or two about the design of information systems. The information system for an organization was often called the management information system or 'MIS'. The MIS is like the nervous system of a living organism: its purpose is to acquire, store, process and convey information wherever it is needed in the organization. The MIS must serve the objectives of the organization, and mirror the organizational structure. For instance, in hierarchical organizations, information was held centrally on a mainframe computer and only released to lower levels through the chain of command – the vertical lines on the tree-like organization chart. The chart had no formal horizontal links on the same level from one department to another, and so the MIS offered no way for the production manager to access sales department information, for instance. Each department used a dumb terminal (a monitor and keyboard) connected directly to the mainframe and was allowed access only to its own data.

In the network organization, however, information is not held centrally, but distributed across different computers on the network, with different types of information held at the points where it is most often needed, to avoid unnecessary network traffic. However, the information system for a network organization can be designed to allow any user (not just 'management') access to any information they are authorized to use, regardless of where it is held on the network. In principle, information should only be held once. For instance, only one list of personnel should be held, accessible by the Finance team for the payroll, and also by the Human Resources team for their functions. A suitable information system for a network organization consists of a network of powerful 'server' computers, one for each team. Each server holds master data and software specific to the needs of the team. Then each team member has a 'client' PC linked to the team server. Thus everyone's PC is linked to everyone else's in the organization and potentially via the Internet to millions of other PCs around the world.

The modern client–server MIS is so much more versatile than the old central mainframe MIS. Its main traffic is now becoming a wide range of unstructured multimedia communications on top of the modest flow of formal, structured data needed for day-to-day management which was the staple of the mainframe. This transformation of MIS is just another example of the Internet phenomenon, in which exciting, user-friendly software converted a computer scientists' network (the pre-1990s Internet) almost overnight into a consumer product. That is why managers now are learning the same skills as their net-head teenage sons and daughters. The global Internet and the organization intranet share the same 'browser' access software and communications protocols.

For an impression of the features available in a modern CPIS, read the boxed examples inserted in the text. They are derived from the publicity material of systems suppliers in 1997. We must remember, however, that systems are continually being enhanced, so these examples may no longer be an accurate guide to the sophistication and functionality available.

Computer-based personnel information systems

Figure 7.2 shows a user's view of a computerized personnel information system.

Small firms of, say, 20 people or fewer can often manage without networking their computers. Everyone knows everyone else and all work under the same roof, so it is easy for people to communicate when they are free to do so. However, connecting up a network is getting to be so straightforward that the payback from

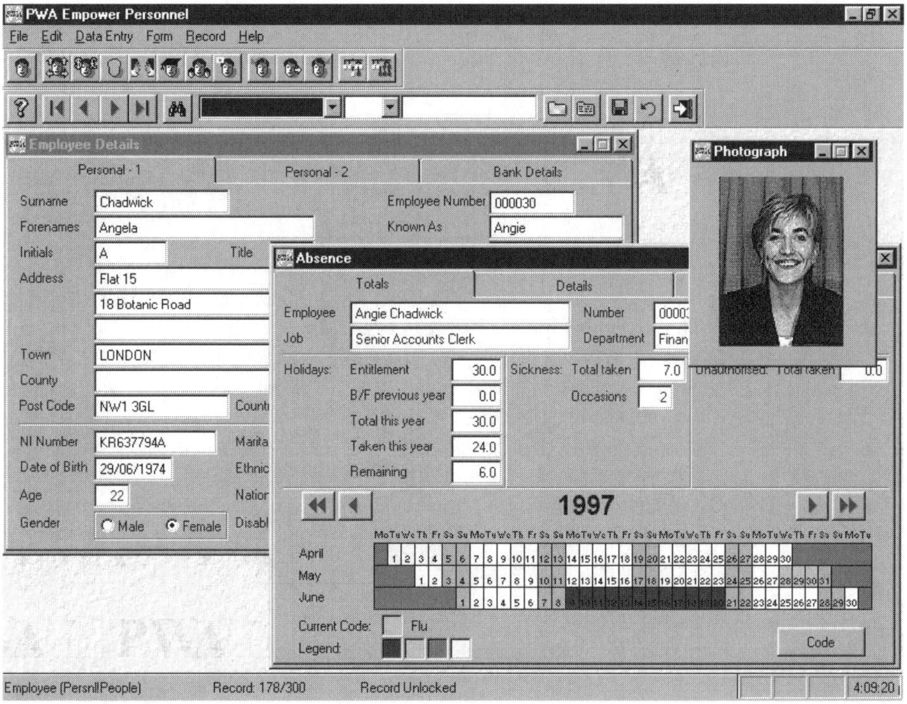

Figure 7.2 A user's view of a computerized personnel system: an example from PWA Personnel Systems Ltd, Marlow, SL7 1BX, England, reproduced with permission.

e-mail alone could still be just a few months. Even so, every organization's needs are unique and separate computers will continue to be installed and used, often as an interim measure before linking them in a network. So let us start with a personnel database on a single PC, set up perhaps to replace the existing paper-based employee records in the filing cabinet. The immediate advantages are:

- Space is saved – no more bulky filing cabinets.
- Time is saved – you can extract and view a person's file in seconds at the click of a mouse.
- Searching and sorting are much easier. You can easily extract the records of everyone in Sales, or everyone who hasn't had a performance review in the past 12 months, or everyone on a salary of less than £16 000 p.a., for instance.
- If you don't know a person's name, you can find someone's record by clicking on a person's picture in a gallery.
- You can set access rights for different users: access can be read-write, read-only or no access. Also, access can be to the whole record, or just to certain parts such as the less sensitive data in a person's records.

These advantages arise from simply automating existing procedures in the HR office. However, when the PC is networked, information which before was only available in the HR office is potentially much more widely available. Of course, just because it is technically possible doesn't mean it will happen in practice. That depends on the culture of the organization and how open it is to changes in working practices.

The process of making information more freely and widely available in an organization is what Shoshana Zuboff (1988) called 'informating' the organization, in

Box 7.8 HR Access: global, enterprise-wide information access

This system, supplied by IBM, offers a single repository for HR information for all the countries in which a company operates. By using a Web browser it allows access to HR information through the Internet or intranet in many languages to authorized users anywhere, including the mobile and external workforce.

'Because today's marketplace is global, international deployment is a major business challenge. Organizations need the capability to manage people in different countries with multiple language, currency, regulatory and cultural requirements. And organizations do not just need to reach people in assigned office locations any more. The virtual organization requires anywhere, anytime access to information.'

HR Access can empower the people in your organization, which means greater efficiency for your operations at all levels:

- HR professionals – can concentrate on core HR functions like building succession plans and developing strategic HR programmes.
- Line managers – can play a fuller role in building employee skills and development plans through performance reviews and salary management.
- Employees – through self-service can update personal and professional information, such as newly acquired skills. They can view job openings, enrol in training programmes, read about corporate policy and consult the employee handbook – all on-line. As well as lightening the administrative workload, self-service builds commitment, strengthens teamwork, motivation and satisfaction because employees are more involved and better informed.

(Edited extracts reproduced with permission from IBM Global Services, Leamington Spa, CV32 4EA, England)

contrast to simply automating the work. A fully informed organization is one in which information permeates the organization, and people can make good decisions instantly by interacting with symbolic representations of business resources, rather than with the resources directly. An example she gives is an operator in a paper-making plant who now gauges a process from a computer screen whereas before he plunged his hand into the vat and rubbed the pulp between his fingers. The nature of the work changes, becoming less physical, more cerebral, and some find this easier to cope with than others.

Technically, once information is coded digitally, informing the organization is straightforward. It is just a question of putting the information on the network.

The additional advantages, then, of putting the CPIS on the network are:

- Remote access is possible – you can view the records without going to the HR office, cutting travelling time.
- More than one person can view the same records at the same time, cutting waiting time.
- Empowerment, teamwork and self-management are strongly supported through free and open access to information that teams need for decision making.

An HRM culture may in theory grant teams access to information, but if the transaction costs – the time and risks – are too high, people just won't bother. A good computer network therefore enhances the HRM approach by eliminating transaction costs, so that decisions can be supported by the best possible information.

Box 7.9 Resumix can double your staffing productivity

This California-based company with offices in London has a client list of 400 global companies including Kodak, Coca-Cola, Ford, IBM and Walt Disney, all using Resumix systems for recruitment. The systems can reduce by at least half the cost-per-hire, which averages over $4000 per employee in the USA – and cut the time-to-fill by half too. How's it done? By re-engineering the recruitment process.

Resumés and CVs received by e-mail and fax can be entered directly into Resumix's Human Skills Management System, and typed or hand-written CVs can be scanned into the system. The information is then categorized by skills, job titles and education, and the applicant records matched to the organization's requirements for particular jobs, skills or experience – all automatically, using the latest expert systems technology. And the system is a natural for interfacing with the Internet.

For instance, at UB Networks, a subsidiary of Tandem

Computers, line managers can fill a job requisition on screen which is then routed for approval signatures, imported into Resumix and the opportunity posted on the Internet. Applicants browsing UB's Web page can simply paste their resumé to the page, where it is downloaded into Resumix without ever being printed.

An organization's competitive advantage today increasingly depends on its ability to attract and retain the most qualified and productive employees. Jon Peters, staffing systems manager for UB Networks, believes that up to 30 per cent of new employees will soon find their jobs through Internet postings. 'When we first started, we found that only young, technical people were applying. Now, we're getting a large pool of non-technical people, showing that Internet usage is expanding into the general population,' Peters says.

(Extracts from material supplied by Resumix, Epsom, KT17 4QJ, England)

Conclusion

The theoretical grounds for implementing the HR approach to managing an organization are impeccable, even though in practice there is little hard evidence that it works. Thus after a decade of exhortation from academics, chief executives remain sceptical. HRM has never been a crowd puller at conferences like TQM and BPR, and it's easy to see why: the up-front risks and costs of making the change loom large but the payoff on the bottom line has never been shown to exist! At least BPR has a 3 in 10 chance of a payoff, and TQM does improve quality and chances of corporate survival. Hardly surprising then, that there are few examples of organizations trumpeting HRM, and of these their motives are sometimes questionable. Do top managers use HR professionals sometimes just to handle the inevitable human problems that arise from downsizing? Is HRM invoked just to put a respectable gloss on crude cost-reduction exercises?

However, let us be unequivocal about HRM: it is essential and will prevail in today's competitive global markets. Those organizations that implement it alongside TQM and BPR will gain an increasing long-term edge on their bureaucratic hierarchical competitors. Why? Because the rules of the game developed in the industrial age no longer apply now. Nearly a century ago, Henry Ford used a command-and-control hierarchy to leverage his knowledge. He and a few top advisers told thousands of factory workers what to do, and the market gratefully purchased 15 million black Model Ts. Of course this is no longer possible today.

Today's products are so sophisticated and competition so fierce that it is quite impossible for a small group at the top of a Ford-like hierarchy to operate successfully. Competition in the global market is in ideas, information and knowledge, and success is achieved by coordinating the brain-power of the whole organization to out-smart the other players. We need the scientific approach and empowerment of TQM, we need the restructuring and computers of BPR, and above all we need the high trust and commitment of HRM. By combining these elements, a new 'inform-and-entrust' team-of-teams organizational form is emerging which may eventually become the dominant structure for knowledge management in the twenty-first century.

Summary

There are many ways in which information technology has and will continue to exert an impact on work organizations. In the chapter, we have reviewed a range of human resourcing options that have been largely triggered through the adoption of information technology.

The manner in which the opportunities for changing employment management policy and practice through the application of information technology is undertaken depends on whether the dominant view lies at the hard or the soft end of the HRM spectrum. There is the potential for enormous efficiency gains but coupled with this is the danger of de-skilling work. Alternatively, there are opportunities to free employees of the routine aspects of their work so that they are able to engage with the more intellectually challenging and satisfying elements of work.

IT also offers the opportunities to operate with a diversity of organizational forms and new ways of working. The lone manager needs not only to be conversant with the opportunities that could arise but also to anticipate the likely benefits and difficulties for the manager and their subordinates associated with such changes.

Questions

1   How far has computerization of the personnel function progressed in your organization? Which of the stages below has been reached?
    Stage 0 – no computerization. Only paper files used.
    Stage 1 – paper files, plus a terminal to access the personnel list used by accounts for wages and salaries.
    Stage 2 – as for stage one, but with a CPIS on a stand-alone PC used only for training and development.
    Stage 3 – a networked system using a single personnel list for wages and salaries, personnel administration, and training and development.
    Stage 4 – as for stage 3, but with line managers authorized to access certain types of personnel information.
    Stage 5 – as for stage 4, but with all employees authorized to access certain types of personnel information, perhaps using an intranet browser.

2   Can you summarize in two or three lines the effects of global markets on:
    (a) your organization – its products and markets;
    (b) your job – how it has changed and is likely to change;
    (c) you – your attitude to your job and your organization.

3   What repetitive tasks at work do you find a chore? List two or three examples. Is it possible that they could be automated or re-engineered out of existence by computer networks? What authorization would be necessary? What technology would be necessary?

4   What are you doing to maintain your employability? How are your team skills? Your self-motivation? Your computer skills?

5   Where does your organization stand on the questions of security of employment and employability? What specific, formal policies does it express in employment contracts or mission statements?

6   Disintermediation is the term used to describe the ability of computer networks to eliminate intermediates, 'middle men' and agents in a wide range of different transactions. Give two examples made possible by the Internet affecting retail services. Give two examples which are used, or could be possible in your organization, to allow line managers to help themselves rather than depend on specialist staff managers.

7   Which of Robert Reich's categories of worker best describes you? Are you a repetitive producer, an in-person server, a symbolic analyser or a government or agricultural worker? What are the implications of your belonging to this category?

8   Has your organization ever implemented TQM, BPR or HRM? If so, what are the most important changes that have occurred in the way the organization is managed?

9   Is access to information strictly on a 'need to know' basis in your organization? Or can you use your computer to reach out through the network to access information on other functions (sales, marketing, production, accounts, personnel etc.) or other products in which you are not directly involved? You may need to log on at work and see what's possible, or speak to your friendly computer adviser before you can answer this question.

10 Try to get access to your CPIS at work through the network, or failing that, get someone in Personnel to demonstrate its basic features to you. Does the system have functionality or potential which is not being used? Is value being lost as a result?

References and further reading

Bridges, William (1995) *Jobshift – How to prosper in a workplace without jobs*, Addison Wesley, London.

Coupland, Douglas (1991) *Generation X. Tales for an accelerated culture*, Abacus. London.

Hammer, Michael (1990) Re-engineering work: Don't automate, obliterate. *Harvard Business Review*, Jul–Aug.

Hammer, Michael & Champy, J (1993) *Re-engineering the corporation – a manifesto for business revolution*, Nicholas Brealey, London.

Hutton, Will (1995) *The State we're in*, Jonathan Cape, London.

Joiner, Brian (1994) *Fourth generation management – the new business consciousness*, McGraw Hill, New York.

Kolb, David A (1984) *Experiential Learning*, Prentice Hall, London.

Oakland, John (1989) *Total Quality Management*, Butterworth Heinemann, Oxford.

Reich, Robert B (1991) *The work of nations: a blueprint for the future*, Simon & Schuster, New York.

Revans, Reginald F (1980) *Action Learning*, Blond & Briggs, London.

Taylor, FW (1911) *Principles of Scientific Management*, Harper, New York.

Wilson, David A (1996) *Managing knowledge*, Butterworth Heinemann, Oxford.

Zuboff, Shoshana (1988) *In the age of the smart machine*, Heinemann, London.

Legal briefing

A. Data Protection Act

There is no generally recognized right to privacy in English law, and the Data Protection Acts do not specifically provide one (but see later in this briefing). An alarming amount of personal information is stored on electronic systems, making retrieval and unauthorized access a simple matter compared to the old-style manual systems. All that the Acts seek to do is to impose some control on the use of stored data.

The Data Protection Act, 1984, requires all data users who hold personal data that may be processed automatically to register with the Data Protection Registrar (now Commission). This includes employers who hold data concerning individual employees, and includes not only factual data, but also expressions of opinion. It is a criminal offence to fail to register.

Data may only be kept for lawful purposes, shall not be disclosed in a manner incompatible with those purposes, or kept for longer than necessary. The individual who is the subject of the information is entitled to be told that such information is being kept, to have access to that information and, if appropriate, to have it amended or deleted. An individual may enforce his or her rights through the court of the Data Protection Commission. Among these rights is a claim for compensation for loss caused by the holding or disclosure of 'inaccurate data'. However, in this context, expressions of opinion, which would include references, are not covered.

A power contained in the Act to regulate the use of information relating to racial origin, political affiliations, religion, mental and physical health and criminal convictions has not, as yet, been exercised.

The Data Protection Act 1998, in force from April 2000, implements an EU Directive on the subject. When taken together with the Human Rights Act, 1998, due to come into force in October 2000, there will be the nearest approximation to a law protecting privacy that there has ever been in the UK. The Directive, in fact, requires the Member Governments of the EU to 'protect the fundamental rights and freedoms of natural persons and, in particular, their right to privacy with respect to the processing of personal data'.

The Act replaces the Data Protection Registrar with a Commissioner. There are some significant changes relating to employment. No one may now require a 'data subject' (that is, a person about whom data are kept) to exercise their personal right of access to the data for the benefit of some third party. In the context of employment, an employer is prevented from requiring an employee, or applicant for employment, to make a 'subject access' request for criminal records. There are exceptions in certain circumstances, for example where there is a legal obligation to disclose the information such as in the case of prison officers or social workers, or 'where it is justified in the public interest'. How this will be interpreted is a matter for speculation. Further, any term in an employment contract requiring a 'data subject' to supply to another person all or part of a record that contains information about that subject's physical or mental health made by a health professional in the course of caring for the individual, will be void.

The protection is extended by the Act to manual filing systems as well as to computerized data.

There still remains the problems of storage of electronic data within large organizations, particularly where the information can be accessed across national boundaries. In large, multi-site organizations, employees are often encouraged to make use of the information available, and it is clearly a very useful commercial

tool. Any individual employee would not, seemingly, be liable under the Act for misusing information, as he or she would not be the 'data controller', and it does not appear that the employer would be answerable for the actions of such a 'rogue' employee. It is, however, open to a court to decide otherwise, and it is always a wise precaution for an employer to have a strict 'privacy' policy in place wherever employees have access to sensitive information. The Access to Medical Records Act, 1988, entitles an employee or prospective employee to see any medical report before it is disclosed to the employer, and this includes information that is not automatically processed. There is a right to correct any errors that appear in the report.

Information technology has also given rise to a number of other employment problems. There has been a spate of recent cases where employees have been dismissed for using the company's e-mail address to send private communications. This is a worse problem for employers than the occasional private telephone call because of the nature of electronic systems and the potential for widespread dissemination of messages that have nothing to do with the employer's business. It is a form of theft, and an increasing number of employers are treating it as such. Another problem is the downloading of material from the Internet by employees. This is praiseworthy if it advances the interests of the employer, but so much of the material downloaded onto office systems does nothing of the sort, and is, on the contrary, of a pornographic nature.

It is highly advisable for employers to have a clear policy, communicated to the employees, on the consequences of the misuse of the company's electronic systems.

B. Protection of computer programs

The legal briefing to Chapter 9 indicates that the scale of protection afforded to intellectual property rights depends very much upon the right being claimed. A grant of patent gives a monopoly right for 20 years, so that the patentee can successfully stop the commercial exploitation of that same device by any other person, even someone who has come up with the same idea quite independently. Copyright, on the other hand, lasts for the lifetime of the creator plus 70 years, but is a right against copying only. There is no protection against a rival who has quite independently given expression to the same idea.

The Patents Act, 1977, provides that it is not possible to patent a computer program as such. Programs are protected by copyright as 'literary works', but this does not, of course, give the owner the perceived commercial advantage of a monopoly right. A policy decision was clearly taken that a grant of patent would be too restrictive to other operators in the field and to the purchasing public.

However, devices that are not computer programs as such, but simply happen to run on a computerized system, are eligible for a grant of patent. A leading example is that of a traffic-lights system that was run by computer, but was held not to be a program as such. The company was granted a patent. There are a number of rather confusing decisions. Compare with the example given above the case of Merrill Lynch, the City finance corporation, which was refused a patent for its system for continuously updating analyses of market information for clients. This was judged to be a computer program as such.

There is some indication that the EU is reconsidering the patentability of computer software.

C. Problems of 'policing' the Internet

It is a trite observation that law trails behind advances in technology, and during an uncomfortable interim period, the judges struggle to find analogies with established principles with which they are familiar, but which have arisen out of very different circumstances. One example is the protection of databases. In one sense, a database is a compilation of material that is itself in the public domain, and which the compiler has not 'created'. But the fact that 'skill, judgement and labour' have been expended upon the compilation itself (the criteria that are required for recognition of copyright) means that copyright is accorded to databases in English law.

The problem with this is that there has to be substantial extraction of the material before it becomes an actionable infringement, and there is seemingly no remedy against a hacker who extracts a small item of information, even assuming one could identify who it was. The EU has recognized the growing importance of digital information systems. A great deal of time, skill and money goes into the compilation of such systems, and the owners are entitled to a return on their investment. In a Directive implemented in January 1998, copyright protection remains, but in addition, a new sui generis

right (relating to itself alone) has been implemented in connection solely with databases.

The following quotation appeared in an article in The Economist of 27 July 1996, itself quoting the words of a Los Angeles intellectual property lawyer: 'The Internet is one gigantic copying machine. All copyrighted works can now be digitized, and once on the Net, copying is effortless, costless, widespread and immediate.'

The basic problem, as the author saw it, is that there is an identity of interest between the pirate and the consumer (who will often be the same person). It is not generally regarded as theft or to be in any other way reprehensible – almost in the same league in the public estimation as getting past customs with an undeclared bottle of cognac. It is not, however, in the 'same league' commercially. The ease and scale of the copying can cause severe financial loss to owners of copyright works who lose the opportunity to charge for the reproduction and distribution of their works. In fact, the traditional notions of 'reproduction and distribution' have no place in digital systems. The problem posed for criminalizing these activities will be discussed in the next section. Each technical advance in this area spawns a number of technical solutions to problems of abuse; for example, IBM has devised a 'security system' for sending digital information over the Internet, and a method of tracing the 'abstraction' of the material. Two problems arise in connection with this; first, no system, however seemingly secure, is proof against 'nobbling' – the counter-security device; second, the service provider who is extracting the material without the authority of the copyright owner and making it available to others may be based in a country that does not enforce international copyright laws.

D. Is there a property right in information?

This seemingly arcane topic is in fact relevant to the problems of legal sanctions relating to the extraction of digital material from the Internet. It is generally conceded that criminal sanctions would be more likely to deter potential pirates than merely civil sanctions. One problem that has already arisen in the English law is that the criminal law of theft is rooted in the taking of property or the obtaining of property by deception. What is being 'stolen' in these circumstances is highly valuable information, which is not regarded as 'property' in the normal sense of that word. There is an equal problem with regard to fraud: the defrauded party is, in essence, a machine! A very similar problem occurs with the unauthorized digital transfer of funds; no 'property', as generally understood, is appropriated, no money is actually handled, there is merely an 'adjustment' to the the banking records. New technology calls for a totally new approach to the imposition of criminal sanctions; trying to squeeze the new situations into the old law is simply not working.

E. Copyright in computer-generated works

The Copyright, Designs and Patents Act, 1988, interprets 'computer-generated works' as those produced in circumstances such that there is no human author. Where such a situation arises, it is the client who commissions a software house to provide a program, for example for technical designs, who is the owner of the copyright. This lasts for 50 years from making the work. There remains the problem of deciding whether a 'human author' can be identified; if so, he or she will hold the copyright in the normal way, and the work will not be 'computer generated'. Further, it remains to be seen how the current law will cope with advances in technology such as 'neural networks'.

Further reading

Bainbridge, DI (1999) *Intellectual Property*, 4th edn, Pitmans.

Cornish, WR (1996) *Intellectual Property*, 3rd edn, Sweet & Maxwell.

Dworkin and Taylot (1989) Copyright and Patents Act, 1988, Blackstone Press.

Human resource management in the smaller business

8

Matthew Lynas and Sheila Healy

Learning objectives

After studying this chapter you should be able to:

- understand the key issues facing small to medium businesses with respect to the area of human resource management;
- appreciate the difficulties small to medium businesses experience in selecting appropriate resources for development, in terms of both personnel and organization;
- identify the problems of growth in smaller businesses and the models which can be used in managing the transition to greater complexity;
- discuss interventions and support which can assist in managing change and in developing an adequate approach to human resource management in the small to medium business.

Introduction

Over the past decade or so the small business sector of the UK economy has gained strength and small to medium businesses have become a significant topic for applied research. By small we mean having fewer than 50 employees and medium having between 50 and 250 employees (Matthews, 1996). Resource issues such as finance and marketing are the focal points of a great deal of research interest from international networks with both academic and agency interest, while organizations with growth potential are central to those concerned with the development of small to medium businesses as part of national policy aspirations. Human resource management (HRM), while being recognized as an important factor in the successful growth and development of the smaller business, has, to a large extent, been neglected.

The limited amount of depth research which has been carried out into HRM in smaller businesses has concentrated essentially on the study of current practice with a view to suggesting improvements, while acknowledging the inherent constraints on resources. The research consistently points to a lack of systematic, defined approaches to the basic people needs of the business, for example the lack of job descriptions and specifications to support the hiring of applicants and the lack of any systematic basis for deciding on pay. In general there has been a lack of adequate concern with HRM as a concept in identifying factors which lead either to growth and success or conversely to decline and failure.

Harvey (1986) suggests that the human resource factor is a key element in small businesses becoming more productive and more competitive. In a study by Foulkes (1980), effective human resource management is highlighted as a key component for organizational success. Despite this, the situation within many smaller businesses, particularly those in the early stages of start-up, often excludes expenditure on what might be regarded as areas of marginal interest, at a time when concentration needs to be devoted to developing product and market. Indeed, writers such as Baumback (1988) and Pickle and Royce (1988) tend to suggest that there is, at least in the early stages, very little interest on the part of small business owners with regard to establishing approved HRM, even simple systems for dealing with human resources issues. Hess (1987) and Kao (1989) further suggest that areas such as marketing and other strategic activities tend to take precedence over any other functional activities, including human resource management, although they may well be critical to the future of the firm. The conclusion tends to be that, although many regard human resource management as critical in the success of a business, it is not often seen that way by those who either start or wish to grow their business. This may be partly attributed to the informal nature of the smaller business, particularly in the early stages of growth, and to interpretations which suggest that formalization of HRM practices could lead to unwanted bureaucracy.

Human resource management in the smaller business

There are a range of areas where small to medium businesses can improve performance without having to employ expensive resources. These include the areas of recruitment and selection, management training, and the utilization and development of employees. We look at each of these in turn. The important point to make is that these areas of managerial responsibility are not the exclusive domain of larger organizations with specialist expertise. They are just as important – perhaps even more so because of limited resources – in the smaller organization where the potential damage can be proportionately greater.

Recruitment and selection of personnel

The main arguments for attention to HRM are normally based on the view that small to medium businesses tend to use marginally qualified workers (Pickle and Royce, 1988). The limited skills which those prepared to work within smaller businesses have to offer is well recognized by practitioners and emphasized as an area for more systematic attention. This is sometimes compounded by the limited scope for picking and choosing employees. Suggestions for countering this have been put forward by some writers such as Wagner and Foolford (1989) who suggest that instead of trying to attract skills which may well be in scarce supply and outside their ability to finance, smaller businesses should concentrate on attracting non–career employees. Rather than being a solution aimed at improving human resource utilization in the smaller business, this alternative tends to reinforce a general belief that human resource issues need not be regarded as a priority area for attention. Scarborough and Zimmer (1988) tend to dispute this, rather suggesting that HRM practice, based on systematic lines, would directly influence the quality of the firms' employees and indirectly impact on the profit of the firm. Such conviction is difficult to instil in the minds of the managers within the smaller business whose priority may be immediate survival in the market place and where, for various reasons, resources may be restricted with particular limitations on finance.

Management training

There are many challenges that face those concerned with the delivery of training suited to the needs of smaller organizations. The widely differentiated nature of these businesses makes it exceptionally difficult to develop an understanding of how skill needs can be met and is compounded by the lack of time for diagnosis of training needs and in many cases the lack of competence to carry out identification of needs for new learning. In addition, the tendency is for managers to learn through exposure and to consider their immediate work situation as providing a learning process which is much more appropriate to their needs than external courses. There is little interest in the acquisition of professional qualifications for their own sake – the learning orientation is towards solving the immediate problems of the business. This means there can be a fundamental clash between the perspectives of those involved with the organization of formal training and any owner-manager's participation in such formalized courses. Finding ways of responding presents some difficult obstacles for those involved with training. Indeed, Gibb (1990) has identified that perhaps the most significant challenge to the training on offer to smaller businesses is not the absence of training material or subject specialization in general but the ability of trainers and organizers to identify needs and demands effectively and develop learning appropriately, in ways that will relate to the problems experienced by small to medium businesses. As he sees it, the delivery of over-elaborate approaches to the smaller firm, which might not be appropriate to its particular stage of development, will mean that it cannot transfer learning into practice. It is his view that there is no shortage of trainers who are 'experts' in a particular discipline – the real challenge is how to deliver subject knowledge at the appropriate level and in a manner appropriate to the participants' needs.

First of all, those who are involved with training need to possess the ability to present the broader aspects of running a business rather than narrow subject specialisms. It is also important to recognize that, in dealing with management of small to medium businesses, there are a wide variety of skill and knowledge levels. The language, content and pace often have to be very flexible and recognize the need to guide managers towards the adaptation of concepts and techniques to meet their own unique business situations. In this sense the creation of learning is often much more difficult than in larger organizations where managers are accustomed to hearing of different concepts, even at the level of simply being familiar with their use. The orientation therefore has to be essentially action learning and linked to a problem-solving approach. There needs to be awareness of the linkages between what is formally taught, and application in the operational situation is an imperative. Thus it is important to have the option of being able to follow up on training with in-house counselling and advice which will help management to apply concepts and principles in a way appropriate to the needs of the business. Converting these suggestions into practice requires awareness of what we mean by stages of growth in small businesses, and from such a model identifying the kind of assistance which can best contribute to assisting those managing small businesses to move from one key stage of growth to another. We will look at growth models in more detail later in this chapter.

The utilization and development of human resources

Received evidence with regard to the smaller business indicates that they are poorly managed in a number of areas but particularly so with regard to the utilization of people capabilities. This can be attributed to inadequate training in management coupled with the restricted resources to do so; the inability of owner-managers to identify what is relevant to their needs and often the inability of the providers to meet what they perceive as the basic requirements. While many problem areas can be dealt with through job clarification, target setting and even the dismissal of unproductive staff if such extreme action is necessary for survival, there is a need for human resource management and the efficient utilization and development of people.

The utilization of human resources means having the right structure and ensuring the operation is tightly staffed. In spite of the claims to the contrary, many smaller organizations are not short of manpower – examination often showing them to be overloaded. The need is for rigour, in the same way as for any other business and the same way as for any other resource acquisition. It is as important in the smaller firm to have clear job criteria to avoid over-selection. It is equally important that there is a process of inducting newcomers into the smaller business. In fact, it is even more imperative to do this in the smaller firm so that newcomers can 'get themselves into' the thinking of the owner-manager as this is a vital aspect of ensuring integration into an organization which may not have formal written guidance on how things are done. Once the employee is established as part of the organization, attention must be focused on his or her effective development within it.

The argument for giving attention to areas such as employee development has been expressed by writers, for example Schuler (1989), justifying such concern on the basis that because of its very nature each employee within the smaller firm interacts with customers and with other employees to a much greater extent than might be the case in larger organizations. Thus the employee's abilities to interact effectively become more significant. Hofer and Sandberg (1987) further support the need for effective employee development with the suggestion that entrepreneurs achieve their success through their employees, seeking out the best people, rewarding them and creating a climate which encourages creativity and performance. Similar views have been expressed by Briscoe and Soukup (1990) who view employees as the firms' most important resource, regarding them as critical to the success of the firm. Further evidence of the possibility that this can be regarded as a key factor can be seen in attempts by larger organizations to create what is essentially a more entrepreneurial environment through decentralizing authority and decision making and encouraging an 'entrepreneurial' spirit in their employees. It would, however, be wrong to conclude that the existing climate in many smaller organizations is always conducive to stimulating and reinforcing such desirable behaviour. The support which this requires through training, equitable reward and results monitoring are often lacking at the earlier stages of start-up and growth and can be neglected even when firms can be seen to be thrusting towards success and growth.

Managing the smaller business

Lack of managerial skills and ineffective delegation are shortcomings in small to medium businesses which have been highlighted across the years – Perrigo (1975) identifying such basic shortcomings as contributing to restrictions on growth. The management training or requirements to overcome such basic shortcomings and the particular problems associated with succession can represent some of the most significant challenges to be overcome in the management of the smaller business.

Managerial skills

Management is not only a process but a relationship between people which is dependent on all sorts of events happening around us. We may choose to adopt a tough confident style when we see difficulties ahead and a different style when matters are running smoothly. It is clearly not possible within the smaller firm to pick and choose managers or supervisors to fit particular situational demands. What is required is the ability to recognize the changes in style needed for different situations and an awareness that subordinates may have different perceptions of their need. In addition, from inception the smaller business should seek to create a working climate where responsibility can be enthusiastically embraced by both managers and subordinates, i.e. an enterprising climate.

Delegation

In developing an enterprising climate in the smaller business, delegation is perhaps one of the most significant issues that the owner-manager needs to confront. In doing so, almost inevitably there is a need for a third-party counselling contribution, which has as its basis the need to demonstrate the relevance of good human resource management principles to the effective management of the business. Delegation of at least some of the operational tasks, which the owner-manager has been accustomed to dealing with, is paramount in ensuring effectiveness in the small firm. This inevitably necessitates organizational changes, with the corresponding need to define areas of authority, responsibility and duties of others within the staff of the firm. Such changes need to be understood and observed throughout the firm but it is also important to understand that they can be more difficult to implement within a smaller business than in a large firm. It is not simply a case of the owner-manager mastering the principles of delegation and organization. It involves changes in habits and in long-standing and deep-rooted assumptions of the owner-manager regarding the relationship with his/her employees and indeed fundamentally among the employees themselves. Such changes may be resisted, especially by those who find themselves for the first time responsible to and receiving instructions from an employee other than the owner-manager. The owner-manager will also need to challenge his or her assumptions about how to manage different situational needs and to develop the degree of flexibility to operate through subordinates – as Perrigo (1975) rightly points out, one should not be surprised that delegation, or lack of it, is usually by far the most difficult limitation for the owner-managers of small businesses to rectify.

Responsibility can be given to subordinates by drawing up simple delegation plans, giving support by counselling and coaching. Responsibilities and authority should be clearly established, preventing unease as to who should or should not take responsibility for particular tasks. This unease could result in underutilization of people and a failure quite often to deliver what is required in relation to the customer. Obviously there is risk in doing this, but the greater risk is that if growth occurs, the firm could be saddled with many incompetent subordinates with little or no commitment.

Example 8.1 highlights some of the difficulties associated with the delegation of responsibility within a small business and suggests a number of ways in which these can be tackled. Note, in particular, the need to realize that some relinquishing of responsibility is necessary in order for the company to continue to operate efficiently.

Succession

One of the lessons of delegation and an integral part of management is the ability to know when to 'bow out'. There are numerous cases in the literature of owner-managers with successful businesses who cling on to the detail of management when they should be relinquishing executive duties in favour of a successor. The resolution of the problem is only facilitated when the owner-manager is able to rec-

Example 8.1: Midshire Minerals

Midshire Minerals is a small company with 15 employees engaged in the extraction of Silica for use in a number of manufacturing areas. The company structure is basic, having an MD, and two supervisors, responsible for supervising extraction and washing operations. In addition to 'overall' management, the MD had responsibility for sales, which involved maintaining close contact with a number of geographically dispersed customers. However, because of the day-to-day detail of managing the plant, each customer visit resulted in a backlog of problems to be dealt with on return. Many of these were routine but involved matters for quick decisions (such as the purchase of replacements for mobile equipment) which the MD kept under his personal control. Both supervisors have been employed at the plant for the past 16 years and are thoroughly familiar with the processing methods. The MD's reluctance to consider involving the supervisors in the wider management stemmed from his perception of the risks involved. The pressures resulting from the MD's attempt to cover marketing/sales, routine administration and overall control led to a breakdown situation and forced a rethink on what needed to be done. Following consultation the suggested solution included:

1   A delegation plan which defined areas of managerial work essential to the continuation of the business as a profitable enterprise. This involved the MD's continued responsibility for sales/marketing and the drawing up of longer-term plans for the business.

2   A restructuring of the supervisory roles to include accountability of the more senior supervisor for stores and immediate purchase of plant spares up to £1000 in value. Additionally responsibility for providing details for wages and bonus computation was delegated to the senior supervisor. The second supervisor was delegated joint responsibility for recruiting and selecting new operatives and dealing with disciplinary matters, short of dismissal.

3   A number of simple systems were introduced covering:

- job analysis
- job specifications for operators
- clearly stated disciplinary steps and documentation
- basic training in skills and safety.

To increase commitment to the suggested changes and help in their implementation, the MD undertook responsibility to counsel each supervisor, ensuring that they were both competent and happy in the new assumed responsibilities.

ognize the difference between his or her own personal desires and the needs of the business. Only when such a challenge to personal assumptions takes place is it possible to achieve an acceptable and satisfactory solution. However, it can be the case that the recruitment of a successor is often carried out with the owner-manager having in mind a model which relates to his or her particular notions of a worthy successor. Such an intuitive approach to the recruitment and selection process can result in a mismatch with the needs of the business. Consequently this can be a significant cost to the small business. It suggests that smaller businesses need to avoid ad hoc decisions which can lead to disruptive situations. It justifies the value of carrying out systematic analysis of skills, knowledge and attitudinal requirements even in the smallest business. Turnover impact is proportionately greater in the smaller business and may result in decreased sales, time loss and lower morale.

Organizational development – the growing business

While acknowledging that many businesses either choose not to grow or are constrained in their growth ambitions, a significant number do grow and develop to greater degrees of complexity. This section considers some of the models used to describe the process of organizational growth.

Growth models

There are numerous models which provide a speculative approach to describing how growing businesses pass through distinctive phases in their life-cycle as they evolve from their 'simple' owner-managed status into functionally organized 'complex' entities. From a human resource point of view, of particular interest are models, such as Francis (1991) and Greiner (1972), which profile the phases in the life-cycle and the kind of organizational development processes which require attention.

The Francis model of organizational growth (1991), illustrated in Figure 8.1, provides a template which can be useful in positioning the firm in a growth cycle. Most small businesses can be classified in the 'Simple Structure' class but often find themselves in the 'Crisis of Disorganization' phase. The dangers are that they will move to formalize structures and systems and as a consequence lose something of the creativity which inspired the business in the first place. The Francis model has a contribution in helping to identify actions which will help to smooth the transition between one phase and the next. This might include clarification of roles, establishing more formal lines of communication and the setting and review of objectives. It may also mean developing a more systematic approach to dealing with basic human resource issues such as recruitment and selection, assessing performance and developing more consistent approaches to discipline.

Greiner (1972) suggests that organizations, from their inception, move through

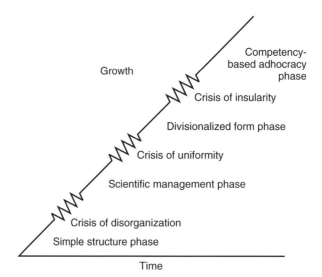

Figure 8.1   The Francis Model of organizational growth. *Source:* Francis (1991). By kind permission of Pearson Professional Ltd.

periods of evolution, followed by 'Crises', which he refers to as 'Revolutions', and which are characterized by problems emanating from the need to reconsider the assumptions underpinning the entrepreneurial phase of the business. The Greiner model sets out a number of key variables which basically characterize the orientation of different stages of growth. The implication is that these variables need to be considered and managed if only because they influence the response capability of the business. There are specific variables which have a direct impact on what can be regarded as human resource utilization constraints or enhancers, including structure, strategy, style of management, culture and reward.

The various models, while invaluable in describing the growth process, fail in their promise of guidance. Mount *et al.* (1993), in providing a comprehensive view of how businesses grow and develop, are critical of the failure of models to project the way in which the transition from the owner-managed state to a professionally managed firm can be effectively managed. They single out the failure to deal with problems of developing systems for marketing information, quality control or internal reporting.

It is notable in all of these models that there is a dominance of attention to marketing and finance with little of direct impact on how to deal with the people issues, which are evident in many smaller businesses within a growth mode. Churchill and Lewis (1983) also support the view that at the early stages of growth, systems development is likely to be basic, with formal planning limited in many cases only to cash forecasting. The centrality of the owner, often synonymous with the business itself, is often put forward as an explanation for this lack of concern with attention to developing more systematic ways of managing. These writers also follow the view that one of the consequences of growth is a move towards functional organization. This is concomitant with perhaps the recruitment of professional staff members into the business, dealing with basic financial, marketing and production systems. The orientation remains very much towards production and the need to sell the company's product. The key issues, which are often people concerns, seldom get systematic attention in this phase. For example, issues such as clarification of roles or delegation of detailed matters to subordinates are seldom considered. The consequences are often lack of clarity and increased stress through retention of unnecessary technical responsibilities at the senior level in such organizations. So important is this aspect of small business management in dealing with the transition from a 'power'-based to a 'role' culture (Handy, 1984) that an attempt to provide a greater understanding of the process is imperative.

Managing the transition from 'simple' to 'complex' organization

In our discussion of the growth models we identified a number of factors which need to be addressed in managing the transition from a 'simple' to 'complex' organization in order to prevent the development of problems which may eventually overwhelm it. These problems, as identified by writers such as Bignell *et al.* (1977) and Child (1984), typically include work overload, poor integration between 'departments', reduced capacity for innovation, weakening control, procedural ambiguities and rigid attitudes. Example 8.2 illustrates some of the problems

Example 8.2: Oilshare

This case relates to a company which has its roots in the oil and gas contracting sector. The organization has been serving the industry in a specific area of North Sea technology for a period of some five years and during that period has experienced a number of take-overs involving only slight changes in management. The organization has a total employee strength of some 80 staff. The three owners have a long association with the industry sector and are not only experienced in their spheres of engineering or design but regard themselves as competent in growing a successful business. Having passed through an intense stage of creativity with very direct involvement from the three owners, the company is in disarray. There is confusion as to who is available to give direction on operational matters. In particular, there exists a degree of day-to-day involvement on the part of at least one of the owners with issues which should have been resolved by the specialist concerned. The image created is one of inadequate belief in and communication with the organization's staff. The consequences of the non-management of change as the organization developed and grew can be summarized by the following:

- Frustration caused by non-conformance to existing systems in the firm with severe effects on morale.
- Time delays with financial implications and a low image with customers due to late delivery. This in turn has had a marked affect on profit margins because of increased labour input due to the need to rework parts supplied.
- A marked reduction in job satisfaction leading to the loss of key personnel. Duplication and confusion in relation to roles because of ad hoc changes in initial agreed plans through interference of owners, intense frustration and the creation of a blame culture.
- Unnecessary unplanned overtime and confusion in priorities, adding considerably to costs.
- An intense lack of confidence between the various departments and sections in the firm.

which can be created when a growing business fails to manage the growth transition effectively. At the root of a great deal of the concerns raised in Example 8.2 are issues of structure and strategy.

Structure

The initial stage of the life-cycle is variously labelled entrepreneurial, pioneer or inception. It is characterized by Handy (1984) as a power-based culture. It may be seen as the ultimate in centralization with decision making vested in the owner-manager. The needs will be technical in the sense of producing a product or service and building up the customer/client base. In meeting such objectives no specific pattern of task allocation or formalized clarity in roles will exist. In fact the founder(s) will almost certainly wish to retain the responsibilities they are comfortable with, whether technical or selling.

As the organization grows, whether through increase in business turnover or in headcount, the senior management may find difficulty in dealing with the increasing complexity. This may force the need to create some degree of specialism as, for example, in accounts, sales or personnel, thus further increasing managerial complexity. This functionalization in effect moves the organization towards a role culture. Quite often the transition is not a consciously systematic process but carried out in a piecemeal fashion, the consequences leading to problems of role and goal clarity and interpersonal and intra-group conflicts. Such situations call for assistance based on behavioural principles which will guide managers on ways of retaining the strengths of the entrepreneurial firm, while avoiding the pitfalls of excessive formalization. Non-cooperation between functions, as a result of differing interpretations of goals and objectives, can create rigidity and hinder growth. Desire for autonomy can result in internal struggles and inter-departmental conflict over strategy. Perhaps most importantly, functional structures provide little opportunity for skill development. These potential barriers require the diagnostic and conceptual skills associated with organizational development and change management. Because of the pressures which have been discussed in relation to the small business in its initial growth phases, combined with a dominant concern with technical and marketing issues, such competencies are unlikely to exist and may have to be provided through appropriate counselling interventions.

Strategy

Writers such as Bamberger (1980), Ansoff (1972) and Herold (1972) advocate strategic planning as a significant contribution to the business and Timmons (1978) suggests planning to be a necessary attribute of entrepreneurship, stating that 'one of the most striking characteristics of the successful entrepreneur is his attitude towards and use of planning'. Despite such positive assertions, there is by no means universal agreement that strategic planning is either necessary or desirable (Karger and Mallik, 1975; Rue and Fulmer, 1973), although there is general agreement that it would be unwise to dismiss planning as a desirable process. However, it is also important to recognize that what might be seen as necessary features of formalized planning may not necessarily be appropriate to the smaller business.

In considering the growing firm, then, there is a need to look at strategic planning as a process which can engage the owner-manager in reflecting on his or her aspirations and what prerequisites need to be met for successful development. These reflections can then be used in the development of a plan to guide the business through its transition from a 'simple' to a more 'complex' organization. Indeed, Gibb and Scott (1985) identify what they refer to as the 'Leadership Base' which incorporates the personal objectives of the owner and his or her interaction with the future direction of the business. Specifically highlighted are the following:

- The influence of families on the objectives of the small firm and generally on the management of the business.
- The personal capability of the owner-manager will have a significant influence on what might or might not be done with regard to the development of skills. The initial stages of the business will draw substantially from previous experience, occupational background and on specific training and education. The adequacy of skills for any business development may therefore be a primary concern in relation to what can be achieved.
- Attitude to change is fundamental in determining what might or might not be done in relation to acquiring the competencies needed for successful development.

This chapter is designed to raise awareness of the specific difficulties small businesses experience in dealing with basic human resourcing issues. It has focused on particular aspects such as resourcing and management training, not in terms of providing specific solutions, but in developing awareness of areas where proactive interventions can be beneficial.

In particular, the problems inherent in handling the transition from the start–up firm to being a small to medium-sized enterprise requires particular attention to succession and to ensuring clarity in roles, objectives and the development of basic systems. From the case examples it is clear that small firms can benefit from approaching such concerns in a systematic way. Preparation and planning are essential in achieving a smooth transition and ensuring the long-term survival and, if desired, growth of the business. Difficulties commonly reside in convincing owner-managers of the need for such a positive approach to regarding human resource actions as a fundamental contribution. The following section offers some basic arguments for developing and integrating HRM concepts into the ongoing processes of the business.

Integrating HRM: some perspectives on implementation

The arguments point to a relatively low interest in human resource management at both the start-up and growth stages of small business. To promote good practice in this area, the link with the perceived day-to-day problems of running the business must be established. Obviously the minimal demands of legislation are unavoidable and it is possible to get the advice needed from readily accessible sources. However, if those managing small businesses are to make effective use of limited resources, they need to be convinced of their level of contribution to survival and development. Most of the arguments for attention to the people dimension fail to do this. The argument here is to find a vehicle which can be acknowledged as being integral to the core competencies of the business, perceived by customers as adding value. This can then be used to link systematic concern for human resource issues to the mainstream needs of the business. The purpose of this section is to provide a basic illustration of how this concept might provide a practical way to convince managers that attention to human resource issues must be a top priority.

Quality: a key focus for human resource development

There are a number of potential vehicles which could be chosen as a focus for integrating human resource management into the effective running of a business. However, the focus on quality is chosen because it is a concern in both service and manufacturing and in private and public sectors. Perception of quality can be linked to perceptions of both employees and customers. The illustrations of below par service are widespread. Even in the higher technology areas of the economy, large clients have to place pressures on small businesses to approach quality standards in a systematic way. Developing an image that will sustain a place in a particular market means giving attention to the skills and knowledge base of the firm!

The argument

Quality has been described as the 'single most important force leading to economic growth of companies in [international] markets' (Feigenbaum, 1982). Buzzell and Gale (1987) suggest that 'in the long run, the most important single factor affecting a business unit's performance is the quality of its products and services, relative to those of competitors'. The PIMS analyses, to which their work relates, assert that companies offering higher quality products and services relative to those of competitors enjoy specific advantages, not least those reflected in customer loyalty. The benefits accruing are not exclusive to any particular size of company! The basic principles that need to be applied are:

● Top management commitment and an understanding by everyone in the business of the centrality of quality to the survival and development of the business. Zeithaml, Parasurman and Berry (1990) argue that 'the absence of total management commitment to service quality virtually guarantees that quality aspirations will not be achieved'. They go on to argue that 'strong management commitment energizes and stimulates an organization to achieve a high level of [service] quality'. The human resource contributions here are to be found in leadership which can:

   1   Recognize the need to clarify roles and responsibilities for each and every employee focused on identified standards.

   2   Provide the coaching and counselling necessary to support the quality process as 'the way things are done' in the business.

   3   Develop basic recruitment and selection procedures which place significant emphasis on the centrality of quality in the business, and the attitudes needed to sustain this.

   4   Develop basic induction procedures where the essential nature of quality to the success of the business is the central theme. The responsibility for delivery should be that of the owner-manager. This should also be linked to clarity on the basic statutory procedures, which will operate in the case of a disciplinary action being required.

   5   Communication and ongoing learning linked to quality and business development can flow from the steps in the above four action areas. Management should integrate mentoring into the ongoing activities. Shetty and Ross (1985) give support to this perspective in arguing that: 'The commitment of management to quality must be reflected in the context of 'total' company strategy and operations. [. . .] must be reflected in the context of the company's other goals and priorities; only then can it be integrated into the company's way of doing business'.

Human resource efforts appropriate to the stage of development, like quality efforts, depend on top management commitment based on the realization that the effectiveness of the business depends on the interaction between both – quality is dependent on the degree to which the human resource contribution is systematically and conciously managed. There is evidence that employee belief in delivering on quality criteria is a function of percieved commitment. This is reinforced by the support actions of managers in their communication, coaching and mentoring processes (Reeves and Hoy, 1993). These authors point to the evidence that little attention is paid to reinforcement derived by attention to appropriate incentives and basic training. The argument is that by focusing on what is readily perceived by management as the keystone of the business, in developing the people capabilities to deliver quality, attention can be more readily directed to reinforcing this through appropriate focus on incentives and competencies enhancement.

Lawler *et al.*'s (1995) study on the basics of high-performance organizations indicates that these are within the capabilities of even the smallest businesses to create. Essentially these cover:

- Generating competencies: which means ensuring that the business has the right mix of skills and knowledge to meet the future needs. Even if the business has only one individual the exercise is still worthwhile, as a reflective, learning exercise.
- Reinforcing competencies: means encouraging individuals to think about what their operational environment requires in terms of skills, knowledge and attitudes. It becomes quite apparent here that such a review can be made an integral part of the process of developing the business.
- Sustaining compentencies: needs to be seen as integral with the operation of the business. This is again a focus for continuous reflection on what changing operational needs demand.
- Servicing competencies: means ensuring that the basic systems are developed to interact and be mutually supportive.
- Deploying competencies: perhaps the most important contribution of all human resource management concepts, clarifying structures and role and optimizing involvement of employees to the maximum extent possible.

These actions do not require elaborate systems but as a process can be seen to create, almost unconsciously, personal learning for the management of small businesses. The essential movement is from a reactive to a proactive approach to thinking about the human resource contribution, commensurate with the specific needs of the business.

Hess (1987) asserts that small business managers in the US ranked personnel management as second most important next to general management. This section argues that with careful choice of the 'vehicle' regarded as central to the success of the enterprise, human resource management can be embedded in the consciousness of even the most sceptical of owner managers.

Conclusion

The measurement and indeed definition of what constitutes success in the smaller business has not been resolved, although there are mechanistic analyses which suggest criteria. What is clear, however, is that the effective management of human resources plays a vital role in achieving such success. Despite this, the evidence suggests that human resources are seldom regarded as a priority but often surreptitiously creep up on managers when they start to expand their business. As internal specialist assistance is not likely to be at hand, the application of systematic processes which ensure that employees are selected to 'fit in' and are given the guidance needed to perform effectively is essential in the smaller business. Perhaps even more important is the need to understand the implications of even modest growth and the need to give careful consideration to human resource factors as the organization develops.

Summary

The discussion here has focused on the importance of HRM to the success of the smaller firm, exploring why, despite its importance, it is often neglected or ignored. We then went on to look at particular aspects of HRM such as resourcing, management training and the utilization of human resources, not in terms of providing specific solutions, but in developing awareness of the areas where proactive interventions can be beneficial. Issues around the general lack of management skills within smaller firms and the need for training to be tailored to the specific, practical needs of the owner-managers are highlighted. While many smaller firms choose not to grow, those that do can encounter problems relating to the transition from a simple, entrepreneurial firm to a more complex organizational entity. As the business develops, delegation of responsibility and in many cases the succession of leadership become significant issues of concern. These are addressed in Example 8.1. To help understand the process of organizational growth, a number of growth models have been discussed with particular emphasis being placed on the Francis model of organization growth (1991), as a useful tool in highlighting potential areas of difficulty. Example 8.2 illustrates some of the difficulties arising from poorly managed growth, the root of which are often failures of strategy and structure.

Questions

1   You are the owner manager in a small start up business which currently employs a competent general clerical assistant, a workshop assistant, a workshop supervisor and four trained pattern makers. You are stretched with day-to-day details of dealing with suppliers, banks, customers and production problems. Draw up a simple plan of delegation which will enable you to service existing customers and generate new business.

2   Consider the variety of experience which you are exposed to in running your own small business, across a range of functions. Reflect on your personal learning over the past two years since the business commenced and consider the best approach to meeting the skills and knowledge gaps you identify (e.g.

planned reading, meeting other owner managers, formal training, combinations of these).

3   You have passed successfully through the start-up phase in establishing your business. Applying the Francis Model, identify the kind of problems you need to be aware of in managing the transitions which unexpectedly rapid growth is now creating.

4   How would you characterize success in small business over and above purely profitability criteria?

5   What particular ethical issues might arise in managing people in the small firm? In what ways might it be more difficult to practice 'ethical' people management in the smaller organization? In what ways might it be easier?

References

Ansoff, IH (1972) Strategy as a tool for coping with change. In *Handbook of Strategic Planning* (B Taylor and K Hawkins eds), Longman, London.

Bamberger, I (1980) *Development and Growth of Firms – A Theoretical Frame of Reference for a Research Project Concerning Small and Medium Firms*, Unpublished Paper, University of Rennes.

Baumback, CH (1988) *How to Organise and Operate a Small Business*, 8th edition, Prentice-Hall, Englewood Cliffs, New Jersey.

Bignell, V, Peters, G and Pym, C (1977) *Catastrophic Failures*, Open University Press.

Briscoe, DR and Soukup, WR (1990) HRM in Small Companies. Paper Presented at the *Association of Management Annual Conference*, Orlando, Florida, August.

Buzzell, R and Gale, B (1987) *The Pims Principles: Linking Strategy to Performance*. The Free Press, New York.

Child, J (1984) *Guide to Organisations*, Harper and Row, London.

Churchill, NC and Lewis, VL (1983) The five stages of small business growth. *Harvard Business Review*, May–June, 36–50.

Feigenbaum, AV (1982) Quality and Business Growth Today. *Quality Progress*, **15**, November, 22–25.

Foulkes, FK (1980) *Personnel Policies in Large Non-union Companies*, Prentice-Hall, Englewood Cliffs, New Jersey.

Francis, D (1991) Francis Model of Organisational Growth. In *Henley Distance Learning Module – Managing People: Creating Successful Organisations*, Henley Distance Learning Limited.

Gibb, A and Scott, M (1985) Strategic awareness, personal commitment and the process of planning in the small business. *Journal of Management Studies*, **22**(6), 597–631.

Gibb, AA (1990) Training for Small Business, DUBS Occasional Paper 9051.

Greiner, L (1972) Evolution and revolution as organizations grow. *Harvard Business Review*, **51**, 37–46.

Handy, C (1984) *Understanding Organisations*, 2nd edition, Penguin, London.

Harvey, LJ (1986) Nine major trends in HRM. *Personnel Administrator*, November, 102–9.

Herold, DM (1972) Long range planning and organisational performance – a cross validation study. *Academy of Management Journal*, **15**, 91–102.

Hess, DW (1987) Relevance of small business courses to management needs. *Journal of Small Business Management*, **25**(1), 29–33.

Hofer, CW and Sandberg, WR (1987) Improving new venture performance: Some guidelines for success. *American Journal of Small Business*, **2**(1), 11–26.

Kao, JJ (1989) *Entrepreneurship, Creativity and Organization*, Prentice-Hall, Englewood Cliffs, New Jersey.

Karger, DW and Malik, FA (1975) Long range planning and organizational performance. *Long Range Planing*, **8**(6), 60–4.

Lawler, EE, Mohrman, SA and Ledford, GE (1995) *Creating high performance organizations: practices and results of employee involvement and Total Quality Management in Fortune 1000 Companies*. Jossey Bass, San Francisco, CA.

Matthews, P (1996) The council redefines small and medium. *The European*, 19 Sept, p. 36 (1).

Mount, J, Zinger, JT and Forsyth, GR (1993) Organising for development in the small business. *Long Range Planning*, **26**(5), 111–20.

Perrigo, AEB (1975) Delegation and succession in the small firm. *Personnel Management*, May.

Pickle, HB and Royce, LA (1988) *Small Business Management*, 4th edition, John Wiley & Sons, New York.

Reeves, C and Hoy, F (1993) Employee Perceptions of Management Commitment And Customer Evaluations of Quality Service in Independent Firms. *Journal of Small Business Management*, **31**(4), October.

Rue, LW and Fulmer, RM (1973) Is long range planning profitable? *Academy of Management Proceedings*, Boston.

Scarborough, NM and Zimmer, TW (1988), *Effective Small Business Management*, 2nd edition, Merrill Publishing Company, Columbus, OH.

Schuler, (1989) *Personnel and Human Resource Management*, 4th edition, West Publishing Company, St Paul, MN.

Shetty, YK and Ross, JE (1985) Quality and it's Management in Service Businesses, *Industrial Management*, **25**, November–December, 7–12.

Timmons, JA (1978) Goal setting and the entrepreneur. *Journal of Small Business Management*, **16**(2), 1–9.

Wagner, RJ and Foolford, MD (1989) Non–career employment decisions and their impact on small business. *Journal of Small Business Management*, **27**(3), 39–47.

Zeithaml, VA, Parasuraman, A and Berry, LL (1990) *Delivering Quality Service: Balancing Customer Perceptions and Expectations*. The Free Press, New York.

Legal briefing

A. Application of employment protection laws

Certain of the employment protection laws apply differently to 'small employers', and indeed some of the laws do not apply at all.

For example, in the written particulars that have to be given to each employee listing the important terms of the contract (see legal briefing, Chapter 1), employers with fewer than 20 employees when the particular individual's employment began, do not have to provide details about disciplinary or grievance procedures. This does not mean that such an employer is not required to act reasonably when dealing with the dismissal of employees.

A female employee on maternity leave has fewer rights to return to work if, immediately before the end of her leave, the employer has five or fewer employees. If it is not reasonably practical to offer her either the old job back or a suitable alternative job, she will have no claim to compensation. One might cynically comment that this provision typifies the fulfilment, in

Continued on page 280

the 1980s, of the then government's promise to help small businesses.

There is a 'small employers' relief in connection with Statutory Sick Pay. The definition of 'small employer' for this purpose relates to the employer's liability to make social security payments; if this liability does not exceed an annual sum of £20 000, the employer is allowed a rebate on SSP paid out to employees. The figure of £20 000 is subject to amendment.

The Disability Discrimination Act, 1995, does not apply to employers with fewer than 20 employees. This figure may be subject to revision downwards in the light of the working of the Act in practice. In addition, when deciding whether it was practical for an employer to make the necessary adjustments to accommodate disabled employees, account will be taken of the employer's financial and other resources.

A similar provision applies to the law of unfair dismissal, where the Tribunal is considering the reasonableness of the employer's action. The words used here are 'size and administrative resources'. An example would be the decision to dismiss an employee who was on long-term sick leave. A large employer might be expected to 'accommodate' such an employee, and to find him work should he eventually return.

In a somewhat different vein, the statutory obligation placed upon company directors to disclose levels of employee information and participation in the annual report to the shareholders only applies to companies with more than 250 employees.

The European Works Council Directive applies only to large-scale multinationals.

The new recognition procedures relating to trades unions do not apply to establishments with 20 or fewer employees.

The preceding three items are discussed in the legal briefing to Chapter 3.

B. Accounting provisions of the Companies Act

Certain small companies, other than charities, are exempt from having their annual accounts audited. The qualifying threshold, expressed in terms of annual turnover, was increased to £350 000 by Regulations that came into force on 15 April 1997.

Small and medium-sized private companies have had the privilege for some years of filing simplified annual accounts at Companies House. For this purpose, a small company is defined as one with a turnover for the financial year, and the preceding one, of not more than £2.8 million, a balance-sheet total of not more than £1.4 million and not more than 50 employees. A company need only meet two of these criteria. For a medium-sized company, the relevant figures are £11.2 million, £5.6 million and 250 employees. The concession is not available to banking or insurance companies.

C Deregulation of private companies

A private company is one that does not state in its Memorandum of Association that it is a public company. The securities of a private company may not be advertised to the public (to do so is a criminal offence) but may only be bought and sold by private contract. Private companies are distinguished by having the word limited (ltd) at the end of their names rather than plc (public limited company). The vast majority of all companies are registered with shareholders' limited liability. In 1980, the old restriction to a maximum of 50 on numbers of shareholders in private companies was abolished, so that it is quite possible to find very large private companies in existence.

However, such companies are normally quite small, and the provisions of the Companies Act, 1989, relieved such companies of many of the administrative burdens laid down by statute. Provided that correct procedures are adopted, such companies can avoid the requirement to hold formal company meetings, including the annual meeting, to lay accounts and directors' reports before the annual meeting, and to re-appoint the auditors. All business that would normally be transacted at a meeting can be conducted by post. The snag is that resolutions circulated in this way must receive the unanimous consent of the shareholders before they can be acted upon. For practical reasons alone, the privilege will only be claimed by companies with relatively few shareholders. Safeguards are built into the system, and there is still some business, such as the dismissal of a director in the course of his or her term of office, where a meeting is still required.

Change and strategy in organizations

9

Nelarine Cornelius with William Scott-Jackson

Learning objectives

After studying this chapter you should be able to:

● understand the different ways in which change and its management in organizations are described and defined;
● understand the nature and variety of change interventions and where and why they are employed;
● understand the role of HRM in corporate and business strategy formulation and implementation;
● understand how strategic human resource management can be conceptualized and proactively managed;
● understand the nature of HRM facilitated versus HRM grounded interventions;
● understand the ways in which line management practice and roles can help or hinder the management of change.

Introduction

Throughout this book, the work of academics, practitioners and commentators has been presented in which it has been suggested that major, **step changes** have taken place in the 'external environment'. This external environment is made up of the competitive market or client community and socio-political, economic and technical climate within which organizations sit. All of these have exerted a substantial influence on the way organizations are structured and managed. Examples of step changes include the following:

● The impact of new technology, in particular information technology
● Globalization
● 'Japanization' of management practice
● Customer focus
● Government policy to increase managerial practice within non-profit organizations
● Demographic changes

Table 9.1 Pressures to change from the external environment: some examples

Pressure	Impact
New technology	The impact of technology in the workplace is discussed in more detail in Chapter 7. However, it should be mentioned here that a number of suggestions have been made regarding the size of the impact. Information technology in particular may be adopted in order to improve technology or to exploit more fully the knowledge that individuals have. New technology has also provided the catalyst for the movement towards new hybrid organizational forms, including different degrees of virtualization of organizational structures.
Globalization	Globalization has come about for a variety of reasons. Within certain industries, it has been part of a gradual development, through local national, then international to multinational and finally, to a globalized organization of operations. In industries such as publishing, this has reflected a desire to exploit differences in labour market conditions (for example, to exploit low wage economies) or avoid 'restrictive' labour practices, while in a number of manufacturing companies, a move from one-site manufacturing of products to assembly provided similar advantages to those encountered in publishing, but also with the flexibility to shift production from country to country, as market demands or employee relations conditions change. Globalization is also considered an imperative for success and domination in certain industries, such as oil and airlines, and is pursued through internal growth or strategic alliances.
Total Quality Management (TQM)	Total quality management (TQM) is an approach developed by the American, Deming, which was exported to Japan and then re-imported to Western organizations along with other 'Japanese' management techniques, such as Just-in-Time (JIT) management and continuous improvement (*Kaizen*). In combination with electronic point of sale (EPOS) systems and changes to transportation and storage practices, JIT has, in particular, radically changed the way warehousing stock control, and logistics are undertaken, greatly influencing and tightening inventory costs, particularly in manufacturing and retailing. However, of greater significance has been the impact of TQM. 'Zero defects' and high quality is no longer an aspiration in many organizations, it is a *pre-requisite* for successful competition. Moreover, TQM is linked closely with globalization in many industries. Specifically, for goods that are essentially standard or 'commodity' based, such as MacDonalds hamburgers or electronic circuit boards, for globalization of operations to succeed, quality of production and service need to be high and guaranteed for all the basic components of a product. Thus, globalized operations are likely to have highly developed and effective quality management systems. However, such systems will only be effective if developed in conjunction with effective HRM policy and practice, the most obvious links being to job design and training and development activities.
Customer focus	The power and influence of consumers have grown over the years. Organizations are far more sensitive to the demands made by specific consumer groups, and the influence of pressure

groups, such as those in the 'green' movement. In addition, many organizations have attempted to differentiate themselves from their competition, in other words a source of potentially sustainable competitive advantage. Many large organizations have undergone major culture change programmes for which a primary objective is the improvement of front line customer care. HRM policy and practice has been central in facilitating such changes.

Managerialism within non-profit and voluntary organizations

In the UK, there have been a number of governmental responses to steadily rising demands on public sector spending. Given its ideological and doctrinal tendencies, between the late 1970s until the early 1980s, there has been a steady increase in the privatization of previously nationalized public services, the 'contracting out' of specific services to the private sector and tight spending limits. In addition, there has been the promotion of managerial practice at the expense of more traditional public sector administrative practice. Shortfalls in domestic provisions of services to the under-privileged (such as public housing) as well as crises which have secured international attention and interest (war and famine) have also heightened the role of the voluntary sector, which, like the public sector, has seen more commercial type practice and market or quasi-market conditions expand. This increased 'managerialsim' has dealt with some deficiencies in practice but also has its critics. Although there are parallels, non-profit organizations also have distinctive characteristics, as their primary concerns are addressing issues of need, rationing and the management of professional and groups, usually in a pluralistic framework. In particular, some management practice does not fit nearly into non-profit organizations (NPOs), given the often unitarist frameworks within which it first developed. However, in spite of the shortfalls, naiveté and criticisms of managerialism, there would appear to be an increase in it in NPOs across the globe.

Demographic changes

Demographic studies indicate that the characteristics of labour markets are changing. In northwest Europe, the population as a whole is aging, a situation which is particularly pronounced in countries such as Germany and Holland, and regions such as Scandinavia, whilst elsewhere, the population is increasing and the age profile falling, such as in Mexico, Africa and India. Also, in much of the Western world, the amount of time spent in full-time employment is decreasing.

A significant change in many Western countries is the activity of women in the labour market, which has steadily increased (see Chapter 1), although typically, women are likely to be less well paid and not achieve the same level of seniority within many organizations, the progress which has resulted from changes in the law, changing societal expectations and increased educational success has been substantial. Slow progress but in a similar direction is being made by those other traditionally disadvantaged groups, such as those from ethnic minorities and those with disabilities.

In many industrialized nations there has been a steady improvement in the educational attainments of the workforce, in terms of both formal academic education and vocational training.

Many of these changes have resulted in the introduction of specific **general management initiatives**, such as Total Quality Management and Business Process Re-Engineering, as well as those related to mainstream HRM functions like training and development and recruitment and selection strategies, in order to cope with these changes. These initiatives may also be regarded as activities requiring the **management of change**. However, there is also a large academic and practitioner literature on **generic change management in organizations**.

In both, the links between specific interventions and their likely impact or interaction with HRM practice are often not drawn. This interaction is explored in some detail within this chapter.

Change often comes about as a result of strategic imperatives. However, the relationship between HRM and strategy, in both theory and practice, is often questionable or unclear. We will consider how HRM's role in strategy formulation, development and implementation has been and could be better elaborated, and also outline more proactive models of strategic HRM.

Furthermore, a range of change interventions is available but which ones are appropriate to given specific circumstances, and why? Issues such as the range and scale of change are discussed and the pros and cons of particular types of intervention are evaluated. In addition, we will consider how line managers can help, hinder and proactively facilitate the effective management of change, and assess the likely success of change *before* they happen.

Change may result in anxiety and stress for some. Attention is paid to how stress can be moderated and managed for the line manager and the subordinate. Although the actions that can be taken by individuals are considered, the roles and responsibilities which can and should be taken by the organization are suggested also. Finally, the relationship between the change management and HRM strategy, policy and practice is outlined.

Environmental factors as organizational drivers

'Environmental' factors such as those listed earlier are likely to have had some impact on organizations, irrespective of the industry or sector that they are located in, and whether the organizations are large or small. They are referred to as **organizational drivers**, as they 'drive' organizations towards reconsidering current practice and ultimately, they are a catalyst for change. Over and above these environmental pressures, other factors may lead to the adoption of change interventions. This may occur as a consequence of a desire to improve, a legislative imperative, or a change in strategy.

Much of the literature on the management of change in organizations has, as its focus, interactions between specific types of interventions and elements of an organization (such as systems or work groups, or the organization as a whole, discussed more fully later in this chapter). The emphasis is often on the specialist change agent (discussed in more detail in Chapter 6 on international HRM), the characteristics of the intervention techniques involved, and the (often rhetorically only) positive outcomes. Inevitably, what gets published in the newspapers, books and journals tends to be biased towards the 'good news' stories. But the reality is usually less tidy and more complex.

Let us take the example of a line manager responsible for a project team. Head offices have decided that the company needs to downsize; an integral part of a high-level decision to change the *strategic direction* of the company. Our line manager has been asked to decide which staff she would like to retain as core within the project teams, and to indicate to the HRM department who should leave. Shortly after these events, it is announced that the company is restructuring. The team's line manager is expected to decide how best to organize her staff and their work in order to satisfy new requirements.

Clearly, the main role of the line manager in this example is to deal with the *operational* aspects of the implementation of change. In the scheme of things, the major decisions have been taken at the top of the organizational hierarchy. However, the 'front line' of the change is at the interface between the line manager and his or her project team, where the changes will succeed or fail. Put another way, *it is the sum total of similar actions taken by line managers across the organization that ensure the downsizing and restructuring, and therefore the corporate strategy overall, become a reality.* Furthermore, these actions contribute *directly* to employee motivation and commitment, especially given the disruption, inevitable worries about job security and potentially negative outcomes on work performance.

One implication is that line managers would be more effective if they had an overview of the change and a strong strategic perspective (irrespective of whether they formally have a strategic role) in order to understand how they and their team will fit into the scheme of things, in terms of the underlying strategic planning and the nature of the change intervention itself. In addition to this, managers will need to be able to cope with anxieties, uncertainties and any disruptions to relations between subordinates and their colleagues or indeed, subordinates and managers, that the changes will create.

Organizational renewal

Not all change comes about as a result of external pressures. It may be that there is a desire to ensure that an organization's people and 'soft systems' do not lose their edge and dynamism through out-of-date skills or complacency. Sound stewardship is needed so that organizational change is not just a result of being forced to change (through external factors) but is where appropriate decisions are made to choose change in order to keep staff and systems at their most efficient and effective. Indeed, often such change is part of a process of continuous improvement which may be interspersed with more major initiatives.

HRM can play a vital role within such processes. Many core personnel as well as more long-term and strategic areas can (and indeed may need to) be addressed. However, failure to read the signs that change is needed is not uncommon. Sometimes, this may be because those who need to make the key decisions are narrow in their outloook, or they may realize what needs to be done but resources are tight. Alternatively, the factors that should signal the need to change are often subtle and part of a web of interconnected factors which, unless one is vigilant, may be difficult to discern and are thus overlooked.

The interconnected nature of change: change and the 'meta-system'

Let us take the example of the directors and associates of a small, networked company in the north of Germany with one overseas operation on each continent, selling Web site development products on the Internet. The company will need to know about how to market and sell their products in Germany, in the rest of Europe and worldwide. They will also need to know how commercial transactions on the Internet can be made effective, which requires constant monitoring and scanning based potentially on information arising from anywhere within the World Wide Web. The relationships between the 'external environment', the market and the macro environment both globally and locally through to work groups and individuals within the company we can regard as a **'meta-system'**, with interrelationships between the various 'elements' within it. Within this world, what lies outside or inside of the 'organizational boundary', indeed the concept of an organizational boundary, potentially may become more fluid and more difficult to define, particularly if an organization is structured virtually.

However, for convenience, we can break down this meta-system into various segments or **domains** and in Figure 9.1, these domains within which change may take place are represented. The basic element is the individual, building up through work groups, the whole organization, and beyond this, to the 'external' environment. It is equally important to remember that the 'world of work' overlaps with 'home and community life' and across both cuts the hopes, fears and expectations for one's employment stability and career or job development and prospects (career dynamics). Any change will generate winners and losers: change in one part of the meta-system is likely directly or indirectly to affect other parts of it. Sometimes the connections are obvious but at other times relationships are less obvious and more subtle. There needs to be care taken if managers and their employees are to interpret the signals accurately rather than misinterpret them.

Within each of these domains are **stakeholders**, individuals or groups who have a direct, specific 'investment' (financial, employment or emotional), a vested interest, in the success and well-being of an organization. Different types of changes are likely to affect a specific combination of stakeholders (the **stakeholder web**) and the relationships between stakeholders (**stakeholder relations**). It is equally important to remember that what is important will depend on where you are standing: although the board of directors may be concerned with the organization's performance overall, for most employees, the most significant domain is likely to be their immediate work group and the prospects for it. When any change is being considered, it is important to judge:

- whether stakeholders are likely to support or object to the change;
- what power they have to resist the change;

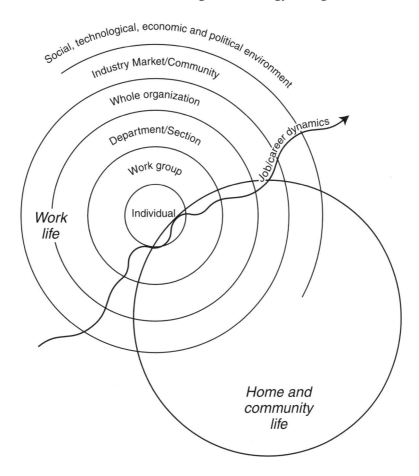

Figure 9.1   Domains of change.

- what leverage or bargaining tools organizations have to counterbalance stakeholder leverage.

Figure 9.2 contains a summary of the questions that should be asked in order to undertake a basic **stakeholder analysis**. Depending upon the character of the organization and the issues under consideration, a more detailed appraisal in which potential sources of common interest between specific stakeholders (including potential unofficial 'alliances of convenience') can be outlined also, in order to achieve a more complex **stakeholder mapping**.

The nature and scale of change

It might be decided that change needs to take place right across the board. Such **organization-wide change** is often difficult to achieve because of factors such as the range of activities, competing personal and political interests, trying to

Stakeholder	Potential/ Likely gains	Potential/ Likely losses	Stakeholder leverage	Organizational leverage	Assess likelihood of change or resistance	Bargaining Tools: Stakeholder	Bargaining Tools: Organization
Work team (in total) Member A Member B Member C ⋮ Member X							
The boss							
Related work team(s) (in total) Member A Member B Member C ⋮ Member X							
Shareholders							
Trade union(s)/ staff representatives							
Board of directors							
Local community							

Figure 9.2 Stakeholder analysis: assessing likely stakeholder reaction to proposed change.

communicate effectively to such a large and disparate audience, and simply maintaining momentum. Nonetheless, organization-wide interventions remain popular, and many large corporations have embarked on such programmes, often on the back of management initiatives. Smaller-scale change activities, or **sub-system changes**, may be either one-off, stand-alone or part of an organization-wide project. An example of a sub-system is a department or division, a hierarchical layer such as junior managers, or a work group.

Within both, the nature of the changes may be **first order**, (requiring small adjustments to work methods) or **second order** (concerned with the belief and assumptions behind work practices: Levy and Merry, 1986) and often, a combination of the two. So, for example, it might be decided to improve customer care provision within the sales team, which requires first-order change (better telephone skills, greater employee freedom to decide on price, and faster response times) but also second-order change (greater awareness of the interaction between employee attitudes and the quality of customer service provision).

Moreover, both first- and second-order changes are likely to require substantial HRM inputs such as training (to use the telephone effectively and modify attitudes), rewards (for example, a bonus for the team that scores best in customer satisfaction surveys) and appraisal (where a key results area might be 'to improve customer response times by 50 per cent' but also to reinforce the new desired attitudes). In other words, HRM provides a potentially powerful **internal lever** for change. Finally, at the level of the smallest unit of currency, the individual, changes here are the ultimate indicator of whether **personal changes** have actually taken place and ultimately, whether over time, change will have to be pushed and coerced or will be sustained willingly.

The implication is that for interventions which have a clear people management component, line managers need to think through how HRM activities can and should help facilitate change, as it is often these inputs that play a vital role in making changes become realities.

What is change? A working definition

Irrespective of the size, rate and pace of change, for people who work in organizations change of some kind is inevitable. Whether it is an organizational or personal response to shifts in the 'external' environment, the exploitation of new technologies, or a simple, small-scale adjustment to working practice, change and its consequences are and should be encountered by all, for the well-being of the organization and the individual. Problems often arise if changes are ill-timed or inappropriate, given the nature of the issues to be dealt with. However, in those work organizations that actively resist or are hostile toward changes, major or minor, over time a crisis point is reached and stark choices faced: radical turnaround, metamorphosis, or an 'end game' strategy, often followed by decline and ultimately the demise of the organization.

Working definition: **Change in organizations** involves the movement or transformation of some factor or factors, which may be tangible (such as a computer system or product portfolio) or more intangible (such as attitudes or beliefs). What changes may centre on the more technical, 'hard' and bounded issues through to those that are more people-centred, messy and 'soft' in nature. However, it is more appropriate to consider change in organizations as a *continuum of types* from hard to soft and also as *dynamic*, with changes that start in one guise (e.g., the introduction of new technology) likely to have associated issues that are not similar in substance or character, albeit that they are related (such as the identification of training and development needs in order that the technology can be exploited).

Change can operate at the level of an individual or group through to that of the whole organization. It requires the mobilization of resources (physical, financial, intellectual and emotional). The larger the change, the more a coordinated managed effort becomes an imperative.

It can be superficial or deep rooted, major or minor, and often requires a catalyst of some kind. It has in-built within it a maximum and minimum speed: if too slow, it may not be perceived as a change at all and may rapidly be perceived as irrelevant or become redundant; if too swift and too detailed, it is likely to tire or alarm those involved with it and thus may stall.

Change is usually introduced to solve actual or potential problems but will inevitably generate them also. As organizations are made up of *people*, any change of any kind will inevitably need to address 'people centred' components. It is unlikely to be welcomed by all who will be affected by it.

A galaxy of meaning clusters around the term 'change'. At its simplest, it implies some form of transformation: movement from A to B; the adoption of new options; a transition. Listed in Figure 9.3 are a number of definitions of change that are particularly pertinent to change within organizational settings.

In this chapter, we will use a working definition of change in organizations, which is not all encompassing but does reflect key elements of many of the definitions of change and its management in organizations.

What is change? Definitions, causes and levels

Change within an organization may be seen to occur at two possible levels. First-order change (the most common) concerns small adjustment to work methods – such as having more team meetings to solve a communications problem. Second-order change looks more deeply at the beliefs and assumptions behind existing work practices, such as why team members are failing to communicate (Levy and Merry, 1986).

How might the beliefs and assumptions of individuals and groups change? The psychologist George Kelly argued that individuals should be thought of as 'personal scientists' attempting to make sense of the world around them. Each individual possesses a system made up of **psychological constructs**, though which information is filtered. Some of these constructs are uniquely held, while others are shared with 'significant groups', such as the family, professional body or local community. For Kelly, *change was a process of reconstructing*, requiring shifts in individual or shared psychological constructions, or in other words, **change is a process of psychological reconstruction**. According to the characteristics of an individual or group, reconstructing occurs with differing degrees of difficulty but always, the more major the shift away from personally important constructs, the more substantial is the intellectual and emotional effort involved.

But how can we be sure that even if people are able to change, they are *willing* to? Carnall's (1990, p. 99) view of change is that typically, an individual will ask the questions 'Should I attempt to make a change?' and 'What more can I do to improve the chances of introducing change effectively?' His views on change have their roots in the **expectancy theories** of motivation, developed by researchers such as the American psychologist Victor Vroom (1964). Specifically, Vroom was interested in the decision-making aspects of motivation, such as the degree of preference an individual had for a particular outcome and the subjective probability that an individual held that particular behaviour would lead to these outcomes. In other words, is it worth my while changing: what are the **costs** and what are the **benefits** and how well do these balance up? The final decision and the 'factors' that contribute to it are summarized in the equations below.

For change to occur

$$EC = Z$$

Where **EC** = **the energy for change** and **Z is the perceived cost of making change**. In other words, the energy required to make the change has to be balanced against the perceived cost of making the change. We 'calculate' how much energy or effort is likely to be involved by assessing three factors, **A**, the **felt dissatisfaction** with the present situation; **B** is the level of **knowledge of the practical steps forward** and **D**, the extent to which our vision of the outcome is shared with that of the sponsor of the change (**shared vision**). This may be summarized as:

$$EC = A \times B \times D$$

Furthermore, Kelman (1969) (cited in Cummings and Huse, 1989) argues that **manipulation** is intrinsic to attempts to change the behaviour of others. Specifically, '(Behaviour change) . . . inevitably involves some degree of manipulation and control, and at least an implicit imposition of the change agent's values on the client or the person that he (or she) is influencing.'

What triggers change? Kurt Lewin (1951) (cited in Buchanan and Huczynski, 1997) suggests that change **is the outcome of opposing forces**, forces for change and forces for maintaining the status quo. Huczynski and Buchanan (1997) argue that **changes are initiated by some 'disorganizing pressure' or trigger** arising either within or outside the organization. Potential sources or disorganizing pressure include:

- **Interdependencies** The various facets of an organization are interdependent. Change in one aspect of an organization creates pressures for adjustments in other aspects.
- **Conflicts and frustrations** Differences between managers and employees may lead to conflicts which in turn create pressures for and resistance to change.

Change rarely takes place smoothly. Instead it happens in an 'untidy' way. Some parts of the organization change more rapidly than others, in other words, there are **time lags**.

Cummings and Huse (1989) argue that many **organizations** are required to undertake fundamental changes due to **environmental pressures**, which in turn, often require a major, sometimes radical, **shift in the basic assumptions** within them. Specifically:

'rapid changes in, for example, technologies, have rendered many organizational practices obsolete, pushing firms to be continually innovative and nimble.' . . . These organizational changes have been characterized by a number of terms including 'double loop learning', 'frame-breaking change', 'reorientation', 'culture change', 'strategic change', 'large scale change', 'quantum change' and 'transformation'. These terms imply fundamental changes in organizational strategies and structures, and in how memb0ers perceive, think and behave at work. The changes go far beyond making the existing organization better or fine tuning the status quo. They are concerned with fundamentally altering the taken-for-granted assumptions underlying how the organization relates to its environment and functions. Changing these assumptions entails significant shifts in corporate philosophy and values, in business strategy, and in the numerous structures and organizational arrangements that shape members' behaviours. Not only is the magnitude of change greater, but the change fundamentally alters the qualitative nature of the organization.

Figure 9.3 Definitions of change.

Strategy, human resource management and change

Strategic issues have been discussed on many occasions earlier in this book, but for our purposes we can define **organizational strategy** as simply that which details the direction pursued in the long to medium term, against a desired future state, which may be deliberate or emergent in origin. It is achieved through major resource mobilization and organization-wide, cross-functional coordination of activities, often outlined in a plan of action to make the vision a reality. Commonly, strategic decisions affect the product–market (or in the case of non-profit organizations, the client–activity mix) of an organization.

What is considered key to successful strategic plans depends upon the latest research, prevailing economic conditions and, like any management activity, fashion. From the heyday of large, highly detailed, structured and rigid corporate plans to interpretations of the strategy development process as a more organic, emergent process, as well as aspects of and issues relating to strategic planning, such as organizational restructuring, product portfolio management, industry structure, value adding activities: various models have all had their moment in the spotlight (Collis and Montgomery, 1995). Currently, an important area of development within the strategy field is around processes, resource evaluation and identification of internal capabilities that provide sustainable competitive advantage (Collis and Montgomery, 1995; Porter, 1996; Ghoshal and Bartlett, 1995). In addition, there is an oscillation between an emphasis on issues internal to the organization (such as capability), external (such as changes in government legislation) or the fit between the two (for example, assessment of the degree of fit or mismatch between current organizational capabilities and new legislation).

For most line managers, it is a change in strategic direction, for example in order to enter new markets or exploit new service opportunities, that is the most frequently encountered basis for major organizational change. However, even if the overall strategic direction is maintained, many organizations are seeking to exploit or develop sources of sustainable competitive advantage, by improving the efficiency and effectiveness of what is increasingly being seen a core differentiating competitive element – its employees. Such thinking, grounded in ideas such as continuous improvement and leverage, has meant that focusing on routinely evaluating and enhancing employee effectiveness is in step with current strategic thinking (Hamel and Prahalad, 1993).

Therefore to reiterate, HRM provides a potentially powerful lever for change, including strategic change, and therefore managers need to be more aware of how HRM policy, systems and practice can be exploited to facilitate change or, potentially, might undermine change. An example in which these issues are outlined is presented in Figure 9.4, in which the case of Japanization of working practice incorporating a shift towards team working is explored. The generic change management and the specific HRM considerations that should be made are mapped out. Put simply, do the culture, climate, communications and work group dynamics on the one hand, and training, orientation, job design, performance management and remuneration policies on the other, provide a suitable foundation for likely success?

How 'strategic does HRM get?

However, how genuinely strategic does HRM get? This is a question that has occupied the minds of writers and researchers in the field of HRM for some time now. At one extreme are those who argue that strategic decision making largely neglects HR issues or, at best, addresses them retrospectively. At the other extreme, it is suggested that strategy is only ever effective if consideration is given to all resources and functional areas, including HRM, although research suggests that there is a gap between what companies assert they do and what happens in practice (see review of discussions in Legge, 1995). Why do these arguments and issues matter? First, changes in the strategy often require substantial changes in HRM policy and work practice. So, for example, changes in the main service delivered by a company will have a significant impact potentially on core business but also on the way in which employees need to function, and the implication is that there may need to be significant changes to HRM policy and strategy. However, a glance through a random sample of annual reports is likely to reveal a much lighter treatment of HRM issues relative to other functional areas such as marketing and finance. Why is HRM so often away from the strategic hub? Listed below are some of the reasons, both speculative and researched, why this might be the case.

● **The relative newness of the discipline**: Relative to other functional activities, human resource management as an academic discipline is a recent development, as are the establishment and evaluation of practice in relation to it. More cynically, it has been argued that '. . . HRM represents the discovery of personnel management by chief executives' (Fowler, 1987 cited in Legge, 1995).
● **'People' issues may be dealt with in an economic focus HRM and often retrospectively**, as the primary focus is on 'hard' rather than 'soft' organizational elements in relation to the strategy process.

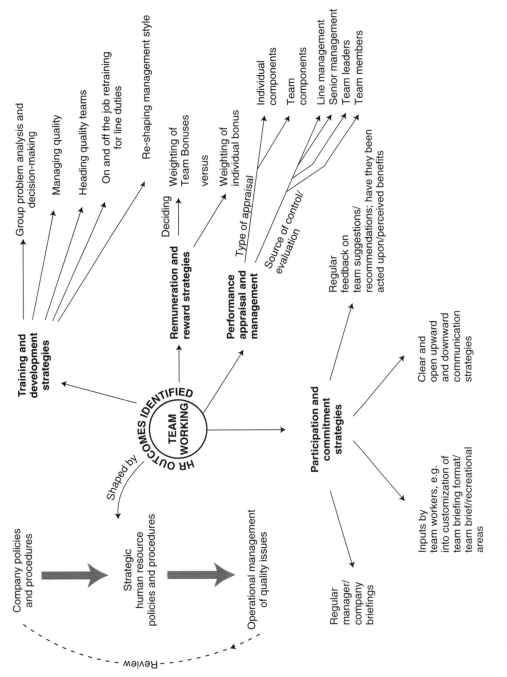

Company policies and procedures

Strategic human resource policies and procedures

Operational management of quality issues

Shaped by

HR OUTCOMES IDENTIFIED

TEAM WORKING

Review

Training and development strategies

Group problem analysis and decision-making

Managing quality

Heading quality teams

On and off the job retraining for line duties

Re-shaping management style

Remuneration and reward strategies

Deciding Weighting of Team Bonuses

versus

Weighting of individual bonus

Performance appraisal and management

Type of appraisal

Source of control/ evaluation

Individual components

Team components

Line management

Senior management

Team leaders

Team members

Participation and commitment strategies

Regular feedback on team suggestions/ recommendations; have they been acted upon/perceived benefits

Clear and open upward and downward communication strategies

Inputs by team workers, e.g. into customization of team briefing format/ team brief/recreational areas

Regular manager/ company briefings

Figure 9.4 Change management: identifying the HRM outcomes.

- A traditional 'administrative orientation' for personnel and human resource management practice in many organizations, leading to a lack of the necessary skills, knowledge and expertise required for effective change awareness and management among HRM professionals (see Storey in Storey, 1995) as well as a lack of expertise in strategic human resource management issues and decision making.
- A perception that HRM practitioners lack a 'managerial' and/ or whole organization and strategic perspective: Therefore, their assistance is often neither sought nor considered likely to be valuable given this credibility gap (Legge, 1995). Indeed, one survey in the UK indicated that only about one-third of large companies had some formal HRM representative on their boards (Purcell in Storey, 1995).
- HRM as a fragmented, 'balkanized' activity (Millward *et al.* 1992): In some organizations, HRM activities are scaled down and HRM outsourced in an ad hoc, fragmented and unsystematic manner. So for example, HRM professionals are simply commissioned by senior management to engage consultants to conduct major change on the behalf of the organization. Therefore, expertise is drawn upon when required but not built up within the organization, as a primary responsibility shifts towards the management of contracts. The result of contracting out coupled with an unsystematic approach undermines the practice of HRM as a holistic activity, and the likelihood of achieving a truly strategic perspective is reduced.
- Separation of strategy formulation and strategy implementation: The acid test of any strategy ultimately is how it operates when it is implemented. However, too often, there is a tendency for the strategies to be developed *without* a clear picture of how they can be implemented. This is unfortunate as the feasibility of implementation is an important assessment of how viable the strategy is likely to be. Further, it is often through careful early consideration of implementation that major HRM issues are unearthed.

Strategic HRM

People 'adding value': the human capital view

It is certainly true that there are examples in the literature of so-called 'strategic HRM' that are nothing of the kind, given our understanding of the terms strategic decision and strategy, and merely present planning of day-to-day, operational issues. This is not to suggest that operational issues are unimportant: indeed, many weaknesses in strategic planning arise because of a lack of attention to the interrelationships between strategic and operational issues. However, the perceived importance of strategic HRM decisions to organizations can be judged in many ways: is there an HR Director on the main board; do board members have a 'watching brief' for HRM issues; what amount of time and resources are channelled into such decisions; is there a clear and understood link between general strategic decisions and specific strategic HRM decisions? For our purposes, we can think of **strategic human resource management** (SHRM) as concerned with the 'people centred' aspects of the corporate strategic activity, and that **strategic HRM decisions** should be made in the key strategic decision-making arena of an organization, such as the main board.

One aspect of a strategic HRM approach that we will be considering in more detail has roots that may be traced back to the Nobel-prizewinning work of Theodore Schultz (1979, cited in Odiorne, 1984) on **investment in human capital**. He considered explicitly the importance of employees to an organization in terms of their economic value, not merely as 'units of production' that converted raw materials to goods, but as possessing skills, knowledge and expertise vital to the success of organizations. He stated that:

> Although it is obvious that people acquire useful skills and knowledge, it is not obvious that these **skills and knowledge are a form of capital**, that this capital is part of a deliberate investment that has grown in Western societies at a faster rate than conventional (non-human) capital, and that its growth may well be the most distinctive feature of the economic system.

In the decades following on from Schultz's work, the cross-over of his theory from economics to strategy models incorporating resource-based views of the firm (Collis and Montgomery, 1995), personnel and the emerging human resource management fields had taken place, driven by the increasing importance of Japanese models of management, central to which is investment in people. In the HR field, this is reflected in the work of George Odiorne (1984) on human resource investments and knowledge and skills' portfolio management, Jack Fitz Enz (1990) on human resource accounting, and from the strategy field, Gary Hamel and CK Prahalad on the potential of human capital as a source of sustainable competitive advantage (1993).

One strategic HRM model that takes into account this 'human capital' dimension has been developed by Lundy and Cowling (1996) (Figure 9.5). They suggest that a key stage in the strategy development process is **internal capability analysis**, part of which entails the definition of core effectiveness criteria which in turn, should lead to the design of mutually supportive human resource activities within a coherent human resource strategy. It is this attention to the issue of mutual support that creates the potential for a coherent human resource strategy.

However, the Odiorne and Fitz Enz models in particular lie very much at the 'hard', fairly utilitarian end of the strategic human resource management spectrum, with the language used to espouse their views that of the balance sheet, and employees considered in terms of costs and liabilities. Within such models, management's role is shaping and dictating formally how skills and knowledge can be made to fit with strategic needs. At the 'softer' end of the spectrum, there is now an interest, derived from the knowledge management and organizational learning field (Quinn *et al.* 1996), in the 'unlocked potential' of skills, knowledge and expertise within organizations. Here, the primary concern is to unlock and exploit these, but within the view that inevitably, control shifts from that of the manager towards the knowledge worker (refer to Chapter 2 on training and development and Chapter 3 on involvement and participation for

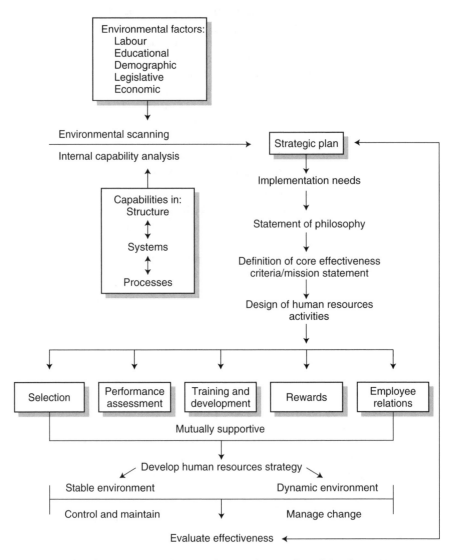

Figure 9.5 Model of strategic HRM diagram. Source: after Lundy and Cowling, 1996.

a fuller discussion of this subject). The belief is that it is the latter that is best positioned to unearth 'organizational knowledge' and identify the best operational strategies, especially at the company–customer interface, often through informal channels of communication where strong relationships can be formed. These views are captured in the statement by Ghoshal and Bartlett (1995) that

> Unlike (non-human) capital, knowledge is most valuable when those on the front line control use of it.

Towards a more robust account of strategic HRM

One response to the need for HR strategy to be discussed at main board level has been to try to position HR directors as being capable of making a valuable strategic contribution. Other functions have achieved this by defining specific strategic elements of their overall role as distinct from more mundane day-to-day activities. In finance, for example, financial management aspects are distinguished from book-keeping and so on. Various authors (e.g. Storey 1992, see Figure 0.10) have provided useful distinctions between various roles of the HR function. Using a synthesis of these models (Figure 9.6), it can be seen that the most strategic of these is that of Business Partner with its high integration with the business and its high perceived value. In practice, several organizations (see Scott-Jackson (1999) for examples) have implemented HR structures that separate operational service delivery (normally centralized) from business partnership. The business partners form part of line management teams providing HR advice and expertise while contracting with the centre for service delivery. The HR Service Centre's role is to provide cost-effective best practice in HR techniques and processes. The Business Partner's role is to provide business-oriented HR guidance and to maximize the business' utilization of its human resources. Thus strategy is separated from day-to-day service delivery but is closely linked to business needs. The Business Partners can report to a central HR Director (who is usually seen as Business Partner to the board) with a 'dotted line' to the relevant line director or vice versa. A common feature of these types of structures is that the reporting lines oscillate between the two alternatives.

The 'Service provider' role requires the effective delivery of cost-effective personnel processes to the organization. This would include the provision of recruitment services, training and compensation and often includes payroll services. This role is seen as having low strategic value and can easily be outsourced. The services are typically expected to continually improve while simultaneously showing a reduction in cost. Thus best practice 'cost per function' in the various service areas is a key concern for this function.

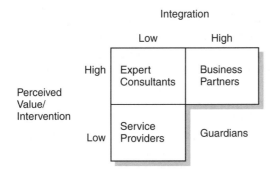

Figure 9.6   Roles of Personnel/HR Departments.

The 'Guardian' role aims to protect the organization from illegal or immoral or unacceptable actions by line management. Very often this prevention is primarily simply legally justified (i.e. stopping illegal sackings) but this can be extended to define and defend organizational principles such as fairness or equity. This 'Guardian' role has power and authority but is not seen as high value. Typically, the role of legal guardian may be recognized but management as a whole take the responsibility of defining and promoting principles and values. These are often ill-defined, incoherent and determined mainly by local management capabilities, styles and preferences. Management's role as guardian is often seen as conflicting with some other objective, such as tactical profit.

'Expert consultants' build a reputation for adding value in their area of expertise (which is normally an area that is seen as the general responsibility of line management) by providing good advice and through marketing that expertise. Examples of this role are less common but would typically focus at an operational level in areas such as competency analysis. In some cases the HR consultants compete internally with external consultants and in rare cases they provide consultancy on the open market as well. The rationale for this is not simply financial but rests on the need for consultants to have wide and continually updated experience in a range of organizations.

'Business Partners' act as a key part of the senior management team to provide tactical and strategic advice from an HR viewpoint. As an example, if a Board were concerned to cut costs, an HR Business Partner would propose measures to do with people such as productivity improvements or lay-offs. She or he would also comment on the feasibility of others' ideas from a people viewpoint. A Service provider, in contrast, might typically be asked simply to implement a decision to make a number of employees redundant. A Group Director of HR often acts as an informal business partner to the Chief Executive but often because of previous business background. His/her advice may be sought despite, rather than because of, HR specialist knowledge. Similarly, some senior HR Directors focus on providing HR advice to the exclusion of the other roles, such as operational service, and run the danger of losing credibility through failing to meet operational needs and increasing cost-effectiveness.

One case study, in a large bank (Scott-Jackson, 1999) found that this structure still meant that HR largely reacted to, but did not contribute to, business strategy. This was partly because long-term business strategy was not formulated in any detail, but took the form of a general strategic intent and a continuous monitoring of the future strategic environment. A further development (Figure 9.7) was to set up a separate HR strategy unit whose job was to consider and recommend long-term HR strategies in the context of a long-term view of the bank's competitive and strategic environment. The long-term HR strategy was based on building key capabilities that would provide competitive advantage (see Resource-based theory below). For example, a strategy to build individual change competence was developed through an analysis of long-term trends. The HR implications of the bank's specific strategies were then managed through the Business Partners. The central service organization provides continually improving best-practice people processes and monitors legal and social constraints to act as the organization's guardian.

Business imperative	HR response	HR function
Long-term strategic intent	Identify and build key capabilities to add competitive advantage	HR Strategy
Specific business strategies	Ensure business strategies can be achieved through effective HRM	Business Partners
Business as usual or short-term tactical projects, e.g. set up new location	Provide best practice, cost-effective HR processes	Central HR Services
Drive corporate values and culture. Protect against legal or social damage	Monitor and manage values, legal changes and social climate(s)	Central HR Services

Figure 9.7   HR Strategy as a distinct function in a large organization.

Main models of strategic HRM

Strategic HRM has been, and is being, developed from several distinct academic frameworks. These range from Personnel/HRM through to economic and strategic perspectives. The main frameworks can be grouped into three strands:

● Universal or 'best practice' – models which suggest that a given set of HR conditions or practices will provide strategic advantage to any firm in any circumstances. These models tend to develop from an HRM perspective, particularly those that suggest that high commitment is always a cause of strategic success. They also arise from the economic measurement perspective where comparative measurement of the impact of HR on shareholder value, for example, proposes that a given bundle of 'best practice' HR processes has a high correlation with strategic success in a set of firms treated as homogenous.
● Contingent or 'best fit' – models emanating from strategy perspectives which suggest that certain types of HR practices will benefit certain types of organization depending on their strategic environment or strategic reaction to it.

- Unique or organization-specific – models emanating from a resource-based view of the firm which suggest that for each organization certain unique and inimitable human capabilities will provide sustainable competitive advantage.

Human resource management 'universal' theories

The basic tenets of HRM, particularly the 'high commitment' or 'soft' model (see Introduction), have been applied in a strategic context to suggest that various generic HR principles, if applied, will have a beneficial impact on the strategic success of any organization. So, for example, consistent systems for generating employee involvement, recruitment based on sound selection methods, development and training, and pay based on performance are likely to lead to competitive advantage. Becker and Huselid (1998) report that firms with a one standard deviation higher value on a group of HR practices (an index) have 24% higher shareholder equity and 25% higher accounting profits. Interestingly, for one particular set of practices indexed as 'management compensation', a one standard deviation difference was equated with an increase in accounting profits of 27%. At a more general level, the typical set of generic practices could be summed up as:

> Employees should be recruited with care, treated as permanent rather than dispensible, seen as a source of continuous improvement in productivity and trained, on an ongoing basis ... A visionary leader should create an atmosphere in which organizational change is normal and expected ... Progressive management will wish to engage the intelligence, expertise and commitment of its employees in achieving the organisation's aims ...
>
> Lundy and Cowling (1996:2)

Thus it is suggested that the application of a set of HR best practices, or 'HRM bundle' as it is increasingly being called, will provide strategic advantage for any organization. There are various ideas on what the ideal 'HRM bundle' might be composed of, but it would typically include the elements most often associated with a high commitment model of HRM. Guest (1987:42) suggests that the main dimensions of HRM are:

- The goal of integration. If human resources can be integrated into strategic plans, if HR policies cohere, if line managers have internalized the importance of HR and this is reflected in their behaviour and if employees identify with the company, then the company's strategic goals are likely to be more successfully implemented.
- The goal of employee commitment.
- The goal of flexibility/adaptability, i.e. organic structures, functional flexibility.
- The goal of quality, i.e. quality of staff, performance, standards and public image.

Grant (1991) suggests the following:

- The training and expertise of employees determine the skills available to the firm.
- The adaptability of employees determines the strategic flexibility of the firm.
- The commitment and loyalty of employees determine the firm's ability to maintain competitive advantage.

From a practitioner viewpoint, this perspective reinforces the argument that HR is important and that HR professionals, as experts in 'best practice', have a major contribution to make. Evidence to support the argument can be developed by showing a linkage between 'best practice' and strategic success. This can be done by modelling causal links between, for example, motivation and customer satisfaction, or by demonstrating correlations between a set of HRM practices and a measure of overall success. Sears, as an example of a causal model (Rucci et al., 1998), demonstrated a relationship between employee satisfaction, employee behaviour, customer satisfaction and profitability. This reflects a general model assumed by many universal theories – that HR processes work because they always enhance commitment and commitment always enhances human performance, and enhanced human performance always enhances profit and shareholder value.

Lundy and Cowling (1996) give a model for determining HR strategy (Figure 9.5) which focuses on the planning of various HRM activities in response to strategic needs. The strategic needs of the business drive the production of value (philosophy) as well as the other activities such as training. This model is really illustrating how strategy can be *implemented* through HR, NOT how strategy can be *determined* by HR factors. The concern of strategic HRM, if it is to be differentiated from HRM in general, should be the latter.

From the perspective of organizational economics, researchers such as Becker and Huselid (1998) have demonstrated correlations between HRM bundles of best practice and outcomes such as retention and productivity. Success, in these models, can be measured by profit, revenue, shareholder value or return or share price. In the USA, these HRM bundles are often referred to as High Performance Work Systems and might include pay for performance, systematic recruitment of senior executives, employee involvement and so on. The methodological basis of these studies has been criticized by, for example, Purcell (1999) in several respects and indeed Becker and Huselid (1998) themselves are careful to advise caution and further research. However, the outputs of these, and other studies in the UK (e.g. West et al., 1997), are being avidly absorbed and reiterated by HR practitioners and other researchers as they purport to provide evidence of causal relationships between HR best practice and strategic performance.

The research agenda for a universal model would logically include:

● the identification of the most important components of the HR bundle, i.e. those HR factors that would help any and every organization to achieve strategic success;
● the processes and conditions in which those factors can be maximized in order to gain most advantage.

It could be argued, from a strategic perspective, that generic HR factors which are important to *any* organization's success (universal) cannot be 'strategic' as they are not determined by, nor do they determine, strategic decisions. This is not to suggest that they are unimportant (the word 'strategic' is sometimes used as a synonym for important), as, if valid, they obviously need to be carefully developed and nurtured.

Contingent or best fit HR strategy

A similar approach is adopted by Fitz Enz (1990) who is building a large database, through his firm Saratoga, of various HR metrics in an attempt to elicit best practice. The Saratoga database is, however, organized by various factors such as industry segment and size of firm so that 'best practice' can be to some extent contingent on the firm's situation. This is an example of a 'best fit' or contingent model which tries to identify a set of practices or resources which would be appropriate for different general categories of organizational situations. Fitz Enz (1990) categorizes organizations by industry type, size and so on whereas Miles and Snow (1984), for example, suggest that specific HR strategies are determined by specific business strategies. The external competitive environment, the industry and indeed the structure of the workforce itself create conditions where unique and valuable skills, knowledge and HR processes add competitive advantage. Purcell (1999) also points out that other internal strategic decisions impact HR strategy, e.g. a strategy to deploy technology would suggest a distinct HR strategy. This type of contingent model has more to do with strategy determination, albeit based on fairly generic categories, and would purport to help organizations to determine the best HR strategy suited to its particular circumstance.

The research agenda here might focus on:

- identifying which HR factors have a varying impact on success dependent on certain organizational situations;
- identifying the categories of organizational situations which moderate the influence of HR factors on strategic success. These might include size, market, workforce factors, competition, geography and so on.

Organization-specific – resource-based strategy

An alternative body of theory derives from the fields of strategy and economics and sees 'human resources' as an important type of strategic resource which, by virtue of its complexity, may provide significant competitive advantage. These models suggest that every aspect of the content of HR strategy is particular to an individual firm and that the most useful academic input is to propose a process by which the content can be worked out (e.g. Scott-Jackson, 1999; Lepec and Snell, 1999). One argument here is that intangible resources explain the differences in success between firms that are apparently similar. Human resources are often intangible, therefore human resources may influence at least some of the difference. A resource meets the criteria for competitive advantage if it is valuable, rare, inimitable and non-substitutable. In these terms, human capital resources might include, for example, experience, judgement, ability to work as teams and intelligence. Competitive advantage occurs only if the resource is differentiated between firms and is non-mobile. Sustained competitive advantage can occur only when other firms are also incapable of duplicating the benefits of the resource.

Under this model, 'human resources' refers to the HR capital under the firm's control and HR practices are the management of that pool. Human resources can certainly add value differentially. Taking 'skills' as an example of a human resource, given the assumption that skill levels follow a normal distribution, then high levels of any particular skill will be rarer than average skill levels. It can also be argued that human resource advantages of skills are difficult to imitate because:

- it is difficult to duplicate a firm's historical position,
- it is difficult to identify exactly what causes its advantage, and
- it is difficult to understand the social complexity of an organization's relations with its human resources.

Human resources can be substitutable by technology but this substitution can be duplicated and any advantage lost. The resource of cognitive ability, for example, can be applied across a number of roles and can be considered to be non-substitutable. The fundamental importance of this perspective, compared to commonly held views, can be seen in several cases. For example, much relevant literature (e.g. Wright *et al.*, 1994) suggests that top management are a primary source of competitive advantage. However, they are most easily identifiable and can be approached and recruited by search consultants. They therefore cannot be a source of *sustainable* competitive advantage. Competitive advantage must be found in the entire pool and particularly interactions and inter-working within the pool. This suggests that:

- firms with higher human capital resources (e.g. cognition) should be more effective;
- human resource *practices and processes* can also add competitive advantage but are imitable *so cannot be a source of sustained advantage* unless they lead to an improved human capital resource;
- a firm that perfects selection and reward will have 'first mover' benefits to the extent that people themselves are not perfectly mobile.

People are not strictly a 'human resource' in themselves. Each 'owning person' is a collection of various types of resource in a package and some human resources result from the interactions of groups of people. The firm effectively hires 'human resources' from the owning person or persons. Human resources are complex and difficult to classify and measure. Their value is extremely variable and is affected by a large number of factors (e.g. mood, social interactions, weather). Unlike most other resources, they are not clearly controlled by or owned by the firm as their use is entirely mediated through a relationship with the 'owning persons'. They are packaged, in the owning person, together with a large number of characteristics that are not resources. Some types of human resource may be incorporated in the wider organization – an innovative culture, for example. All this means that human resources are not easy to analyse in a cost–benefit equation. Unfortunately the view of human resources as simply 'the people' means that their (wage) costs can be identified and measured, whereas their benefits are less measurable. Many downsizing decisions (Scott-Jackson, 1998) are made because of the lack of data on the revenue impact of people, compared to the easily available and presented data on their costs. In a recent board meeting, the author challenged this view by proposing that, if revenue benefits of people were to be ignored, then the board itself should be the first to go, representing, as they did, by far the largest per capita cost!

It is observed that firms in the same industry sector can operate at different levels of profitability for long periods. Thus each enterprise is unique, with different types and amounts of resources arising from different histories. Each resource, be it a process or a resource, is also unique.

Part of the difficulty from an academic standpoint is that heterogeneous resources may be useful to a firm but cannot be easily understood, analysed or compared. If they could, they would no longer be inimitable. The main aim of research is to illuminate those factors that provide competitive advantage, but from a commercial viewpoint, the more obscure the characteristics the better.

Some authors (e.g. Hamel and Prahalad, 1993) have identified knowledge as the major differentiating skill. In this way, one version of the resource-based view can be considered as universal – the ability to build, develop, retain and share knowledge is proposed as a universal source of competitive advantage. This approach could be used to discuss the resource itself, e.g. knowledge, or the processes by which the resource is utilized, e.g. knowledge management.

In any event, even if the firm-specific, resource-based view of strategic HR is valid, there are (at least) two difficulties to be overcome by future research:

- If current sources of a firm's competitive advantage are rare and inimitable then they are not likely to be easy to analyse or compare and their advantages are likely to be the result of causally ambiguous, complex, interrelated resources built up over time. A reductionist methodology is therefore unlikely to yield useful results.
- If one objective of academic theory were to help firms compete then a key research area would be how to build future sources of competitive advantage. This has been handled in at least two ways. It might be possible to identify a major type of resource that would add advantage in most circumstances. The uniqueness of this advantage would derive from the way in which the resource was developed, deployed and managed. Candidates for this universally advantageous resource would include 'knowledge' (Hamel and Prahalad, 1993) and 'culture' (Guest, 1987). Another approach would be to develop a process by which future sources of competitive advantage could be identified and developed by firms. This approach has been adopted by Scott-Jackson (1999) and required a seven-year single-firm case study. The result was a process model (Figure 9.8) which identified four candidate sources of advantage and which suggested ways in which they could be developed to be unique and inimitable.

Synthesis and research implications

It can be seen that theories of strategic HRM can be positioned along a continuum from universal to organization-specific, with contingent in the middle. As in most academic polarizations, it is worth considering whether the various theories really conflict or whether they can operate together to give a more complete picture.

There are several ways in which the models could be seen as complementary:

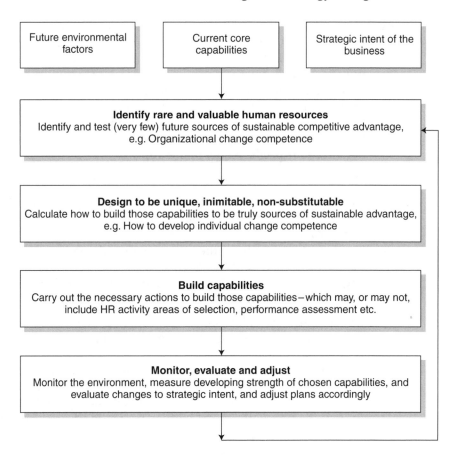

Figure 9.8 Process for formulating HR strategy through identifying organization-specific human resources.

- The models may apply to the different roles of HR. For example, the universal best practice model applies to the service provider and guardian roles whereas a contingent model might apply to the consultant role and the organization-specific model applies to the business partner role.
- The models may apply to different components of the HR bundle. For example, commitment may well be a universally useful component whereas pay for performance might be organization-specific or contingent.
- The models might focus on the difference between strategy formulation and implementation. The universal model might determine the major human capabilities that could provide the basis for competitive advantage (such as high commitment or knowledge). The organization-specific, resource-based model might describe how, or prescribe that, they should be developed in ways that are unique and difficult to replicate. The universal model tells us what and the resource-based model tells us how.

- The models might simply operate at different levels of granularity. Becker and Huselid (1998), for example, utilize an overall index of the high performance work system (HPWS) to correlate firm performance with HR in a seemingly universal conclusion that HPWS correlates with organizational success. However, the HPWS is composed of many individual factors so that although many firms could achieve similarly high scores, the individual components making up their scores could vary substantially. Thus, at the top-level index, the universal model applies whereas at the level of individual HR factors, an organization-specific model might apply.

In either case, the research agenda would now include:

- Universal – Identifying and building those components of the HR bundle that are necessary for the competitive success of any organization in any circumstance.
- Contingent – Identifying the main driving criteria by which identified components add value differentially.
- Organization-specific – Developing a process by which differentiating human resources can be identified and built.

The last of these areas of investigation would add a new element to the process of strategy formulation. The other two would provide generally applicable content to any strategy.

The end result could suggest that, for example: high commitment is necessary for the competitiveness of any organization, pay for performance is necessary for strategic success in the consumer retail market and, as a result of a process for determining key capabilities, individual innovation is a source of competitive advantage in a specific retail firm in a specific competitive environment.

It can be seen that the universal and contingent contributions tend to lead to HR components *necessary* for success whereas the organization-specific model leads to sources of unique competitive advantage. It is easier (but by no means easy) to correlate the presence or absence of HRM components to organizational performance than it is to demonstrate the efficacy of a process which results in unique capabilities which cannot be compared within or across organizations. It is likely therefore that comparative, quantified data and research will continue to be accumulated for the universal and contingent models. Until a number of firms apply a resource-based HR strategy process, comparative data will be hard to identify and case studies (e.g. Scott-Jackson, 1999) will provide the main research input for the resource-based organization-specific model.

Initial assessments of coming change: context and intervention type

There are plenty of reasons why change is likely to occur in any organization. Some of these, for example the introduction of specific systems of management such as TQM or BPR, or strategic change, have already been mentioned. More generally, we can identify the following additional items also:

- A desire to secure gains in efficiency and effectiveness
- Changes in the attitudes and beliefs of staff towards key stakeholders or customer/client groups
- 'Negative work environment' characterized by under-performance, employee dissatisfaction, business failures or dysfunctional behaviour
- Exploitation of market opportunities
- Renewal or transformation of the organization as a whole or of key parts of it
- A desire to secure increased employee compliance

However, many people rightly hold a cynical attitude towards changing anything at all in their organizations. Too often, change interventions are warmly embraced as the new 'quick fix', only to be derided a few years later as simplistic, passé or faddish. All models of change and their associated interventions have inherent strengths and weaknesses, but because of the enthusiasm of senior management or the persuasive powers of an external consultant, the downsides can be easily overlooked. This is not to suggest that all the outcomes of a change intervention can be anticipated, but some certainly can. Managers need to assess preparedness of the organization generally and themselves and their subordinates specifically, given the reasons for the intervention and the nature of the intervention to be undertaken. Also, they need to be clear about the help and support that they are likely to need, and whether such expertise can be found within the organization or will need to be sought externally.

Listed below are some of the most important considerations that should be made in order to understand the strengths, limitations and difficulties associated with change in the 'soft systems' or people-centred parts of organizations. The list includes elements that can be readily managed and also those that cannot but which are, nonetheless, informative.

Organizational preparedness can be evaluated by considering the following:

- **Anticipated change or unexpected change**: Is the change sudden or unexpected, or incremental and planned? Typically, how well do you think the organization deals with these types of change, and why?
- **Analysis of strengths and weaknesses**: What are the specific strengths and vulnerabilities located within an organization and how do these interrelate with each other?
- **Commitment and compliance**: To what extent is the change dependent on the agreement and 'buy in' of key individuals and groups? What sources of power and influence does each of these have?
- **Visioning and sense making**: How well equipped is the organization and its members to make use of the information (hard, soft, formal, informal) in order to make sense of the current situation and to create new options? Is expert help required?
- **Problem analysis and decision making**: What are the problem analysis and decision-making strategies employed, both formally and informally? How effective or appropriate are they? For 'hard' interventions, is sufficient attention paid to people-centred issues: for 'people centred' interventions, are technical issues being neglected? As any change will inevitably generate new

problems, have these been considered, or is a naïve, laissez faire or utopian position being adopted?

- **Resources**: What can and should be marshalled to help with the changes?
- **Preparedness and planning**: How well prepared are employees for the change? What planning processes are used to develop, outline and plan the detail of the change? Have contingencies been built in at the development stage in case things do not go to plan?
- **Key roles**: Who is going to sponsor (provide the necessary resources), champion (promote and drive the change) and facilitate the change? Are they the most appropriate people for these roles? Beyond instigation, who else is essential for the facilitation of the change and do they possess the necessary skills and expertise?
- **Facilitating and managing the change**: Can the design and implementation of the change be facilitated and managed by staff in the organization or is external support needed?
- **Outcomes**: What is wanted from the change? What are the actual and perceived benefits? Were there any unanticipated benefits? How optimistic, 'utopian', cautious or negative are the views among key individuals and groups?
- **Rational and emotional responses**: What are the anxieties, hostilities and sources of resistance to change (justified and unjustified) that are likely to be encountered? How could these be handled?
- **Coping strategies**: What will be the response if things go wrong? What **potential problem analysis and contingency planning** has been undertaken? To what extent can the organization's members cope with uncertainties, inconsistencies and paradox? Can specific sources of anxiety or stress be anticipated and managed? How able is the organization and its members to cope with the inevitable stress that will result from any major change?
- **Implementation**: Has consideration been given to how the plans could be implemented? Are these considerations an integral part of the assessment of the suitability, feasibility and acceptability of the change, given knowledge of environmental factors, internal assessment and stakeholder analysis?

The **appropriateness** or **fitness for purpose** of interventions can be assessed by considering:

- What is the information on which the choice of intervention has been made? Is this information reliable?
- What are the areas that need to be addressed? Broadly speaking, is it *knowledge*, *skills*, or *attitudes and beliefs*?
- Is the intervention appropriate given what needs to be shifted (i.e. knowledge, skills or attitudes and beliefs?)
- Who is going to fund the intervention? Is the resource level sufficient?
- Who are 'the clients'? Senior management, departmental managers, line managers and so on.
- Who is going to 'champion' the change and keep the momentum going?
- Do we possess the skills internally to manage the intervention or do we need to draw on external expertise?

● How will we know if things have changed? How are we going to evaluate and monitor the impact of the change?

Examples of change interventions: 'Organizational development'-type initiatives

In earlier chapters (see in particular Chapter 2 on training and development and Chapter 3 on generating comment through involvement and participation processes) the studies of FW Taylor and his theories of Scientific Management, along with the application of such practices within the context of the Ford Motor Company in the early part of this century, are outlined. To recap briefly, with a Scientific Management approach, jobs are broken down into simple tasks that are easy to execute and automated whenever possible. The organization of work is regarded as the responsibility of managers, while workers are 'hired hands', motivated solely by money. Changes to work practice centre largely around 'task centred' improvements in efficiency, with the emotional needs of workers largely ignored. The de-skilling, alienation and demotivation experienced by many workers in such 'Taylorist' or 'Fordist' organizations have been written about extensively, as is the reaction against such ideas about organizations and workers, as highlighted by the researchers in the 'Human Relations' school, in particular from the 1940s through to the 1960s (for a review, see Buchanan and Huczynski, 1997) and in more recent times in the criticism of Taylorist-like or 'Neo-Taylorist' practices, as characterized by the close electronic surveillance, tight managerial controls and limited worker autonomy in some call management centres (Arkin, 1997).

Over the years, there have been a number of schools of thought concerning the appropriateness of specific actions in order to facilitate change in organizations. In the United States, emphasis from the 1940s onwards saw major steps forward in the application of the social sciences (and in particular, psychology and sociology) towards a better understanding of workers and organizations. On the other side of the Atlantic, Eric Trist and colleagues at the Tavistock Institute in London were conducting studies into the relationship between technology and social factors in the workplace. The interventions that arose from these early investigations into organizational effectiveness by researchers such as Kurt Lewin and his colleagues in the 1940s rapidly developed into one of the most influential types of intervention, referred to as **organizational development** (see review of the evolution of organizational development in French and Bell, 1995).

There are many definitions of organizational development, or OD. One definition that highlights concisely the main elements of many of the OD interventions undertaken was written by Richard Beckard (1969):

Organizational development is an effort (1) planned, (2) organization-wide, (3) managed from the top, (4) to increase organizational effectiveness and health through (5) planned interventions in the organization's 'processes' using behavioural science knowledge.

The reference to 'organizational health' can be seen as an indirect reference to an organization's climate or motivational status.

At the heart of 'traditional' OD is:

- organizational diagnostics and large-scale social-science based survey work;
- laboratory training grounded in sensitivity training based activities, such as T-groups or team building. More recently, such approaches have been developed further into human processes' interventions, at the interpersonal and group levels, and also organization-wide;
- action research (where research is closely linked to action of organizational members who in turn are able to use the findings of the research to action change);
- productivity and quality of work life initiatives;
- socio-technical systems analysis and interventions.

A more recent definition of OD is offered by the British academic, Ralph Stacey (1993):

> (Organizational development) ... is the long-term programme of interventions in the social, psychological and cultural belief systems of an organization. These interventions are based on certain principles and practices that are assumed to lead to greater organizational effectiveness.

It is worth raising a number of points in relation to Stacey's definition. First, OD-type interventions are usually long-term, therefore assessment of the final impact of such interventions will be long-term also. Therefore, it is unlikely that there will be a quick return on investment. Secondly, Stacey makes explicit that OD is a type of intervention that can be employed to influence an organization's culture.

The culture school

A second wave of social-science-grounded whole organization interventions surfaced in the 1980s. Core to many of these interventions associated with this second wave was culture change. The importance of culture was implicit within many of the OD strategies that were employed in the more 'traditional' approaches in the early years (see in particular Margulies and Raia, 1978): for many of these interventions there was more of a focus on inter- and intra-group dynamics. However, it was made more explicit in many of the OD-type interventions that occurred during the 1980s. This renewed interest was prompted significantly by the 'culture school' of consultants and academics such as Tom Peters and his colleagues and Rosabeth Moss Kanter (their main positions summarized in their books *In Search of Excellence* and *A Passion for Excellence* (Peters and Waterman, 1982 and Peters and Austin, 1985) and *The Change Masters* (Moss Kanter, 1983)). Put simply (and indeed by other writers and practitioners, simplistically), they argued that the wrong sort of culture (which we can regard as a system of attitudes, beliefs and basic assumptions) could get in the way of organizational effectiveness, while the right sort of culture could provide a source of sustainable competitive advantage.

Many large organizations undertook major culture change programmes during this period, and the results of these interventions were mixed. Indeed, at least 50 per cent of the companies that were identified as 'excellent' by Peters and Waterman's own criteria were no longer found to be so five years later (Pascale, 1990). Although by no means all of these failures centred around cultural factors, it was argued that an important key success factor was the strength and robustness of the company culture. There are many reasons why a number of these interventions may have been only partially successful or, indeed, largely failures, which include:

- over-simplistic descriptions or understanding of the nature of organizational culture;
- off-the-shelf interventions applied without reference to a detailed and robust understanding of socio-behavioural issues within organizations;
- poor research and data collection;
- a tacit assumption that organizational cultures are in some way uniform, or can be made so;
- the belief that changes in behaviour are rapidly followed by changes in attitudes, beliefs and basic assumptions;
- a lack of fit between changes to organizational culture and changes to related HRM systems;
- a failure to address the political and power-play-centred issues that can undermine such interventions, with in particular the 'traditional' approaches to OD erring towards the 'conflict aversive'. A quote by Burke (1982, cited in French and Bell, 1995)

   Organization development signifies change, and for change to occur in an organization, power must be exercised.

- over-ambitiousness: Major change within any organization requires skillful handling. It is unlikely that proposed change will meet with universal acceptance or that those who undertake the change will possess all of the skills and knowledge to make the change work. Often, a more realistic approach is to undertake a 'test run' or pilot of the change that is to be extended to the whole organization, with a view to learning what initial ideas about the change are wrong, or what problems are likely to be encountered when trying to scale up the change, in terms of logistics and resources. Targeting the change at key departments or sections within an organization provides the interventionists with useful options. Departments which are most enthusiastic, high status or, most importantly, key to the change, can become involved in the early stages, thus reducing possible resistance, drawing the change to the attention of many and creating the maximum movement for the minimum input respectively.

However, beyond naïveté (Dawson, 1994) or unscrupulous 'hard sell', there is another side to understanding the rhetoric and 'over-simplification' that it has been suggested can be associated with OD. Rhetoric may flatter to deceive but it may also have a more noble role. Specifically, no matter how simplified the message, OD interventions often signal strongly that there is a need to do

Mr Robert Horton looks determined to live up to his American-earned sobriquet as the "hatchet gentleman." This was the friendly term applied to an Englishman who managed to chop out jobs in Cleveland when he was chairman of Standard Oil (the forerunner of BP America) and retain community support at the same time.

After just one week as Chairman of British Petroleum he is drastically cutting back the company's head office, and eliminating 1,150 jobs, with up to 900 redundancies over the coming year. Whether the "gentle" part of the appellation will still apply after this exercise in radical central office reshaping remains to be seen.

Most people losing jobs will be cleaners, building maintenance staff and computer specialists – services to be contracted for on a reduced scale when BP moves to its smaller corporate offices at Finsbury Circus, a stone's throw from its current skyscraper headquarters in the City of London.

Yet a significant number of managers from the core of the corporate centre are also going – 160 jobs out of the current 540.

And while a 30 per cent job loss at the centre is severe enough, the guts of Mr Horton's programme are far more sweeping than the implications of cutting a thousand jobs in a company with a staff of 120,000.

"What I'm trying to do," he says, "is to simplify, refocus, make it clear that we don't need any longer to have hierarchies. We don't need any longer to have baronial head office departments. This is a fundamentally different way of looking at the way that you run the centre of the corporation."

Mr Horton accepts the achievements of his predecessor, Sir Peter Walters, who is widely credited with helping BP out of financial difficulties in his 10 years in office, while restructuring and fixing a forward-looking stratgegy for the group. "This is not a reorganisation." Mr Horton insists. "And I'm not

restructuring BP." However, "After 20 years, organisations build up an accretion of barnacles on their hull and need a jolly good scrape," he adds.

With a good scrape in his second week in office, Mr Horton aims to clarify and simplify the role of the corporate centre, devolve financial authority and responsibility down a flattened corporate hierarchy and eliminate committees and layers of control and planning – all of which is intended to force individuals to take responsibility and initiative – throughout BP, not just in Britannic House.

He wants BP to be more flexible and responsive in what is likely to be a turbulent decade. And he is in effect telling people in the operating businesses: I'm going to get off your backs and stop second guessing your decisions.

"What I want to get away from is a culture where the chairman says, 'I really want to know why the lavatories at the service station in Shiplake are not adequately stocked with toilet paper."

BP's basic business structure will continue to be dominated by four business divisions: exploration and production, oil refining and marketing, chemicals, and nutrition. The plan will lead to the final integration of the old Standard Oil business into the BP system. The Cleveland headquarters, where Mr Horton played a key role turning Standard Oil around, will be gutted of its operational role, although Mr Horton insists it will be even more important in strategic terms and in presenting the corporation's public face. Europe is being upgraded as a region, headquartered in Brussels.

Investment sums that can be spent without referral up the bureaucratic chain will be increased throughout the group. BP will, none the less, still be a far cry from the oil industry's paradigm of decentralisation, Shell, which vests almost complete autonomy in its nationally based, integrated operating companies.

BP is by no means the first giant multinational to attempt to redefine the

centre and eliminate hierarchies in Britain. ICI began the process eight years ago, under the redoubtable Sir John Harvey-Jones.

What is unusual is the spectacle of a mammoth preparing the revolution so thoroughly as BP – especially the "soft", human aspects of radical change. In America, General Electric concentrated for its first few years under the abrasive, but inspirational, leadership of Jack Welch from 1981 on the "hard" aspects: job cutbacks, simplified structures and streamlined processes – leaving executives to fend for themselves and causing much disaffection among middle management.

Horton plans to make hard and soft go almost together, with job cutbacks followed swiftly by programmes right across the group aimed directly at changing attitudes and behaviour to fit with the changed work relationships. Mr Horton expects, perhaps optimistically, that this will take two or three years.

It is a vision that is far more easily articulated than achieved. Employees will have to prise themselves from a comforting bureaucratic womb and learn to take risks.

Horton recognises this: "The system will fight back because there are people who are comfortable with this. All their life has been trained for another sort of way of doing things."

And there is a danger not just that the programmes might fail, but that if handled insensitively, it could provoke confusion and increase the cynicism that has accumulated in recent years inside the company, all of which was throughly documented in two opinion surveys last year that shocked the BP management.

What is proposed at the centre shows fully the potential for disarray. Some 70 corporate centre committees, 90 per cent of the total, are gone – closed, plain and simple – with individuals taking responsibility instead. Hierarchically structured departments are out – replaced by small flexible teams. Mr Horton and his close advisers evidently

Figure 9.9 Cutting down and reshaping the core. *Source:* Financial Times, 20 March 1990.

see the difference, but what about others in BP?

The first day-on-the-job question – "Who do I report to?" – no longer has an answer at BP's corporate headquarters. The new "organisation chart" consists of ovals floating inside a larger oval (dubbed The Egg, by the Project 1990 team), with the chairman and chief operating officer sitting on top of it, and managing directors from the operating businesses hovering outside. Instead of structured hierarchy, managers will network – create their own patterns of interaction.

Mr David Simon will keep a steady hand on the tiller as chief operating officer, giving Mr Horton time to devote himself to strategy and external relations.

It all spells flexibility, but it may just as easily spell confusion unless responsibility is delegated precisely to individuals and teams. It will fail unless BP employees are conditioned to accept this new responsibility.

Mr Horton is probably well equipped to lead such a change. He is an extremely ambitious man whose character is not flawed by a lack of self-esteem. He rose rapidly to the top and, perhaps not unexpectedly, has won his share of detractors inside the company. He is, none the less, recognised as a highly capable man with an expansive personality and an appealing public face. He is willing to wade into the thick of controversy, as he did in Cleveland, and plead his case. As he jets around the world in the coming months and years, arguing his corner face-to-face with many BP employees, he will surely win many converts.

One need not be cynical to notice that the changes are also certain to bolster Mr Horton's powers in the job by centralising head office authority around himself and Mr Simon, with whom he is sharing some of the traditional job of chairman. As much as the old committees and departments at the corporate centre served as an extension to the chairman's office they also buffered the chairman from a direct relationship with the departments and

the operating divisions. With traditional hierarchies cut away managers will become beholden to Mr Horton and, to a lesser extent, M. Simon. If Mr Horton succeeds, BP will truly become his oyster and a gentleman he will remain.

Mr Horton laid exceptionally careful plans to stage the corporate revolution he has now unleased within BP, writes Christopher Lorenz. He got the BP Board to commission "Project 1990" – a research and consultation process which prepared the revolution – last July, eight months before the retirement 10 days ago of Sir Peter Walters, and even before Mr Horton had been confirmed officially as heir apparent.

Yet the need for change had become patently obvious. BP was bogged down in its own bureaucracy, and its senior staff were becoming increasingly disgruntled – as was revealed at the beginning of 1989 in an opinion survey of its top 150 managers. The survey shocked Sir Peter and his managing directors, not least because more than half of the senior staff was unclear about the BP group's five year mission and strategy. Many of the 150 also felt that BP's structure impeded both operational flexibility and collaboration between different businesses.

Such internal criticisms of the effects of BP's near-military regime of committees, commands and controls were taken much further by the 4,000 lower-level respondents to a broad-ranging questionnaire which was carried out by the Project 1990 team last autumn.

The Walters regime, introduced in 1981 shortly after his accession, was vital in its day: his erection of myriad checks and balances both across BP, and up-and-down its steep hierarchy, resuced the company from its flaccid state at the turn of the decade: before then, much of it had been run, like may large European companies of the time, on an integrated basis which was unwieldy, in spite of the fact that diversification had turned it into an exceedingly complex construct.

The basic elements of the structure which Walters introduced were: clearly-

separated international "business streams" (divisions) with their own boards; and negotiated financial relationships at all levels across the business streams, and between them and head office. "It was exactly the right medicine," said one senior American BP manager today.

Yet, as the 1980s progressed, bureaucracy grew as committee was piled on committee, and as the head office involved itself with operational issues in addition to strategic and financial ones.

A hectic divestment programme was meanwhile rendering the degree of complexity and control increasingly inappropriate. By the late 1980s, from having encompassed as many as 11 "business streams" in 70 countries, BP's spread and managerial complexity had been stripped back to only four streams: exploration ("BPX"), oil (refining and marketing), chemicals and nutrition. With increased emphasis on regional management in Europe, America and the Far East, "an 11×70 matrix can now move towards a 4×3 one," as Mr Horton puts it.

Still, old managerial structures, information flows, procedures and styles remained largely unchanged. "We spent more time dividing up the pie than trying to make it bigger," said the US executive. The medicine which had once been so potent was turning sour.

The head office also seemed to have become preoccupied with "asset-trading" – in other words, with portfolio management through acquistions and divestitures. The effect on internal morale was inevitable, as last autumn's staff questionnaire showed only too clearly. There was a financial penalty too. Instead of the size and cost of the London head office falling as the portfolio of businesses shrank, it increased by 10 per cent between 1987 and 1989, to more than 5,800 people (2,500 excluding engineering and research). Total UK corporate costs were up from £94m a year to more than £130m last year. They were heading for £150m in 1990 before Mr Horton got to work.

things differently, and are often vital in creating a 'can do' mindset and challenging the status quo.

Moreover, Henry Mintzberg, Professor of Strategic Management at McGill University in Canada, has suggested that there are different ways in which the manner in which corporate strategies unfold can be considered (Mintzberg and Waters in Bowman and Asch, 1988). He suggests that what emerges from the strategy process is likely to differ from the original intention. Indeed, the unintended order that unfolds in such **emergent strategies** not only implies a pragmatic response to the unexpected once strategies are implemented, but also that strategic learning is taking place; that is, those responsible for managing the development and implementation of the strategy are '**learning what works**'.

In practice, organization development initiatives are likely to reflect this 'learning what works'. Therefore, not all deviations from the intended are due to a lack of foresight, knowledge or skill on the part of the intervention programme or over-ambition inherent within such programmes, but often reflects a realistic approach to managing what is, in practice, a process which naturally emerges once the intention is stated.

The term OD is probably less commonly used these days. Nonetheless, the second wind provided by the organizational culture interventions discussed above and other management-centred and more OD-type initiatives has created what is sometimes referred to as '**second-generation organization development** (French and Bell, 1995). Not only has much of the methodology established with the development of traditional OD been recast and redefined but new approaches have been adopted also. In Figure 9.10, a number of OD-type and other general 'people-centred' change interventions are outlined (which would now be most closely associated with 'soft' models of HRM), along with the benefits and potential problems associated with each. Moreover, these interventions clearly highlight the potentially important role for HRM in the maintenance or shaping of organizational culture, with behaviours, beliefs and assumptions shaped through the careful use of, for example, training and development programmes, reward strategies and recruitment and selection policy and practice.

Images of the person and of organizations

Before considering the strengths and weaknesses of any specific change model or process, it is important to consider the image of the person that lies within it, implicitly or explicitly. At first, this might appear to be a rather esoteric consideration. However, a considerable debate has raged among researchers and practitioners over this question. Perhaps the most widely known clash has already been mentioned earlier in this chapter, around challenges to Scientific Management. It has been argued that the images of the person associated with Scientific Management include that of a 'cog within a machine', with little or no attention paid to the personal and social needs of the individual: workers are 'hired hands', the 'industrial brawn' which needs to be lead by the 'industrial brains' or 'thinking elite' within the organization, the managers. Pioneering work by researchers such

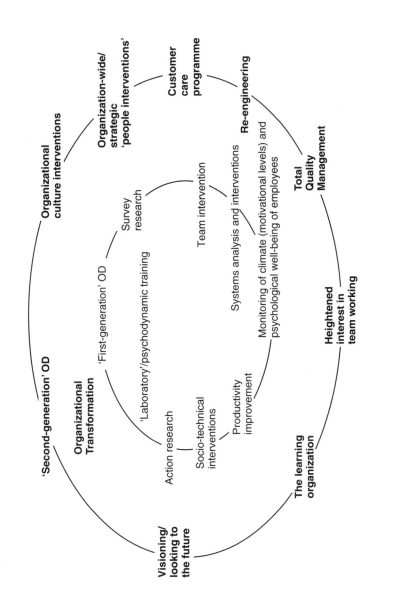

'Second-generation' OD

Organizational
Transformation

'First-generation' OD

Organizational
culture interventions

Organization-wide/
strategic
'people interventions'

Customer
care
programme

Re-engineering

Total
Quality
Management

Heightened
interest in
team working

The learning
organization

Visioning/
looking to
the future

'Laboratory'/psychodynamic training

Survey
research

Team intervention

Systems analysis and interventions

Monitoring of climate (motivational levels) and
psychological well-being of employees

Productivity
improvement

Socio-technical
interventions

Action research

Figure 9.10   First and second-generation organization development.

as the Australian George Elton Mayo highlighted the importance of group dynamics and interpersonal relationships in the workplace. Spurred on by such studies, alternative images of the employee that challenged this then dominant view and, specifically, the 'Human Relations' school emerged, within which employees were considered to be self-motivated with a wish to be self-fulfilled (see Buchanan and Huczynski, 1997; French and Bell, 1995 for more detailed accounts).

Similarly, there are many who would argue that 'human resource management' as modelled and practised often reflects an instrumental view of employees, with people merely malleable and expendable resources. Furthermore, it would be fair to say that too often, what is 'espoused best practice' for the management of change using HRM-based strategies does little more than mirror the worst excesses of Scientific Management, with people regarded as expendable, merely costs on the balance sheet. However, as with HRM practice generally, there is a continuum of HRM-based approaches to change that can be identified and different issues and problems are likely to be tackled in different ways.

Clearly, organizational development is only one example of a category of people-centred change intervention. There are a number of general and HR-specific approaches to management, many of them discussed in more detail earlier in the book, and these management approaches all have implications for HR policy, line managers and the successful management of change. Moreover, each of these approaches will possess specific underlying assumptions and also different forms of potential resistance to change.

Let us take the example of a team-working-based total quality management. It is assumed that individuals can and should be allowed the autonomy to make decisions about quality relating to the tasks that they are allocated and to select the appropriate means to make good most of the deficiencies in quality where necessary. Previously, a supervisor would have undertaken the role of controlling quality.

Sources of resistance to change may lie with:

- **supervisors** who may lose their seniority or who find their jobs significantly re-modelled;
- **employees** who:
  - regard taking on additional responsibilities as additional work without additional pay;
  - may be uncomfortable with the new team-working approaches;
- **trade unions** who will share and promote a number of employee concerns, including:
  - reductions in traditional lines of demarcation;
  - the introduction of new work practices which reduce the opportunities for union representatives to act as a liaison between management and employees;
  - changes to work practice which may potentially reduce headcount;
- **line managers** who are concerned that their authority, as well as parts of their job, are being devolved down the line.

Clearly, there are changes in the tasks people have to complete, and changes in expectations, relationships and individual responsibilities. In this instance, the management of change will need to include a range of activities which may help to address the concerns that stakeholders have. Moreover, there are significant implications for HR policy and practice, many of which are outlined in Figure 9.3, which include making the following considerations:

- Have the appropriate **job analyses** for the new roles and responsibilities been undertaken?
- Have new **person specifications** been drawn up?
- Have adjustments been made to our **recruitment and selection policy and practice**, given the new person specifications?
- What **training and development** activities are needed for employees, supervisors and managers?
- How much of **employee pay and bonuses** should be individually or group based?
- What weighting of **employee performance** should be individually or group assessed?

Resistance to change

Resistance to change is a fact of life. For any change, some will gain from it while others will lose out and the resistance that may occur may reflect this. However, others may resist simply because they are unclear what the likely outcomes of the change will be, so that the source of resistance is grounded in anxiety. Alternatively, it may be that the outcome genuinely cannot be predicted or that the nature of the changes has been communicated poorly.

Sources of resistance to change include:

- Personal losses that will occur as a result of the change, such as status, resources, or autonomy
- Poor communication of the reasons for, and outcomes of, the change, from head office, senior or line managers
- Generalized anxiety about the change: people do not know what the outcomes will be and more specifically, the implications for them
- A preference for the status quo
- Lack of trust by employees of senior members of the organization
- Concern by employees that they will not be able to meet the 'new requirements' of the change; for example, if they are required to work in new ways, especially if they have not received training
- The organizational climate, and the degree of trust or mistrust that exists
- The economic climate and security or insecurity of employment

For those involved in the management of change, it is important to identify:

- the factors that are likely to **drive the change forward**;
- those that are likely to **restrain it**;
- the likely outcome or **equilibrium point** (Lewin, 1947 in Buchanan and Huczynski, 1997).

There is no magic formula for managing resistance to change, as the most appropriate response is determined by a combination of the nature of the resistance and the skills and organizational resources available to the line manager to deal with the situation. Let us take the example of the introduction of an organization-wide initiative to improve performance which is underpinned with new performance appraisal systems where previously there were none. Sources of resistance could include the fear of assessment, fear of having to discuss one's performance formally with the boss or fear of unfair treatment. These anxieties could be managed through:

- **briefing sessions**: letting employees know well in advance of the first appraisal interviews what the process will entail and the safeguards that will be put into place;
- **line manager training** to ensure that managers are clear about how appraisals should be conducted, in terms of both the administrative and the interview process;
- **allowing employees the opportunity to have a say in their appraisal**; for example, being able to formally record how they feel they have performed over a period of time and what has helped or hindered their performance;
- **appeals procedures** for employees who feel that they have been unfairly treated: a safeguard for the employee and an important signal for line managers, regarding their conduct for appraisals.

Within such an approach is the preparation of those affected for the changes that lie ahead, and a sense of control or influence over some of the key activities associated with the change, with a clear idea of the activities that need to be undertaken in order to ensure that the change takes place. In other words, managing resistance can be helped by careful forward planning, management, and the building in of contingencies in case things go wrong.

Line managers need to be aware that resistance to change may not be due to intransigence or fear on the part of colleagues, superiors or subordinates. There are often genuine reasons why people resist change which are not always easily or readily expressed but which may not only have implications for the likely success of the intervention but also serve to highlight areas or issues that have been neglected or overlooked altogether. Care and thorough forward planning will help in the anticipation of likely sources and causes of resistance to change, which has implications also for employee commitment. However, one should also be aware that *inevitably*, some will resist change. If job losses are an option, employees are unlikely to act like 'turkeys voting for Christmas'. Also, for some, if 'new ways of working' are to be introduced, the implication is that the old ways, and also those employees associated with them, are no longer valued. Negative messages will be read by some into any intervention, whether they are stated, implicit or not really there at all.

In all organizations, there are tacit expectations on the part of senior managers, line managers and subordinates: an 'unwritten' contract, often referred to as the 'psychological contract' that exists between the company and employees. (The psychological contract is discussed in more detail in Chapter 3 on generating commitment through involvement and participation processes). Such contracts are rarely acknowledged explicitly, but they are nonetheless understood by both employees and management (Argyris, 1960; Etzioni, 1964).

Often, changes that are introduced into organizations impact in some way upon the psychological contract. This may arise in a variety of ways. For example, it may be that supervisory relationships are recast, or that job security is challenged, or that training and development strategy is altered in some way. In essence the relationship between 'the organization' and the employees, along with mutual expectations, is changed.

However, there may be a 'lag' between the actions of management and the perceptions by employees that the 'rules of the game' have changed. In a number of organizations, the psychological contract is handled explicitly, and rather than hope that there is a gradual realization that, say, security of tenure is no longer the company policy, a range of actions are taken to ensure that clear policy statements are developed and backed by a coherent practice, underpinned with guidelines for line managers and employees.

Nonetheless, there are many instances of where such approaches still fail to persuade. This might arise for a variety of reasons.

- The company's managers may be sending out 'mixed messages'. So for example, written policy outlines one managerial position, while line managers behave in a manner that contradicts this.
- HRM systems that have been developed within systems and strategies prior to the change remain unaltered after it. For example, performance review systems developed for assessment of individual employees remain unaltered in the face of new team-working practices.
- The nature of the proposed changes are difficult to accept (e.g. increased job insecurity) and employees resist the change psychologically. This psychological resistance may manifest itself in a variety of ways, obvious or hidden.
- The management of the activities needed to facilitate the transition is handled badly, resulting in inconsistencies of implementation across the organization, amd more mixed messages.

Figure 9.11 The psychological contract.

The 'Shadowlands' of change: coping with anxiety and stress

One way in which complex ideas and relationships have been represented for thousands of years is through stories of one kind or another. You may be familiar with the Greek myths, some of which have been identified as graphic illustrations of the political, social and moral realities of the times. For example, in the story of the Judgment of Paris, while Paris slept he dreamt that the god Mercury appeared to him demanding which of three goddesses was the most beautiful – an allegory for the political choices and discord associated with the Trojan War.

Allegories, analogies, metaphors and proverbs – they all allow us to highlight specific aspects of characteristics or issues, which may be complex, and then figuratively, in words or pictures, tell us something about a situation, but also about the ways in which the 'storyteller' chooses to make sense of things.

One saying frequently heard in relation to the management of change is, 'You can't make an omelette without breaking eggs'. One interpretation of this might be that in the transformation from one thing to another, you may have to change things by breaking or undoing them. A more cynical view is that it is not inanimate objects, but people, who *need* to feel the pain of change: no pain, no gain. However, those on the receiving end of change management programmes often feel less as if the sacrifice is worthy as they are being led to the promised land, and more like soldiers in the blood bath of the First World War: stressed, tired, scared; merely dispensable cannon fodder in the push to gain ground in the battlefield of organizational life.

Irrespective of the reasons for a change, whether it is to improve 'organizational well-being' as in the case of traditional organizational development, or radical strategic change, employees are not always treated as carefully as they should be.

There are a range of factors that can result in anxiety and stress among employees, some of which are inevitable, but also those that can and should be anticipated and better managed.

The point at which work becomes challenging, healthy pressure for one employee but unmanageable and stress inducing in another varies between individuals, according to factors such as one's personality and other predispositions: willingness and ability to complete a job, and the degree of control the employee feels he or she is gaining or losing. Traditionally, stress has been described as a legacy of primitive physiological 'flight or fight' responses. Specifically, in work organizations, we often do not have the option to do either, and therefore become distressed. Engineering analogies have been used, where each individual reaches a 'breaking point' beyond coping with challenges or pressure and becomes stressed. In reality, stress is channelled through the physiological and the psychological, brought about by factors such as a personal predisposition which results in an inability to cope, specific events, or factors such as an excessive workload, excessive noise, a bullying boss, or having to do things in a way that runs counter to your natural predisposition. It can manifest itself in many ways, such as an inability to think clearly, make decisions or manage emotions. Other indicators include heightened blood pressure, sleep disorders, eating disorders, and maladaptive behaviours such as excessive drinking and smoking, and behaving 'out of character'. How precisely it manifests itself varies from person to person: what is likely to be common to those experiencing stress is **the anticipation of imminent psychological disorder**. This is not to suggest that one experiences major clinical breakdown such as depression or burnout (though these can occur), but simply that it becomes difficult to cope. See Figure 9.12 for a cautionary tale.

Sources of stress

There are many sources of stress, often referred to as **stressors** (see Figure 9.13). These include:

- **psychological and social factors**, such as negative team dynamics, uncertainties or confusion about the employer–employee relationship (for example in the psychological contract), or personal dispositions or vulnerabilities.
- The **work environment** (such as excessive noise or heat, or physical and chemical hazards) which has the potential to affect all employees.

It was Saturday morning in executive land. Michael, a top-flight, 55 year-old manager was breakfasting late with his daughters. "Your mother tells me," he said, turing to his 23-year-old, "that you have been burning the candle at both ends – work all day and play all night. It won't do you any good in the end," he chided her gently. "And what about you, Dad?" she replied. "When are you going to slow down?"

"In this business," he said, "it's like riding a bicycle. If you stop pedalling, you fall off. But I'm planning to retire when I'm 60 and then we can do all the things your mother and I have been dreaming of together. And now – once I've cleared my desk – I'm going to have a game of tennis!"

Three hours later the phone rang. It was the hospital. Michael had suffered a massive heart attack on the tennis court and had died by the time he reached the hospital. His last check-up had found nothing wrong with him, except exhaustion and a touch too much cholesterol. His wife is sure that it was work that killed him.

What are we doing to ourselves? Consider these numbers: 42 per cent of all workers feel "used up" by the end of the day; 69 per cent would like to live a more relaxed life; parents spend 40 per cent less time with their children than they did 30 years ago; the rise in per capita consumption in the last 20 years is 45 per cent, but the decrease in the quality of life, as measured by the Index of Social Health, is 51 per cent; only 21 per cent of the young now think they have a very good chance of achieving "the good life", com-

pared with 41 per cent 20 years ago.

We already work longer, but not necessarily better, than every other country in Europe. Thirty six per cent of non-manual staff work more than 48 hours every week. In a survey of managers by the Institute of Management, 77 per cent considered their hours were stressful, 77 per cent worried about the effect on their families and 74 per cent about their relationship with their partner. Stress, they say, costs us 40 million working days a year and £7bn.

So why do we do it? It can't be to increase efficiency. If it were, we would be out-performing the Germans by more than 10 per cent, because we work much longer than they do. Could it be that we actually prefer our work to the other bits of our lives, or was Michael right in thinking that if once you relax, you'll be lost forever? Have we exchanged the over-comfortable cushion of the lifetime job for the philosophy of a corporate marketplace in which you are only as good as your last project or report, where the best will thrive and the less good will be ejected? Have we decided that creative destruction, the principle at the heart of market capitalism, is also appropriate to its people, and that for the best to grow, the rest must be neglected?

If this is what is happening, the consequences are worrying. Leaving aside the stress which inevitably follows, a market philosophy within the firm will encourage people to look first to their own interests and their own skins, and only second to the firm for which they work. The short term will dominate

their thinking, while the competition for personal recognition will splinter group loyalties and make cooperation even more difficult than it already is.

More insidiously, people will lose their objectivity over time, as they focus down more narrowly on the immediate task, losing touch with the world outside, the markets beyond their focus and the way more ordinary mortals think and feel. Insensitivity is as bad for business as it is for relationships. "Blinkered, bigoted and boring" was the comment by a group of friends on one of their number who was flying high in his corporation. It could have been jealousy, but was more likely to be a prediction of problems to come. Who would want to live with, or work for, a boring, blinkered bigot?

Corporate Darwinism, the survival of the fittest, has much to commend it as a personnel philosophy in uncertain times, when even the wisest would find it hard to predict what skills will be most needed in the future, or who will succeed. But individuals, like new species, need a modicum of protection to allow them to grow, and they need space and time in which to do it. Learning, moreover, is largely a matter of experimentation, mistakes and honest reflection. If we punish the mistakes too heavily or allow too little time for reflection, the experimentation will disappear as we seek to play it safe.

We would do well to remember the axiom of William Gore, founder of W L Gore, who said that mistakes "above the water-line" are the things we learn from; it is only the ones "below the waterline" that sink the ship.

Figure 9.12   Life's a job and then you die. *Source:* Handy (1997).

- Lack of fit between the individual and the work group or the work environment (person–environment fit, where 'the environment' may be the physical environment, the 'psychological environment' of psychological and social factors, or both), referred to as **the person–environment (P–E) fit** (Van Harrison in Cooper and Payne, 1978; EU Working Time Directive, 1998).
- **Poor HRM policy and practice**, such as poor work design or employee-unfriendly shift patterns.
- **Factors that originate outside the workplace** but influence work performance (for example, pressures at home such as financial problems or marital difficulties).

It can be seen from this list that a number of stressors may be due to vulnerabilities of the individual or factors that originate from home life. However, there are also clearly a number of areas that lie within the remit and responsibility of the managers of organizations, practically, ethically and legally. In the United Kingdom, the latter is reflected in the employer's duty to provide a safe system of work, and through European Health and Safety legislation, which requires employees to undertake no more than 48 hours work a week (there is both UK and US data that suggests that working in excess of this significantly increases the likelihood of suffering from cardio-vascular disease (Kasl in Cooper and Payne, 1978 and EU Health and Safety Directive, 1998)).

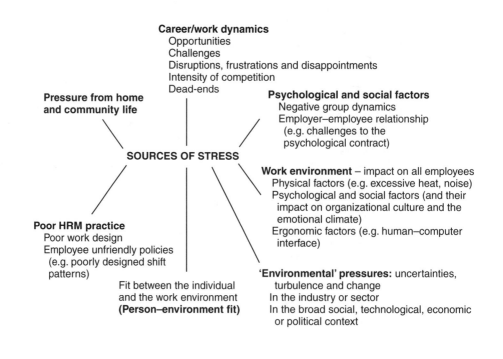

Figure 9.13 Sources of stress.

Managing stress – a shared responsibility

HRM inputs can have a critical role in the moderation of potential stressors in the workplace through activities such as job design, training and development, and policy development in the areas of codes of conduct to moderate culture and climate and contracts of employment. However, all too often, the management of stress is at the margins of activity undertaken only when stress has taken hold. And although the value of occupational health specialists, stress counselling (face-to-face or telephone-based Employee Assistance Programmes or EAPs) can and do play a vital role (see Figure 9.14), their use primarily is when the stress has already caused the damage to employee health and morale. At worst, stress management may be ignored altogether and, too often, its victims are stigmatized as suffering because of personal frailties, as 'stress is for wimps'.

Within the context of the management of change in particular, there is often an opportunity to manage the change that helps to moderate the impact and make it less stressful for employees. Across an organization, this could entail audits of employee morale, training and heightening the awareness of employees and managers to detect and manage stress in themselves and in others, and reviews of HRM policy and practice and its impact on physical and psychological well-being. But what about the detail of what can be done? In one small study, it was found that the profile of the sources of stress was characteristic of an organization although the individual stressors were rarely unique to it (Cornelius and Duignan, 1996). The greatest source of difference was the attitude held towards stress

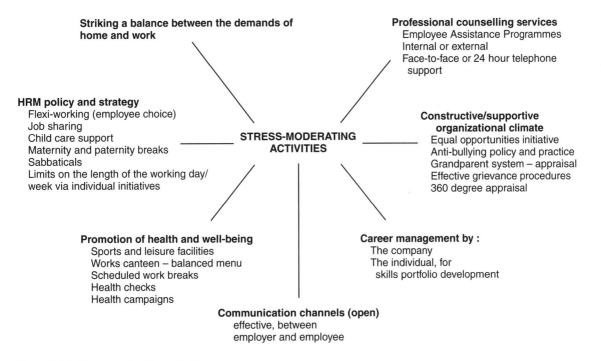

Figure 9.14   Stress-moderating activities.

and its management and, at its most mature, this was represented as a shared responsibility between management and employees and a reality that required *proactive* management, not a laissez faire approach or outright denial and avoidance.

A constructive, organization-wide policy towards the management of stress provides a sound framework in which individual managers can deal with stress-related issues as they arise in themselves or among their subordinates. Indeed, managers have a central role in the management of organizational stress, as it is through their example and their actions that team climate and attitudes towards stress are fostered. Moreover, it is through the line management application of HRM policy and practice (for example, the volume and type of work that employees have to undertake) that stress can be moderated.

Agents for change: Expanding roles and responsibilities for the line manager

We have already outlined some of the environmental changes that are likely to make their mark on organizations. Many of these have potentially a significant impact on what is expected of the line manager. For example, many HRM departments have been downsized or downgraded to more basic operations and HRM activities largely automated or outsourced (Millward *et al.*, 1992). Increasingly therefore, managers are required to undertake HRM activities that would have more traditionally been undertaken by specialist staff (Brewster and Hegewisch, 1994; Millward *et al.*, 1992). The implication of the latter in particular is that line managers are more likely to be required to deliver or coordinate activities such as training and development and recruitment and selection, and have a more central role in performance management.

Many aspects of the nature of the jobs of managers and their relationship to others are likely to change. This includes functional and role redesignation, change at key interfaces such as those between subordinates, superiors, and the 'home and community' domain, and the role of change facilitator. The facilitation of change is something in which, traditionally, line managers have had a subordinate role: specialist change interventionists or agents set out the strategy and define the nature of the interventions and their management, down to the operational details. Increasingly, there is a realization that change interventions succeed or fail on the ability of organizations to marshall more explicitly their line managers as an integral and driving force in the management of change, rather than being regarded as a barrier to change, a difficult group to be changed or an adjunct to the real efforts of change interventions.

Some managers may have a designated role in the management of change (for example, they may be required to train staff); it could be argued that it is more likely that their role will be about facilitating change in a different way. Specifically, this is likely to centre around *the management of the anticipations, uncertainty and outcomes of change.*

Pressures on the line manager

So far, we have discussed the issue of stress in general terms. However, there is an increasing awareness of the **stresses associated with change that concern line managers in particular** (see Figures 9.15a and 9.15b).

Corporate downsizing and delayering have placed progressively heavy burdens on the shoulders of line managers, who are having to make do with fewer employees and other resources. Furthermore, there are a number of dilemmas that line managers may face as a result of change interventions. You may be aware of stories of line managers who feel uneasy at the demands that they are required to place on their subordinates, or are uneasy as they are being asked by Personnel to decide who should be retained or made redundant. Some of the stress that may result from these or other equally difficult decisions may arise because of their newness: a manager may not have had to make such decisions before. Or, having built a good team spirit, there may be genuine concern that all this hard work will be undermined, both for those concerned about their job security before the axe falls and, as well as the 'survivors', those who remain after the redundancies have taken place. The relationship between a manager and his or her subordinates is altered in a way that leaves both sides feeling uncomfortable.

Whether they like it or not, most employees will expect that their line managers will to some extent be able to influence a situation, no matter how apparently hopeless the cause. This **influencing role** has less to do with the formal expectations of the administrative and decision-making roles that managers have and is more concerned with the **inspirational character** that **leadership** entails (Zalesnik, 1977). Leaders require followers and if employees feel that their corner is not being fought, their commitment is likely to wane rapidly.

It is important that line managers themselves prepare adequately for change, particularly if the nature of the changes is likely to generate anxiety and stress. For example, interviewing is never easy but giving someone the bad news that he or she has been made redundant is a particularly difficult task, and many line managers would benefit from specialist guidance and training. In addition, one has to be prepared to **set personal boundaries**.

- What is it that it can be reasonably expected that you could be asked to do?
- Are there some actions that you have been asked to undertake that lie outside your experience? What guidance and help can the organization provide?
- Have any of your colleagues gone through such experiences previously? What help and guidance can they provide?
- How will you respond if asked to do something that you consider to be wrong or unethical?

Change, role choice and the line manager

For the line manager, change and its management is likely to exert its presence on him or her in a variety of ways. One way in which this can be examined is by considering the *roles* that managers may choose or be required to adopt which can

In the cult of delayering, middle managers were the chosen sacrifice. Now research suggests that it may all have been a mistake. By Roger Trapp

In recent years, middle managers have become corporate whipping boys. Generally accused of intransigence and unreasonable loyalty to the old ways, they are blamed for putting up barriers that prevent senior executives communicating their go-getting visions to the rank and file.

But new research from the Cranfield School of Management offers a few crumbs of hope to this much-maligned species. Steven Floyd claims his studies show that far from being corporate dinosaurs and a burden on company resources, middle managers can play an important strategic role.

"Companies engaged in across-the-board downsizing and delayering may be throwing the baby out with the bath water," Floyd says. "They are ridding themselves of what they think is dead wood but are in fact losing vital strategic capability.

"Ironically, restructuring is linked with re-engineering but, in ditching middle managers,

companies are losing the very people who have capacity to re-engineer its processes."

Floyd, associate professor of strategic management at Connecticut University and a visiting professor at Cranfield, has identified four strategic roles for middle managers; championing innovative initiatives, facilitating adaptability to new behaviour, synthesising information (both within and outside the organisation) and implementing strategy.

How well middle managers perform these roles has a direct bearing on a company's overall ability to pursue its strategies and maintain its competitive advantage, according to the professor.

Moreover, the study of 250 managers in 25 organisations highlights the importance of middle management involvement in the formulation of new strategies as well as in the implementation of existing strategies, says Floyd, who – with Bill Wooldridge – has written a book, The Strategic Middle Manager (published last year by Jossey Bass), that explains why the old model of middle management no longer works.

They conclude: "Organisations need to understand the

potential strategic value of middle management. They cannot rely solely on top managers to create successful strategies as they are often not sufficiently in touch with changes in the market or in technology.

"Instead, alternative strategies need to emerge from the middle up: top management's role is to recognise when a good strategy comes along and find the resources to support it." they write.

The suggestion that middle managers are not necessarily as doomed as has been thought should come as a welcome surprise to young people who have been brainwashed into thinking they are being prepared for a world with no promise of work.

Eighty-one per cent of final-year undergraduates feel insecure about the world of work, according to a survey published today by recruitment specialists Reed Graduates. Even once they find work, more than half remain insecure in their first jobs.

Yet about half of final-year students are excited about the world of work and nearly 90 per cent feel they will gain work with opportunities for advancement.

Figure 9.15a Stress control and intervention activities: 'Defending the middle ground'. *Source:* The Independent, 19 June 1997.

facilitate or impede change. Examples of the roles that managers may take on include the following:

● **Role of leader**: Much of the literature on the management of change in organizations focuses in particular on the leadership qualities of managers. It is certainly an important consideration: at times of uncertainty, clear leadership is vital, especially for subordinates. Specifically, for most employees, the work group is regarded as a *psychologically significant group* (Tannenbaum and Davies, 1969 in French and Bell, 1995). Therefore, it is a potential source of stability, self-esteem, support and friendship. With work groups, roles, responsibilities and behaviour are shaped by it and it also greatly influences the way in which work group members relate to the requirements of the organization,

Today's managers are stressed out, kept in the dark by their seniors and suffer from constant insecurity about their jobs, according to a new survey which aims to track the progress of 5,000 managers over five years.

The Quality of Working Life, produced by Professors Les Worrall and Cary Cooper of the University of Manchester Institute of Science and Technology (UMIST), in conjunction with the Institute of Management, found that two out of three British managers in companies of all sizes had coped with organisational restructure in the past year.

Professor Cooper, who lectures in organisational psychology, said managers' low morale was directly linked to the stress of rapid change. "We are moving into a short-term contract, freelance culture. The next generation might get used to that, but the problem is with people in their thirties, forties and fifties. Job insecurity levels, even among senior management, are quite high," he said.

"There has been a lot of downsizing, which has caused enormous problems. It's worse than the 1980s enterprise era when the stress was self-induced. What we have been seeing is more worrying, because the stress is not in people's control."

The survey, funded by the Post Office, garnered 1,361 replies and found that two-thirds of British households had two working partners. One-third of households comprises partners who both work full time. Eighty-two per cent of managers reported that they regularly worked more than 40 hours per week, with 41 per cent often taking work home at weekends. Meanwhile, nearly 65 per cent said they were under constant time pressure; a similar percentage said they felt guilty for staying in bed because of illness.

Peter Khoury of International Consulting Services said top managers should set an example. "Communication is critical. It's more than e-mail or a newsletter; it's the way you behave. What does that say to the people who look up to you?"

He said his company, which provided staff with a counselling service, free sports club membership and medical cover, tried to encourage managers' competencies over and above hard-line objectives.

Roger Young, an Institute of Management director, added: "Managers are somewhat down in the mouth. Top bosses need to find the balance between meeting individual and company needs."

Professor Cooper said the survey produced two surprising results: a high proportion of male managers (one in four) are now given paid paternity leave; but despite the technology revolution, just four per cent of managers work from home.

Information overload was a huge stress-factor for managers, said Professor Cooper, who still managed a 20 per cent response to his 5,000 questionnaires in just three weeks. "What we need is to manage the new technology rather than let the new technology manage us. We have to see how to prioritise our e-mails, the Internet and mobile phones."

He predicted companies would become more family-friendly and flexible towards working hours in the coming years. "These are critical years for Britain. We have revolutionised our industry; we now have to manage our human resources so they don't burn out," he said.

Figure 9.15b Stress control and intervention activities: 'Too much pressure?' *Source:* Independent on Sunday, 19 October 1997.

be it positively, negatively or with indifference. More generally, for certain organizational change interventions, changes to leadership (or more generally, management style) are often *central* to the change. Moreover, the members of the line manager's team will often expect him or her to defend their interests.

- **Role of catalyst**: Depending upon the nature of the intervention, line managers may have a central, *transforming* role in change interventions. This may be achieved in a number of ways, including facilitating change awareness and competence of subordinates, passing on skills, knowledge and expertise to enable subordinates to change their work practices, or simply making subordinates more comfortable with and accepting of change.

- **Role of gatekeeper**: Managers may be required to undertake a 'gate keeping' role that requires them to act as a conduit for directives and information that is passed directly or indirectly from the top of the organizational hierarchy through to the managers' subordinates. This is often paradoxical, as the role may be viewed in a variety of ways: as an important mechanism for the transmission of new ideas and practices, as key negotiators between senior management and workers or as an *important communications conduit* but also as a source of conflict and tension, with the manager cast as 'player-manager' or 'piggy in the middle', attempting to satisfy the sometimes conflicting needs of subordinates and superiors. The compromises struck in order to satisfy the needs of the various stakeholders requires more than the ability to 'obey orders': political skills and fixes and 'unofficial' actions are, in practice, often the only way of maintaining a difficult balancing act. In the extreme, official or unofficial middle management intransigence may be how managers respond to decisions made up the hierarchy that are a source of anxiety, threat or hostility to themselves or their subordinates.
- **Role of organizational symbol**: For many change interventions, the manager is an important, symbolic focal point, signalling some significant departure from a previously held position. Positive symbolic roles designated to managers include that of 'hero', 'saviour' or 'champion', while more negative implicit roles include 'Luddite' and 'old timer'. The symbolism is often reflected in the rhetorical position of the organization, which can be interpreted in a cynical, pejorative sense or in a noble, aspirational one (Sims *et al.*, 1993).
- **Role of 'mobster'**: This is a more manipulative, negative role, in which the manager is cast as a 'heavy', a bodyguard who is expected to protect the interests of the organization, whatever it takes; a position sanctioned directly or indirectly by senior management. It is expected that if initial persuasion fails, subordinates 'deserve whatever they get', and officially or unofficially, tangible or psychological rewards are offered to the compliant or those viewed as desirable by the organization, while intimidation, punishment, insecurity and the threat of or actual job losses are meted out to those who are not.

These and other possible roles are summarized in Figure 9.16. The danger for the line manager, especially given the range of roles that could be undertaken, is that the roles become ambiguous, come into conflict with one another or overload the line manager through sheer weight of numbers, resulting in role overload, ambiguity, confusion, and ultimately stress, unless clarity about which role combination will work is achieved.

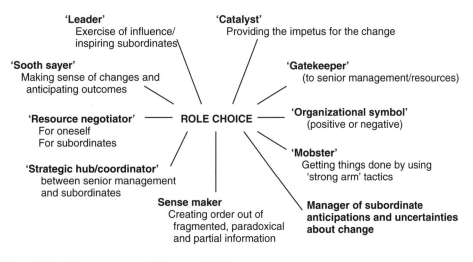

Figure 9.16   Line managers and change: role change.

Conclusion

Changing our 'psychological maps'

Managing change in organizations is an activity that all line managers will have some involvement with. Ultimately, changing the way people behave, believe or think is never a straightforward or, indeed, a necessarily viable task. Sometimes, it may prove simply too difficult for employees to do things differently, and hard decisions will need to be made about redeployment or even outsourcing.

Everybody has his or her own way of viewing and understanding the world – his or her own personal construct system – in which beliefs and values, uniquely held or to some degree shared with others, will determine the likely acceptance and commitment towards change or reluctance or rejection of it (Kelly, 1991). The outcome of many change interventions is to help employees see that it is possible to see and do things differently, resulting in the loosening up or even the reconstruction of key parts of these construct systems, our personal road map of how to make sense of the world around us. Many also struggle because some people genuinely find it easier than others to cope with limited information and limited structure, while others find it difficult to create their own or share in others' alternative scenarios of the future. Understanding that these difficulties may manifest themselves in a variety of ways, including stress and resistance to change, is something that needs to be understood, anticipated and proactively managed.

Evaluation before the change

However, this is not merely a theoretical debate about how and why we do or do not change. There are many practical activities, such as the assessment of preparedness for change, stakeholder analysis and careful planning, which are essential to the design, development and implementation of change interventions. You should draw up a list of questions if you or your organization is contemplating or actively planning change initiatives, in order to assist your understanding and to help you plan. The list below is a distillation of such considerations that appear throughout this chapter. You should:

- **understand the nature of the change and the reasons for it**;
- **assess the preparedness** of relevant stakeholders, including yourself;
- be clear about the sources of, and reasons for, **resistance to change**;
- assess the **costs and benefits** of change overall, and for specific stakeholders;
- identify mechanisms for **coping with anxiety and uncertainties**;
- develop a **changeover plan**. What is in place to help cope with the change from, for example, an old to a new way of working? Will you need to keep the old systems in place for some time, either while the changeover progresses or in order to ensure that there is the necessary backup?
- **clarify roles and responsibilities** in relation to the intervention, and those that will be required or will emerge as a result of the intervention;
- identify which **other functional activities related to the change**, directly or indirectly, will also need to be addressed/reviewed and how;
- assess what **contributions** the organization expects **the line manager to make** towards the change: what contributions will you need in practice to undertake in order to manage change in your patch?
- undertake **contingency planning** and **potential problem analysis**: what needs to be put in place?
- consider how you will **evaluate** and **monitor** the development, progress and outcomes of the change;
- evaluate what **the HRM contribution** should be in order **to help facilitate the change**, through established or new policies and practice.

Towards a human resource management-based model of organizational change

HRM policy and practice may facilitate change or provide the primary basis for it. So, for example, a change intervention targeted at changing customer care practice may draw on a range of activities to facilitate the change, such as training and development events, and alterations to the reward and appraisal systems. By contrast, a directive to improve the quantity and change the nature of training and development activities is not only an HRM-grounded initiative but will also be facilitated through training and development (i.e. HRM) based policies, procedures and activities.

Figure 9.17 contains a schema which represents an idealized version of **a human resource management-based model of organizational change**. The reasons for, or **drivers of, change** reside in one or more **organizational domains**, from the

DOMAINS OF CHANGE: CORPORATE POLICY AND HRM POLICY
SOURCE OF CHANGE STRATEGY AND STRATEGY DRIVERS

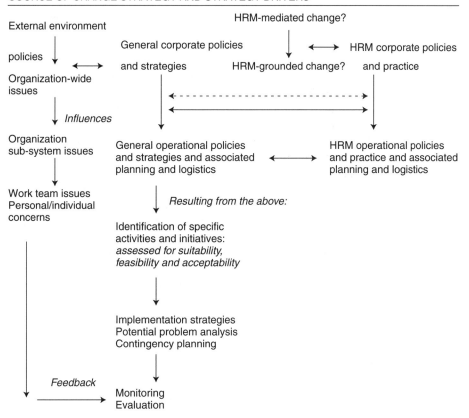

Figure 9.17   A human resource management-based scheme of organizational change.

external environment through to the individual (most often, 'the individual' is likely to be a senior manager or executive). These drivers lead to **development of general corporate policy and strategy** of which either an integral element or a retrospective development is associated HRM corporate policy and strategy. The precise nature of the HRM policy and strategy will in part be determined by whether the change desired is to be **HRM mediated** or **HRM grounded**.

In turn, what results from these will be **general and HRM-based operational policy and strategy**, for which a timetable and sequence of key events, planning and logistics need to be developed.

The precise nature of the policies, strategies and plans that are developed is '**contextual**', and it is only against contextual factors such as time scales and resources available that **fitness for purpose** can be evaluated.

Summary

Changes in the external environment of organizations have resulted in a number of changes within organizations. A range of change interventions is available to help facilitate change, but which ones are appropriate to given specific circumstances, and why? Issues such as the range and scale of change were discussed and the pros and cons of particular types of intervention evaluated. In addition, we considered how line managers can help, hinder and proactively facilitate the effective management of change, and assess the likely success of change programmes *before* they happen.

The role of HRM in the development of organizational strategy and indeed, more proactive approaches to strategic HRM were introduced. The reasons why the impact of HRM on strategy processes often fails, and the ways in which a clearer role can be made for HRM within organizational strategy, were considered also.

Change may result in anxiety and stress for some. Attention was paid to how stress can be moderated and managed for the line manager and the subordinate. Although the actions that can be taken by individuals were considered, the roles and responsibilities that can and should be taken by the organization were suggested also. Finally, the relationship between change management and HRM strategy, policy and practice was outlined.

Questions

Review

1   You have been asked to introduce major revisions to your organization's Business Process Re-engineering programme for your work team, one year after BPR's initial introduction. What are the main considerations you make in order to ensure effective take-up of this management initiative?
2   A company's head office has decided to reduce the head count in your department by 30 per cent over the next 18 months as part of an attempt to recoup financial losses. What are the implications for managing work teams?
3   Can organizations be made ready for change? Discuss.
4   How could the strategic impact of HRM be improved?
5   How should major change interventions be assessed and why?
6   Many ethical dilemmas may arise for the manager responsible for managing a change programme; identify some of these given the material in this chapter, and consider how the organization might act to anticipate these.

Project-based activities

1   Identify case examples or short accounts of change interventions in books, journals, newspapers or on the Internet.
     (a) What appear to be the most popular types of intervention? Why do you think this is so?

(b) What is not said within these cases and accounts that would provide you with a more rounded insight into the 'real story' of change?

2 Choose a major strategic change intervention that has taken place or is taking place in your organization. Gather information around the following:

(a) How was the strategic change communicated? What were the strengths and weaknesses?

(b) Who were/are the key stakeholders? What influence are they able to exert over the intervention and will they be able to affect the change, officially or unofficially and if so, how?

(c) Overall, what were the strengths and weaknesses of the strategic change?

(d) How could the intervention have been improved? Are there issues that have never been resolved to the satisfaction of specific stakeholders? How were/should these have been dealt with?

(e) Outline and evaluate the contribution made by (i) line managers and (ii) HRM specialists to the development and implementation of the organizational strategy.

3 (a) What are the sources of stress that you are aware of (i) for employees, (ii) for managers, in your organization?

(b) How could the HRM function help combat stress?

References

Argyris, C (1960) *Understanding Organizational Behaviour*, Dorsey Press, Homewood, Ill.

Arkin, A (1997) Hold the production line. *People Management* February, 22–7.

Becker, BE and Huselid, MA (1998) High performance work systems: A synthesis of research and managerial implications. *Research in Personnel and Human Resources Management*, 16, 53–101.

Beckhard, R (1969) *Organization Development: strategies and models*, Addison-Wesley, Reading, Mass.

Brewster, CJ and Hegewisch, A, eds (1994) *Policy and practice in European human resource management: The Price Waterhouse Cranfield survey*, Routledge, London.

Buchanan, D and Huczynski, A (1997) *Organizational Behaviour*, 3rd edition, Prentice-Hall, Hemel Hempstead.

Burke, W (1982) cited in French, WL and Bell, CH (1995) *Organization Development: Behavioural science interventions for organization improvement*, Prentice-Hall, Englewood Cliffs , NJ.

Carnall, C (1990) *Managing Change in Organisations*, Prentice-Hall, Hemel Hempstead.

Collis, DJ and Montgomery, CA (1995) Competing on resources: strategy in the 1990s. *Harvard Business Review*, July–August, 119–28.

Cornelius, NE and Duignan, K (1996) HRM and the stress paradox: models of the person and the organisation. Conference proceedings, Open University Business School International Conference 'HRM – The inside story', Milton Keynes.

Cummings, TG and Huse, EF (1989) *Organizational Development and Change*, 4th edition, West Publishing, Minnesota.

Dawson, P (1994) *Organizational change: a processual approach*, Paul Chapman, London.

Etzioni, A (1964) *Modern Organizations*, Prentice-Hall, Englewood Cliffs, NJ.

European Union (1998) Working Time Directive.

Fitz Enz, J (1990) *Human value management*, Jossey Bass, London.

French, WL, and Bell, CH (1995) *Organization Development: Behavioural science interventions for organization improvement*, Prentice-Hall, Englewood Cliffs, NJ.

Ghoshal, S and Bartlett, CA (1995) Changing the role of top management: beyond structure to processes. *Harvard Business Review*, January–February, 87–96.

Grant, RM (1991) The resource based theory of competitive advantage: implications for strategy formation. *California Management Review*, 33, 3.

Guest, DE (1987) Human Resource Management and Industrial Relations. *Journal of Management Studies*, 24, 5:48–51.

Hamel, G and Prahalad, CK (1993) Strategy as stretch and leverage. *Harvard Business Review*, March–April, 75–84.

Handy, C (1997) Lifes a job and then you die. *The Director*.

Kasl, S (1978) Epidemiological contributions to the study of work stress. In *Stress at Work* eds C Cooper, and RL Payne, John Wiley & Sons, Chichester.

Kelly, GA (1991) *A theory of personality: the psychology of personal constructs*, Routledge, London.

Legge, K (1995) *Human Resource Management: Rhetorics and realities*, Macmillan, Basingstoke.

Lepac, DP and Snell, SA (1999) The human resource architecture: Toward a theory of human capital allocation and development. *Academy of Management Review*, 24:1, 31–48.

Levy, A and Merry, U (1986) *Organizational Transformation*, Praeger, New York.

Lewin, K (1947) cited in Buchanan, D and Huczynski, A (1997) *Organizational Behaviour*, 3rd edition, Prentice-Hall, Hemel Hempstead.

Lundy, O and Cowling, A (1996) *Strategic Human Resource Management*, Routledge, London.

Margulies, N and Raia, AP (1978) *Conceptual Foundations of Organizational Development*, McGraw-Hill, New York.

Miles, RE and Snow, CC (1984) Designing strategic human resource management systems. *Organizational Dynamics*, 13(1): 36–52.

Millward, N, Stevens, M, Smart, D and Hawes, WR (1992) *Workplace Industrial Relations in Transition*, Gower, Aldershot.

Moss Kanter, R (1983) *The Change Masters*, Simon and Schuster, New York.

Odiorne, G (1984) *The Strategic Management of Human Resources: a portfolio approach*, Jossey Bass, San Francisco.

Pascale, R (1990) *Managing on the Edge: how successful companies use conflict to stay ahead*, Penguin, London.

Peters, TJ, and Austin, NK (1985) *A Passion for Excellence*, Random House, New York.

Peters, TJ and Waterman, RH (1982) *In Search of Excellence*, Harper Row, New York.

Porter, ME (1996) What is strategy? *Harvard Business Review*, November–December, 61–78.

Purcell, J (1995) Corporate strategy and its link with human resource management. In *Human Resource Management: A critical text*, ed. J. Storey, Routledge, London.

Purcell, J (1999) Best practice and best fit: chimera or cul de sac. *Human Resource Management Journal* 9:3 26–41.

Quinn, JB, Anderson, P and Finkelstein, S (1996) Managing Professional Intellect: making the most of the best. *Harvard Business Review*, March–April, 71–80.

Rucci, AJ, Kirn, SP and Quinn, RT (1998) The employee-customer-profit chain at Sears. *Harvard Business Review*, January–February, 82–97.

Scott-Jackson, WB (1998) Maximise flexibility, minimise redundancy: Achieving sustainable competitive advantage through organisational and individual change competence. In C Armistead (ed.) *Effective Organisations*, Cassells, London.

Scott-Jackson, WB (1999) *Individual change competence: development of a strategic human resource*, PhD Thesis, Oxford Brookes University.

Schultz, T (1979) cited in Odiorne, G (1984) *The Strategic Management of Human Resources: a portfolio approach*, Jossey Bass, San Francisco.

Sims, D, Fineman, S and Gabriel, Y (1993) *Organizing and Organizations*, Sage.

Stacey, R (1993) *Strategic management: Management and Organisational Dynamics*, Pitman, London.

Storey, J (1995) Human Resource Management: Still marching on or marching out? In *Human Resource Management: A critical text*, ed. J Storey, Routledge, London.

Van Harrison, R (1978) Person–Environment Fit and Job Stress. In *Stress at Work*, eds C Cooper, and RL Payne, Wiley.

Vroom, V (1964) *Work and motivation*, John Wiley, New York.

West, MA, Nickell, S, Patterson, MG and Lawthom, R (1997) *Impact of people management practices on business performance*, IPD, London.

Wright, P, McMahan, G and McWilliams, A (1994) HRM as a competitive advantage: a resource based perspective. *International Journal of Human Resource Management*, 5, 2.

Zalesnik, A (1977) Managers and Leaders: Are they different? *Harvard Business Review*, May–June, 67–78.

Legal briefing

A. The effect of stress at work

Dealing with stress at work is now seen as part of the employer's contractual duty to provide employees with a 'safe system of work'. See the legal briefing to Chapter 1. A number of significant cases have arisen recently, which may be indicative of an increase in stressful situations in the workplace, or may simply reflect an increased willingness on the part of employees to sue. In *Johnstone v. Bloomsbury Area Health Authority* [1992], excessive hours required by the employee's contract led, foreseeably, to physical illness. The employer was judged to be at fault. The judges in the Court of Appeal did not agree on their reasons for their opinion but the soundest reason, arguably, was the failure of the employer to provide a safe system of work. In the later case of *Walker v. Northumberland County Council* [1995], a senior social services manager, who had already suffered one nervous breakdown, was put back to work with inadequate backup staff. He suffered another breakdown which rendered him incapable of further employment. The employer was held liable for failing to do all that was reasonble to protect the health and safety of the employee.

This does pose a problem with regard to staff of managerial level who realize that stress is part of the job and who are, presumably, adequately remunerated for it.

Even in these cases, it would be possible to find an employer liable for physical or mental breakdown through stress where this was foreseeable and adequate precautions were not taken. Connected to this is the problem posed by jobs that are inherently stressful, such as the police, fire service, ambulance service etc. Here the stress is caused not so much by overwork as by the situations that the employees are called upon to deal with. It was at one time suggested that where the stress was exacerbated by the conduct of the employer (as claimed after the Hillsborough Football Stadium disaster), the employer would be legally liable for foreseeable illness or incapacity as a result.

The case of *White v. Chief Constable of West Yorkshire* [1999] illustrates some conflict of policy with the case of *Walker* above. The House of Lords held, by a majority of 3–2, that the police officers present at the Hillsborough football stadium disaster could not recover compensation from their employer for psychiatric injury caused by witnessing harrowing scenes of death and injury. The police authority had already been found negligent in the way that it had attempted to control events on that day, and there was no question concerning liability for death and injury caused to spectators. It remains to be seen how the law relating to non-physical injury, particularly that caused to employees in the course of their employment, will

Continued on page 336

develop in the future. The employer's obligation to provide a safe system of work is briefly referred to in the legal briefing to Chapter 1.

B. The Transfer of Undertakings (Protection of Employment) Regulations, 1981

These Regulations, known colloquially as 'TUPE', were passed as a result of an EU Directive aimed at preserving the contractual rights of employees where the business for which they worked, or part of it, was transferred to another enterprise. The new law signalled a profound shift in traditional thinking on the employment relationship. In essence, where the 'undertaking' is to be transferred to another owner (other than by take-over by share purchase), the employees are automatically transferred with the rest of the assets together with their present contracts (including rights against their former employer) and trade union recognition, if any. The cost of dismissing any of these employees will fall upon the transferee employer, and will be treated as unfair dismissal. The only exception is where the dismissal is for an 'economic, technical or organizational reason', in which case it will be treated as a case of redundancy. This subject is treated at more length in the legal briefing to Chapter 1. One of the more intractable problems to which TUPE has given rise is the harmonization of terms and conditions of employment between groups of employees working for the same employer, where one group has been transferred from another enterprise with statutory protection for their former contracts.

Where part of an undertaking is to be transferred, TUPE will apply as long as that part of the undertaking is discrete and identifiable. Contrary to what the UK government originally understood, the Directive applies to non-commercial as well as commercial enterprises, and the UK law had to be amended to bring it into line with EU law. TUPE therefore applies to the hiving-off of cleaning and catering services by local authorities, hospital trusts, etc. This acted as something of a blow to the policy, implemented by the former Conservative administration, of Compulsory Competitive Tendering (CCT) in the public sector. The intention was to reduce public expenditure by introducing competition into the awarding of service contracts; this goal was more difficult to achieve if successful contractors found themselves the proud employers of the former workforce with their previous contract terms, including pay, intact.

A significant exception to this emerged from a 1997 European Court of Justice case involving a school cleaning contract in Germany. Seven cleaners, including a Mrs Suzen who was the plaintiff in the case, worked for the company that had the cleaning contract. When the contract terminated, it was not renewed but awarded to another company, and the seven cleaners were dismissed. They claimed that this contravened EU law, and that their employment contracts were automatically transferred to the new contractor. The Court held that where there is a transfer of a contract *from one contractor to another*, the Directive requiring the protection of contracts of employment does not automatically apply. It will only apply if the second contractor takes over significant tangible or intangible assets, OR, a major part of the workforce, in terms of their numbers or skills used by the former employer in the performance of the contract. In other words, if the second contractor takes over significant property, or commercial contracts, or a significant part of the workforce, then the contracts of the rest of the employees are automatically transferred as well. The crucial criterion is: does an identifiable entity, including assets and personnel, retain its identity when the transfer takes place? Every case will turn upon its own facts!

This case was only concerned with the transfer of a contract from one contractor to another; it made no pronouncement upon the first contracting-out of services, where, presumably, TUPE still applies. Where a contract is purely of a service character, does not involve the transfer of significant assets and relies upon the services of a largely unskilled workforce, the incoming contractor can avoid TUPE by electing not to take any of them on.

The Employment Relations Act, 1999, has empowered the Secretary of State to make Regulations to clarify further the law relating to TUPE. Some uncertainties have arisen out of the decided cases. In particular, the Regulations should deal with the contracting out of services, with transfers affecting public bodies, and with the situation where the transferee employer wishes to negotiate a change of employment terms with the transferred employees.

It has been held in a recent Court of Appeal case, *Bolwell v. Redcliffe Homes Ltd.* [1999], that employees have a right to be informed of any proposed transfer.

As in the case of collective redundancies (please see legal briefing to Chapter 1), the obligation on the part of the employer to consult with appropriate trades unions on matters relating to a proposed transfer has been extended to elected representatives of the workforce.

The Collective Redundancies and TUPE Amendment Regulations came into force on 28 July 1999. They provide that where there is a recognized trade union, the TU representatives have priority over employee-elected representatives in collective consultations on redundancies and transfers.

C. Patents Act, 1977 – employee rights

This section, and the ones following, is concerned with an area of law known as 'intellectual property'. This briefing will concentrate on the aspects of greatest relevance to the employment relationship, namely patents, copyrights, registered and unregistered designs. These all represent significant asset value to any business, and affect employees who may have contributed to that value by their talents.

The topic has also attracted the attention of the EU, since the exercise of these rights must necessarily detract from free competition in the market. The European policy to date has been to implement a programme of harmonizing measures to ensure that, as far as possible, each member state has in place laws on these matters that do not differ too widely from one another.

To begin with patents: a grant of patent is a very valuable commercial right. It is granted in respect of an invention that is novel, represents an 'inventive step' and can be applied in an industrial context. An application to the Patent Office is subjected to a long period of scrutiny to ensure that the invention complies with the criteria. The process can also be expensive. The advantage gained by a grant of patent is that the patentee obtains a monopoly right to exploit the invention for gain, or to license others to exploit it for a fee. This monopoly lasts for 20 years, and is territorial in application. That is, it operates within the territory for which it is registered, and a patent may be registered in several different countries – for an appropriate fee, of course. The current statute in force in the UK is the Patents Act, 1977, as amended by the Copyrights, Designs and Patents Act, 1988. The 1977 Act brought the UK law into line with the European Patent Convention.

In one respect this Act departs from the provisions of the Convention, in that the rights of employee-inventors are recognized and provided for, although, as will be

seen, this is more apparent than real. The basic legal rule, and a similar provision applies to all intellectual property rights, is that if an employee invents a device or process in the course of his or her employment, the patent right belongs to the employer, and if the employee happens to apply for and be granted a patent in his or her own name, he or she can be required to assign it to the employer.

The Patents Act provides as follows: an employer is entitled to the patent rights where the employee is in the course of his or her duties and the circumstances are such that an invention might reasonably be expected. It may be difficult on occasion to determine when an invention 'might reasonably be expected' from an individual's employment. The problem is illustrated by the pre-Act case of *Electrolux Ltd v. Hudson* [1977], where the defendant, a storeman employed by the plaintiffs, invented in his own time a special adaptor for use in vacuum cleaners. The court rejected the employer's claim for the assignment of the patent rights. If the employee had been a 'general technical advisor', or if the invention had been devised during the employer's time and using his facilities, the outcome might have been different. Employers are well advised to make explicit in employees' contracts exactly what is expected of them as regards inventions, although if a 'blanket' obligation is placed on all employees to assign patent rights to the employer, this may well be struck down as being in unreasonable restraint of trade.

The Act further provides that an employer is entitled to the patent rights where the employee, in the course of his or her employment, has a 'a special obligation to further the interests of the employer's undertaking'. An employee may well fall into both categories, such as the head of an R&D division. This second category will certainly include company directors and senior managers who owe a fiduciary duty to the company, that is, a duty to act in good faith arising from their position of trust within the company.

Perhaps the most controversial part of the Patents Act relates to employees' rights, as distinct from obligations. An employee is entitled to apply for an award of compensation if the patent, having regard to the size and nature of the employer's undertaking (among other things), is of outstanding benefit to the employer. This provision does not apply if there is a collective agreement (between employer and unions) providing for payment to employees in these circumstances. The wording of this section of the Act means that an

Continued on page 338

employee's right to compensation does not depend upon his or her genius and the quality of the invention, but on the overall contribution that the invention makes to the employer's profits. In general, the employee in a large company is less likely than one working in a small company to receive an award under the Act.

In all cases, there is nothing to stop individual employees from entering into a patent-sharing agreement with the employer.

D. Copyright

Unlike a patent, a copyright arises automatically in favour of the creator of a literary, dramatic, musical or artistic work, and lasts for the lifetime of the creator plus 70 years. Again, unlike a patent, copyright does not confer absolute monopoly rights, but only a right to prevent copying. In theory, two individuals could, quite independently of one another, produce the same, or a very similar, book, article, play, piece of music, etc., each of which is entitled to its own copyright. As with patent rights, an employee whose work includes the production of written material, or, indeed, anything else that may attract copyright, will be under an obligation to assign the right to the employer. The same obligation, as with all other aspects of intellectual property, does not affect an independent contractor. The case of Stevenson, *Jordan & Harrison Ltd v. MacDonald & Evans Ltd* [1952] provides a good illustration. An employee of the plaintiffs, engaged to write scientific texts, was held to be entitled to the copyright in a set of lectures that he gave in the evenings as an independent activity, and so he was entitled to assign **that** copyright to the defendants, another publisher.

E. Rights in registered and unregistered designs

With design assuming an ever-higher profile in the marketability of goods, the protection of original designs against unauthorized copying is a valuable property right for the creator. Designs that are judged by, and appeal to, the eye, such as surface decoration on porcelain, are protected by registration under the Registered Designs Act, 1949, as amended by the Copyright, Designs and Patents Act, 1988. The Act of 1988 also created a new unregistered design right, relating to any aspect of the shape or configuration (whether internal or external) of the whole or any part of any article. Monopoly rights are accorded for varying lengths of time in registered and unregistered designs. The policy underlying design rights is the encouragement of good industrial design by protecting designers from unauthorized copying by others.

As with other aspects of intellectual property, an employee-designer cannot exercise these rights on his or her own behalf. Legally, they belong to the employer.

It is always open to the parties to enter into an agreement for the sharing of these rights.

Negotiation and HRM 10

Alan Blackburn

Learning objectives

After studying this chapter you should be able to:

- understand the process of negotiation;
- explain the differences between integrative and distributive negotiation;
- prepare for a negotiation encounter;
- advise others on the effective behaviours used by negotiators.

Introduction

People negotiate regularly in a variety of different contexts and often without realizing they are negotiating. For example, over domestic chores: if you wash the dishes then I will dry them, or better still, if I dry the dishes and put them away does that mean I can go out for a drink with my friends! Young children are most effective negotiators as they do not see the need to retain ongoing friendly relations with parents. Sanctions parents use to support their own positions fall on deaf ears and parental concessions are often given to children whatever the result of the negotiation encounter. This chapter concentrates not on the informal everyday negotiation practice but on the more formal style of negotiation practised in the workplace between parties who have different views.

Negotiation may be described as a process where parties to a potential conflict attempt to resolve that conflict by coming to an agreement. Negotiating within an organizational context can be differentiated from other types of negotiation for the following reasons:

1   People in an organization have an ongoing relationship; they belong to the same organization but remain independent. The implications of this are that once the negotiation is over, people return to their normal activity set that involves interacting to a greater or lesser extent with people with whom they were negotiating. Negotiation therefore is simply a behavioural episode within an ongoing relationship. If a person feels aggrieved with the conduct and/or outcome of the negotiation then they may look for opportunities in future negotiations to get their own back.

Outside an organizational context, negotiations can be one-off encounters in which a different style of negotiation practice may be used, ensuring wherever possible that you come out of the encounter winning. Selling a motor car may be one example of this, as it is unlikely that we would ever want to meet the buyer of our car again. This type of negotiation is called direct negotiation as people negotiate on their own behalf.

2   In negotiations between organizational and employee representatives, negotiators need to sell any resulting agreement to their constituents. This type of negotiation is called indirect representative negotiation as negotiators who may be elected to their positions are acting as representatives of a constituency to put forward a point of view on the constituents' behalf. Negotiators, however, are not in a position to agree negotiated outcomes without referring back to the people they represent.

Definition
Negotiation is a process of changing positions and making concessions from initial positions in the course of moving towards agreement (Dunlop, 1984).

The key words in this definition are 'changing positions' and 'making concessions', which highlight during the negotiation process that negotiators must be prepared to offer concessions to receive any concessions of their own. This is not to say that a compromise will always be reached mid-way between the original positions of the negotiators but that if concessions are offered on both sides then the chances are that an agreement will be reached. The process was summed up effectively by a trade union leader who was quoted as saying, 'Negotiation is like two people standing at opposite sides of a room and walking towards one another trading concessions as they walk. The trick is to make the other person walk faster than you, so the eventual settlement is more towards the terms you want, rather than the terms they want'.

Negotiators have clear reasons why concessions are being made. Concessions must be linked to achieving the overall objective from the negotiation, hence concessions must be aimed to encourage the other party to move their position in a particular direction. The skill of the negotiator is to marshal the presentation of their arguments to achieve overall objectives while obtaining more concessions than they themselves provide.

Two types of negotiation practice

There are two distinct types of negotiation as follows;

- The first is called **distributive negotiation**. In this situation, a negotiator will attempt to win as much as they can at the expense of the other negotiator. This is a 'win-lose' situation where one negotiator coerces the other to agreement.
- The second is called **integrative negotiation**. In this situation, both negotiators adopt a joint problem-solving approach to reaching agreement while ensuring that both sides make concessions to foster a feeling by both parties that they have gained from the negotiation. This is a 'win-win' situation.

Negotiators tend not to declare the type of negotiation practice they are engaging in, hence it is important to identify the type of practice early in the proceedings by attempting to identify the practice of your opponent through behavioural and communication signs; a joint problem-solving approach may turn out to be distributive. If the style is not identified early enough, it may have a detrimental effect and lead to concessions being given up needlessly.

Outcomes of the negotiation process

The following three figures show some possible outcomes of a negotiation. Each diagram shows two oblong boxes which represent a negotiator or team of negotiators. Each oblong runs across the page from the right- and left-hand side respectively. The Ideal Settlement Point (ISP) for each negotiator is the position furthest away from the other negotiator, i.e. at the extreme left- or right-hand side of the diagram. The ISP is indicated on the diagram. At the other end of each box is the Fallback Position (FP) of each negotiator, which is marked on the boxes as FP. The fallback position indicates the minimum objectives a negotiator must achieve if an agreement is to be achieved. Some way between these extremes is the Likely Settlement Point (LSP), which may be realistically achieved if both negotiators 'walk towards each other' offering concessions as they walk. The relative positions of each negotiator overlap, indicated by the overlapping boxes in the picture. This area may be called the bargaining zone, which is shaded in the diagram to indicate the area in which agreement is likely to be reached.

Figure 10.1 shows what happens during negotiation when agreement can be reached. The bargaining zone of both negotiators overlap, hence agreement will be reached between the fallback position and likely settlement point. The location of the settlement will depend upon how effectively each side marshals their argument.

Figure 10.2 shows what happens during negotiation when agreement cannot be reached. This is not necessarily a fault of the negotiators but may be a structural problem caused where the bargaining zone of each negotiator does not overlap. Reaching agreement becomes difficult, and negotiations end in deadlock, much to the frustration of the negotiators. In these situations it becomes important to check back with the original objectives set for the negotiation. Reviewing the

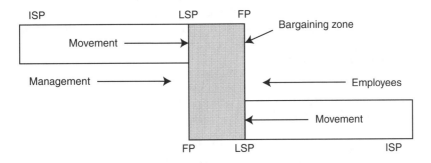

Figure 10.1 What happens during negotiation when agreement *can* be reached.

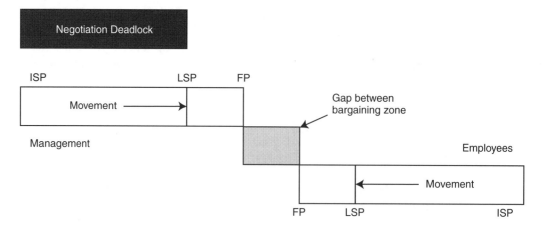

Figure 10.2   What happens during negotiation when agreement *cannot* be reached.

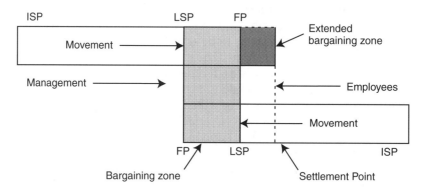

Figure 10.3   What happens during negotiation when a fallback position is not identified.

objectives may reveal that they were unrealistic, but it is important too to check that negotiators are not tempted into offering concessions that would take them beyond their bottom line, which would mean sacrificing original objectives.

Figure 10.3 shows what can happen if a fallback position is not clearly and accurately identified and/or arguments that make your case have not been presented effectively. One negotiator has been pulled way beyond their bottom line towards the ideal settlement point of the other negotiator.

The negotiation process is an expensive business both in terms of concessions given away that may have been unnecessary but also in terms of personal credibility as a negotiator.

The process of negotiation

The negotiation process is divided into a number of phases and often presented as such by commentators. The phases vary from four to nine depending upon the fine distinctions made between each stage. To further complicate the issue, each stage is called a slightly different name. Consensus suggests that the process may be most usefully divided into four stages noted below. Each stage, however, is far from watertight and in reality the process often reverts to earlier stages before moving towards agreement.

Stage 1.   Prepare your case
Stage 2.   Explore key issues in your respective cases
Stage 3.   Bargain to develop an acceptable package
Stage 4.   Close the negotiation by reaching agreement

The tactics used in each of these stages are discussed below.

Stage 1. Prepare your case

Preparing a case is the most crucial stage of any negotiation. The preparation stage is where a negotiator sets overall objectives for the negotiation and then collects and marshals facts to construct a case that will help achieve the objectives set. This means collecting relevant information, which includes issues comprising the outer and inner context of the case. For example, an overall objective for a negotiation which many of us can share may be set in the context of trying to sell a motor car. The overall objective is to sell the car at an acceptable rate of return. The outer context may be considered as the environmental issues which impact on the negotiation overall; when selling a motor car the average price of vehicles within a particular class, vehicle age, overall availability and special offers by motor traders will impact on the selling price. The inner context is the issues that affect your negotiation specifically; for example, the rarity, overall condition, mileage, colour, tyre wear and fitted extras will also affect vending price.

Negotiators must use facts to present their case in the strongest possible way by producing a compelling argument which cements facts of the case together. When constructing a case it is useful to put yourself in the other negotiator's position, which allows you to think through counter-arguments and develop a response to them, which in turn makes your case seem stronger. The process also helps to identify possible areas of weakness in their position which can be checked out while negotiating. Progress towards reaching a settlement is helped if negotiators prioritize sub-objectives in relation to their overall objective. One way to achieve this is to prioritize the sub-objectives within your overall objective by 'MIL'ing objectives, i.e. M is objectives that Must be achieved that helps identify your bottom line, I is objectives that are Intended to be achieved which identifies your likely settlement points and L is objectives that you would Like to achieve, which can be a 'wish list' that identifies your ideal settlement point. Prioritizing objectives helps identify tradables that can be offered during face-to-face negotiation. Tradables are concessions which can be offered to the other side who should in theory offer concessions in return. During the preparation stage it is useful to prioritize concessions that you may be prepared to make. This can be done by identifying concessions that for you are of low value and therefore inexpensive to give but are of high value to the other negotiator. For convenience, objectives and concessions can be organized using the matrix shown in Figure 10.4. Thinking through concessions helps identify the ideal

Objectives that Must be achieved (fallback position)	Concessions you will not make
Objectives that you Intend you achieve (likely settlement point)	Concessions you can make
Objectives that you would Like to achieve (ideal settlement point)	Concessions you can make

Figure 10.4   Negotiation objectives and concession matrix.

settlement point, your bottom line and therefore the limits of your bargaining arena. A matrix can also be constructed for the opposing negotiator, which helps think through issues within their case too.

Stage 2. Explore key issues in your respective cases

The second stage in negotiation is to exchange information about one another's case, which encourages exploration of the issues. Of importance is the way a case is presented to best advantage.

Negotiations often open when one negotiator makes a statement about their negotiating stance. Early exchanges often begin by noting broad issues based upon underlying principles, which are likely to differ between the parties. It is useful during these presentations to note potential areas of common ground, principles over which both parties are likely to agree, which helps move the process of reaching agreement forward. Both parties will present arguments that add justification to their opening positions while withholding information that the other party can use against them. Statements and arguments offered at this time reflect the ideal settlement point for each team. It can also be useful to indicate the areas in which you are prepared to make some concessions while taking care to withhold the extent to which you are prepared to move. This sends signals to the other party from which they try to gauge the boundaries around the potential bargaining arena. The style and tone used by negotiators during these opening statements set the tone for subsequent dialogue and often the remainder of the encounter.

The process then moves through an argumentative stage where both parties try to spot weaknesses in the other party's position. Each party tries to develop its own case while undermining the arguments put forward by the other. During this process more information will be revealed by each party in order to justify the case they are making. This information has value and should be assessed as to the likelihood that it can be used back against the party who revealed it. It is important to uncover the premises on which a case is constructed. If the underlying premises can be destabilized, it weakens the other party's argument, which in turn opens the potential that they will reconsider their opening position and movement may occur by concessions being tentatively offered. This process attempts to adjust the other negotiator's attitude over what may be achieved at the end of the negotiation process; once expectations are reduced, concessions received will seem even more valuable than they otherwise would.

Stage 3. Bargain to develop an acceptable package

During Stage 2, both parties normally accept there is a need to move away from their respective ideal settlement points towards the ISP of the other side. The question of how far you need to move to reach agreement is the issue that needs careful consideration during this phase of the process. Bargaining is where a likely settlement point is identified within the bargaining arena. The process involves packaging concessions which you may consider exchanging with the other side to reach an acceptable settlement point while staying within your bargaining arena. All concessions offered during this stage must be made conditional on obtaining something in return. The words 'if' and 'then' are key to this process.

For example, when selling a car you may propose, '**If** you want me to drop my price by £500, **then** I will remove my CD player and road fund licence.' But to keep the negotiation positive you may also try a counter-offer; for example, '**If** you will pay the full asking price for the car, **then** I will pay for a Ministry of Transport Certificate of roadworthiness, a full service at my local garage and also provide you with a receipt.'

Giving and receiving counter-offers in this way gradually narrows the range of likely settlement points to a settlement point which is acceptable to both parties. In the cut and thrust of bargaining the negotiation process can revert back to Stage 2 before moving forward. Summarizing tentative agreements helps slow the pace of negotiation, and can provide space and therefore thinking time for negotiators. Emphasizing common ground by summarizing the points to which you both agree also retains the positive outlook of the process overall. During bargaining it can be useful to link or separate concessions during argument. For example, when offering a concession you should ask for a specific concession in return. Concessions are therefore made conditional and of course can be withdrawn again if the concession offered in return is of insufficient value to comprise an acceptable package. As the bargaining process moves forward it may be useful to call adjournments, which allows you to check back that you are achieving what you want out of the negotiations and, more importantly, that the likely settlement point remains within your bargaining arena and above the bottom line set at the preparation stage.

Stage 4. Close the negotiation by reaching agreement

The final phase of the process is deciding, closing and agreeing the package of proposals by finalizing the agreement. In employee relations negotiations this would involve committing the proposals to paper by writing them down. This can spark another round of negotiating as negotiators struggle to give meaning to their agreements using appropriate language. It can be in the interests of both negotiators to use clear language to express their agreements; however, negotiators may also deliberately use ambiguous language, allowing some degree of flexibility as proposals are implemented. In choosing to use clear or confused language each situation will differ according to the perceived advantage created for the respective parties.

The point at which to close negotiations is another important consideration. When selling a car, it is unlikely that another negotiation will be conducted with the same person, hence the conduct and close of negotiations become less important. For negotiations in organizations, however, negotiators are likely to have a continuing relationship and once negotiations are complete it is important that negotiators part on amicable terms. Judging the close is important to this aspect. It is important to close the negotiations when both parties feel they are gaining appropriately from the agreed bargain. This means driving a hard bargain but allowing the other negotiator to leave the negotiating table with their self-esteem intact. Push too far and the other negotiator is likely at some point in the future to try to get their own back. Judging the close appropriately is therefore a key consideration for maintaining effective ongoing relationships between negotiators who work together regularly.

In employee relations, negotiators are elected/appointed to represent the interests of their constituency. Before the outcomes of negotiations can be agreed in fine detail, the negotiators must refer back to their constituents to ratify the agreement. At the end of the negotiations it is usual that a joint statement will be constructed and released by the negotiators to disseminate the broad terms of the agreement. The final decision to accept or reject the agreement is taken by constituents; however, it is likely that a number of minor issues will be raised which can be dealt with by the negotiators. Where there is a failure to agree, the negotiators will be mandated to continue the process.

Organization of negotiations

To date, we have considered the process of negotiation but paid scant attention to the organization of those who negotiate. A brief overview is provided under the following headings:

1   Power and negotiation
2   Roles of negotiators
3   Behaviours of negotiators
4   Outcomes of negotiations

1. Power and negotiation

Perception of which negotiator holds the most bargaining power relative to the other has a major influence on the conduct of negotiation. Power is a relative concept which exists in the minds of negotiators through conditioning and stimuli gleaned from the environment of the negotiation. It is the relative perceived power imbalance between the parties to the negotiation that can affect the process. Power can offer perceived bargaining advantage or disadvantage, which in turn can affect the behaviour of negotiators. Inappropriate, blatant use of power during negotiation stimulates 'low trust' relations that can spread beyond the immediate forum of the negotiations into the larger constituency. The style used during negotiation of this type is distributive: I win and you lose. On the other hand, using power through a joint problem-solving approach can develop 'high trust' relations for the overall benefit of the organization.

2. Roles of negotiators

Negotiations can be conducted either as an individual or as a member of a negotiation team. For individual negotiation, the roles undertaken by a negotiation team fall to one person; the amount of data processed during negotiation is extremely high, hence preparation for the negotiation encounter becomes vitally important. For team negotiations, preparation remains important but for slightly different reasons. Individuals within the team are likely to have slightly different agendas, hence agreeing and maintaining a party line can be tricky. For success, a common line must be agreed before meeting the other side.

In team negotiations, people are allocated different roles to help the process. For example, teams can allocate roles of Lead Negotiator, Back-Up Negotiator, Note Taker/Observer. The latter can be separated if there are four people in the team. Once roles are allocated it is important they are adhered to. The Lead Negotiator is responsible for presenting the case, to the other side and therefore acts as spokesperson for the team. The Back-Up Negotiator acts as assistant in presenting the case, particularly where the lead becomes tired or begins to lose momentum. The Back-Up Negotiator also listens carefully to the arguments and can advise during adjournments. The Note Taker/Observer maintains records of progress and advises which proposals may be attractive to the other party, but also looks for potential weaknesses in the case of the other side. Finally, the Observer is a tactician who watches for conscious or subconscious signals issued by the other side which can reveal sticking points or signs of weakness in the way the case is presented through body language or speech intonations.

Using adjournments appropriately keeps negotiations moving and team negotiations on line.

3. Behaviours of negotiators

Behaviours used by people during negotiations can either help or hinder the process overall while preparing and when facing the other side. Inappropriate behaviour is largely in the eyes of the beholder; however, Walton (1965) identified through research behaviours that could help or hinder the process of negotiation. Walton noted that inappropriate behaviour generates a similar response by the other party and the conduct of the negotiation can rapidly degenerate into a downward spiral of deteriorating response and counter-response.

Behaviours used by effective negotiators were:

- listening and showing that you are listening;
- questioning for clarification;
- summarizing issues neutrally;
- challenging the other party to justify their case;
- being non-committal about proposals made or received;
- seeking and giving information;
- not rejecting proposals out of hand but using the proposal to build a package around by linking the proposal to another issue.

Behaviours avoided by experienced negotiators were:

- interrupting;
- talking over the top of the opposing negotiator;
- point-scoring by referring back to previous, often historical, issues not relevant to the discussions;
- talking too much but not listening;
- shouting or shouting down the other party;
- sarcasm, threats, personal verbal attacks;
- finally, accusing the other side of lying.

Once negotiator behaviour embarks on a downward spiral it is difficult to remedy. It is much easier and more productive to avoid it initially.

4. Outcomes of negotiations

There are four possible outcomes to a negotiation:

You lose: They lose
You lose: They win
You win: They lose
You win: They win

The last outcome in the list above is the most productive for maintaining effective working relationships. Winning and losing, however, are perceptions. The presentation of the case and the behaviours of the parties during the negotiation can give the impression to the other team that the negotiation process has been a positive experience, with both teams feeling they have gained something of value. The reality may remain in the presentation of proposals rather than the content of the package itself. The final outcome is likely to be of high value to each team and constituents where the bargaining power of teams is perceived to be equal, and of relatively low value to the teams and constituents where the bargaining power of the teams is perceived to be unequal. Perception, image management and presentation remain central to the process of negotiation.

Summary

This chapter has discussed both the stages of negotiation and conduct of negotiators. The examples used for discussion, however, are taken from a general context as most people have experienced the trials and tribulations of selling a motor car and experienced first hand the emotions involved when there is a perceived power imbalance between two parties to a negotiation. We also distinguished employee relations negotiation from others as there is a need to maintain an ongoing relationship with work colleagues if employee relations are to remain positive. Negotiation is a skill we use regularly, often informally in our day-to-day work. Discussions here have concerned themselves with more formal negotiations that take place during a meeting or a series of meetings which may spread over several hours or even days. The experience of negotiating can generate feelings of elation and satisfaction but can also generate resentment and anger. Because of this it is important to set an appropriate tone from the outset and take pains to identify the style of negotiation being used by your opponents.

Questions

1   What advice would you give to an inexperienced colleague who is to prepare for a formal negotiation for the first time?
2   During negotiations, what tactics would you use to keep the process moving forward on a positive note?
3   What are the four possible outcomes of a negotiation?

4   You are planning to sell a motor car. Use the matrix and model suggested to generate your bargaining arena, ideal settlement point, bottom line and likely settlement point.

References

Dunlop, JT (1984) *Dispute Resolution*, Auburn, London.
Walton, R and McKersie, R (1965) *Behavioural Theory of Labour Negotiations*, McGraw Hill, New York.

Conclusions

Nelarine Cornelius

Throughout this book, we have attempted to highlight what we believe to be a number of key areas within the management of human resources from a line management perspective. Throughout, there is a sense that the roles and responsibilities of the line manager (and indeed the HRM specialist) are ripe for review, redefinition and recasting, given a backdrop of significant organizational restructuring, 'new' organizational forms and the continued evolution of human resource management theory and practice. In reality, it is neither appropriate nor desirable for there to be 'one kind' of 'idealized' HRM specialist or line management practice, no more than it is for there to be 'one type' of engineer. As with any functional activity, there is likely to be *a diversity of forms that the line manager's role in HRM could take,* which will in part be shaped by variables such as pressure from the external environment and organizational responses to these, tasks that need to be completed and reflected upon in employment management.

At this point, we would like to revisit two of the themes that run through all of the chapters. One dominant theme is that of **the downward pressure on line managers towards greater responsibility for managing HR issues**. This downward pressure is the result of downsizing and associated reductions in central specialist support services, restructuring and the impact of information technology. Increasingly, the expectation is that managers need to be effective 'people managers' irrespective of whether or not they welcome the shift. Coupled with another pressure – that of more systematic evaluation of managers and the performance of their subordinates – if managers wish to be regarded as competent people managers they will need to possess a basic portfolio of skills and knowledge in the area of managing human resources. This developmental input will have to be acquired *over and above* the specific area of technical expertise that they may have been primarily employed for. Managers will require systematic and professional programmes of continuous development: a laissez faire or ad hoc approach is unlikely to be adequate.

Another dominant theme centres **around looking towards and managing the future**. In order to stay ahead of the competition, managers and their organizations need to scan the world around them actively and try to anticipate possible outcomes: not only from events already in train but also those which may not have an immediate impact but for which any future impact could be substantial.

Understanding how organizations could deal with the future can be approached in many ways. One useful array of ideas and approaches is encapsulated within **scenario planning** literature and technology (see Schwartz, 1991; Wack, 1985a, b). Put simply, scenario planning is concerned with *the generation of viable alternative future scenarios which organizations need to explore and assess their* *potential readiness for*. A key purpose for such exploration is to establish how well or how badly organizations would be able to cope with significant changes in the 'external environment' – be it within specific industries or sectors, or social, technological, economic or political changes – and to identify current or future organizational strengths and weaknesses as well as strategies that enable preparedness to be developed.

An important aspect of scenario planning is **scenario learning**, which we can consider to be the process of learning which accompanies scenario planning (Wood, 1997). Scenario learning enables us to become more exploratory and less constrained in the way that we develop views of the future. There are many developmental techniques and inputs that help to facilitate flexibility of thought and force us out of the straightjacket of the current dominant ways of thinking about things (see Schwartz, 1991). The learning therefore not only centres around the organization and the environment but also helps us identify *our* personal strengths and limitations when understanding and coping with alternative views of the future (Cornelius, 1997). For some, it may be that exploring the future is an uncomfortable experience. Specifically, there may be an unwillingness or a limited ability to create visions of the future, particularly if one is unsure of one's likely position in it.

For others, there is rightly a fear that a 'reality check' will be absent from the process, allowing utopian views at one extreme or gloom and doom at the other to flourish unchecked (though in well-managed scenario planning this is rarely the case in practice). Like all thinking about the future, the 'negative–positive' caricature outlined above, with the glass either half empty or half full, merely outlines the ends on a continuum, with many more balanced positions between the extremes. In the first half of the twentieth century, there were many who argued that technological advances would lead to a shorter working day and week and increased leisure time, while others feared that 'Big Brother' totalitarians would exploit the new technology and enslave us all. At the end of the twentieth century, for the majority of us both views would probably be regarded as extreme. However, the feeling that technological change meant that the world of work would change significantly, *that we would be doing things differently*, is core to both views and, indeed, many technologically driven changes in the world of work have come about.

We all have our views on what the future might be like. To conclude, we have outlined areas within line management-centred HRM which we believe should be addressed in the near future, in order to improve our practical and theoretical understanding of line management-centred HRM. These views are presented in the form of **personal commentaries** developed by the contributors to the book.

Personal commentaries on the future of HRM

Recruitment, selection and workforce diversity

Managers now are taking increasing responsibility for recruiting, selecting and inducting within their organizations. We now operate in a global environment, with many leading organizations operating internationally and recruiting, selecting and working with diverse workforces around the world. In addition, workforces reflect changing social and demographic patterns. Organizations that harness the 'diversity advantage' will be those that benefit from harvesting this diversity of talent and it is likely that they will gain competitive advantage.

If organizations are to become truly diverse and achieve a culture in which diversity thrives, then there need to be strong links between diversity objectives and the corporate plan. This requires not only commitment from the top of the organization but also the support and 'ownership' of diversity by the line manager. Traditionally, managers have neither understood the meaning of diversity nor seen it as their responsibility. Nonetheless, diversity is the responsibility of all and particularly of line managers, who are at the 'sharp' end and can make diversity work for them and their departments.

Recruitment and selection processes play a key role in creating a diverse organization but can only succeed if diversity is part of the business culture. For example, an applicant who is not from the majority culture will not stay long in an environment which is clearly hostile to diversity. The manager has a clear role (and indeed, responsibility):

- to be committed to the achievement of diversity;
- to auditing and assessing needs;
- to be clearly accountable;
- to communicate effectively policies and practices;
- to champion diversity;
- to coordinate activity;
- to evaluate and monitor progress towards diversity.

Further research is needed to investigate the expectations of individuals from diverse backgrounds and the reality of organizational life. The induction crisis highlights the impact of 'formal' and 'informal' practices in organizations. 'Hard' information on the reasons why people from diverse backgrounds do not apply to organizations and in particular, their experience within them is limited by the lack of available research data, especially concerning those from ethnic minorities. Further research is also needed into the reasons for 'management reluctance' to tackle diversity issues.

With the increasing devolving of human resource policies and practices to line managers, the human resource management of the organization is going to be very dependent on the willingness and ability of line managers to manage and own these policies and practices. The current drive of many line managers is the bottom line, and this is often in the form of short-term budget cuts. Under such pressures, longer-term or broader issues are frequently side-lined or seen as part of specialist Personnel activities. However, what is becoming increasingly clear is that organizations that value and invest in their employees attract their commitment and are more likely to achieve competitive edge.

Knowledge and learning in the 'new order'

The perceived importance of training and development to the organization has now taken hold due to a variety of factors: specific management interventions to which continuous learning is central, an increased interest in employee competence as one form of organization competence, and the real difficulties encountered in deciding on the best approach to employee development in 'new' organizational forms, such as networked or virtual organizations. For the latter there is an increasing realization that the knowledge acquired by employees is not just what they have learned through formal systems of education, and professional and management development. Much employee learning takes place informally, through the acquisition of tacit knowledge, developed on the job, and often transmitted socially through formal and informal contacts with colleagues. This tacit knowledge is potential intellectual gold, which could provide sources of ideas which fuel creativity and, specifically, new product and service development.

Although mechanisms are in place in some highly networked organizations to attempt to avoid losing this vital knowledge, in the form of social meeting places set up to encourage informal contacts and to kindle the flames of tacit knowledge and learning, our understanding of how best to develop employees given these new circumstances is limited, and requires far more detailed research.

Who is responsible for employee training and development? Usually, attention is focused on the organization and the government, though increasingly the need for the individual to take control of their own destiny, through self-managed learning, is likely to gain in popularity. Training and development will increasingly be viewed as a vital *reward* for organizational membership; given increasingly short-term contracts of employment, employability is more likely to be achieved through possessing a portable portfolio of skills and knowledge that can be taken from company to company.

The challenge to society will be to ensure that as many as possible of those active in the labour market are able to participate in the post-industrial, knowledge-based economies that we are shifting towards, and given the 'knowledge intensive' nature of much new work and the traditional reluctance of employers to foot more than a minimal bill for those who are not viewed as 'core' employees, government initiatives and increased participation by further and higher educational institutes in this skilling for the second industrial revolution are likely to gain momentum.

Participation, involvement and commitment

The landscape of personnel and human resource management practice is a mixture of sectional developments. Many companies that operate HRM are typified by private sector, transnational corporations which open greenfield sites and take the opportunity to change management practices wholesale when commissioning operations. This often happens in areas of high unemployment. This can involve issuing new standard and non-standard employment contracts to employees who willingly accept working practices designed to incorporate many of the processes known as involvement and participation. In some cases unions are recognized, in many they are not. Where unions are recognized, membership is patchy and numerically weak.

To separate a discrete set of managerial practices from wider production and organizational technology is problematic. On greenfield sites, the process of HRM therefore tends to be the accepted 'way we do things around here', incorporating both management processes and job design.

For brownfield sites the approach is different. Brownfield sites are more likely to have a trade union presence. Unilateral changes to operating practice are likely to be a slower process than on greenfield sites. Here incremental change is more likely to be applied by management to adjust operating practices. There is more likely to be a challenge from employee representatives if the status quo is threatened. For HRM a mixture of practices, combining some elements of traditional personnel processes with human resource management, may result in employee representation operating side by side with participation and involvement processes. Redesigning jobs is likely to be a collaborative issue between management and employees. Involvement and participation processes could help facilitate change.

The public sector shows a different picture. Here there remains a strong trade union presence where we are more likely to find established collective organization. Since the publication of the Rayner Reviews of the mid-1980s, the government has continually set efficiency targets for public sector organizations to work to. These relatively large centres of employment make the sustainability of trade union organization easier to maintain than in the private sector. It is here that we see more traditional personnel management practices operating. There also remains division, due to professional job boundaries and contracting-out policies. To overcome these boundaries, communication processes need to be elaborate and accurate. In these areas we are less likely to find sophisticated involvement and participation processes beyond established collective bargaining and joint consultation. These, however, do not in themselves help to establish partnership and common goals.

The development of partnership, breaking down barriers between managers and employees and between professional groups, may be an important challenge ahead for managers of public sector organizations. To this extent, it is the public sector organization and the use of involvement and participation processes in these key areas that seem the most neglected in terms of research.

For HRM in general and involvement and participation in particular, it is largely down to managers to choose which set of practices they prefer: pure HRM, a mixture of personnel and HRM or a new set of innovative ideas which are yet to be categorized.

Managing performance and flexibility

The popularity of workplace flexibility is unlikely to wane, given the drivers of cost controls and, increasingly, access to 'global' labour markets. However, many of the changes in work practice for those on the periphery of organizations have less of the glamour of the brave new world of knowledge-based working and are more like a return to the bad old days. Twenty-four hour working is on the increase, and Taylorist-type working practices, characterized by de-skilling of jobs, tight managerial control, and electronic surveillance and monitoring of performance, are increasingly the norm in the service arms of many industries.

We have previously considered the important links between effective management performance and employee commitment. It has been suggested by many that these new work practices, at the 'hard' end of HRM practice, are already creating anxiety and stress among employees (Arkin, 1997) and with the first wave of Taylorism at the beginning of the twentieth century as our benchmark, are likely to lead to alienation, frustration and limited job satisfaction. Moreover, consistent with the first Taylorist organizations, unions are often marginalized or absent; such employees are more likely to be 'peripheral' than core and they are unlikely to enjoy security of tenure. History really does repeat itself.

Eventually, work redesign may soften the manner in which staff in such organizations are expected to work. However, more research needs to be done on the impact of such work practices on the performance of the organization as a whole, and individual and team performance specifically, beyond the first years of start-up when downsizing and lower building costs are among the short-term attractions.

International human resource management

In many ways, the future of international human resource management is bound up with the changing nature and characteristics of the global economy itself. As mentioned in the summary to Chapter 6 on international human resource management, it is not possible to be prescriptive, nor should writers attempt to be so, about the role that management with responsibility for international human resource management should take. Different organizations and different sectors will develop in varied ways, each requiring an approach to international human resource management that best reflects their industry or organizational practice. The future of international human resource management does, however, appear to be developing around a number of common themes and determinants, each of which may be applied to different organizations in a way that suits them best.

These common themes include:

● The increasingly important role of international management development in developing core skills and competencies
● The interdependence of decision making within the transnational corporation
● The role of technology as an important aid to the production processes, management information systems and general communication processes

- The demise of the expatriate manager
- The development of cross-cultural teams
- A situation where all human resource management is international human resource management

I will address all of these in turn, albeit briefly.

The increasingly important role of international management development in developing core skills and competencies

International management development has an important role to play in the development of a 'cadre' of international managers, who fit most closely into Howard Perlmutter's (1969) 'geocentric' category relevant to staffing strategy. Here, the ideal is to develop managers who can operate effectively anywhere in the world, without being weighed down by the cultural baggage of their home country. Managers will possess the important competence of cross-cultural sensitivity: the facility to readily appreciate both the hard (social, economic and political infrastructure) and soft (language, attitudes and behaviours) cultural issues from one region to another.

The interdependence of decision making within the transnational corporation

In the future, decisions, affecting international human resource management issues may be taken as a result of a consultation process involving the sharing of information, views of expertise and so on, across subsidiaries. The IHRM strategy will draw heavily upon a range of expertise and will no longer be the prerogative of management operating from a centralized position. Indeed, many subsidiaries may have their own IHRM specialists who assist in the design and implementation of strategy at the local level.

The role of technology as an important aid to the production processes, management information systems and general communication processes

Technology enhances production and service delivery processes, bringing with it the imperative to secure appropriate skills levels at different operations around the world, and communication processes that aid management decision-making processes across national and cultural borders. IHRM, operating in an increasingly integrative way, will draw upon this facility in respect of skills development for staff and management alike, particularly within the activity of international human resource planning.

The demise of the expatriate manager

Expatriate managers, if not already a phenomenon of the past, are unlikely to last in their current state much beyond the millennium. Where the emphasis is on the development of a cadre of international managers who possess a tool bag of transferable, multicultural skills that they carry with them from one location to another, the company compound and the expatriate on the two- to three-year 'posting' may no longer be a viable proposition.

The development of cross-cultural teams

An essential part of international management development will be the acquisition of cross-cultural skills by exposure to the different national and business cultures through cross-cultural teams. The 'action learning' approach to international management development will obviate the necessity for extensive travel and relocation from one subsidiary to another for any lengthy period of time.

A situation where all human resource management is international human resource management

As the world becomes even more of a 'global village', in a sense all human resource management will become 'international'. Global companies are now comprised of small, medium-sized and large enterprises. Companies operating previously in exclusively domestic markets now find themselves competing with a variety and complexity of international operators. The HRM issues that pertain to the global company, in time, become the same issues for the local operation conducting business at the national level.

'Employee-centred' HRM and the death of hierarchy

Trying to get a CEO or Managing Director to embrace HRM can be a bit like trying to get a totalitarian state to adopt democracy – almost everyone can see the advantages except the few in control at the top who have the most to lose. So what can be done to speed up the revolution? In the short term (without resorting to Madame Guillotine) the answer is very little. In the longer term, however, time is on the side of the angels. If education does not work, global markets will – because the old command-and-control organizations will be unable to compete with the smarter network organizations based on the principles of HRM.

The people at the top of an organizational hierarchy – usually men – are there as a result of the 'Darwinian' selection processes which take place when each rung of the ladder is scaled. They got there usually because they are brilliant at politics, greedy for power and suspicious of anyone bright enough to beat them to the next rung. They want to make all the decisions and tend to surround themselves with 'yes-men': they see the hierarchy as a mechanism for implementing their own ideas, and see other people's ideas as a threat to their authority. Naturally, this is extremely frustrating for anyone else with thoughts on running the business. Eventually, most staff with initiative or creativity will be forced out or have left through frustration – at which point the whole organization will be incapable of acting without someone at the top to tell them what to do.

This may be an unfair caricature, but in some organizations perhaps it is nearer the truth than we care to admit. Then what chances are there of introducing empowerment, or self-managed teams?

Any radical reform in a hierarchy must always be wholeheartedly approved at the top if it is to have any chance of succeeding – and reforms do not come any more radical than HRM. As we have argued in this book, HRM will inevitably prevail in most organizations, but in the meantime, many good organizations will fail in the market and disappear, simply because the hierarchy encourages secrecy, stifles initiatives and denies access to the knowledge resources of the organization. Good, smart employees will lose their jobs, and the economies of regions will suffer as a result. What can be done to speed up the transition of organizations into forms more suited to the needs of post-industrial, knowledge-based societies? Is this a valid area for academic research? Should academics refrain from an opinion on what should be done by managers, and restrict themselves to analysing what managers have done, and explaining why they did it? In most other disciplines, researchers look backwards and forwards: explaining what has been, and investigating what might be. If business schools adopt a similar, more proactive approach, perhaps there will be less incentive for businesses to set up their own company universities.

With this frame of reference in mind, key areas for research should be as follows:

1   To seek evidence that the HRM approach does improve the performance of organizations. So far, most investigations have failed to reveal any evidence at all, except for weak positive results from new businesses in greenfield sites. However, most studies have been conducted within the context of existing hierarchies.
2   To investigate the hopes and fears that top managers have about implementing the HRM approach. How may these be addressed in putting the case for HRM?
3   To investigate the influence of the existing culture and structure in an organization on the chances of successful introduction of HRM. What influence do the following factors have?

● A culture of openness or secrecy
● A tall or flat hierarchy
● A history of trust or mistrust
● Much or little experience of working in teams
● The existence or non-existence of a policy of respect for individuals

What are the implications for HRM?

Business education has blossomed in the past ten years, and HRM now has prominence on most courses. A growing wave of better educated middle managers is moving upwards through the hierarchy of most organizations, as these managers gain experience and promotion. Eventually, there will be more top managers with knowledge of the HRM approach and its advantages, and the old industrial paradigm of the brainy few at the top doing all the thinking for the brawny many lower down will be swept away. The hierarchy and its emphasis on controlling people will be seen as an expensive alternative to trusting people to use their initiative and get on with their jobs.

In the meantime, line managers should judge how far they dare implement some of the principles of HRM, but keep their powder dry and demonstrate the effectiveness of the new philosophy in the context of their own situation, wherever possible.

Future developments in the management of human resources in the smaller business

The need is for continued research into the identification of 'winners': that is, smaller businesses which are capable of growth and development. From a human resource perspective the emphasis needs to be on releasing human potential and finding more effective ways of encouraging relevant self-development. There will continue to be a need to research and develop models which will enhance understanding of the processes of growth that make small businesses successful.

In particular, human resource issues in the smaller business need to be researched not only in terms of making systems more relevant but also in developing guidance, policies and practice which can support growth aspirations and assist in managing the transitions attendant on growth. Finally, the competencies needed for effective advisory work in small firms require greater research, both from a national point of view and towards the development of small business on a global basis.

Managing change

A number of issues are worthy of much closer attention in this field. Previously, the importance of more work on the ways in which human resource management-centred initiatives can be a vehicle for managing change was raised, but this is one area in particular which merits more formal research.

As in some of the other commentaries, the importance of increasing our understanding of employment management theory, policy and practice in 'new' organizational forms is relevant to change management. Many of the changes already in train in networked and virtualized organizations will have a profound effect on social interactions and the relationships between subordinates and managers, and indeed, the role of managers has already been defined in organizations that have trodden this particular path.

However, it would be easy to overlook the fact that many of the 'new' organizational forms are often part of a more traditional, bureaucratic organization: the greenfield edge to a predominantly brownfield site. Managing change in these hybrid organizations, given the differences in policy, practice and outlook that are likely to be established in the old and emerge at arms length in the new, will require knowledge about the interactions of the elements that we are just beginning to understand.

Many organizations have opted to 'contract out' the knowledge-based, and often high-cost, activities within their organizations. This has implications for organizational competence, tacit knowledge, and the development of reward and commitment strategies to retain those on a series of short-term contracts, and managing change given this kind of workforce will explicitly require greater expertise in the manipulation of HR strategies to facilitate change.

The trend to 'outsource' is increasingly being applied to the HR function itself. Organizations from the smallest to the largest are operating with a few 'specialist' HR staff; much of the traditional HR administrative information has been knowledge engineered into software, and operational duties are now the responsibility of the line manager. Little is known about the relative losses and gains in such organizations, though such practices certainly increasingly merit the attention of scholars and practitioners. Our main interest here is the impact that such changes might have on the HR components of managing change, as a real concern might be that without proactive stewardship, HR issues in relation to change might become sidelined. Finally, whither strategic human resource management? Many of the actual developments outlined in the chapter and the future developments proposed in these concluding sections imply that the need to elaborate 'hard' and 'soft' models of strategic HRM is urgent. The empirical investigation of the work organizations whose strategic HRM has genuinely strategic characteristics, from small through to large enterprises, would also help to better put into context the theoretical developments in this field.

Negotiations – the impact of new organizations and ways of working

Much of what was outlined earlier in the book, in the chapter on Negotiations and HRM, relates to negotiations conducted face-to-face. Information technology changes and more virtualization of organizations means that we will need to revisit the extent to which more familiar strategies for negotiations are transferable, given new organizational forms and new ways of working. However, this is not to suggest that we should throw the baby out with the bath water. The Negotiations and HRM chapter emphasizes the importance of effective management group dynamics and inter-personal relations, and understanding how remoteness of those with whom we are negotiating may change some of the 'rules' is an important area for future research.

Future developments in ethics and HRM

Research and theory-building in the area of ethics and HRM is continuing to grow. One key issue under consideration is the role of classical ethical theory in assisting practitioners to resolve ethical dilemmas. Some have made an argument that these classical theories are products of the cultures and politico-economic systems in which they arose, which limits to a degree their applicability to present-day ethical concerns (Winstanley and Woodall, 2000). These writers have pointed to the relevance of discourse ethics and the ethics of care as new areas of theory that may be helpful in understanding ethics and HRM. Others have argued that laboured analysis using classical theory is not necessary – what is in the common interest is 'known' and does not require reference to the relative merits of, for example, deontology versus utility (Kaler, 1999).

Still others have argued that much more rigorous empirical research into the 'ethical landscape' of organizations and how this shapes individual decision making or 'ethics in action' is important to our understanding of ethics and HR practice (Cornelius and Gagnon, 1999). External, 'first principles' analysis of the ethical nature of the conduct of organizations is important but may bring limited value to the practitioner engaged in attempting to improve ethical conduct within his or her organization. This requires a clearer recognition that the individual is an ethical actor but that this individual operates within a landscape which he or she may both shape, and be shaped by.

Final comments

The personal commentaries have generated a number of alternative scenarios, snatches of future possibilities, for the field of employment management. Although a very partial selection, there are a number of emergent ideas from this range with which we would like to conclude, and whose progress the line manager in particular would do well to follow.

First, there is a feeling that the role of the line manager has become more intense. This is a result of a combination of factors, including downsizing in general and the stripping out of layers of management specifically: managers are expected to do more and deliver more with less. This is coupled with a sense of heightened expectations on the part of the line manager, in terms of competence, knowledge and functional flexibility. The manager is expected to be more entrepreneurial, closer to the market and the customer.

However, this is coupled with a sense of decreasing support for the line manager from internal specialists, many of whom disappeared with the downsizing when head office departments were seen as contributing minimal amounts to the line and to the direct production of goods and services: less expert help than unnecessary overheads. With this has come about an increase in responsibility among line managers for employment management roles and responsibilities, but as we have discussed earlier, the devolution of HR responsibility often looks more like haphazard, opportunistic devolution, and the devolution is often more balkanization than systematic or strategic delegation.

Under such pressures, line managers may increasingly find that a form of **partnership management** is a way of ensuring a balance is struck. Specifically, employment management specialists act as facilitators and internal consultants who are able to advise managers in an 'internal consultancy' mode of operation.

In turn, the line manager is the one with the 'local knowledge' of employees and teams, and it is *cooperative action* that becomes central to operations. Thus the line manager is not over-burdened with activities that require detailed, specialist knowledge (some of which are likely to have legal implications) and the expertise of managing a workforce does not become so dissipated that, potentially, knowledge and expertise in relation to managing a key strategic resource, employees, cannot develop and grow within the organization.

The relatively unfamiliar territory of the networked or virtual organization could be considered in one of two ways. The first is as an extrapolation of the flexible organization approach, and within this, ensuring that the knowledge expertise drain is not soaked up by an often less nurtured peripheral organization is important. The second is more concerned with maintenance of the vital social processes of any organization. As a phenomenon driven by technology and the desire to exploit global markets, the financial attractiveness of the gains that can be achieved in the short term through 'optimization' of workforce numbers has two potential stings in the tail. First, when is an organization too small, lacking in the critical mass to build up expertise and 'presence' in the market? The second point is most easily built on the analogy of maintaining contacts between family and friends. Over time, families and friends are likely to disperse, but through various efforts, it can remain possible to create 'a sense of belonging'. Phone calls, family videos, cards posted to loved ones for high days, holidays, weddings and births, and visits, albeit infrequent, maintain the links, but require effort. Organizations' work groups moving towards the networked/virtual position are likely to face similar dilemmas, and the initiative for maintaining a sense of belonging and commitment will have to be driven. Employment management specialists may be able to reinforce these important, informal networks, in a variety of ways, including training and development initiatives, reward packages and briefing sessions, but 'informal arenas' of interaction will also be needed, in which employees meet primarily to exchange ideas and maintain social contacts, actions which are already in place in some networked organizations. Moreover, one might speculate that such social contacts are most likely to flourish where the bonds are already strong and interpersonal relationships well established. It is here that the line manager is likely to have a key role in maintaining a sense of esprit de corps and commitment to the organization.

We have presented many examples of academics and practitioners who have argued strongly that there is limited evidence of a move towards more strategy-centred employment management practice. Perhaps it is international HRM that will provide the best framework for further development of strategic approaches, as international strategic activity, particularly for joint ventures or strategic alliances, is highly dependent upon effective alignment of human resources. Moreover, potentially, international HRM pushes us away from the Anglo-American axis of understanding of employment management practice, and towards an appreciation of differences and diversity of practice, given the range that exists within highly successful economies around the world.

Strategic activity follows trends and fashions. In the 1970s, there was much activity centred around setting up conglomerates in order to spread risk. In the boom of the early 1980s, there were numerous mergers and acquisitions followed in the recession of the late 1980s by a trend towards demergers. In the 1990s, the trend is towards mergers and strategic alliances on a more global scale. The paradox of downsizing is that it is often a precursor to scaling up.

Given a current view, that employees are a source of sustainable competitive advantage, against a background of increasing outsourcing of employment management activities, it is important that companies keep their eyes on the prize. New approaches and new systems of employment management will be needed in order to address a number of newly emerging challenges. However, the reality is that there has always been and always will be a range of options, from the traditional to the radical. Diversity provides choice: what matters is that appropriate choices are made.

References

Arkin, A (1997) Hold the production line. *People Management*, February, 22–27.

Cornelius, NE (1997) *Developing Views of the Future through Scenario Planning: A constructivist perspective*. Proceedings of the European Institute for Advanced Studies in Management Conference 'Social Construction, Innovation and Organizational Change', Leuven, Belgium.

Cornelis, N and Gagnon, S (1999) From ethics 'by proxy' to ethics in action: new approaches to understanding HRM and ethics. *Business Ethics: A European Review* **8**(4) pp 225–235.

Kaler, J (1999) What's the good of ethical theory? *Business Ethics: A European Review* **8**(4) pp206–213.

Perlmutter, HV (1969) The tortuous evolution of the multinational corporation. *Columbia Journal of World Business*, January–February, 9–18..

Rayner Security Reports, 1976–1986, Her Majesty's Treasury, London.

Schwartz, P (1991) *The Art of the Long View: Scenario planning – protecting your company against uncertainty*. Century Business, London.

Wack, P (1985a) Scenarios: unchartered waters ahead. *Harvard Business Review*, **63**(5).

Wack, P (1985b) Scenarios: shooting the rapids. *Harvard Business Review*, **63**(6).

Winstanley, D and Woodall, J (eds) (2000) *Ethical Issues in Contemporary Human Resource Management* London: MacMillan Business

Wood, W (1997) So where do we go from here? *Across the Board*, March issue.

Glossary

Assessment centres

Assessment centres are a way of providing a more 'complete' picture of the applicant through the use of a range of evaluation techniques. Typical assessment centre activities include psychometric testing, observation of group-based activities, and interviewing applicants.

Behavioural questions

These are questions which seek evidence of past behaviour as a predictor of future performance, in particular the presence or absence of a skill or competence. For example:

> 'Describe a time in any job you have held when you were faced with problems or pressures which tested your ability to cope. What did you do?'

Biodata

Biodata is an abbreviation for the term biographical data. Biodata analysis involves examining the biographical data of an applicant, often through analysis of application forms, curriculum vitae and references. Though useful, biodata provided by applicants needs to be scrutinized carefully. Useful safeguards can be built in through cross-referencing different biodata sources, e.g. application form data with information obtained from referees or through additional scrutiny in the selection interview.

Broad banding pay

Broad banding is the compression of pay grades into a small number of wide bands. Such systems facilitate lateral career moves in delayered (flatter) organizations by providing rewards for sideways moves; less emphasis is placed on promotion. Administration of reward processes is also considerably simpler and more clearly understood under this system. Progression through the pay band may be linked to achievement of competence, skills and performance.

Business growth

Business growth refers to the aspiration to expand a business in terms of its turnover. There are various models of growth, usually highlighting the growth of companies from a start-up operation to more complex business operations.

Business Process Reengineering (BPR)

The name coined by Michael Hammer to describe a business improvement method which sets out to analyse the core business of a company, and then redesign the mechanism for delivering the product or service without reference to existing methods, staffing or structures, but taking the fullest advantage of modern information technology. The method has been shown capable of dramatic, often ten-fold improvements in financial performance and cost efficiency.

Capability

Within the field of performance management, capability analysis is concerned with the identification of employee under-performance that may be due to a lack of willingness or skills and ability, which persists over a substantial period of time. Capability procedures can be used if more informal discussions between manager and employee have not resulted in an improvement in performance to the required standards. Capability procedures are a method of ensuring that employees have the chance to 'get back on track' without having to resort to disciplinary procedures.

Change in organizations

Change in organizations relates to the movement or transformation of some factor or factors. People-centred change may operate at the level of the individual or the group through to the whole organization. It can be superficial or deep rooted, and minor or major. Change may solve but inevitably creates problems also. It is unlikely to be welcomed by all who will be affected by it (see also **First-order and Second-order change**).

Change intervention

A change intervention is a structured, planned programme of activities which is introduced into an organization with a view to creating movement or transformation. In relation to people-centred interventions, some combination of skills, knowledge, attitudes and behaviour among specific groups of employees is the target of such interventions. Major change interventions are often implemented by 'change agents' or 'interventionists' who possess specialist knowledge or expertise.

Competence

Competence is the characteristic set of knowledge, skills, abilities, motivations and procedures that individuals working in specific jobs bring with them to allow them to perform their work to minimum standards.

Criteria

Criteria are standards against which judgments are made. In recruitment and selection, criteria are used to assess whether applicants are likely to be suitable for the positions available. The criteria can be developed from information gathered from a variety of sources, including job/role analysis.

Cultural diversity

Cultural diversity is the range and variety of attitudes and behaviours that are culturally determined (see also **Diversity**).

Culture

Culture is the determinant that shapes attitudes and behaviour at community, national and organizational levels.

Direct participation

'Opportunities which management provide, or initiatives to which they lend their support, at workplace level for consultation with and/or delegation of responsibilities and authority for decision making to their subordinates either as individuals, or as groups of employees relating to their immediate work task, work organisation and/or working conditions' (Geary and Sisson 1994).

Discipline

Within organizations, discipline takes different forms: self-discipline stemming from personal values, skills training and strength of character; team discipline arising from mutual control and peer pressure; and managerial discipline – managerial control where a team is responsible and answerable to a team leader, and the leader is directive and responsible for the behaviour and performance of the team. Formal disciplinary action centres around managerial discipline and is the last resort when self and team discipline and more informal managerial disciplinary approaches have failed. Disciplinary action may be required when an individual performs at below required work standards or behaves in a manner that contravenes an organization's codes of conduct. The disciplinary action taken must be based on hard evidence, and in the first instance is normally aimed at formally acknowledging poor performance and behaviour but with the intention of rectifying the situation. However, where gross misconduct (see **Misconduct**) has taken place, employees may face instant dismissal.

Diversity

Diversity is concerned with understanding that there are differences among employees and that these differences, if properly managed, contribute to the achievement of organizational objectives. Diversity factors include race, culture, ethnicity, gender, age, disability and work experience.

Diversity advantage

The diversity advantage is achieved by openly acknowledging, understanding and valuing differences and recognizing that they provide a dimension which contributes to achievement of organizational objectives.

Employee appraisal

Employee appraisal concerns the evaluation of individual or team performance. There are many kinds of employee appraisal. These include:

- individual appraisal which centres around the appraisal of employees by their line managers;
- 360 degree appraisal which entails the collection of information from superiors, subordinates and peers about performance – it is most likely to be a form of manager appraisal;
- team appraisal that requires members of a work team to evaluate the performance of themselves and their work colleagues.

Employee benefits

Employee benefits are that part of reward that is provided in addition to cash payments. The main types of employee benefits are those which are deferred, e.g. pension; those which are immediate, e.g. company car; and those which are cyclical, e.g. holidays.

Employee development

Employee development concerns the full range of strategies, tools, processes, procedures and structures that are employed in a given organization aimed at improving the capability (long and short term) of the organization's members.

Employee involvement

Employee involvement may be defined as the range of processes designed to engage the support, understanding, and optimum contribution of all employees in an organization and their contribution to its objectives.

Employee participation

Employee participation may be defined as the process of employee involvement designed to provide employees with the opportunity to influence and, where appropriate, take part in decision making on matters which affect them. Participation may be further categorized into **direct participation**, where opportunities or initiatives are provided by management. These may take the form of workplace-level consultation, or delegation of responsibilities and authority for decision making to their subordinates, either as individuals or as groups of employees, and relating to their immediate work task, work organization or working conditions. **Indirect participation** is where representatives of employees meet with representatives of management, within a predetermined and agreed forum, to discuss matters of mutual interest to both groups.

Ethnic monitoring

Ethnic monitoring involves collecting and analysing statistical data on the percentage of employees from the majority population and those from ethnic minorities. It can be used, for example, to establish the representation of those from ethnic minorities at different levels within an organization. Within recruitment and selection it is used to monitor the percentage of those from ethnic minorities who apply and are selected for specific positions.

Ethnocentric

An ethnocentric approach is one in which there is a focus on the attitudes, behaviours and practices of a single ethnic group.

Euromanager

Euromanagers are those whose primary experience and responsibility lie within the confines of Europe.

Existential views of learning (see Instrumental versus existential learning)

Expatriate manager

An expatriate manager is a manager from the home country sent to manage an overseas subsidiary of the home country operation.

Federation

An amalgam of states or organizations each of which has the authority to operate autonomously from one another.

First-order change

First-order changes are those that require relatively small adjustments, such as to working methods. These are the most common sorts of changes. An example of a first-order change would be having more team meetings in order to ensure that staff received more regular briefings in order to overcome a minor communication problem (see **Second order change**).

Flexible working practices

Flexible working practices are working practices which are not covered by standard full-time work contracts, e.g., part-time working, job sharing and temporary and contract work.

Functional flexibility (see Flexible working practices)

Geocentric manager

In management terms, a manager who has the facility and competence to operate anywhere in the world without being unduly influenced by the cultural baggage of his or her home country.

Global

The term global concerns the treatment of some aspect of organizations or commercial activity as an operational whole.

Globalization

Globalization refers to the process of becoming global.

Goal achievement (see Organizational goal achievement)

Grandparent

Within some staff appraisal schemes, grandparents have a 'third party' role in evaluating the performance of managers handling appraisals. Their primary responsibilities include ensuring that appraisals are conducted efficiently, effectively and fairly. They also have responsibility for handling concerns raised by appraisees who feel that these concerns cannot be dealt with objectively by their line managers and therefore forward them to the grandparent for adjudication. Typically, a grandparent is a line manager's line manager.

Gross misconduct (see Misconduct)

Growth (see Business growth)

Heterarchy

In organizational terms, a heterarchy is where no one component of the organization dominates another and where there is no clear organizational hierarchy.

Hierarchy

A hierarchy is an organizational structure founded on power relationships between clearly defined tiers of management. In international management specifically, it is usually where the home country dominates the international operation.

Home country

The home country is the country of origin, usually where the company head office is based.

Host country

The host country is where an overseas subsidiary is located.

Indirect participation

Defined by the Institute of Personnel and Development as 'where representatives of employees, meet with representatives of management, within a predetermined and agreed forum, to discuss matters of mutual interest to both groups' (IPD 1990).

Instrumental versus existential views of learning

In the instrumental view of learning, the learner is seen to be a vessel into which ideas are poured. The teacher is seen as the font of knowledge which must be imparted to the learner. In the existential view of learning, the learner is seen to be a 'self-in-process'. The role of the teacher in this view is seen to be that of the facilitator of the learner's processes of becoming aware.

Integration

Integration is said to have occurred where one part of the organization physically becomes part of another.

Interdependency

In international management, interdependency is said to occur where different components of the organization cannot operate without a degree of dependence upon one another.

Internal capability analysis

Internal capability analysis is an assessment integral to the development of strategic human resource management. It involves the definition of core effectiveness criteria which, in turn, should lead to the design of mutually supportive human resource activities within a coherent human resource strategy.

International company

An international company is any enterprise that has interests overseas, in a single country or a number of different countries around the world.

International joint venture

An international joint venture is where two or more international companies come together to form a third-party company which then operates autonomously in a particular region of the world.

Investors in People (IIP)

A system of accreditation of organizational processes that places emphasis upon the links between organizational purpose and the competence needed by employees of a given organization. The system is in use in the United Kingdom.

Job evaluation

Job evaluation is concerned with systematically evaluating jobs to determine their relative worth. It provides the basis for grading and pay structures within organizations.

Just-in-time (JIT)

Just-in-time (JIT) is a method of manufacture which sets out to achieve the economies of mass production for products which used to be made in batches. It allows manufacture without the use of large stocks of raw materials, work-in-progress or finished goods. It operates on the principle of transferring products from one stage in manufacturing to the next in batches of one, as soon as they are processed, instead of larger batches, calculated from the economic batch quantity formula. Products are never made for stock, but only just in time for when they are needed.

Kaizen

Kaizen is a Japanese term which translates as 'continual improvement'. A philosophy for improving the quality of a manufactured product through encouraging everyone at work to seek small improvements in the processes, and the working environment. In the western world, the philosophy is known as Total Quality Management.

Kanban

Kanban is a Japanese term which translates as 'visual record'. It is an essential element in the JIT method of manufacture, and operates as a signal from one stage of manufacture to the previous stage, to flag that another item of production will soon be needed. It can be a simple square painted on the floor between stages, just large enough for one item of work-in-progress, to be filled by the earlier stage as soon as the later stage withdraws from it.

Key performance indicator (see Performance indicator)

Key results area

A key results area (KRA) is a key activity or activities within a person's job where particular actions must be taken to ensure the success of producing goods or achieving effective service delivery for customers.

Kolb's learning cycle

Kolb's learning cycle is a way of understanding adult learning that emphasizes the circular links between concrete experience, reflective observation, abstract conceptualization and active experiment.

Managerial mindset

Managerial mindset refers to the way in which managers think and behave. The implication is that this thinking is partial and with a fairly firm structure, which is not readily amenable to change although change is possible. The 'mindset' concept is grounded in the psychological processes of cognition and perception. It can be also thought of as a 'mental map' commonly shared by managers (see also **Personal constructs**).

Meta-system

The meta-system is a way of describing the complex mesh of relationships that impinge on organizations internally (represented by the dynamics of interpersonal, inter-departmental or other interrelationships within) and externally (in the guise of a market, sector or industry or broader environmental factors such as the economy, or wide-ranging technological change).

Sections or levels within the meta-system may be considered as domains, such as the individual, the work group, or the market.

Misconduct

Misconduct is said to have taken place when there is a deviation in performance or behaviour from the standards set down by an organization in its employees' contract of employment and its codes of conduct. Minor offences such as lateness and persistent substandard work are technically misconduct but are likely to be treated more informally or may be dealt with through corrective measures such as capability procedures. More usually, the term misconduct is reserved for more significant events such as unauthorized absence, persistent poor time keeping, or a continued failure to carry out duties to a satisfactory standard. **Gross misconduct** is said to have occurred when there is a more serious breach, such as theft of company property, fraud, assault on colleagues or repeated acts of misconduct.

Multi-domestic company

A multi-domestic company is one where the subsidiary operations are an exact duplicate of the home country operation.

Multinational corporation

A multinational company is one that has operations in a variety of countries around the world.

National Vocational Qualifications (NVQs)

National Vocational Qualifications (NVQs) form the basis of a system of accreditation of job competence in the United Kingdom. There are five levels within the current system; the achievement of each certifies increasing levels of job competence.

Networked organizations (see Organizational structure)

Numerical flexibility (see Flexible working practices)

Organizational development

There are many definitions of organizational development. It has been described as planned, organization-wide effort which is managed from the top, to increase organizational effectiveness and health (i.e. the organization's climate or motivational status) throughout. Others have described it as a long-term programme of interventions in the social, psychological and cultural belief systems of an organization and it is assumed to lead to greater organizational effectiveness.

Organizational goal achievement

Broadly, there are two popular areas in which the manner in which organizations set out to achieve goals are considered. In the first, the focus is on strategy, systems and structure, and this is the one that traditionally has been used by organizational strategists. In the second, the focus is one of purpose, process and people.

Organizational structure

Organizational structure can be considered in a variety of ways, but typically refers to the relationships between activities in an organization and the levels of authority and formal power, as represented in an organizational chart. Typically an organization will also have an 'informal' structure of unofficial relationships and sources of power. Although there are various typologies of organizational structure, many large organizations in particular are **hybrid structures**, made up of a variety of forms. Recent additions to the typology of organizations are **networked organizations** in which connections between key activities are facilitated through the use of information technology, and **virtual organizations**, where the networking concept is pushed even further and both their activities and their employees are remote and the majority of connections and communications take place via the Internet. In reality, organizations are more likely to possess a virtualized element within their more traditional profile of types within a hybrid organizational structure, and both afford a degree of flexibility to organizations which enables them to shift more rapidly the numbers of employees at the flexible periphery of their core workforce.

Pay structures

Pay structures define different levels of pay for jobs or groups of jobs by reference to, firstly, their internal value – often determined by job evaluation, and secondly, the market rate – often determined by market surveys.

In general, payment structures provide for pay progression in accordance with performance, skill, competence or service.

Performance appraisal

Performance appraisal concerns the evaluation of performance at any level within an organization.

Within performance appraisal is the activity of staff appraisal, which concerns the evaluation of individual or team performance. Such appraisals are undertaken in order to identify excellent, good and below-standard performance. Activities that are commonly associated with employee appraisal (see **Employee appraisal**) include objective setting, appraisal interviewing, and the identification of training and development needs.

Performance indicator

Performance indicators are quantitative or qualitative 'measures' which provide information about some aspect of performance of an organization and its members. Human resource corporate performance indicators provide information about key aspects of performance in relation to strategic human resource management areas and provide an indication of their contribution to overall strategic performance. Within performance management, the term key performance indicator (KPI) is more commonly associated with individual and team performance. KPIs provide an indication of the extent to which a key performance area has been addressed.

Performance management

Performance management may be viewed as a means of getting improved results from the whole organization, by focusing at different levels (from the whole organization through to the work group and its members) through coordinated, holistic activities. It is a broad, systematic approach to the achievement of organizational objectives by providing an interconnected set of goals which are linked at the organizational, departmental, work team and individual levels.

Performance-related pay

Performance-related pay offers pay incentives in return for the achievement of performance levels. The most common methods of performance-related pay are: profit sharing – a percentage of annual profit is paid as a bonus; merit pay – an increase on basic pay is determined by an assessment of individual performance at work; individual bonuses – based on assessment of individual performance and not normally integrated into basic pay; team bonuses – based on assessment of team performance; share options – based on awarding shares in the business with tax-free advantages on their sale.

Personal constructs

Everyone has his or her unique way of viewing and making sense of the world around them. The psychologist George Kelly argued that all people possess a unique system of personal constructs, which are used as a filtering mechanism through which information is filtered. Embedded within this system are beliefs and values, some of which are uniquely held by an individual and others which may be shared with friends, family, work colleagues or the community. Aspects of our construct system are open to change while others are highly resistant to change, as such changes are likely to challenge our personal beliefs and the image of ourselves that we hold or our 'core personality'.

Personal development plan

A personal development plan is an individualized plan of action created for all members of the organization that sets forth development plans in two areas: personal development and career development. They are based on a needs assessment that is itself the result of some combination of self, supervisor and peer assessment of the individual employee's goals, strengths, and the gaps between skills that employees have now and those that they may need or want to develop in the future. The personal development plan is under the control of the individual. Within it, the needs for development are highlighted, and individual development targets, proposed strategies for meeting needs, and the means for monitoring progress towards targets are all identified.

Pluralist perspective

Within a pluralist perspective, organizations are viewed as coalitions of separate interest groups presided over by a top management which serves the long-term needs of the organization. In such organizations, conflicts of interest are seen as inevitable, but these conflicts can be used creatively for the overall good of the organization.

Polycentric management

Polycentric management concerns leaving management up to the locals, centred around local management practice. It creates a variety of different management systems around the world.

Power hub

A power hub is where power is concentrated, for example, within the head office.

Psychological contract

A psychological contract can be described as the tacit assumptions that are held on the part of members of an organization. It differs from a formal contract of employment as it is not necessarily written down, but it is nonetheless commonly understood. An example of a psychological contract would be that employees might expect a job for life if they work hard and remain loyal to the company, while the management of that same organization offer jobs for life and a fair day's pay for a fair day's work, but expects employees to demonstrate that they are 'loyal company workers'.

Psychometric test

A psychometric test is a written instrument designed to assess some aspect of an individual, such as motor skills, verbal or numerical reasoning or personality. Such instruments are normally designed by psychologists. The worth of a psychometric testing depends upon the robustness of the test (see Reliability and Validity) and the appropriate application and administration of the test.

Radical perspective

Within a radical perspective, the employment relationship is viewed as conflictual, with management possessing more power than employees. A worker's ability to work is a commodity that can be bought and sold by managers. Individual employees who rely on managers for employment are relatively powerless to influence working arrangements but such a relationship generates cynicism and mistrust which is never far below the surface.

Reliability

Reliability is the extent to which a psychometric test can be used repeatedly yet give the same or similar results. For example, if a group of managers were tested for numerical reasoning, their test scores should be similar if they were retested.

Results areas (see also Key results area)

Results areas are areas within an employee's work responsibilities which have been designated those in which specific achievements or targets should be met.

They can provide an indication of how stretching future job goals or targets should be.

Reward management

Reward management is concerned with the management of the way people are rewarded in relation to their value to an organization. It is concerned with the management of financial and non-financial rewards and with the link between strategies, values, policies, plans and processes. Reward includes pay, additional payments, performance-related pay and employee benefits.

Reward package

The reward package includes all elements of pay, e.g. bonus, performance-related pay, shift payments and employee benefits such as holidays, sick pay, medical insurance and discounts.

Second-order change

Second-order change involves change to deep-rooted issues such as the attitudes, beliefs and assumptions behind existing work practices. If a particular problem persists and worsens over time, for example there is a failure for the members of a department to communicate with each other, it may be that attitudes towards certain members of staff are getting in the way of open communication. To change the behaviour (poor communication) one would need to change the underlying attitudes. (see **First order change**)

Small to medium-sized business (SMB)

The definition of a small to medium-sized business (SMB) varies from country to country. In the United Kingdom, a small business is defined as having fewer than 50 employees and a medium-sized business as having between 50 and 250 employees.

Stakeholder

A stakeholder is an individual or group which has a direct, specific investment (for example, financial, employment or emotional) in the success and well-being of an organization. Different types of changes are likely to affect a specific combination of stakeholders within the broader set of relationships (stakeholder relationships) that exist within this network of relationships, referred to as the stakeholder web.

Standardization

Standardizing concerns the creation of duplicates, such as products or systems, with common features, around the world.

Strategic alliance

A strategic alliance concerns cooperation between two or more companies for a specific purpose, e.g. research and development.

Structure (see Organizational structure)

Team reward

Team rewards are payments to teams which link to the performance of that team. The purpose of team rewards is to reinforce the value of team working in the organization. Team reward may involve the whole team receiving the same reward or individuals in a team receiving different rewards.

Total Quality Management

A management approach based on the Japanese Kaizen philosophy (see **Kaizen**), for improving the quality of product or service, by improving the processes involved. There are three cornerstones to the approach: an obsession with quality, a scientific approach, and teamwork.

Transnationality

A worldwide operation where there is a high degree of interdependence between the different subsidiaries around the world and between the subsidiaries and the home country. It will often be characterized by the devolution of different functional areas to different regions or locations around the world.

Unitarist perspective

Within a unitarist perspective, an organization is viewed as a unified whole; all employees who work there have a sense of common purpose within an overall paternalistic style of management. In such an organization, conflict is seen as unhelpful and caused by troublemakers.

Universalism

Universalism refers to the provision of a universal approach to management.

Validity

Validity is the extent to which a psychometric test measures what it is designed to measure. It is established by statistical analysis and is usually undertaken by a trained occupational psychologist.

Virtual organizations (see Organizational structure)

Work sample

A work sample is a test in which one or more practical tasks which are part of the job itself are performed. For example, giving a presentation where the job involves giving presentations.

Index